CW00517352

VW Owners Workshop Manual

I M Coomber

Models covered

Volkswagen Passat Saloon, Hatchback (inc. GT) & Estate, including
limited edition models; 1588 cc, 1595 cc, 1781 cc, 1921 cc, 1994 cc
Volkswagen Santana Saloon; 1595 cc, 1781 cc, 1921 cc, 1994 cc

Does not cover Diesel engine models, or 'Series 3' Passat range introduced May 1988

ISBN 1 85010 502 2

© Haynes Publishing Group 1990

All rights reserved. No part of this book may be reproduced or transmitted in any form or by
any means, electronic or mechanical, including photocopying, recording or by any information
storage or retrieval system, without permission in writing from the copyright holder.

Printed in England *(814–2S9)*

ABCDE

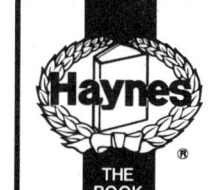

THE
BOOK

Haynes Publishing Group
Sparkford Nr Yeovil
Somerset BA22 7JJ England

Haynes Publications, Inc
861 Lawrence Drive
Newbury Park
California 91320 USA

British Library Cataloguing in Publication Data
Coomber, Ian. *1943-*
VW Passat & Santana owners workshop manual.
1. Cars. Maintenance & repair – Amateurs' manuals
I. Title II. Series
629.28'722
ISBN 1-85010-502-2

Acknowledgements

Thanks are due to Duckhams Oils who provided lubrication data and to the Champion Sparking Plug Company Limited who supplied the illustrations showing the various spark plug conditions, and to Sykes-Pickavant Limited who provided some of the workshop tools.

Special thanks are also due to all those people at Sparkford who helped in the production of this manual.

About this manual

Its aim

The aim of this manual is to help you get the best value from your vehicle. It can do so in several ways. It can help you decide what work must be done (even should you choose to get it done by a garage), provide information on routine maintenance and servicing, and give a logical course of action and diagnosis when random faults occur. However, it is hoped that you will use the manual by tackling the work yourself. On simpler jobs it may even be quicker than booking the car into a garage and going there twice, to leave and collect it. Perhaps most important, a lot of money can be saved by avoiding the costs a garage must charge to cover its labour and overheads.

The manual has drawings and descriptions to show the function of the various components so that their layout can be understood. Then the tasks are described and photographed in a step-by-step sequence so that even a novice can do the work.

Its arrangement

The manual is divided into thirteen Chapters, each covering a logical sub-division of the vehicle. The Chapters are each divided into Sections, numbered with single figures, eg 5; and the Sections into paragraphs (or sub-sections), with decimal numbers following on from the Section they are in, eg 5.1, 5.2, 5.3 etc.

It is freely illustrated, especially in those parts where there is a detailed sequence of operations to be carried out. There are two forms of illustration: figures and photographs. The figures are numbered in sequence with decimal numbers, according to their position in the Chapter — eg Fig. 6.4 is the fourth drawing/illustration in Chapter 6. Photographs carry the same number (either individually or in related groups) as the Section or sub-section to which they relate.

There is an alphabetical index at the back of the manual as well as a contents list at the front. Each Chapter is also preceded by its own individual contents list.

References to the 'left' or 'right' of the vehicle are in the sense of a person in the driver's seat facing forwards.

Unless otherwise stated, nuts and bolts are removed by turning anti-clockwise, and tightened by turning clockwise.

Vehicle manufacturers continually make changes to specifications and recommendations, and these, when notified, are incorporated into our manuals at the earliest opportunity.

This manual is not a direct reproduction of the vehicle manufacturers' data, and its publication should not be taken as implying any technical approval by the vehicle manufacturers or importers.

Whilst every care is taken to ensure that the information in this manual is correct, no liability can be accepted by the authors or publishers for loss, damage or injury caused by any errors in, or omissions from, the information given.

Introduction to the Volkswagen Passat and Santana

The 'new' Volkswagen Passat was introduced in September 1981, with revised body and trim features being the main visual differences from the earlier range of models. Mechanically very few alterations were necessary, the engines fitted being of 1.6 and 1.8 (four-cylinder) or 1.9 and 2.0 litre (five-cylinder) capacity. A four- or five-speed manual gearbox or three-speed automatic transmission is fitted according to model, and drive is to the front wheels.

The body, whether Saloon, Hatchback or Estate, has four doors, is of steel monocoque construction and has full underbody protection when new.

Full instrumentation is provided together with electric windows, power steering and a centralised locking system according to model.

Details of later models, and modifications which may affect procedures covered in the main chapters, are given in the Supplement at the end of the manual.

Contents

4

Volkswagen Passat GL5

Volkswagen Santana GX5i

6

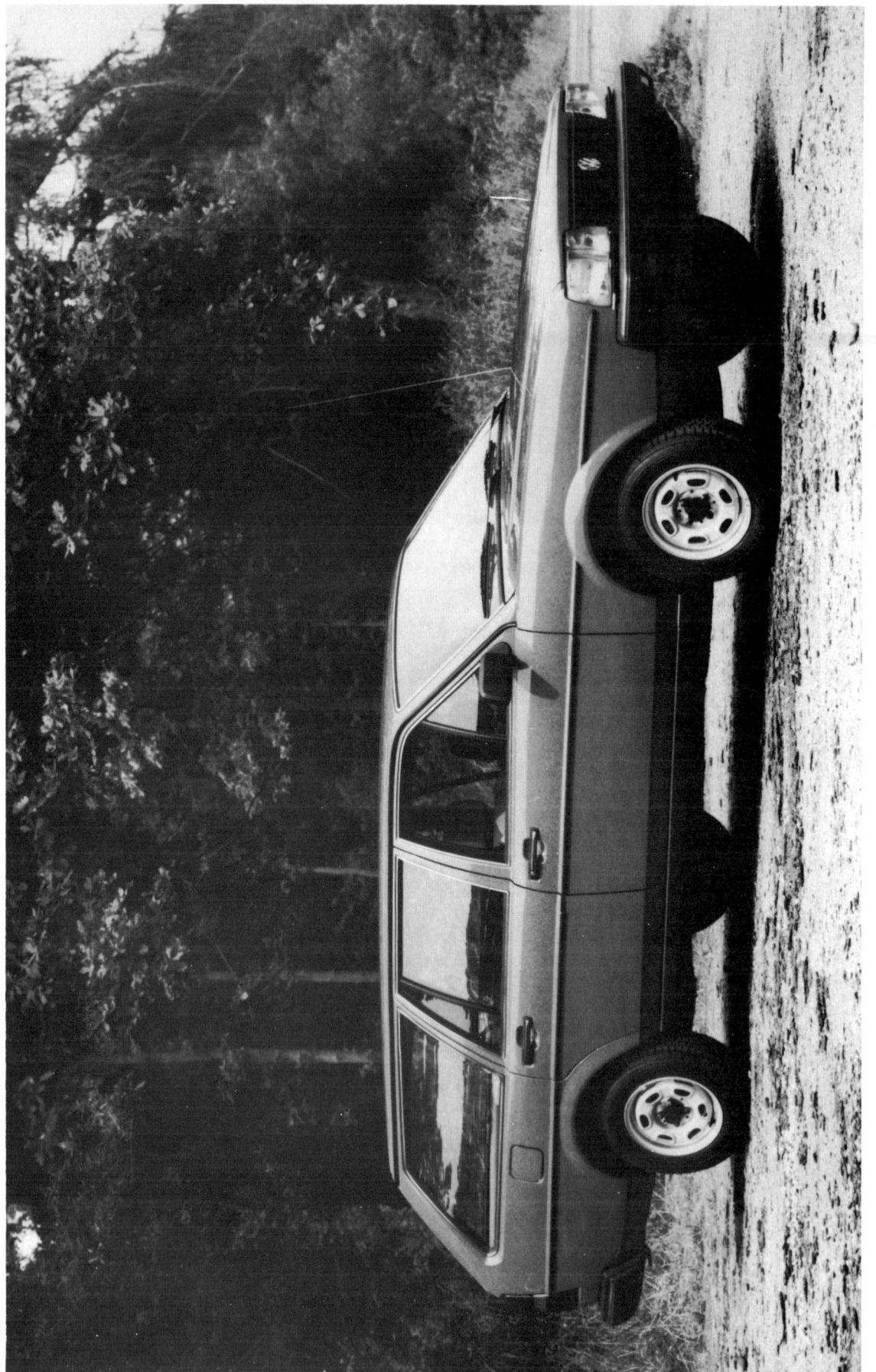

Volkswagen Passat CL Estate

General dimensions, weights and capacities

Dimensions

	Passat Saloon	Passat	Passat Estate	Santana
Overall length	4530 mm (178.4 in)	4435 mm (174.6 in)	4540 mm (178.7 in)	4545 mm (178.9 in)
Overall width	1710 mm (67.3 in)	1685 mm (66.3 in)	1685 mm (66.3 in)	1695 mm (66.7 in)
Overall height (unladen)	1395 mm (54.9 in)	1385 mm (54.5 in)	1385 mm* (54.5 in)	1400 mm (55.1 in)
*Overall height with roof rails			1455 mm (57.6 in)	
Wheelbase	2550 mm (100.3 in)	2550 mm (100.3 in)	2550 mm (100.3 in)	2550 mm (100.3 in)
Track – front	1414 mm (55.6 in)	1414 mm (55.6 in)	1414 mm (55.6 in)	1414 mm (55.6 in)
Track – rear	1422 mm (56.0 in)	1422 mm (56.0 in)	1422 mm (56.0 in)	1422 mm (56.0 in)

Weights

	Passat Saloon	Passat	Passat Estate	Santana
Gross vehicle weight:				
1.6 and 1.8 litre	1460 kg (3218 lb)	1460 kg (3218 lb)	1520 kg (3350 lb)	1460 kg (3218 lb)
1.9 and 2.0 litre	1580 kg (3483 lb)	1580 kg (3483 lb)	1620 kg (3571 lb)	1580 kg (3483 lb)
Kerb weight (manual gearbox models*):				
1.6 and 1.8 litre	985 kg (2171 lb)	985/960 kg (2171/2116 lb)	1085 kg (2391 lb)	1005 kg (2215 lb)
1.9 and 2.0 litre	1085 kg (2391 lb)	1085 kg (2391 lb)	1105 kg (2436 lb)	1125 kg (2480 lb)

	All models
*Add the following for automatic transmission models:	
With four-cylinder engine	25 kg (55 lb)
With five-cylinder engine	15 kg (33 lb)
Maximum roof rack load (gutter rail fixing only)	75 kg (165 lb)
Maximum trailer weight (trailer without brakes):	
1.6 litre	500 kg (1102 lb)
1.8 litre	500 kg (1102 lb)
1.9 and 2.0 litre	550 kg (1212 lb)
Maximum trailer weight (trailer with brakes) – (12% gradient):	
1.6 litre	1200 kg (2645 lb)
1.8 litre	1200 kg (2645 lb)
1.9 and 2.0 litre	1500 kg (3306 lb)
Maximum trailer nose weight on ball coupling:	
All models	75 kg (165 lb)

Capacities

Engine oil:	
1.6 and 1.8 litre with filter	3.0 litre (5.3 Imp pint)
1.6 and 1.8 litre without filter	2.5 litre (4.4 Imp pint)
1.9 and 2.0 litre with filter	3.5 litre (6.2 Imp pint)
1.9 and 2.0 litre without filter	3.0 litre (5.3 Imp pint)
Difference between engine oil dipstick minimum and maximum marks	1.0 litre (1.8 Imp pint)
Cooling system (with heater):	
1.6 and 1.8 litre	6.0 litre (10.6 Imp pint)
1.9 and 2.0 litre	8.0 litre (14.1 Imp pint)
Fuel tank:	
All models	60 litre (13.2 Imp gal)
Manual gearbox:	
Type 014	1.7 litre (3 Imp pint)
Type 013	2.0 litre (3.5 Imp pint)
Type 093	2.4 litre (4.1 Imp pint)
Automatic transmission:	
Type 089 and 087 (total) – ATF	6.0 litre (10.6 Imp pint)
Type 089 and 087 (Service) – ATF	3.0 litre (5.3 Imp pint)
Type 089 final drive – SAE 90	0.75 litre (1.3 Imp pint)
Type 087 final drive – SAE 90	1.0 litre (1.8 Imp pint)

Buying spare parts and vehicle identification numbers

Buying spare parts

Spare parts are available from many sources, Volkswagen have many dealers throughout the country and other dealers, accessory stores and motor factors will also stock Volkswagen spare parts. Our advice regarding spare part sources is as follows:

Officially appointed vehicle main dealers – This is the best source of parts which are peculiar to your vehicle and are otherwise not generally available (eg complete cylinder heads, internal transmission components, badges, interior trim etc). It is also the only place at which you should buy parts if your vehicle is still under warranty. To be sure of obtaining the correct parts it will always be necessary to give the storeman your car's engine and chassis number, and if possible, to take the 'old' parts along for positive identification. Remember that many parts are available on a factory exchange scheme – any parts returned should always be clean! It obviously makes good sense to go straight to the specialists on your vehicle for this type of part for they are best equipped to supply you.

Other dealers and accessory shops – These are often very good places to buy materials and components needed for the maintenance of your vehicle (eg oil filters, spark plugs, bulbs, fan belts, oils and grease, touch-up paint, filler paste etc). They also sell general accessories, usually have convenient opening hours, charge lower prices and can often be found not far from home.

Motor factors – Good factors will stock all of the more important components which wear out relatively quickly (eg clutch components, pistons, valves, exhaust systems, brake cylinders/pipes/hoses/seals/shoes and pads etc). Motor factors will often provide new or reconditioned components on a part exchange basis – this can save a considerable amount of money.

Vehicle identification numbers

Modifications are a continuing and unpublicised process in vehicle manufacture. Spare parts manuals and lists are compiled upon a numerical basis, the individual vehicle numbers being essential to identify correctly the component required.

The vehicle identification plate is located in the engine compartment on the right-hand side.

The chassis number is stamped on the rear panel of the engine compartment.

The engine number is stamped on the left-hand side of the cylinder block.

Vehicle chassis number/identification plate location

Vehicle identification plate location

Engine number location – 1.6 litre shown

Tools and working facilities

Introduction

A selection of good tools is a fundamental requirement for anyone contemplating the maintenance and repair of a motor vehicle. For the owner who does not possess any, their purchase will prove a considerable expense, offsetting some of the savings made by doing-it-yourself. However, provided that the tools purchased meet the relevant national safety standards and are of good quality, they will last for many years and prove an extremely worthwhile investment.

To help the average owner to decide which tools are needed to carry out the various tasks detailed in this manual, we have compiled three lists of tools under the following headings: *Maintenance and minor repair, Repair and overhaul,* and *Special.* The newcomer to practical mechanics should start off with the *Maintenance and minor repair* tool kit and confine himself to the simpler jobs around the vehicle. Then, as his confidence and experience grow, he can undertake more difficult tasks, buying extra tools as, and when, they are needed. In this way, a *Maintenance and minor repair* tool kit can be built-up into a *Repair and overhaul* tool kit over a considerable period of time without any major cash outlays. The experienced do-it-yourselfer will have a tool kit good enough for most repair and overhaul procedures and will add tools from the *Special* category when he feels the expense is justified by the amount of use to which these tools will be put.

It is obviously not possible to cover the subject of tools fully here. For those who wish to learn more about tools and their use there is a book entitled *How to Choose and Use Car Tools* available from the publishers of this manual.

Maintenance and minor repair tool kit

The tools given in this list should be considered as a minimum requirement if routine maintenance, servicing and minor repair operations are to be undertaken. We recommend the purchase of combination spanners (ring one end, open-ended the other); although more expensive than open-ended ones, they do give the advantages of both types of spanner.

Combination spanners - 10, 11, 12, 13, 14 & 17 mm
Adjustable spanner - 9 inch
Transmission filler/drain plug key
Spark plug spanner (with rubber insert)
Spark plug gap adjustment tool
Set of feeler gauges
Brake bleed nipple spanner
Screwdriver - 4 in long x $\frac{1}{4}$ in dia (flat blade)
Screwdriver - 4 in long x $\frac{1}{4}$ in dia (cross blade)
Combination pliers - 6 inch
Hacksaw (junior)
Tyre pump
Tyre pressure gauge
Oil can
Fine emery cloth (1 sheet)
Wire brush (small)
Funnel (medium size)

Repair and overhaul tool kit

These tools are virtually essential for anyone undertaking any major repairs to a motor vehicle, and are additional to those given in the *Maintenance and minor repair* list. Included in this list is a comprehensive set of sockets. Although these are expensive they will be found invaluable as they are so versatile - particularly if various drives are included in the set. We recommend the $\frac{1}{2}$ in square-drive type, as this can be used with most proprietary torque wrenches. If you cannot afford a socket set, even bought piecemeal, then inexpensive tubular box spanners are a useful alternative.

The tools in this list will occasionally need to be supplemented by tools from the *Special* list.

Sockets (or box spanners) to cover range in previous list
Cylinder head bolt splined socket
Reversible ratchet drive (for use with sockets)
Extension piece, 10 inch (for use with sockets)
Universal joint (for use with sockets)
Torque wrench (for use with sockets)
'Mole' wrench - 8 inch
Ball pein hammer
Soft-faced hammer, plastic or rubber
Screwdriver - 6 in long x $\frac{5}{16}$ in dia (flat blade)
Screwdriver - 2 in long x $\frac{5}{16}$ in square (flat blade)
Screwdriver - 1$\frac{1}{2}$ in long x $\frac{1}{4}$ in dia (cross blade)
Screwdriver - 3 in long x $\frac{1}{8}$ in dia (electricians)
Pliers - electricians side cutters
Pliers - needle nosed
Pliers - circlip (internal and external)
Cold chisel - $\frac{1}{2}$ inch
Scriber
Scraper
Centre punch
Pin punch
Hacksaw
Valve grinding tool
Steel rule/straight-edge
Allen keys
Selection of files
Wire brush (large)
Axle-stands
Jack (strong scissor or hydraulic type)

Special tools

The tools in this list are those which are not used regularly, are expensive to buy, or which need to be used in accordance with their manufacturers' instructions. Unless relatively difficult mechanical jobs are undertaken frequently, it will not be economic to buy many of these tools. Where this is the case, you could consider clubbing together with friends (or joining a motorists' club) to make a joint purchase, or borrowing the tools against a deposit from a local garage or tool hire specialist.

The following list contains only those tools and instruments freely available to the public, and not those special tools produced by the vehicle manufacturer specifically for its dealer network. You will find occasional references to these manufacturers' special tools in the text of this manual. Generally, an alternative method of doing the job without the vehicle manufacturers' special tool is given. However, sometimes, there is no alternative to using them. Where this is the case and the relevant tool cannot be bought or borrowed, you will have to entrust the work to a franchised garage.

Valve spring compressor
Piston ring compressor
Balljoint separator
Universal hub/bearing puller
Impact screwdriver
Micrometer and/or vernier gauge
Dial gauge
Stroboscopic timing light
Dwell angle meter/tachometer
Universal electrical multi-meter
Cylinder compression gauge
Lifting tackle
Trolley jack
Light with extension lead

Buying tools

For practically all tools, a tool factor is the best source since he will have a very comprehensive range compared with the average garage or accessory shop. Having said that, accessory shops often offer excellent quality tools at discount prices, so it pays to shop around.

There are plenty of good tools around at reasonable prices, but always aim to purchase items which meet the relevant national safety standards. If in doubt, ask the proprietor or manager of the shop for advice before making a purchase.

Care and maintenance of tools

Having purchased a reasonable tool kit, it is necessary to keep the tools in a clean serviceable condition. After use, always wipe off any dirt, grease and metal particles using a clean, dry cloth, before putting the tools away. Never leave them lying around after they have been used. A simple tool rack on the garage or workshop wall, for items such as screwdrivers and pliers is a good idea. Store all normal wrenches and sockets in a metal box. Any measuring instruments, gauges, meters, etc, must be carefully stored where they cannot be damaged or become rusty.

Take a little care when tools are used. Hammer heads inevitably become marked and screwdrivers lose the keen edge on their blades from time to time. A little timely attention with emery cloth or a file will soon restore items like this to a good serviceable finish.

Working facilities

Not to be forgotten when discussing tools, is the workshop itself. If anything more than routine maintenance is to be carried out, some form of suitable working area becomes essential.

It is appreciated that many an owner mechanic is forced by circumstances to remove an engine or similar item, without the benefit of a garage or workshop. Having done this, any repairs should always be done under the cover of a roof.

Wherever possible, any dismantling should be done on a clean, flat workbench or table at a suitable working height.

Any workbench needs a vice: one with a jaw opening of 4 in (100 mm) is suitable for most jobs. As mentioned previously, some clean dry storage space is also required for tools, as well as for lubricants, cleaning fluids, touch-up paints and so on, which become necessary.

Another item which may be required, and which has a much more general usage, is an electric drill with a chuck capacity of at least $\frac{5}{16}$ in (8 mm). This, together with a good range of twist drills, is virtually essential for fitting accessories such as mirrors and reversing lights.

Last, but not least, always keep a supply of old newspapers and clean, lint-free rags available, and try to keep any working area as clean as possible.

Spanner jaw gap comparison table

Jaw gap (in)	Spanner size
0.250	$\frac{1}{4}$ in AF
0.276	7 mm
0.313	$\frac{5}{16}$ in AF
0.315	8 mm
0.344	$\frac{11}{32}$ in AF; $\frac{1}{8}$ in Whitworth
0.354	9 mm
0.375	$\frac{3}{8}$ in AF
0.394	10 mm
0.433	11 mm
0.438	$\frac{7}{16}$ in AF
0.445	$\frac{3}{16}$ in Whitworth; $\frac{1}{4}$ in BSF
0.472	12 mm
0.500	$\frac{1}{2}$ in AF
0.512	13 mm
0.525	$\frac{1}{4}$ in Whitworth; $\frac{5}{16}$ in BSF
0.551	14 mm
0.563	$\frac{9}{16}$ in AF
0.591	15 mm
0.600	$\frac{5}{16}$ in Whitworth; $\frac{3}{8}$ in BSF
0.625	$\frac{5}{8}$ in AF
0.630	16 mm
0.669	17 mm
0.686	$\frac{11}{16}$ in AF
0.709	18 mm
0.710	$\frac{3}{8}$ in Whitworth; $\frac{7}{16}$ in BSF
0.748	19 mm
0.750	$\frac{3}{4}$ in AF
0.813	$\frac{13}{16}$ in AF
0.820	$\frac{7}{16}$ in Whitworth; $\frac{1}{2}$ in BSF
0.866	22 mm
0.875	$\frac{7}{8}$ in AF
0.920	$\frac{1}{2}$ in Whitworth; $\frac{9}{16}$ in BSF
0.938	$\frac{15}{16}$ in AF
0.945	24 mm
1.000	1 in AF
1.010	$\frac{9}{16}$ in Whitworth; $\frac{5}{8}$ in BSF
1.024	26 mm
1.063	$1\frac{1}{16}$ in AF; 27 mm
1.100	$\frac{5}{8}$ in Whitworth; $\frac{11}{16}$ in BSF
1.125	$1\frac{1}{8}$ in AF
1.181	30 mm
1.200	$\frac{11}{16}$ in Whitworth; $\frac{3}{4}$ in BSF
1.250	$1\frac{1}{4}$ in AF
1.260	32 mm
1.300	$\frac{3}{4}$ in Whitworth; $\frac{7}{8}$ in BSF
1.313	$1\frac{5}{16}$ in AF
1.390	$\frac{13}{16}$ in Whitworth; $\frac{15}{16}$ in BSF
1.417	36 mm
1.438	$1\frac{7}{16}$ in AF
1.480	$\frac{7}{8}$ in Whitworth; 1 in BSF
1.500	$1\frac{1}{2}$ in AF
1.575	40 mm; $\frac{15}{16}$ in Whitworth
1.614	41 mm
1.625	$1\frac{5}{8}$ in AF
1.670	1 in Whitworth; $1\frac{1}{8}$ in BSF
1.688	$1\frac{11}{16}$ in AF
1.811	46 mm
1.813	$1\frac{13}{16}$ in AF
1.860	$1\frac{1}{8}$ in Whitworth; $1\frac{1}{4}$ in BSF
1.875	$1\frac{7}{8}$ in AF
1.969	50 mm
2.000	2 in AF
2.050	$1\frac{1}{4}$ in Whitworth; $1\frac{3}{8}$ in BSF
2.165	55 mm
2.362	60 mm

General repair procedures

Whenever servicing, repair or overhaul work is carried out on the car or its components, it is necessary to observe the following procedures and instructions. This will assist in carrying out the operation efficiently and to a professional standard of workmanship.

Joint mating faces and gaskets

Where a gasket is used between the mating faces of two components, ensure that it is renewed on reassembly, and fit it dry unless otherwise stated in the repair procedure. Make sure that the mating faces are clean and dry with all traces of old gasket removed. When cleaning a joint face, use a tool which is not likely to score or damage the face, and remove any burrs or nicks with an oilstone or fine file.

Make sure that tapped holes are cleaned with a pipe cleaner, and keep them free of jointing compound if this is being used unless specifically instructed otherwise.

Ensure that all orifices, channels or pipes are clear and blow through them, preferably using compressed air.

Oil seals

Whenever an oil seal is removed from its working location, either individually or as part of an assembly, it should be renewed.

The very fine sealing lip of the seal is easily damaged and will not seal if the surface it contacts is not completely clean and free from scratches, nicks or grooves. If the original sealing surface of the component cannot be restored, the component should be renewed.

Protect the lips of the seal from any surface which may damage them in the course of fitting. Use tape or a conical sleeve where possible. Lubricate the seal lips with oil before fitting and, on dual lipped seals, fill the space between the lips with grease.

Unless otherwise stated, oil seals must be fitted with their sealing lips toward the lubricant to be sealed.

Use a tubular drift or block of wood of the appropriate size to install the seal and, if the seal housing is shouldered, drive the seal down to the shoulder. If the seal housing is unshouldered, the seal should be fitted with its face flush with the housing top face.

Screw threads and fastenings

Always ensure that a blind tapped hole is completely free from oil, grease, water or other fluid before installing the bolt or stud. Failure to do this could cause the housing to crack due to the hydraulic action of the bolt or stud as it is screwed in.

When tightening a castellated nut to accept a split pin, tighten the nut to the specified torque, where applicable, and then tighten further to the next split pin hole. Never slacken the nut to align a split pin hole unless stated in the repair procedure.

When checking or retightening a nut or bolt to a specified torque setting, slacken the nut or bolt by a quarter of a turn, and then retighten to the specified setting.

Locknuts, locktabs and washers

Any fastening which will rotate against a component or housing in the course of tightening should always have a washer between it and the relevant component or housing.

Spring or split washers should always be renewed when they are used to lock a critical component such as a big-end bearing retaining nut or bolt.

Locktabs which are folded over to retain a nut or bolt should always be renewed.

Self-locking nuts can be reused in non-critical areas, providing resistance can be felt when the locking portion passes over the bolt or stud thread.

Split pins must always be replaced with new ones of the correct size for the hole.

Special tools

Some repair procedures in this manual entail the use of special tools such as a press, two or three-legged pullers, spring compressors etc. Wherever possible, suitable readily available alternatives to the manufacturer's special tools are described, and are shown in use. In some instances, where no alternative is possible, it has been necessary to resort to the use of a manufacturer's tool and this has been done for reasons of safety as well as the efficient completion of the repair operation. Unless you are highly skilled and have a thorough understanding of the procedure described, never attempt to bypass the use of any special tool when the procedure described specifies its use. Not only is there a very great risk of personal injury, but expensive damage could be caused to the components involved.

Jacking and towing

The jack supplied in the vehicle tool kit by the manufacturer should only be used for emergency roadside wheel changing unless it is supplemented by safety stands.

The jack supplied is of the half scissors type. Check that the handbrake is fully applied before using the jack, and only jack the vehicle up on firm level ground. If the ground is not firm you will need to position a large flat packing piece under the jack base to provide additional support.

Chock the wheel diagonally opposite the one to be changed. Using the tools provided remove the hub cap where necessary, then loosen the wheel bolts half a turn. Locate the lifting arm of the jack beneath the reinforced seam of the side sill panel (photo) directly beneath the wedge shaped depression nearest to the wheel to be removed. Turn the jack handle until the base of the jack contacts the ground directly beneath the sill (photo) then continue to turn the handle until the wheel is free of the ground. Unscrew the wheel bolts and remove the wheel. On light alloy wheels prise off the centre trim cap and press it into the spare wheel.

Locate the spare wheel on the hub, then insert and tighten the bolts in diagonal sequence. Lower the jack and fully tighten the bolts. Refit the hub cap where necessary, remove the chock and relocate the tool kit, jack and wheel in the luggage compartment.

When jacking up the car with a trolley jack, position the jack beneath the reinforced plate behind the front wheel (see illustration) or beneath the reinforced seam at the rear of the side sill panel. Use the same positions when supporting the car with axle stands. *Never jack up the car beneath the suspension or axle components, the sump, or the gearbox.*

Towing

Towing eyes are fitted to the front and rear of the vehicle (photos) and a tow line should not be attached to any other points. It is preferable to use a slightly elastic tow line, to reduce the strain on both vehicles, either by having a tow line manufactured from synthetic fibre, or one which is fitted with an elastic link.

When towing, the following important precautions must be observed:

(a) Turn the ignition key of the vehicle being towed, so that the steering wheel is free (unlocked).

(b) Remember that when the engine is not running the brake servo will not operate, so that additional pressure will be required on the brake pedal after the first few applications.

(c) On vehicles with automatic transmission, ensure that the gear selector lever is at 'N'. Do not tow faster than 30 mph (50 kph), or further than 30 miles (50 km) unless the front wheels are lifted clear of the ground.

Front jacking point when using a trolley jack

Rear jacking point when using a trolley jack. Place trolley jack head 50 mm (2.0 in) in front of the side member vertical reinforcement

Jack location on the reinforced seam

Front towing eye

Rear towing eye

Recommended lubricants and fluids

Component or system	Lubricant type/specification	Duckhams recommendation
Engine (1)	Multigrade engine oil, viscosity SAE 10W/40 or 15W/40, to VW 500.00 and 505.00, or 501.01 and 505.00	Duckhams QXR or Hypergrade
Manual gearbox/final drive (2)	Hypoid gear oil, viscosity SAE 80 or 80W/90, to API-GL4	Duckhams Hypoid 80
Final drive – automatic transmission (3)	Hypoid gear oil, viscosity SAE 90, to API-GL5, MIL-L-2150B	Duckhams Hypoid 90S
Automatic transmission (4) and power steering (5)	Dexron type ATF	Duckhams D-Matic
Brake fluid (6)	Hydraulic fluid to FMVSS 116 DOT 3 or DOT 4	Duckhams Universal Brake and Clutch Fluid

Safety first!

Professional motor mechanics are trained in safe working procedures. However enthusiastic you may be about getting on with the job in hand, do take the time to ensure that your safety is not put at risk. A moment's lack of attention can result in an accident, as can failure to observe certain elementary precautions.

There will always be new ways of having accidents, and the following points do not pretend to be a comprehensive list of all dangers; they are intended rather to make you aware of the risks and to encourage a safety-conscious approach to all work you carry out on your vehicle.

Essential DOs and DON'Ts

DON'T rely on a single jack when working underneath the vehicle. Always use reliable additional means of support, such as axle stands, securely placed under a part of the vehicle that you know will not give way.

DON'T attempt to loosen or tighten high-torque nuts (e.g. wheel hub nuts) while the vehicle is on a jack; it may be pulled off.

DON'T start the engine without first ascertaining that the transmission is in neutral (or 'Park' where applicable) and the parking brake applied.

DON'T suddenly remove the filler cap from a hot cooling system – cover it with a cloth and release the pressure gradually first, or you may get scalded by escaping coolant.

DON'T attempt to drain oil until you are sure it has cooled sufficiently to avoid scalding you.

DON'T grasp any part of the engine, exhaust or catalytic converter without first ascertaining that it is sufficiently cool to avoid burning you.

DON'T allow brake fluid or antifreeze to contact vehicle paintwork.

DON'T syphon toxic liquids such as fuel, brake fluid or antifreeze by mouth, or allow them to remain on your skin.

DON'T inhale dust – it may be injurious to health (see *Asbestos* below).

DON'T allow any spilt oil or grease to remain on the floor – wipe it up straight away, before someone slips on it.

DON'T use ill-fitting spanners or other tools which may slip and cause injury.

DON'T attempt to lift a heavy component which may be beyond your capability – get assistance.

DON'T rush to finish a job, or take unverified short cuts.

DON'T allow children or animals in or around an unattended vehicle.

DO wear eye protection when using power tools such as drill, sander, bench grinder etc, and when working under the vehicle.

DO use a barrier cream on your hands prior to undertaking dirty jobs – it will protect your skin from infection as well as making the dirt easier to remove afterwards; but make sure your hands aren't left slippery. Note that long-term contact with used engine oil can be a health hazard.

DO keep loose clothing (cuffs, tie etc) and long hair well out of the way of moving mechanical parts.

DO remove rings, wristwatch etc, before working on the vehicle – especially the electrical system.

DO ensure that any lifting tackle used has a safe working load rating adequate for the job.

DO keep your work area tidy – it is only too easy to fall over articles left lying around.

DO get someone to check periodically that all is well, when working alone on the vehicle.

DO carry out work in a logical sequence and check that everything is correctly assembled and tightened afterwards.

DO remember that your vehicle's safety affects that of yourself and others. If in doubt on any point, get specialist advice.

IF, in spite of following these precautions, you are unfortunate enough to injure yourself, seek medical attention as soon as possible.

Asbestos

Certain friction, insulating, sealing, and other products – such as brake linings, brake bands, clutch linings, torque converters, gaskets, etc – contain asbestos. *Extreme care must be taken to avoid inhalation of dust from such products since it is hazardous to health*. If in doubt, assume that they *do* contain asbestos.

Fire

Remember at all times that petrol (gasoline) is highly flammable. Never smoke, or have any kind of naked flame around, when working on the vehicle. But the risk does not end there – a spark caused by an electrical short-circuit, by two metal surfaces contacting each other, by careless use of tools, or even by static electricity built up in your body under certain conditions, can ignite petrol vapour, which in a confined space is highly explosive.

Always disconnect the battery earth (ground) terminal before working on any part of the fuel or electrical system, and never risk spilling fuel on to a hot engine or exhaust.

It is recommended that a fire extinguisher of a type suitable for fuel and electrical fires is kept handy in the garage or workplace at all times. Never try to extinguish a fuel or electrical fire with water.

Note: *Any reference to a 'torch' appearing in this manual should always be taken to mean a hand-held battery-operated electric lamp or flashlight. It does NOT mean a welding/gas torch or blowlamp.*

Fumes

Certain fumes are highly toxic and can quickly cause unconsciousness and even death if inhaled to any extent. Petrol (gasoline) vapour comes into this category, as do the vapours from certain solvents such as trichloroethylene. Any draining or pouring of such volatile fluids should be done in a well ventilated area.

When using cleaning fluids and solvents, read the instructions carefully. Never use materials from unmarked containers – they may give off poisonous vapours.

Never run the engine of a motor vehicle in an enclosed space such as a garage. Exhaust fumes contain carbon monoxide which is extremely poisonous; if you need to run the engine, always do so in the open air or at least have the rear of the vehicle outside the workplace.

If you are fortunate enough to have the use of an inspection pit, never drain or pour petrol, and never run the engine, while the vehicle is standing over it; the fumes, being heavier than air, will concentrate in the pit with possibly lethal results.

The battery

Never cause a spark, or allow a naked light, near the vehicle's battery. It will normally be giving off a certain amount of hydrogen gas, which is highly explosive.

Always disconnect the battery earth (ground) terminal before working on the fuel or electrical systems.

If possible, loosen the filler plugs or cover when charging the battery from an external source. Do not charge at an excessive rate or the battery may burst.

Take care when topping up and when carrying the battery. The acid electrolyte, even when diluted, is very corrosive and should not be allowed to contact the eyes or skin.

If you ever need to prepare electrolyte yourself, always add the acid slowly to the water, and never the other way round. Protect against splashes by wearing rubber gloves and goggles.

When jump starting a car using a booster battery, for negative earth (ground) vehicles, connect the jump leads in the following sequence: First connect one jump lead between the positive (+) terminals of the two batteries. Then connect the other jump lead first to the negative (–) terminal of the booster battery, and then to a good earthing (ground) point on the vehicle to be started, at least 18 in (45 cm) from the battery if possible. Ensure that hands and jump leads are clear of any moving parts, and that the two vehicles do not touch. Disconnect the leads in the reverse order.

Mains electricity and electrical equipment

When using an electric power tool, inspection light etc, always ensure that the appliance is correctly connected to its plug and that, where necessary, it is properly earthed (grounded). Do not use such appliances in damp conditions and, again, beware of creating a spark or applying excessive heat in the vicinity of fuel or fuel vapour. Also ensure that the appliances meet the relevant national safety standards.

Ignition HT voltage

A severe electric shock can result from touching certain parts of the ignition system, such as the HT leads, when the engine is running or being cranked, particularly if components are damp or the insulation is defective. Where an electronic ignition system is fitted, the HT voltage is much higher and could prove fatal.

Routine maintenance

Maintenance is essential for ensuring safety and desirable for the purpose of getting the best in terms of performance and economy from your car. Over the years the need for periodic lubrication has been greatly reduced, if not totally eliminated. This has unfortunately tended to lead some owners to think that because no such action is required, the items either no longer exist, or will last for ever. This is certainly not the case; it is essential to carry out regular visual examination as comprehensively as possible in order to spot any possible defects at an early stage, before they develop into major expensive repairs.

Under-bonnet view of the engine compartment – four-cylinder Formel E model shown

1 Engine oil filler cap and dipstick
2 Air filter and carburettor
3 Brake master cylinder and servo unit
4 Ignition coil
5 Ignition distributor
6 Battery
7 Engine oil filter
8 Windscreen washer reservoir
9 Alternator
10 Cooling fan (electric)
11 Alternator drive belt
12 Radiator filler cap

Front suspension and associated components viewed from beneath

1	Brake caliper	3	Exhaust system	5	Suspension arm	7	Engine sump and drain plug
2	Gearbox/axle unit	4	Driveshaft	6	Anti-roll bar		

Rear suspension and associated components viewed from beneath

1	Brake pressure regulator unit	2	Rear axle unit	4	Shock absorber lower mounting	6	Handbrake cable
		3	Rear drum brakes	5	Fuel tank	7	Handbrake compensator unit

1   Brake pressure regulator unit   2   Rear axle unit   4   Shock absorber lower mounting   6   Handbrake cable

3   Rear drum brakes   5   Fuel tank   7   Handbrake compensator unit

Every 250 miles (375 km) or weekly – whichever comes first

Engine
Check the level of engine oil and top up if necessary (photo)
Check the coolant level and top up if necessary (photo)
Check the battery electrolyte level and top up if necessary

Tyres
Check and adjust the tyre pressures. Don't forget the spare

Lights and wipers
Check that all the lights work
Clean the headlamps
Check the washer fluid level(s) and top up if necessary (photos)

Brakes
Check the level of fluid in the brake master cylinder reservoir – the level will drop slightly as the disc pads and rear brake linings wear, but if topping up is necessary the hydraulic circuit should be checked for leaks (photo)

MODELS UP TO AND INCLUDING MODEL YEAR 1985

Every 5000 miles (7500 km) or 6 months – whichever comes first

Engine
Change engine oil
Brakes
Check front disc pads for wear (photo)

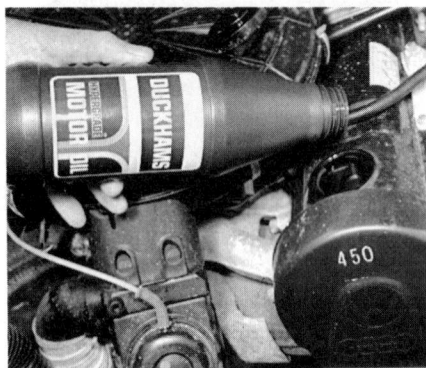

Topping up the engine oil level (four-cylinder engine)

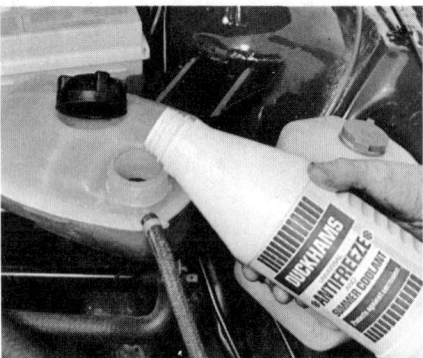

Topping up the coolant level

Top up the windscreen/headlamp washer fluid reservoir

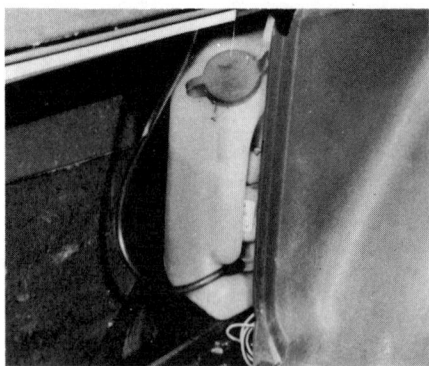

Check/top up if necessary the rear window washer fluid reservoir

Topping up the brake master cylinder fluid level

Check the brake disc pads for wear

Check the drivebelt tension adjustment and the belt for wear

Check the driveshaft rubber boots

Body
Lubricate the bonnet lock and hinges
Grease the door check straps

Every 10 000 miles (15 000 km) or 12 months – whichever comes first

---

Engine
Check antifreeze strength and add as necessary
Check drivebelts for condition and tension, and adjust if necessary (photo)
Renew the spark plugs
Check and adjust the ignition timing
Check and adjust the engine idling speed and exhaust CO content
Check the engine for oil, coolant and fuel leaks
Change engine oil and renew the oil filter
Check the exhaust system for security and leakage

Transmission
Adjust clutch play, where applicable
Check the driveshaft rubber boots for damage and leaks (photo)
Check level of oil/fluid in gearbox/transmission and final drive and top up if necessary
Check transmission for leaks

Brakes and tyres
Check operation of brake pressure regulator where applicable
Visually check the brake hydraulic circuit lines, hoses and unions for damage, deterioration and leaks
Check front disc pads and rear brake shoes for wear
Check the tyres for wear and tread depth

Lights
Check the headlight beam alignment and adjust if necessary

Suspension and steering
Check the steering tie-rod end balljoints for wear, and damage to the dust covers
Check the suspension balljoints for wear, and damage to the dust covers
Check the steering gear bellows for damage and leaks
Check the power-assisted steering fluid level and top up if necessary

Body
Check the body underseal for damage and apply more if necessary

General
Road test car and check the operation of all systems, in particular brakes and steering

---

Every 20 000 miles (30 000 km) or 2 years – whichever comes first

---

Engine
Renew the fuel filter
Renew the air cleaner element and clean the body
Adjust valve clearances and renew valve cover gasket

Every 2 years

Brakes
Change the brake hydraulic fluid, bleed the system and check the operation of the brake system warning device

---

Every 30 000 miles (45 000 km) or 3 years – whichever comes first

---

Transmission
Change the automatic transmission fluid

MODELS FROM MODEL YEAR 1986 ONWARDS

Every 10 000 miles (15 000 km) or 12 months – whichever comes first

---

Engine
Check antifreeze strength and level, and top up if necessary
Check battery electrolyte level and top up if necessary
Check the engine for oil, coolant and fuel leaks
Change engine oil and renew oil filter
Check engine idling speed and CO content

Transmission
Check clutch play and adjust if necessary, where applicable
Check gearbox and driveshafts for leaks
Check automatic transmission fluid level, where applicable

Brakes and tyres
Check the brake hydraulic circuit lines, hoses and unions for damage, deterioration and leaks
Check disc pads and brake shoes for wear
Check brake fluid level and top up if necessary
Check operation of footbrake and handbrake
Check tyres for wear and damage

Lights, wipers and horn
Check headlight beam alignment and adjust if necessary
Check operation of all lights and horn
Check operation of windscreen wipers and washers, and top up fluid if necessary

Suspension and steering
Check steering tie-rod ends for wear
Check front suspension lower balljoints for wear
Check operation of steering

Body
Grease door check straps

Every 20 000 miles (30 000 km) or 2 years – whichever comes first

---

Engine
Check condition and tension of alternator drivebelt and adjust if necessary
Renew the spark plugs
Check and if necessary adjust the valve clearances (except on engines with hydraulic tappets)
Renew air filter element
Renew fuel filter

Transmission
Clean automatic transmission sump and filter, and change fluid

Steering
Check power steering fluid level and top up where necessary

Body
Check underbody sealant and apply where necessary

Every 2 years

Brakes
Renew the brake hydraulic fluid

Fault diagnosis

Introduction

The vehicle owner who does his or her own maintenance according to the recommended schedules should not have to use this section of the manual very often. Modern component reliability is such that, provided those items subject to wear or deterioration are inspected or renewed at the specified intervals, sudden failure is comparatively rare. Faults do not usually just happen as a result of sudden failure, but develop over a period of time. Major mechanical failures in particular are usually preceded by characteristic symptoms over hundreds or even thousands of miles. Those components which do occasionally fail without warning are often small and easily carried in the vehicle.

With any fault finding, the first step is to decide where to begin investigations. Sometimes this is obvious, but on other occasions a little detective work will be necessary. The owner who makes half a dozen haphazard adjustments or replacements may be successful in curing a fault (or its symptoms), but he will be none the wiser if the fault recurs and he may well have spent more time and money than was necessary. A calm and logical approach will be found to be more satisfactory in the long run. Always take into account any warning signs or abnormalities that may have been noticed in the period preceding the fault – power loss, high or low gauge readings, unusual noises or smells, etc – and remember that failure of components such as fuses or spark plugs may only be pointers to some underlying fault.

The pages which follow here are intended to help in cases of failure to start or breakdown on the road. There is also a Fault Diagnosis Section at the end of each Chapter which should be consulted if the preliminary checks prove unfruitful. Whatever the fault, certain basic principles apply. These are as follows:

Verify the fault. This is simply a matter of being sure that you know what the symptoms are before starting work. This is particularly important if you are investigating a fault for someone else who may not have described it very accurately.

Don't overlook the obvious. For example, if the vehicle won't start, is there petrol in the tank? (Don't take anyone else's word on this particular point, and don't trust the fuel gauge either!) If an electrical fault is indicated, look for loose or broken wires before digging out the test gear.

Cure the disease, not the symptom. Substituting a flat battery with a fully charged one will get you off the hard shoulder, but if the underlying cause is not attended to, the new battery will go the same way. Similarly, changing oil-fouled spark plugs for a new set will get you moving again, but remember that the reason for the fouling (if it wasn't simply an incorrect grade of plug) will have to be established and corrected.

Don't take anything for granted. Particularly, don't forget that a 'new' component may itself be defective (especially if it's been rattling round in the boot for months), and don't leave components out of a fault diagnosis sequence just because they are new or recently fitted. When you do finally diagnose a difficult fault, you'll probably realise that all the evidence was there from the start.

Electrical faults

Electrical faults can be more puzzling than straightforward mechanical failures, but they are no less susceptible to logical analysis if the basic principles of operation are understood. Vehicle electrical wiring exists in extremely unfavourable conditions – heat, vibration and chemical attack – and the first things to look for are loose or corroded connections and broken or chafed wires, especially where the wires pass through holes in the bodywork or are subject to vibration.

All metal-bodied vehicles in current production have one pole of the battery 'earthed', ie connected to the vehicle bodywork, and in nearly all modern vehicles it is the negative (–) terminal. The various electrical components – motors, bulb holders etc – are also connected to earth, either by means of a lead or directly by their mountings. Electric current flows through the component and then back to the battery via the bodywork. If the component mounting is loose or corroded, or if a good path back to the battery is not available, the circuit will be incomplete and malfunction will result. The engine and/or gearbox are also earthed by means of flexible metal straps to the body or subframe; if these straps are loose or missing, starter motor, generator and ignition trouble may result.

Assuming the earth return to be satisfactory, electrical faults will be due either to component malfunction or to defects in the current supply. Individual components are dealt with in Chapter 10. If supply wires are broken or cracked internally this results in an open-circuit, and the easiest way to check for this is to bypass the suspect wire temporarily with a length of wire having a crocodile clip or suitable connector at each end. Alternatively, a 12V test lamp can be used to verify the presence of supply voltage at various points along the wire and the break can be thus isolated.

If a bare portion of a live wire touches the bodywork or other earthed metal part, the electricity will take the low-resistance path thus formed back to the battery: this is known as a short-circuit. Hopefully a short-circuit will blow a fuse, but otherwise it may cause burning of the insulation (and possibly further short-circuits) or even a fire. This is why it is inadvisable to bypass persistently blowing fuses with silver foil or wire.

Spares and tool kit

Most vehicles are supplied only with sufficient tools for wheel changing; the *Maintenance and minor repair* tool kit detailed in *Tools and working facilities,* with the addition of a hammer, is probably sufficient for those repairs that most motorists would consider attempting at the roadside. In addition a few items which can be fitted without too much trouble in the event of a breakdown should be carried. Experience and available space will modify the list below, but the following may save having to call on professional assistance:

Spark plugs, clean and correctly gapped
HT lead and plug cap – long enough to reach the plug furthest from the distributor
Drivebelt(s) – emergency type may suffice
Spare fuses
Set of principal light bulbs
Tin of radiator sealer and hose bandage
Exhaust bandage

Carrying a few spares may save you a long walk!

Roll of insulating tape
Length of soft iron wire
Length of electrical flex
Torch or inspection lamp (can double as test lamp)
Battery jump leads
Tow-rope
Ignition waterproofing aerosol
Litre of engine oil
Sealed can of hydraulic fluid
Emergency windscreen
Wormdrive clips
Tube of filler paste

If spare fuel is carried, a can designed for the purpose should be used to minimise risks of leakage and collision damage. A first aid kit and a warning triangle, whilst not at present compulsory in the UK, are obviously sensible items to carry in addition to the above.

When touring abroad it may be advisable to carry additional spares which, even if you cannot fit them yourself, could save having to wait while parts are obtained. The items below may be worth considering:

Clutch and throttle cables
Cylinder head gasket
Alternator brushes
Tyre valve core

One of the motoring organisations will be able to advise on availability of fuel etc in foreign countries.

Jump start lead connections for negative earth – connect leads in order shown

Engine will not start

Engine fails to turn when starter operated
Flat battery (recharge, use jump leads, or push start)
Battery terminals loose or corroded
Battery earth to body defective
Engine earth strap loose or broken
Starter motor (or solenoid) wiring loose or broken
Automatic transmission selector in wrong position, or inhibitor switch faulty
Ignition/starter switch faulty
Major mechanical failure (seizure)
Starter or solenoid internal fault (see Chapter 10)

A simple test lamp is useful for checking electrical faults

Starter motor turns engine slowly
Partially discharged battery (recharge, use jump leads, or push start)
Battery terminals loose or corroded
Battery earth to body defective
Engine earth strap loose
Starter motor (or solenoid) wiring loose
Starter motor internal fault (see Chapter 10)

Starter motor spins without turning engine
Flywheel gear teeth damaged or worn
Starter motor mounting bolts loose

Engine turns normally but fails to start
Damp or dirty HT leads and distributor cap (crank engine and check for spark)
No fuel in tank (check for delivery at carburettor)
Automatic choke faulty (carburettor engine)
Fouled or incorrectly gapped spark plugs (remove, clean and regap)
Other ignition system fault (see Chapter 4)
Other fuel system fault (see Chapter 3)
Poor compression (see Chapter 1)
Major mechanical failure (eg camshaft drive)

Engine fires but will not run
Automatic choke faulty (carburettor engine)
Air leaks at carburettor or inlet manifold
Fuel starvation (see Chapter 3)
Ballast resistor defective, or other ignition fault (see Chapter 4)

Engine cuts out and will not restart

Engine cuts out suddenly – ignition fault
Loose or disconnected LT wires
Wet HT leads or distributor cap (after traversing water splash)
Coil failure (check for spark)
Other ignition fault (see Chapter 4)

Engine misfires before cutting out – fuel fault
Fuel tank empty
Fuel pump defective or filter blocked (check for delivery)
Fuel tank filler vent blocked (suction will be evident on releasing cap)
Carburettor needle valve sticking
Carburettor jets blocked (fuel contaminated)
Other fuel system fault (see Chapter 3)

Engine cuts out – other causes
Serious overheating
Major mechanical failure (eg camshaft drive)

Engine overheats

Ignition (no-charge) warning light illuminated
Slack or broken drivebelt – retension or renew (Chapter 2)

Ignition warning light not illuminated
Coolant loss due to internal or external leakage (see Chapter 2)
Thermostat defective
Low oil level
Brakes binding
Radiator clogged externally or internally
Electric cooling fan not operating correctly
Engine waterways clogged
Ignition timing incorrect or automatic advance malfunctioning
Mixture too weak

Note: *Do not add cold water to an overheated engine or damage may result*

Low engine oil pressure

Gauge reads low or warning light illuminated with engine running
Oil level low or incorrect grade
Defective gauge or sender unit
Wire to sender unit earthed
Engine overheating
Oil filter clogged or bypass valve defective
Oil pressure relief valve defective
Oil pick-up strainer clogged
Oil pump worn or mountings loose
Worn main or big-end bearings

Note: *Low oil pressure in a high-mileage engine at tickover is not necessarily a cause for concern. Sudden pressure loss at speed is far more significant. In any event, check the gauge or warning light sender before condemning the engine.*

Engine noises

Pre-ignition (pinking) on acceleration
Incorrect grade of fuel
Ignition timing incorrect
Distributor faulty or worn
Worn or maladjusted carburettor
Excessive carbon build-up in engine

Whistling or wheezing noises
Leaking vacuum hose
Leaking carburettor or manifold gasket
Blowing head gasket

Tapping or rattling
Incorrect valve clearances (where applicable)
Worn valve gear
Worn timing chain or belt
Broken piston ring (ticking noise)

Knocking or thumping
Unintentional mechanical contact (eg fan blades)
Worn drivebelt
Peripheral component fault (generator, water pump etc)
Worn big-end bearings (regular heavy knocking, perhaps less under load)
Worn main bearings (rumbling and knocking, perhaps worsening under load)
Piston slap (most noticeable when cold)

Chapter 1 Engine

For modifications, and information applicable to later models, see Supplement at end of manual

Contents

Specifications

Part A – Four-cylinder engines

General

	1.6 litre	1.6 litre	1.8 litre
Engine code letters	WV, YN, YP	DT	DS
Capacity	1588 cc (96.9 cu in)	1595 cc (97.29 cu in)	1781 cc (108.6 cu in)
Bore	79.5 mm (3.13 in)	81.0 mm (3.16 in)	81.0 mm (3.18 in)
Stroke	80.0 mm (3.15 in)	77.4 mm (3.02 in)	86.4 mm (3.40 in)
Compression ratio	8.2 : 1	9.0 : 1	10.0 : 1
Firing order	1 - 3 - 4 - 2 (No 1 at timing belt end)		

Cylinder compression – bar (lbf/in²)

	WV, YN, YP	DT	DS
Compression pressure	10 to 12	9 to 12	10 to 13
	(145 to 174)	(131 to 174)	(145 to 188)
Minimum allowable pressure	7.5 (109)	7 (102)	7.5 (109)
Maximum pressure difference between cylinders	3 (44)	3 (44)	3 (44)

Lubrication system
Oil type/specification .... Multigrade engine oil, viscosity SAE 10W/40 or 15W/40, to VW 500.00 and 505.00 or 501.01 and 505.00 (Duckhams QXR or Hypergrade)

Oil capacity:
    Including filter .... 3.0 litre; 5.3 Imp pt
    Excluding filter .... 2.5 litre, 4.4 Imp pt
Difference between dipstick minimum and maximum marks .... 1.0 litre; 1.8 Imp pt
Oil pressure (minimum) at 2000 rpm .... 2 bar (29 lbf/in^2)
Oil pump:
    Gear backlash .... 0.05 to 0.20 mm (0.002 to 0.008 in)
    Gear endplay .... 0.15 mm (0.006 in)

Intermediate shaft
Endplay .... 0.25 mm (0.010 in)

Crankshaft
Needle bearing depth .... 1.5 mm (0.059 in)
End play:
    New .... 0.07 to 0.17 mm (0.003 to 0.007 in)
    Wear limit .... 0.25 mm (0.010 in)
Maximum main bearing running clearance .... 0.17 mm (0.007 in)
Main bearing journal diameter:
    Standard size .... 53.958 to 53.978 mm (2.1243 to 2.1251 in)
    1st undersize .... 53.708 to 53.728 mm (2.1145 to 2.1153 in)
    2nd undersize .... 53.458 to 53.478 mm (2.1047 to 2.1054 in)
    3rd undersize .... 53.208 to 53.228 mm (2.0948 to 2.0956 in)
Big-end bearing journal diameter – 1.6 engine (except 1.6 DT):
    Standard size .... 45.958 to 45.978 mm (1.8094 to 1.8102 in)
    1st undersize .... 45.708 to 45.728 mm (1.7995 to 1.8003 in)
    2nd undersize .... 45.458 to 45.478 mm (1.7897 to 1.7905 in)
    3rd undersize .... 45.208 to 45.228 mm (1.7798 to 1.7806 in)
Big-end bearing journal diameter – 1.6 DT and 1.8 engine:
    Standard size .... 47.758 to 47.778 mm (1.8802 to 1.8810 in)
    1st undersize .... 47.508 to 47.528 mm (1.8704 to 1.8712 in)
    2nd undersize .... 47.258 to 47.278 mm (1.8606 to 1.8613 in)
    3rd undersize .... 47.008 to 47.028 mm (1.8507 to 1.8515 in)

Pistons and rings
Piston-to-bore clearance
    New .... 0.03 mm (0.0012 in)
    Wear limit .... 0.07 mm (0.0028 in)
Groove-to-ring clearance:
    New .... 0.02 to 0.05 mm (0.0008 to 0.0020 in)
    Wear limit .... 0.15 mm (0.0059 in)

	Piston diameter	Bore diameter
Piston size – 1.6 engine (except 1.6 DT):		
Standard size	79.48 mm (3.1291 in)	79.51 mm (3.1307 in)
1st oversize	79.73 mm (3.1390 in)	79.76 mm (3.1042 in)
2nd oversize	79.98 mm (3.1488 in)	80.01 mm (3.1500 in)
3rd oversize	80.48 mm (3.1685 in)	80.51 mm (3.1697 in)
Piston size – 1.6 DT and 1.8 engine:		
Standard size	80.98 mm (3.1881 in)	81.01 mm (3.1893 in)
1st oversize	81.23 mm (3.1980 in)	81.26 mm (3.1992 in)
2nd oversize	81.48 mm (3.2078 in)	81.51 mm (3.2090 in)
3rd oversize	81.98 mm (3.2275 in)	82.01 mm (3.2287 in)

Cylinder bore
Maximum allowable deviation .... 0.08 mm (0.0031 in)
Piston ring endgap clearance (ring 15 mm/0.6 in from bottom of bore):
    New .... 0.30 to 0.45 mm (0.012 to 0.018 in)
    Two section scraper rings .... 0.25 to 0.40 mm (0.0098 to 0.0157 in)
    Three section scraper rings .... 0.25 to 0.50 mm (0.0098 to 0.0196 in)
    Wear limit .... 1.0 mm (0.040 in)

Connecting rods
Maximum endplay .... 0.37 mm (0.015 in)
Big-end bearing running clearance:
    New .... 0.028 to 0.088 mm (0.0011 to 0.0035 in)
    Wear limit .... 0.12 mm (0.0047 in)

Camshaft
Maximum endplay .... 0.15 mm (0.006 in)

Valves

Valve clearances:	
Engine warm:	
Inlet	0.20 to 0.30 mm (0.008 to 0.012 in)
Exhaust	0.40 to 0.50 mm (0.016 to 0.020 in)
Engine cold:	
Inlet	0.15 to 0.25 mm (0.006 to 0.010 in)
Exhaust	0.35 to 0.45 mm (0.014 to 0.018 in)
Adjusting shim thicknesses	3.00 to 4.25 mm (0.118 to 0.167 in) in increments of 0.05 mm
Valve guides:	
Maximum valve rock (measured at head):	
Inlet	1.0 mm (0.039 in)
Exhaust	1.3 mm (0.051 in)

Valve timing at 1 mm lift/zero clearance

	1.6 except DT	1.6 DT	1.8 DS
Inlet opens BTDC	4°	5°	1°
Inlet closes ABDC	46°	21°	37°
Exhaust opens BBDC	44°	41°	42°
Exhaust closes ATDC	6°	3° (BTDC)	2°

Cylinder head

Minimum height (between faces)	132.60 mm (5.220 in)
Maximum gasket face distortion allowable	0.1 mm (0.004 in)
Valve seat angle (inlet and exhaust)	45°

Part B — five-cylinder engines

1.9 litre engine

General

Engine code	WN
Capacity	1921 cc (117.2 cu in)
Bore	79.5 mm (3.13 in)
Stroke	77.4 mm (3.05 in)
Compression ratio	10.0 : 1
Cylinder compression:	
Compression pressure	10.0 to 14.0 bar (145 to 203 lbf/in^2)
Minimum pressure	8 bar (116 lbf/in^2)
Maximum pressure difference between cylinders	3 bar (44 lbf/in^2)
Firing order	1 - 2 - 4 - 5 - 3 (No 1 at timing belt end)

Lubrication system

Oil type/specification	Multigrade engine oil, viscosity SAE 10W/40 or 15W/40, to VW 500.00 and 505.00 or 501.01 and 505.00 (Duckhams QXR or Hypergrade)
Oil capacity:	
Including filter	3.5 litre; 6.1 Imp pt
Excluding filter	3.0 litre; 5.2 Imp pt
Difference between dipstick minimum and maximum marks	1.0 litre; 1.76 Imp pt
Oil pressure (minimum) at idle	1 bar (14.5 lbf/in^2)
Oil pressure (minimum) at 2000 rpm	2 bar (29 lbf/in^2)

Crankshaft

Needle bearing depth	5.5 mm (0.217 in)
Endplay:	
New	0.07 to 0.18 mm (0.003 to 0.007 in)
Wear limit	0.25 mm (0.010 in)
Maximum main bearing running clearance	0.16 mm (0.006 in)
Main bearing journal diameter:	
Standard size	57.958 to 57.978 mm (2.2818 to 2.2825 in)
1st undersize	57.708 to 57.728 mm (2.2719 to 2.2727 in)
2nd undersize	57.458 to 57.478 mm (2.2621 to 2.2629 in)
3rd undersize	57.208 to 57.228 mm (2.2522 to 2.2530 in)
Big-end journal diameter:	
Standard size	45.958 to 45.978 mm (1.8093 to 1.8101 in)
1st undersize	45.708 to 45.728 mm (1.7995 to 1.8003 in)
2nd undersize	45.458 to 45.478 mm (1.7896 to 1.7904 in)
3rd undersize	45.208 to 45.228 mm (1.7798 to 1.7806 in)
Maximum journal out-of-round	0.03 mm (0.0012 in)

Pistons and rings

Piston-to-bore clearance:	
New	0.025 mm (0.001 in)
Wear limit	0.07 mm (0.0028 in)
Groove-to-ring clearance:	
New	0.02 to 0.08 mm (0.0008 to 0.0032 in)
Wear limit	0.1 mm (0.004 in)

Piston rings endgap clearance (ring 15 mm/0.6 in from bottom of bore):
　New .... 0.25 to 0.50 mm (0.010 to 0.020 in)
　Wear limit .... 1.0 mm (0.040 in)

Piston size	Piston diameter	Bore diameter
Standard size	79.48 mm (3.1291 in)	79.51 mm (3.1303 in)
1st oversize	79.73 mm (3.1389 in)	79.76 mm (3.1401 in)
2nd oversize	79.98 mm (3.1488 in)	80.01 mm (3.1499 in)
3rd oversize	80.48 mm (3.1684 in)	80.51 mm (3.1696 in)

Cylinder bore
Maximum allowable deviation .... 0.08 mm (0.0031 in)

Connecting rods
Maximum endplay .... 0.4 mm (0.016 in)
Big-end bearing running clearance:
　New .... 0.015 to 0.062 mm (0.0006 to 0.0024 in)
　Wear limit .... 0.12 mm (0.0047 in)

Camshaft
Maximum endplay .... 0.15 mm (0.006 in)

Valves
Valve clearances .... As 1.6 and 1.8 four-cylinder engines
Adjusting shim thicknesses .... 3.00 to 4.25 mm (0.118 to 0.167 in) in increments of 0.05 mm
Valve guides .... As 1.6 and 1.8 four-cylinder engines

Valve timing at 1 mm valve lift/zero clearance
Inlet opens BTDC .... 10°
Inlet closes ABDC .... 36°
Exhaust opens BBDC .... 45°
Exhaust closes ATDC .... 3°

Cylinder head
Minimum height (between faces) .... 132.75 mm (5.2264 in)
Maximum gasket face distortion .... 0.1 mm (0.004 in)
Valve seat angle .... 45°

2.0 litre engine

At the time of publication, limited information was available for the 2.0 litre engine. With the exception of those items listed below, specifications are generally as for the 1.6 DT and 1.9 engines. If in doubt, contact your dealer for further information.

General
Engine code .... JS (from July 1983 on)
Capacity .... 1994 cc
Bore .... 81 mm (3.19 in)
Stroke .... 77.4 mm (3.05 in)
Compression ratio .... 10.0 : 1

Valve timing at 1 mm valve lift/zero clearance
Inlet opens BTDC .... 1°
Inlet closes ABDC .... 43°
Exhaust opens BBDC .... 43°
Exhaust closes ATDC .... 1°

Torque wrench settings
Part A – 1.6 and 1.8 litre

	Nm	lbf ft
Cylinder head bolts:		
Stage 1	40	29
Stage 2	60	43
Stage 3	75	54
Stage 4	Tighten a further quarter turn (90°) – in one movement	
Note: *Do not retighten the socket-head bolts during servicing*		
Engine to transmission	55	40
Engine mountings	35	25
Engine support to block	25	18
Main bearing caps	65	47
Crankshaft front oil housing	10	7
Intermediate shaft flange	25	18
Crankshaft rear oil seal housing	10	7
Big-end nuts:		
M9 (rigid bolts)	45	33
M8 (stretch bolts):		
Stage 1	30	22
Stage 2	Tighten a further quarter turn (90°) – in one movement	
Camshaft gear	80	58
Timing cover (upper, lower and rear sections)	10	7
Crankshaft pulley to gear	20	14

	Nm	lbf ft
Crankshaft gear bolt:		
M12 (with thread locking compound)	80	58
M14 (oiled threads)	200	148
Intermediate shaft gear	80	58
Tensioner nut	45	33
Valve (cylinder head) cover	10	7
Camshaft bearing cap	20	14
Oil pressure switch	25	18
Oil filter head	25	18
Oil pump to block	20	14
Oil pump cover	10	7
Sump bolts	20	14
Sump drain plug	30	22
Engine to gearbox cover plate	10	7
Exhaust pipe to manifold	30	22
Starter motor	20	14
Flywheel bolts – early (non-shouldered) type	75	54
Flywheel bolts – late (shouldered) type	100	72

Part B – 1.9 and 2.0 litre

	Nm	lbf ft
Engine to gearbox:		
M8	20	14
M10	45	32
M12	60	43
Exhaust pipe to manifold	30	21
Subframe to body	70	51
Engine support to mounting	45	32
Cylinder head bolts:		
Stage 1	40	29
Stage 2	60	43
Stage 3	75	54
Stage 4	Tighten a further quarter turn (90°) – in one movement	
Note: *Do not retighten the socket-head bolts during servicing*		
Main bearing caps	65	47
Oil pump to block:		
Bolt (long)	20	14
Stud and bolt (short)	10	7
Oil pick-up	10	7
Crankshaft rear oil seal housing	10	7
Big-end nuts	50	36
Valve (cylinder head) cover	10	7
Timing cover	10	7
Camshaft bearing cap	20	14
Camshaft gear	80	58
Oil pump pressure relief valve	40	29
Crankshaft pulley vibration damper bolt	450	332
Sump bolt	20	14
Sump drain plug	40	29
Flywheel cover bolts	25	18
Flywheel bolts – early (non-shouldered) type	75	54
Flywheel bolts – late (shouldered) type	100	72

Part A – Four-cylinder engines

1 General description

The engine is of four-cylinder, in-line overhead camshaft type mounted conventionally at the front of the car. The crankshaft is of five-bearing type and the centre main bearing shells incorporate flanged or separate thrust washers to control crankshaft endfloat. The camshaft is driven by a toothed belt from the crankshaft sprocket, and the belt also drives the intermediate shaft which is used to drive the distributor, oil pump and on carburettor engines, the fuel pump. The valves are operated from the camshaft through bucket type tappets, and valve clearances are adjusted by the use of shims located in the top of the tappets.

The engine has a full-flow lubrication system from a gear type oil pump mounted in the sump, and driven by an extension of the distributor which is itself geared to the intermediate shaft. The oil filter is of the cartridge type, mounted on the left-hand side of the cylinder block. The oil pressure switch is located on the rear of the cylinder head (photo).

1.2 Oil pressure switch location on rear face of cylinder head (1.6 litre)

Fig. 1.1 Exploded view of the major components of the four-cylinder engine (Sec 1)

Cap

Cylinder head cover

Reinforcement strip

Plug

Gasket for cylinder head cover

Cylinder head bolt

Camshaft gear

Cylinder head

Distributor

Cylinder head gasket

Intermediate flange

Fuel pump

Oil filter bracket

Sealing ring

Gaskets

Woodruff key

Oil filter

Left support

Sump

Hammer head screw

Gasket for sump

Coolant pump

Toothed belt

Plug

Belt guard rear

Upper belt guard

Plug

Tensioning roller

Intermediate shaft gear

Crankshaft gear

Belt guard lower

Belt pulley

V belt

Fig. 1.2 Exploded view of the timing assembly components (four-cylinder engine) (Sec 1)

2 Engine – routine maintenance

The following routine maintenance procedures should be undertaken at the specified intervals given at the start of this manual. The intervals given are those for a vehicle used in normal driving conditions. Where the vehicle is subject to more severe daily use, such as city driving or in a hot dusty climate, then it is advisable to reduce the maintenance intervals accordingly.

Engine oil check: Check the engine oil with the vehicle parked on level ground, the engine switched off and having been stationary for a short period. This will allow oil in the lubrication circuits to return to the sump to provide a true level reading. The dipstick should be withdrawn, wiped clean, fully inserted then withdrawn again to take the oil level reading. The oil level must be kept between the maximum and minimum markings on the dipstick at all times. If the oil level is down to the minimum mark, it will need a litre (1.7 Imp pint) to raise the oil level to the maximum mark. Do not overfill the engine. Top up through the oil filler neck in the cylinder head cover (photo). Check that the cover is firmly refitted and wipe clean any oil spillage. Recheck the oil level on completion.

Engine oil change: With the vehicle standing on level ground, remove the drain plug from the sump and drain the old engine oil into a container of suitable capacity. Draining is best undertaken directly after the vehicle has been used when the engine oil will be hot and will flow more freely. When draining is complete, refit the drain plug and top up the engine oil to the correct level with the specified grade and quantity of engine oil.

Engine oil filter: The oil filter must be renewed at the specified intervals. The filter is best removed whilst waiting for the engine oil to drain. Renewing the oil filter is described in Section 28 of this Chapter.

Engine general checks: Inspect the engine regularly for any signs of oil, coolant or fuel leaks and if found attend to them without delay.

2.2 Topping up engine oil

3 Major operations possible with the engine in the car

The following operations can be carried out without having to remove the engine from the car:

(a) *Removal and servicing of the cylinder head and camshaft*
(b) *Removal of the timing belt and gears*
(c) *Removal of the flywheel or driveplate (after first removing the transmission)*
(d) *Removal of the sump (after first lowering the subframe)*
(e) *Removal of the oil pump, pistons and connecting rods*

4 Major operations only possible after removal of the engine from the car

The following operations can only be carried out after removal of the engine from the car:

(a) *Removal of the intermediate shaft*
(b) *Removal of the crankshaft and main bearings*

5 Method of engine removal

The engine can be lifted from the car either separately or together with the manual gearbox. On automatic transmission models it is recommended that the engine is removed separately because of the extra weight involved.

6 Engine – removal and refitting

1 Remove the bonnet as described in Chapter 12 then position it out of the way in a safe place, standing it upright on cardboard or rags.
2 Disconnect the battery earth lead.
3 Remove the radiator as described in Chapter 2.
4 Unclip and detach the wiring connector from the rear face of the alternator.
5 Remove the air cleaner unit from the carburettor as described in Chapter 3.
6 Identify those coolant, fuel and vacuum hoses affecting engine removal, label or mark them with masking tape then disconnect them. These will include the fuel hose to the fuel pump and the return hose from the filter unit, the vacuum hose at inlet manifold (to servo) and the vacuum line from the reserve chamber to the carburettor.
7 Identify all wiring for location using masking tape, then disconnect those affecting engine removal. These may include the wiring to the oil pressure switch, temperature sender, distributor coil and inlet manifold pre-heater.
8 On manual gearbox models disconnect the clutch cable from the release lever and cable bracket. Disconnect the throttle cable, as described in Chapter 3. Disconnect the hose from the inlet manifold (where applicable) and the heater hoses from the bulkhead. Also disconnect the heat exchanger hose from the outlet connection at the rear of the cylinder head. Be prepared for additional coolant spillage when disconnecting this hose.
9 Unscrew the left-hand side engine mounting nut from the top and the right-hand side engine mounting from the bottom (photo).
10 Unscrew the nuts and separate the exhaust downpipe from the exhaust manifold.
11 Unbolt the support arm from the front of the engine (at the front) (photo).
12 Disconnect the wiring from the starter motor (with reference to Chapter 10).
13 On models with power steering remove the power steering pump and tie it to one side, with reference to Chapter 11.

Removing engine without transmission
14 Remove the starter motor, as described in Chapter 10.
15 On automatic transmission models unscrew the three torque converter-to-driveplate bolts while holding the starter ring gear stationary with a screwdriver. It will be necessary to rotate the engine to position the bolts in the starter aperture, using a socket on the crankshaft pulley bolt (Figure 1.3).
16 Unbolt the cover plate from the front of the transmission (photo).
17 Detach the exhaust downpipe from the front mounting and tie the pipe to one side.
18 Connect a hoist and take the weight of the engine – the hoist should be positioned centrally over the engine.
19 Support the weight of the transmission with a trolley jack.
20 Unscrew and remove the engine-to-transmission bolts noting the location of the brackets and earth strap.
21 Lift the engine from the mountings and reposition the trolley jack beneath the transmission.
22 Pull the engine from the transmission – make sure on automatic transmission models that the torque converter remains fully engaged with the transmission splines.
23 With the aid of an assistant lift and guide the engine upwards from the engine compartment taking care not to snag it on surrounding components, the brake lines in particular. With the engine lifted clear of the vehicle, lower it to the ground or preferably onto an engine trolley if available.
24 The rear engine plate can be removed at this stage for protection by simply easing it rearwards off its locating dowels and then withdrawing it from between the engine and flywheel/driveplate.

Removing engine with manual transmission attached
25 Detach the exhaust downpipe from the front mounting and tie the pipe to one side.
26 Disconnect the reverse light/gearshift indicator/econometer wiring multi-plug connector above the clutch housing.
27 Unscrew the nut and disconnect the speedometer cable from the differential case.
28 Disconnect the driveshafts from the drive flanges with reference to Chapter 8. Tie them up and support to the side out of the way.

6.9 Engine mounting (right-side) viewed from below (1.6 litre)

6.16 Cover plate removal (1.6 litre)

6.11 Engine front support (1.6 litre)

29 Disconnect the gearshaft rod coupling from the internal selector lever by unscrewing and removing the location bolt then levering the support strut from the balljoint. The shift rod can then be pulled free from the selector lever.

30 Disconnect the earth lead from the upper bellhousing bolt on the left-hand side.

31 Support the transmission with a trolley jack.

32 Loosen the bolt securing the gearbox stay to the underbody. Unscrew and remove the stay inner bolt and pivot the stay from the gearbox.

33 Unbolt the bonded rubber mounting from the gearbox and also unbolt the front gearbox support bracket.

6.35 Engine and gearbox removal (1.6 litre)

34 Connect a hoist and take the weight of the engine – the hoist should be positioned near the front of the engine so that the engine and gearbox will hang at a steep angle (photo).

35 Lift the engine from the mountings and move it forwards, then lower the trolley jack and lift the engine and gearbox from the engine compartment while turning it, as necessary, to clear the body. Lower the engine and gearbox to the floor (photo).

36 If necessary, separate the gearbox from the engine by removing the starter (Chapter 10), gearbox front cover, and engine-to-gearbox bolts. Remove the rear engine plate.

Fig. 1.3 Torque converter to drive plate bolt (automatic transmission model) – remove through starter motor aperture (Sec 6)

Refitting

37 Refitting is a reversal of the removal procedure, but before starting the engine check that it has been filled with oil and also that the cooling system is full. Delay tightening the engine and gearbox mountings until the engine is idling – this will ensure that the engine is correctly aligned. Make sure that the starter cable is not touching the engine or mounting bracket, and is clear of the exhaust system.

38 Adjust the accelerator cable as described in Chapter 3.

39 Adjust the clutch cable as described in Chapter 5.

40 Tighten the engine to gearbox and engine mounting bolts to the specified torque wrench settings.

7 Engine dismantling – general

1 If possible position the engine on a bench or strong table for the dismantling procedure. Two or three blocks of wood will be necessary to support the engine in an upright position.

2 Cleanliness is most important, and if the engine is dirty, it should be cleaned with paraffin before commencing work.

3 Avoid working with the engine directly on a concrete floor, as grit presents a real source of trouble.

4 As parts are removed, clean them in a paraffin bath. However, do not immerse parts with internal oilways in paraffin as it is difficult to remove, usually requiring a high pressure hose. Clean oilways with nylon pipe cleaners.

5 It is advisable to have suitable containers to hold small items according to their use, as this will help when reassembling the engine and also prevent possible losses.

6 Always obtain complete sets of gaskets when the engine is being dismantled, but retain the old gaskets with a view to using them as a pattern to make a replacement if a new one is not available.

7 When possible, refit nuts, bolts, and washers in their location after being removed, as this helps to protect the threads and will also be helpful when reassembling the engine.

8 Retain unserviceable components in order to compare them with the new parts supplied.

8 Ancillary components – removal and refitting

With the engine removed from the car, the externally mounted ancillary components in the following list can be removed. The removal sequence need not necessarily follow the order given:

Inlet and exhaust manifolds (Chapter 3)
Fuel pump or warm-up regulator, as applicable (Chapter 3)
HT leads and spark plugs (Chapter 4)
Oil filter cartridge (Section 28 of this Chapter)
Distributor (Chapter 4)
Dipstick
Alternator (Chapter 10)
Engine mountings (Section 29 of this Chapter)

9 Cylinder head and camshaft – removal

Note: *If the engine is still in the car, first carry out the following operations:*

(a) Disconnect the battery negative lead
(b) Drain the cooling system
(c) Remove the alternator
(d) Remove the inlet and exhaust manifolds
(e) Remove the HT leads and spark plugs
(f) Disconnect all wiring, cables and hoses
(g) Disconnect the exhaust downpipe from the exhaust manifold

CAUTION: *To avoid possible damage to the valves and piston crowns on 1.8 litre engines, do not rotate the crankshaft or camshaft with the timing belt removed.*

1 Unscrew the nuts and lift off the upper timing cover, using an Allen key where necessary (photos).

2 Unscrew the nuts and lift off the valve cover, together with the reinforcement strips and gaskets (photos).

3 Unbolt the outlet elbows and remove the gaskets if necessary (photo).

4 Using a socket on the crankshaft pulley bolt, turn the engine so

9.1A Upper timing cover top nuts

9.1B Upper timing cover bottom nut

9.2A Remove the reinforcement strips ...

9.2B ... and valve cover

9.3 Cylinder head side outlet

9.2C Remove the valve cover from the front gasket ...

9.4 Crankshaft pulley notch aligned with the TDC arrow on lower timing cover

9.2D ... and the rear plug (this must be renewed)

that the piston in No 1 cylinder is at TDC (top dead centre) on its compression stroke. The notch in the crankshaft pulley must be in line with the arrow on the lower timing cover (photo), and both No 1 cylinder valves must be closed (ie cam peaks away from the tappets). The notch on the rear of the camshaft gear will also be in line with the top of the timing belt rear cover.

5   Loosen the nut on the timing belt tensioner, and using an open-ended spanner, rotate the eccentric hub anti-clockwise to release the belt tension.

6   Remove the timing belt from the camshaft gear and tensioner and move it to one side while keeping it in firm contact with the intermediate and crankshaft gears. *The intermediate gear must not be moved, otherwise the ignition timing will be lost and the lower timing cover will have to be removed.*

7   Unscrew the nut and remove the timing belt tensioner.

8   Unscrew the bolt securing the timing belt rear cover to the cylinder head.

9   Using a splined socket unscrew the cylinder head bolts a turn at a time in reverse order to that shown in Fig. 1.9.

10   With all the bolts removed lift the cylinder head from the block. If it is stuck, tap it free with a wooden mallet. *Do not insert a lever into the gasket joint.*

11   Remove the cylinder head gasket.

Bearing caps

Camshaft

Woodruff key

Adjustment shim

Bucket tappet

Spring seat

Lower spring seat

Outer valve spring

Inner valve spring

Valve stem seal

Plug

Valve guide

Oil seal

Cylinder head

Valves

Fig. 1.4 Cylinder head, valves and camshaft components (four-cylinder engine) (Sec 10)

10.3A Remove the camshaft gear

10.3B Camshaft gear Woodruff key

10.4A The number 3 camshaft bearing cap

10.4B Removing No 1 camshaft bearing cap

10.6 Removing the camshaft

10.7 Removing a tappet together with its shim

10 Camshaft and tappets – removal

Note: *If the engine is still in the car, first carry out the following operations:*

   (a) Disconnect the battery negative lead

   (b) Disconnect the wiring, cables and hoses which cross the engine valve cover – remove the air cleaner on carburettor models

   (c) Remove the alternator/water pump drivebelt

1 Follow paragraphs 1 to 6 of Section 9, excluding paragraph 3.
2 Unscrew the centre bolt from the camshaft gear while holding the gear stationary with a bar through one of the holes.
3 Withdraw the gear from the camshaft and extract the Woodruff key (photos).
4 Unscrew the nuts from bearing caps 1, 3 and 5. Identify all the caps for position then remove caps 1, 3 and 5 (photos).
5 Loosen the nuts on bearing caps 2 and 4 evenly until all valve spring tension has been released, then remove the caps.
6 Lift out the camshaft and discard the oil seal (photo).
7 Have ready a board with eight pegs on it, or alternatively use a box with internal compartments, marked to identify cylinder numbers and whether inlet or exhaust or position in the head, numbering from the front of the engine. As each tappet is removed (photo), place it on the appropriate peg, or mark the actual tappet to indicate its position. *Note that each tappet has a shim (disc) fitted into a recess in its top. This shim must be kept with its particular tappet.*

11 Valves – removal and renovation

1 With the cylinder head removed as previously described, the valve gear can be dismantled as follows. Because the valves are recessed deeply into the top of the cylinder head, their removal requires a valve spring compressor with long claws or the use of some ingenuity in adapting other types of compressor. One method which can be employed is to use a piece of tubing of roughly the same diameter as the valve spring cover and long enough to reach above the top of the cylinder head. To be able to remove the valve collets, either cut a window in the tube on each side, or cut a complete section away, so that the tube is about three quarters of a circle.
2 Have ready a board with holes in it, into which each valve can be fitted as it is removed, or have a set of labelled containers so that each valve and its associated parts can be identified and kept separate. Inlet valves are Nos. 2-4-5-7, Exhaust valves are Nos 1-3-6-8, numbered from the timing belt end of the engine.
3 Compress each valve spring until the collets can be removed (photo). Take out the collets, release the spring compressor and remove it.

11.3 Compressing a valve spring for collet removal

4   Remove the valve spring cover, the outer and inner spring and the valve (photos). Thread the springs over the valve stem to keep them with the valve, and put on the valve spring cover. It is good practice, but not essential, to keep the valve springs the same way up, so that parts are refitted exactly as they were before removal.

5   Prise off the valve stem seals, or pull them off with pliers and discard them, then lift off the valve spring seat and place it with its valve (photos).

6   Examine the heads of the valves for pitting and burning, paying particular attention to the heads of the exhaust valves. The valve seats should be examined at the same time. If the pitting on the valve and seat is only slight, the marks can be removed by grinding the seats and valves together with coarse and then fine grinding paste. Where bad pitting has occurred, it will be necessary to have the valve seat re-cut and either use a new valve, or have the valve re-faced.

7   The refacing of valves and cutting of valve seats is not expensive and gives a far better result than grinding in valves which are badly pitted. Exhaust valves, if too worn for grinding in, must be discarded. Re-machining of exhaust valves is not permissible.

8   Valve grinding is carried out as follows: Smear a small quantity of coarse carborundum paste around the contact surface of the valve or seat and insert the valve into its guide. Apply a suction grinder tool to the valve head and grind in the valve by semi-rotary motion. This is

11.5A Remove the valve stem seal ...

11.4A Remove the valve spring cover, springs ...

11.5B ... and spring seat

11.4B ... and valve

produced by rolling the valve grinding tool between the palms of the hands. When grinding action is felt to be at an end, extract the valve, turn it and repeat the operation as many times as is necessary to produce a uniform matt grey surface over the whole seating area of the valve head and valve seat. Repeat the process using fine grinding paste.

9   Scrape away all carbon from the valve head and valve stem. Carefully clean away every trace of grinding paste, taking care to leave none in the ports, or in the valve guides. Wipe the valves and valve seats with a paraffin soaked rag and then with a clean dry rag.

12 Cylinder head – examination and renovation

1   Check the cylinder head for distortion, by placing a straight edge across it at a number of points, lengthwise, crosswise and diagonally, and measuring the gap beneath it with feeler gauges. If the gap exceeds the limit given in the Specifications, the head must be refaced by a workshop which is equipped for this work. Re-facing must not reduce the cylinder head height below the minimum dimension given in the Specifications (Figure 1.5).

2   Examine the cylinder head for cracks. If there are minor cracks of not more than 0.5 mm (0.020 in) width between the valve seats, or at

Fig. 1.5 Check cylinder head for distortion (Sec 12)

Fig. 1.6 Check valve guide wear by measuring valve movement using a dial gauge (Sec 12)

the bottom of the spark plug holes, the head can be re-used, but a cylinder head cannot be repaired or new valve seat inserts fitted.
3   Check the valve guides for wear. First clean out the guide and then insert the stem of a new valve into the guide. Because the stem diameters are different, ensure that only an inlet valve is used to check the inlet valve guides, and an exhaust valve for the exhaust valve guides. With the end of the valve stem flush with the top of the valve guide, measure the total amount by which the rim of the valve head can be moved sideways. If the movement exceeds the maximum amount given in the Specifications, new guides should be fitted, but this is a job for a VW dealer, or specialist workshop (Figure 1.6).

13 Camshaft and bearings – examination and renovation

1   Examine the camshaft for signs of damage or excessive wear. If either the cam lobes or any of the journals have wear grooves, a new camshaft must be fitted.
2   With the camshaft fitted in its bearings, but with the bucket tappets removed so that there is no pressure on the crankshaft,

measure the endfloat of the camshaft, which should not exceed the limit given in the Specifications.
3   The camshaft bearings are normally part of the cylinder head and cannot be renewed. The bearing clearance is very small and the clearances can only be checked with a dial gauge. *If there is excessive looseness in the camshaft bearings, do not attempt to decrease it by grinding or filing the bottoms of the bearing caps.*
4   Where an exchange engine or cylinder head has been fitted at some time it may be possible that the camshaft bearings are of shell type. If the shells are to be renewed, be sure to order the correct size as the camshaft may be of standard or undersize type. A cylinder head with an undersize camshaft will have a yellow identification paint mark over the VW – Audi marking.
5   If renewing the camshaft note that the 1.8 engine camshaft can be identified by a blue line between the 1st and 2nd cams, whilst later 1.6 models (from August 1983 on) have a yellow marking in this position (engine code DS), (Figure 1.7).

Fig. 1.7 Camshaft identification points on the 1.8 litre engine (Sec 13)

A   *Shoulder*   B   *Blue line*

14 Valves – refitting

1   Locate the valve spring seats over the guides, then press a new seal on to the top of each valve guide. A plastic sleeve should be provided with the valve stem seals, so that the seals are not damaged when the valves are fitted.
2   Apply oil to the valve stem and the stem seal. Fit the plastic sleeve over the top of the valve stem and insert the valve carefully. Remove the sleeve after inserting the valve. If there is no plastic sleeve, wrap a piece of thin adhesive tape round the top of the valve stem, so that it covers the recess for the collets and prevents the sharp edges of the recess damaging the seal. Remove the tape after fitting the valve.
3   Fit the inner and outer valve springs, then the valve spring cover. If renewing springs, they must only be renewed as a pair on any valve.
4   Fit the spring compressor and compress the spring just enough to allow the collets to be fitted. If the spring is pressed right down there is a danger of damaging the stem seal.
5   Fit the collets, release the spring compressor slightly and check that the collets seat properly, then remove the compressor.
6   Tap the top of the valve stem with a soft-headed hammer to ensure that the collets are seated.
7   Repeat the procedure for all the valves.

15 Camshaft and tappets – refitting

CAUTION: *To avoid possible damage to the valves and piston crowns on 1.8 litre engines, do not rotate the crankshaft or camshaft with the timing belt removed.*

1   Fit the bucket tappets to their original positions; the adjustment shims on the top of the tappets must be fitted so that the lettering on them is downward. Lubricate the tappets and the camshaft journals.
2   Lay the camshaft into the lower half of its bearings so that the lowest point of the cams of No 1 cylinder are towards the tappets, and fit the bearing caps in their original positions, making sure that they are the right way round before fitting them over the studs.
3   Fit the nuts to bearing caps Nos 2 and 4 and tighten them in diagonal sequence until the camshaft fully enters its bearings.

15.4 Tightening the camshaft bearing cap nuts

15.5 Installing the camshaft oil seal

15.8 Tightening the camshaft gear centre bolt

4   Fit the nuts to bearing caps Nos 1, 3 and 5, then tighten all the nuts to the specified torque in diagonal sequence (photo).
5   Smear a little oil onto the sealing lip and outer edge of the camshaft oil seal, then locate it open end first in the cylinder head No 1 camshaft bearing cap (photo).
6   Using a metal tube, drive the seal squarely into the cylinder head until flush with the front of the cylinder head – *if the seal is driven in further, it will block the oil return hole.*
7   Fit the Woodruff key in its groove and locate the gear on the end of the camshaft.
8   Fit the centre bolt and spacer and tighten the bolt to the specified torque while holding the gear stationary with a bar through one of the holes (photo).
9   Turn the camshaft gear and align the rear notch with the top of the timing belt rear cover (Figure 1.8).

Fig. 1.8 Camshaft gear TDC mark aligned with top of timing belt rear cover (Sec 15)

10   Without disturbing the intermediate gear setting, and keeping the timing belt in firm contact with the intermediate gear and crankshaft gear, locate the timing belt on the camshaft gear and tensioner. The crankshaft must be positioned with No 1 cylinder at TDC. If the position of the intermediate gear is in doubt, it must be checked with reference to Section 18.
11   Turn the timing belt tensioner clockwise and tension the timing belt until it can just be twisted 90° with the thumb and index finger midway between the camshaft and intermediate gears. Tighten the nut to secure the tensioner.
12   Check and, if necessary, adjust the valve clearances, as described in Section 17.
13   Refit the valve cover and reinforcement strips, together with new gaskets and seals, and tighten the nuts.
14   Refit the upper timing belt cover and tighten the nuts.
15   If the engine is in the car, reverse the preliminary procedures given in Section 10.

16 Cylinder head and camshaft – refitting

CAUTION: *To avoid possible damage to the valves and piston crowns on 1.8 litre engines, do not rotate the crankshaft or camshaft with the timing belt removed.*

1   Check that the top of the block is perfectly clean, then locate a new gasket on it with the words OBEN - TOP facing upward (photos).
2   Check that the cylinder head face is perfectly clean. Place two long rods or pieces of dowel in two cylinder head bolt holes at opposite ends of the block, to position the gasket and give a location for fitting the cylinder head. Lower the head on to the block (photo), remove the guides and insert the bolts and washers. Do not use jointing compound on the cylinder head joint.

16.1A Locate new cylinder head gasket onto the block ...

16.1B ... with words OBEN – TOP uppermost

16.2 Lower cylinder head into position

Fig. 1.9 Cylinder head bolt tightening sequence (Sec 16)

3   Tighten the bolts using the sequence shown in Fig. 1.9 in the four stages given in the Specifications to the specified torque (photo).
4   Insert and tighten the bolt securing the timing belt rear cover to the cylinder head.
5   Refit the timing belt tensioner and fit the nut finger tight.
6   Follow paragraphs 9 to 14 inclusive of Section 15.
7   Refit the outlet elbow together with a new gasket and tighten the bolts.
8   If the engine is in the car, reverse the preliminary procedures given in Section 9.

17 Valve clearances – checking and adjustment

1   Valve clearances are adjusted by inserting the appropriate thickness shim to the top of the tappet. Shims are available in thicknesses from 3.00 to 4.25 mm (0.118 to 0.167 in) in increments of 0.05 mm (0.002 in).
2   Adjust the valve clearances for the initial setting-up after fitting a new camshaft, or grinding in the valves with the engine cold. The valve clearances should be re-checked after 620 miles (1000 km), with the engine warm, and the coolant over 35°C (95°F).
3   On 1.8 litre engines it is important to note that the valve clearance adjustment must not be made when the piston is at TDC position, but at 90° before TDC. This ensures that the valves miss the pistons if the tappets are depressed. Remove the valve cover after removing the upper timing cover.
4   Fit a spanner to the crankshaft pulley bolt and turn the crankshaft until the highest points of the cams for one cylinder are pointing upwards and outwards at similar angles. Use feeler gauges to check the gap between the cam and the tappet and record the dimension (photo).
5   Repeat the operation for all four cylinders and complete the list of clearances. Valves are numbered from the timing belt end of the engine. Inlet valves are Nos 2-4-5-7, exhaust valves are Nos 1-3-6-8.
6   Where any tolerances exceed those given in the Specifications, remove the existing shim by placing a cranked dowel rod with a suitably shaped end between two tappets with the rod resting on the edge of the tappets (photo). With the piston for the relevant cylinder

16.3 Tighten the cylinder head bolts

17.4 Checking the valve clearances

17.6A Use a cranked dowel rod to depress the tappets

17.6B Removing a shim from a tappet (tappet removed)

17.6C Notches (arrowed) machined in tappet for removing the shim

at TDC compression, lever against the camshaft to depress the tappets sufficiently to remove the shim(s) from the top of the tappet(s). Do not overdepress the tappets so that the valves touch the pistons. Note that each tappet incorporates a notch in its upper rim so that a small screwdriver or similar tool can be used to remove the shim (photos).

7   Note the thickness of the shim (engraved on its underside), and calculate the shim thickness required to correct the clearance (photo). For example, if the measured clearance on an inlet valve (warm engine) is 0.35 mm (0.014 in) this is outside the tolerance specified for inlet valves which is 0.20 mm to 0.30 mm (0.008 to 0.012 in). The best adjustment is the mid-point of the range i.e. 0.25 mm (0.010 in) and the measured gap of 0.35 mm (0.014 in) is 0.1 mm (0.004 in) too great. If the shim which is taken out is 3.05 mm (0.120 in), it should be replaced by one of 3.15 mm (0.124 in).

8   Provided they are not worn or damaged, shims which have been removed can be re-used in other positions if they are of the correct thickness.

9   Refit the valve cover and upper timing cover, together with new gaskets, after checking and adjusting the valve clearances.

17.7 Engraved thickness in mm on the tappet shim underside

18 Timing belt and gears – removal and refitting

CAUTION: *To avoid possible damage to the valves and piston crowns on 1.8 litre engines, do not rotate the crankshaft or camshaft with the timing belt removed.*

1   If the engine is still in the car, disconnect the battery negative lead.
2   Remove the alternator drivebelt, with reference to Chapter 10.
3   Unscrew the two upper retaining bolts and the single nut (from the front face) and lift off the upper timing cover.
4   Unbolt and remove the pulley from the water pump.
5   Using a socket on the crankshaft pulley bolt, turn the engine so that the piston in No 1 cylinder is at TDC (top dead centre) on its compression stroke. The notch in the crankshaft pulley must be in line with the arrow on the lower timing cover, and both No 1 cylinder valves must be closed (ie cam peaks away from the tappets).
6   If it is required to remove the crankshaft gear, loosen the centre bolt now. Hold the crankshaft stationary with a wide-bladed screwdriver in the starter ring gear (starter motor removed) or engage top gear and apply the handbrake if the engine is still in the car.
7   With the TDC marks aligned unbolt the crankshaft pulley from the gear.
8   Unbolt and remove the lower timing cover.
9   Loosen the nut on the timing belt tensioner, and using an open-ended spanner rotate the eccentric hub anti-clockwise to release the belt tension (photo).
10   Remove the timing belt from the crankshaft, camshaft and intermediate gears, and from the tensioner.
11   Unscrew the nut and remove the timing belt tensioner (photo).
12   Unscrew the centre bolt and withdraw the intermediate gear (photo). Remove the Woodruff key. When loosening the centre bolt,

18.9 Turn the timing belt tensioner anti-clockwise to release the belt tension

18.11 Removing the timing belt tensioner

18.12 Removing the gear from the intermediate shaft

hold the gear stationary with a socket and bar on the rear timing cover bolt.

13 On early models, remove the centre bolt and withdraw the crankshaft gear (photos). Remove the Woodruff key. On models produced from October 1982, the crankshaft gear is located by means of a lug which engages with an angled slot on the end of the

18.13A On early models, remove the centre bolt ...

Fig. 1.10 Crankshaft gear location method on later models (Sec 18)

A   Angled slot   B   Sprocket lug

crankshaft. This modification replaced the Woodruff key engagement method used on earlier models, see Figure 1.10.

14 Unscrew the centre bolt from the camshaft gear while holding the gear stationary with a bar through one of the holes. Withdraw the gear and remove the Woodruff key.

15 Unbolt and remove the rear timing cover together with the alternator mounting bracket from the block and cylinder head (photos).

18.13B ... and withdraw the crankshaft gear

18.15A Remove the rear timing cover ...

18.15B ... and the alternator mounting bracket

18.18 Tightening the crankshaft gear centre bolt

18.19 Tightening the intermediate shaft gear centre bolt

16 Commence refitting by locating the alternator mounting bracket and rear timing cover on the engine and tightening the bolts.

17 Locate the Woodruff key and camshaft gear on the camshaft, insert the centre bolt and washer, and tighten the bolt.

18 Locate the Woodruff key (earlier models) and crankshaft gear on the crankshaft. On later models engage the crankshaft gear lug with the angled slot in the end of the crankshaft. Where an M12 bolt is used, apply a thread locking compound and insert the bolt and washer; where an M14 bolt is used, apply a little engine oil to the thread then insert the bolt and washer. While holding the crankshaft stationary, *tighten the bolt to the appropriate torque* (photo).

19 Locate the Woodruff key and intermediate gear on the intermediate shaft, then insert the centre bolt and washer, and tighten the bolt (photo).

20 Refit the timing belt tensioner and fit the nut finger tight.

21 Make sure that the notch on the rear of the camshaft gear is aligned with the top of the timing belt rear cover.

22 Temporarily fit the crankshaft pulley to the gear then, with No 1 piston at TDC, turn the intermediate gear so that the indentation is aligned with the notch in the pulley (photo). If the distributor has not been disturbed the rotor arm will point in the direction of No 1 distributor cap segment.

18.22 Crankshaft pulley TDC notch aligned with the indentation in the intermediate gear (arrowed)

23 Locate the timing belt on the gears and tensioner, turn the tensioner clockwise to pretension the timing belt, and check that the TDC marks are still correctly aligned.

24 Turn the tensioner clockwise until the timing belt can just be twisted 90° with the thumb and index finger midway between the camshaft and intermediate gears. Tighten the nut to secure the tensioner.

25 Remove the crankshaft pulley, fit the lower timing cover, and tighten the bolts.

26 Refit the crankshaft pulley and tighten the bolts.

27 Locate the pulley on the water pump and tighten the bolts.

28 Refit the upper timing cover and tighten the nuts.

29 Refit the alternator drivebelt, with reference to Chapter 10.

30 Reconnect the battery negative lead, where necessary.

19 Flywheel/driveplate – removal and refitting

Note: *If the engine is still in the car, first carry out the following operations:*

> (a) *On manual gearbox models, remove the gearbox (Chapter 6) and clutch (Chapter 5)*
>
> (b) *On automatic transmission models, remove the automatic transmission (Chapter 7)*

1   The flywheel/driveplate bolts are offset to ensure correct refitting. Unscrew the bolts while holding the flywheel/driveplate stationary (photos).

19.1A Remove the flywheel bolts

19.1B Use a bar and piece of angle iron to hold the flywheel stationary

19.2 Removing the flywheel

2   Lift the flywheel/driveplate from the crankshaft (photo). If removing a driveplate note the location of the shim and washer (Fig 1.11).
3   If the flywheel or driveplate are to be renewed you will need to make the appropriate timing mark for your model on the periphery of

Fig. 1.11 Drive plate components (automatic transmission models) (Sec 19)

1   Washer (chamfer to plate)   2   Shim

Fig. 1.12 Flywheel/driveplate ignition timing mark position – distance (a) to be 21 mm (0.82 in) left of the TDC mark (Sec 19)

Fig. 1.13 Check driveplate to block rear face distance (a) (Sec 19)

the new flywheel/driveplate, since the replacement will only be marked with the TDC mark (0). Measure to the left of centre from the TDC index then mark as shown by scribing or punching the timing index reference at the set distance specified for your model – see Figure 1.12.
4   Refitting is a reversal of the removal, but note that the retaining bolts must be renewed. Two bolt types have been fitted, the later type being identified by a shouldered head. On earlier and late models renew with this later type bolt where possible. It should be noted that the torque wrench setting for the two bolt types differs.
5   Coat the bolt threads with a locking agent prior to fitting and tightening to the specified torque.
6   If a replacement driveplate is fitted, its position must be checked and adjusted if necessary. The distance from the rear face of the block to the torque converter *mounting face* on the driveplate (Fig. 1.13) must be between 30.5 and 32.1 mm (1.20 and 1.26 in). If necessary, remove the driveplate and fit a spacer behind it to achieve the correct dimension.

20 Intermediate shaft – removal and refitting

1   Remove the distributor (Chapter 4), and the fuel pump (Chapter 3).
2   Remove the timing belt and intermediate gear as described in Section 18.
3   Remove the two bolts from the sealing flange, take off the sealing flange and the O-ring (photos).
4   Withdraw the intermediate shaft from the block (photos).
5   With the flange removed, the oil seal can be removed (photo). Fit

20.3A Removing the intermediate shaft sealing flange ...

20.3B ... and O-ring

20.4A Withdraw the intermediate shaft

20.4B The intermediate shaft

20.4C Showing intermediate shaft front bearing

20.5 Levering the intermediate shaft oil seal out from the flange

a new seal with its open face towards the engine and use a block of wood to drive the seal in flush. Oil the lips of the seal before fitting the sealing flange.

6   Refitting is a reversal of removal, but fit a new O-ring and check that the shaft endfloat does not exceed the amount given in the Specifications. Refer to Section 18 when refitting the timing belt and intermediate gear, and to Chapters 3 and 4 when refitting the fuel pump and distributor.

21 Sump – removal and refitting

Note: *If the engine is still in the car, first carry out the following operations:*

(a) Jack up the front of the car and support it on axle stands
(b) Support the weight of the engine with a hoist
(c) Unbolt and remove the transmission front cover

(d) Drain the engine oil
(e) Unscrew the subframe front bolts and lower the subframe

1   Unbolt and remove the sump, using an Allen key where necessary. Remove the dipstick.
2   Remove the gasket.
3   Refitting is a reversal of removal, but use a new gasket without adhesive (photo), and tighten the bolts evenly to the specified torque.

22 Crankshaft oil seals – renewal

Front oil seal
1   Remove the timing belt and crankshaft gear, as described in Section 18.
2   If an extractor tool is available the seal may be renewed without removing the housing, otherwise unbolt and remove the housing (including the relevant sump bolts) and remove the gasket (photo). If

21.3 Locating a new sump gasket on the block (do not use any sealant)

22.2 Removing the crankshaft front oil seal housing

22.3A Using a socket to fit a new crankshaft front oil seal

22.3B Crankshaft front oil seal correctly located in its housing

22.7A Removing the crankshaft rear oil seal housing

22.7B Locate the new crankshaft rear oil seal housing gasket on the dowels

the sump gasket is damaged while removing the housing it will be necessary to remove the sump and fit a new gasket. However, refit the sump *after* fitting the housing.

3   Drive the old seal out of the housing then dip the new seal in engine oil and drive it into the housing with a block of wood or a socket until flush (photos). Make sure that the closed end of the seal is facing outwards.

4   Fit the housing together with a new gasket and tighten the bolts evenly in diagonal sequence.

5   Refit the crankshaft gear and timing belt, as described in Section 18.

Rear oil seal

6   Remove the flywheel or driveplate, as described in Section 19.

7   Follow paragraphs 2 to 4 inclusive (photos).

8   Refit the flywheel or driveplate, as described in Section 19.

23 Oil pump – removal, examination and refitting

1   Remove the sump, as described in Section 21.

2   Using an Allen key unscrew the socket-headed bolts and withdraw the oil pump and strainer from the cylinder block (photo).

3   Remove the two hexagon-headed bolts from the pump cover and lift off the cover (photo).

4   Bend up the metal rim of the filter plate so that it can be removed and take the filter screen out (photo). Clean the screen thoroughly with paraffin and a brush.

5   Clean the pump casing, cover and gears.

6   Check the backlash of the gears with a feeler gauge (photo) and with a straight edge across the end face of the pump, measure the endplay of the gears (photo). Examine the pump cover grooves worn by the ends of the gears, which will effectively increase the endplay of

23.2 Removing the oil pump and strainer

23.3 Removing the oil pump cover

23.4 Oil pump filter screen

23.6A Checking the oil pump gear backlash ...

23.6B ... and endplay

the gears. If the wear on the pump is beyond the specified limits a new pump should be fitted.

7   Fill the pump housing with engine oil then reassemble and refit it using a reversal of the removal and dismantling procedure. Refer to Section 21 when refitting the sump.

24 Pistons and connecting rods – removal and dismantling

1   Remove the cylinder head (Section 9), timing belt (Section 18) and oil pump (Section 23).
2   Mark each connecting rod and cap in relation to its cylinder and position.
3   Turn the crankshaft so that No 1 piston is at the bottom of its bore, then unscrew the nuts/bolts and remove the big-end bearing cap (photo).
4   Using the handle of a hammer, push the piston and connecting rod out of the top of the cylinder. Put the bearing cap with its connecting rod and make sure that they both have the cylinder number marked on them. If any of the bearing shells become detached while removing the connecting rod and bearing cap, ensure that they are placed with their matching cap or rod (photo).
5   Repeat the procedure given in paragraphs 3 and 4 to remove the remaining pistons and connecting rods.
6   Before removing the pistons from the connecting rods, if necessary mark the connecting rods to show which side of them is towards the front of the engine. The casting marks on the rod and cap face towards the front of the engine (photo).
7   Remove the circlips from the grooves in the gudgeon pin holes and push the pin out enough for the connecting rod to be removed (photo). Do not remove the pins completely unless new ones are to be fitted, to ensure that the pin is not turned end for end when the piston is refitted. If the pin is difficult to push out, heat the piston by immersing it in hot water.
8   New bushes can be fitted to the connecting rods, but as they need to be reamed to size after fitting, the job is best left to a VW agent.
9   Using old feeler gauges, or pieces of rigid plastic inserted behind the piston rings, carefully ease each ring in turn off the piston. Lay the

rings out so that they are kept the right way up and so that the top ring can be identified. Carefully scrape the rings free of carbon and clean out the ring grooves on the pistons, using a piece of wood or a piece of broken piston ring.

25 Pistons and cylinder bores – examination

1   Examine the pistons and the bores for obvious signs of damage and excessive wear. If they appear to be satisfactory, make the following checks.
2   Measure the piston diameter at a position 15 mm (0.60 in) from the lower edge of the skirt and at 90° to the axis of the piston and compare this with the information in the Specifications.
3   Push a piston ring into the cylinder bore and use a piston to push the ring down the bore so that it is square in the bore and about 15 mm (0.6 in) from the bottom of the cylinder. Measure the ring gap using a feeler gauge (photo). If the gap is above the top limit, look for obvious signs of bore wear, or if a new piston ring is available, measure the gap when a new piston ring is fitted to the bore.
4   To measure the bore diameter directly a dial gauge with an internal measuring attachment is required. If one is available, measure each bore in six places and compare the readings with the wear limit given. Bore diameter should be measured 10 mm (0.4 in) from the top of the bore, 10 mm (0.4 in) from the bottom and at the mid-point. At each of the three stations, measure in-line with the crankshaft and at right angles to it. If the bores are worn beyond the limit, they will need to be rebored and new pistons fitted.
5   If one bore is oversize, all four must be rebored and a new set of pistons fitted, otherwise the engine will not be balanced. Connecting rods must only be fitted as complete sets and not be replaced individually.
6   Fit the rings to the pistons and use a feeler gauge to measure the gap between the piston ring and the side of its groove (photo). If the gap is beyond the wear limit, it is more likely that it is the piston

24.3 Removing a big-end bearing cap

24.4 Big-end bearing components

24.6 The casting marks (arrowed) which must face the front of the engine

24.7 Location of gudgeon pin circlip (arrowed) in piston

25.3 Checking a piston ring gap

25.6 Checking the piston ring clearance in its groove

Fig. 1.14 Checking the piston diameter (Sec 25)

groove rather than the ring which has worn, and either a new piston or a proprietary oversize ring will be required. If new piston rings are fitted the wear ridge at the top of the cylinder bore must be removed, or a stepped top ring used.

26 Piston and connecting rods – reassembly and refitting

1   Heat each piston in hot water, then insert the connecting rod and push in the pin until central. Make sure that the casting marks on the connecting rod and the arrow on the piston crown (photo) are facing the same way, then refit the circlips.
2   Before refitting the piston rings, or fitting new rings, check the gap of each ring in turn in its correct cylinder bore using a piston to push the ring down the bore, as described in the previous Section. Measure the gap between the ends of the piston ring, using feeler gauges. The gap must be within the limits given in the Specifications.
3   If the piston ring gap is too small, carefully file the piston ring end until the gap is sufficient. Piston rings are very brittle, so handle them carefully.
4   When fitting piston rings, look for the word TOP etched on one side of the ring and fit this side so that it is towards the piston crown. The outer recessed edge on the centre ring must face the gudgeon pin (photo).
5   Unless the big-end bearing shells are known to be almost new, it is worth fitting a new set when reassembling the engine. Clean the connecting rods and bearing caps thoroughly and fit the bearing shells so that the tang on the bearing engages in the recess in the connecting rod, or cap, and the ends of the bearing are flush with the joint face.
6   To refit the pistons, first space the joints in the piston rings so that they are at 120° intervals. Oil the rings and grooves generously and fit a piston ring compressor over the piston. To fit the pistons without using a piston ring compressor is difficult and there is a high risk of breaking a piston ring.

26.1 The arrow on the piston crown (arrowed) must face the front of the engine

7   Oil the cylinder bores and insert the pistons (photo) with the arrow on the piston crown pointing towards the front of the engine. Make sure that the relevant crankpin is at its furthest point from the cylinder.
8   When the piston is pushed in flush with the top of the bore, oil the two bearing halves and the crankshaft journal and guide the connecting rod half-bearing on to the crankpin.
9   Fit the big-end bearing cap complete with shell and tighten the nuts/bolts to the specified torque wrench setting (photo). Note that the contact surfaces of the conrod nuts must be lubricated with oil before fitting and tightening. New nuts/bolts are only required if the existing ones are damaged.
10   Rotate the crankshaft to ensure that everything is free, before fitting the next piston and connecting rod.
11   Using feeler gauges between the machined face of each big-end bearing, and the machined face of the crankshaft web, check the endplay, which should not exceed the maximum amount given in the Specifications.
12   Refit the oil pump (Section 23), timing belt (Section 18), and cylinder head (Section 16).

27 Crankshaft – removal, examination and refitting

1   With the engine removed from the car, remove the pistons and connecting rods, as described in Section 24.
2   Reassemble the big-end bearings to their matching connecting rods to ensure correct refitting.
3   Remove the crankshaft oil seals complete with housings, as described in Section 22.

26.4 Piston with all rings fitted correctly

26.7 Inserting a piston into its bore using a ring compressor

26.9 Tightening the big-end bearing cap bolts

4   Check that each main bearing cap is numbered for position.

5   Remove the bolts from each bearing cap in turn, then remove the caps and lift out the crankshaft (photos).

6   If the bearings are not being renewed, ensure that each half-bearing shell is identified so that it is put back in the same place from which it was removed. This also applies to the thrust washers if fitted – see paragraph 7. If the engine has done a high mileage and it is suspected that the crankshaft requires attention, it is best to seek the opinion of a VW dealer or crankshaft re-finishing specialist for advice on the need for regrinding. Unless the bearing shells (and thrust washers if applicable) are known to be almost new, it is worth fitting a new set when the crankshaft is refitted. If available, Plastigage may be used to check the running clearance of the existing bearings – a strip of Plastigage is placed across the crankshaft journal and then the bearing is assembled and tightened to the specified torque. After dismantling the bearing the width of the strip is measured with a gauge supplied with the strip, and the running clearance read off (photo).

7   Clean the crankcase recesses and bearing caps thoroughly and fit the bearing shells so that the tang on the bearing engages in the recess in the crankcase or bearing cap. Make sure that the shells fitted to the crankcase have oil holes, and that these line up with the drillings in the bearing housings. The shells fitted to the bearing caps do not have oil holes. Note that the bearing shells of the centre bearing (No 3) may either be flanged to act as thrust washers, or may have separate thrust washers. These should be fitted oil groove outwards as shown. Fit the bearing shells so that the ends of the bearing are flush with the joint face (photos).

8   Oil the bearings and journals (photo) then locate the crankshaft in the crankcase.

9   Fit the main bearing caps (with centre main bearing thrust washers if applicable) in their correct positions.

10   Fit the bolts to the bearing caps and tighten the bolts of the centre cap to the specified torque (photo), then check that the crankshaft rotates freely. If it is difficult to rotate the crankshaft, check that the bearing shells are seated properly and that the bearing cap is the correct way round. Rotation will only be difficult if something is

27.5A Removing a crankshaft main bearing cap

27.5B Removing the crankshaft

27.6 Using Plastigage to check a crankshaft journal running clearance

27.7A Fitting the flanged type centre main bearing to the cap

27.7B Fitting the centre main bearing and separate thrust washers to the cap

27.7C Fitting the flanged type centre main bearing into the crankcase ...

27.7D ... ensuring that the ends of the bearing are flush with the joint face

27.7E Fitting the alternative type centre main bearing into the crankcase ...

27.7F ... together with its thrust washers

27.8 Lubricate the main bearing shells

27.10 Tightening the main bearing cap bolts

27.12 Checking the crankshaft endfloat

27.13A Location of spigot needle roller bearing in rear end of crankshaft

27.13B Check position of spigot needle roller bearing

incorrect, and the fault must be found. Dirt on the back of a bearing shell is sometimes the cause of a tight main bearing.

11 Working out from the centre, tighten the remaining bearing caps in turn, checking that the crankshaft rotates freely after each bearing has been tightened.

12 Check that the endfloat of the crankshaft is within specification, by inserting feeler gauges between the crankshaft and the centre bearing thrust face/washer while levering the crankshaft first in one direction and then in the other (photo).

13 On manual transmission models only, the rear end of the crankshaft carries a needle roller bearing (photo) which supports the front end of the gearbox input shaft. Inspect the bearing for obvious signs of wear and damage. If the gearbox has been removed and dismantled, fit the input shaft into the bearing to see if there is excessive clearance. If the bearing requires renewing, insert a hook behind the bearing and pull it out of the end of the crankshaft. Install the new bearing with the lettering on the end of the bearing outwards. Press it in until the end of the bearing is 1.5 mm (0.059 in) below the face of the flywheel flange (photo).

14 Fit new crankshaft oil seals (Section 22) then refit the pistons and connecting rods, as described in Section 26.

28 Oil filter and housing – removal and refitting

1 Place a suitable container beneath the left-hand side of the engine.
2 Unscrew the filter cartridge and discard it – it will be necessary to use a filter strap or special spanner, although if neither of these items is available drive a long screwdriver through the cartridge.
3 If it is required to remove the housing, use an Allen key to unscrew the bolts, then withdraw the housing and gasket (photos).

4 Clean the mating faces of the housing and block then refit the housing, together with a new gasket, and tighten the bolts. Reconnect the oil pressure switch wiring, where applicable.
5 Clean the mating faces of the new oil filter cartridge and housing, and smear a little engine oil on the filter seal.
6 Screw the cartridge onto the housing and tighten it by hand only (photo).

28.3A Unscrew the socket head bolts ...

28.3B ... and remove the oil filter housing

28.6 Fitting a new oil filter cartridge

29.2A Left-hand side engine mounting bracket

29.2B Right-hand side engine mounting

29 Engine mounting – removal and refitting

1   The engine front support bar can be unbolted from the block and removed. When refitting the bar check the engine alignment, as described in Section 6.
2   To remove the left and right engine mountings (photos) first remove the front support bar, then unbolt the mountings using a hoist to support the weight of the engine. When refitting the mountings, check the engine alignment, as described in Section 6.

Part B – Five-cylinder engines

30 General description

The engine is of five-cylinder, in-line, overhead camshaft type, mounted conventionally at the front of the car. The crankshaft is of six-bearing type and the No 4 (from front) main bearing shells incorporate flanged thrust washers to control crankshaft endfloat. The camshaft is driven by a toothed belt from the crankshaft gear and the belt also drives the water pump mounted on the left-hand side of the block. A gear on the rear of the camshaft drives the distributor, and on carburettor models the camshaft also drives the fuel pump.
The valves are operated from the camshaft through bucket type tappets, and valve clearances are adjusted by the use of shims located in the top of the tappets.
The engine has a full-flow lubrication system. A gear and crescent type oil pump is mounted on the front of the crankshaft. The oil filter is of the cartridge type, mounted on the right-hand side of the cylinder block.

31 Engine routine maintenance

The maintenance procedures for the five-cylinder engine are the same as for the four-cylinder unit described in Section 2 of Part A in this Chapter.

32 Major operations possible with the engine in the car

The following operations can be carried out without having to remove the engine from the car:

(a) Removal and servicing of the cylinder head and camshaft
(b) Removal of the timing belt and gears
(c) Removal of the flywheel or driveplate (after first removing the transmission)
(d) Removal of the sump (after first lowering the subframe)

(e)   Removal of the oil pump
(f)   Removal of the pistons and connecting rods

33 Major operation only possible after removal of the engine from the car

The following operation can only be carried out after removal of the engine from the car:

Removal of the crankshaft and main bearings

34 Method of engine removal

The engine must be disconnected from the transmission then lifted from the car.

35 Engine – removal and refitting

1   Remove the bonnet, as described in Chapter 12, and stand it on cardboard or rags in a safe place.
2   Disconnect the battery negative lead.
3   Drain the cooling system, as described in Chapter 2.
4   Unscrew the bolt securing the coolant pipe to the left-hand side of the engine, then disconnect the pipe from the front hose. On some models the coolant pipe is attached to a transmission bellhousing bolt.
5   Remove the screws and withdraw the upper radiator cover.
6   Disconnect the top hose from the cylinder head.
7   Prise the one-way valve and hose from the brake vacuum servo unit.
8   Remove the power steering pump (where applicable), with reference to Chapter 11, but leaving the hoses connected. Tie the pump to the bulkhead (Fig 1.15).

Fig. 1.15 Remove pulley cover and power steering pump (where applicable) (Sec 35)

9   Disconnect the bottom hose from the thermostat housing on the block.
10 Disconnect the wiring from the oil pressure switch on the left-hand side of the engine (photo) and on fuel injection models from the warm-up regulator. Unclip the wiring and place it to one side (photo).
11 Remove the air cleaner unit as described in Chapter 3 (Part A). On fuel injection models remove the air cleaner and air flow meter as described in Chapter 3 (Part B).
12 Identify all fuel and vacuum hoses using masking tape, then disconnect those affecting engine removal. These will include, where applicable:

Fuel hoses to the fuel pump and non-return valve
Vacuum hose to the warm-up valve (fuel injection)
Vacuum hose to the vacuum reservoir and distributor
Crankcase emission control hoses

35.10A Oil pressure switch (five-cylinder)

35.10B Warm-up regulator and wiring

13 On fuel injection models detach and remove the warm-up regulator (leaving the fuel lines connected).
14 Identify all wiring for location using masking tape, then disconnect those affecting engine removal. These will include, where applicable:

Fuel injection wiring to cold start valve, thermo-time switch, auxiliary air valve, and throttle switch
Wiring to temperature sender, distributor, coil, oil temperature switch, inlet manifold preheater and by-pass air cut-off valve

15 On fuel injection models detach the injectors from their seats, remove the cold start valve and the mixture control unit. Plug all fuel lines and connections to prevent the ingress of dirt.
16 Disconnect the accelerator cable as described in Chapter 3 (Fig. 1.16).
17 On manual gearbox models disconnect the clutch cable from the release lever and cable bracket.
18 Remove the alternator, as described in Chapter 10, and where necessary unbolt the alternator bracket from the block.
19 Unscrew and remove the upper transmission-to-engine bolts noting the location of any brackets, but leave the bolt adjacent to the clutch lever in position.
20 Disconnect the heater hoses from the engine block.

Fig. 1.16 Disconnect the accelerator cable (carburettor engine shown) (Sec 35)

Fig. 1.18 Crankshaft damper removal. Insert socket and extension through front aperture (Sec 35)

Fig. 1.17 Unbolt the stop shell from the front crossmember (Sec 35)

Fig. 1.19 Special tool 2084 attached to crankshaft damper (Sec 35)

21 Unbolt and detach the stop shell from the front crossmember (Fig. 1.17).

22 Loosen off but do not remove at this stage the engine bearer/mounting nuts/bolts.

23 Unbolt and remove the starter motor.

24 Unbolt and detach the exhaust downpipe from the manifold joint and at the gearbox bracket. Tie the exhaust to one side out of the way.

25 On automatic transmission models disconnect the coolant hoses from the oil cooler and remove the flange. Also on automatic transmission models unscrew the three torque converter-to-driveplate bolts while holding the starter ring gear stationary with a screwdriver. It will be necessary to rotate the engine to position the bolts in the starter aperture.

26 For additional room when removing the engine, it is recommended that the vibration damper on the front of the crankshaft is removed. Access to the centre bolt is gained by removing the front grille and the number plate. To remove the damper the crankshaft must be held stationary using VW tool 2084 and the centre bolt loosened (Figs 1.18 and 1.19). The bolt is tightened to a high torque and it is therefore better to use the correct tool. However, it may be possible to loosen the bolt while an assistant engages top gear and applies the brakes (manual gearbox) or by holding the starter ring gear stationary using a wide-bladed screwdriver.

27 With the centre bolt removed, loosen two diagonally opposite bolts using an Allen key and remove the remaining two bolts. Release

Fig. 1.20 Damper to gear retaining bolts (Sec 35)

the vibration damper from the crankshaft gear by tapping the bolts and removing them – do not pull off the gear (Fig. 1.20).

28 Connect a hoist and take the weight of the engine – the hoist should be positioned centrally over the engine.

29 Unscrew and remove the subframe front mounting bolts.

30 Support the weight of the transmission with a trolley jack.

31 Unscrew and remove the lower transmission-to-engine bolts.

32 Where necessary unbolt and remove the left-hand side engine mounting bracket – on some models it will first be necessary to remove the radiator panel.

33 Lift the engine from the mounting(s) and reposition the trolley jack beneath the transmission.

34 Further loosen off but do not remove the remaining engine to transmission bolt adjacent to the clutch lever.

35 Pull the engine from the transmission – make sure on automatic transmission models that the torque converter remains fully engaged with the transmission splines.

36 Lift the engine further and then fully remove the remaining engine to transmission bolt, simultaneously raising the jack supporting the transmission.

37 Turn the engine slightly and lift it from the engine compartment then lower it to the floor.

38 Refitting is a reversal of the removal procedure, but before starting the engine check that it has been filled with oil, and that the cooling system is full. Make sure that the starter cable is not touching the

engine or mounting bracket. Delay tightening until the engine is idling – this will ensure that th aligned, as shown in Figs. 1.21, 1.22 and 1.23. If ne transmission mounting bolts before tightening all of t

39 When refitting the crankshaft damper align it with hole in the crankshaft gear (Fig. 1.24). Coat the threads a surfaces of the crankshaft damper centre bolt with an anti-o compound before inserting it and tightening to the specified t

Fig. 1.23 Front engine support (stop shell) check. Stop shell (a) to contact rubber (b), but (b) must not touch crossmember towards the front or side edges of stop shell (Sec 35)

Fig. 1.21 Engine and gearbox alignment dimensions (Sec 35)

Manual gearbox (a) = 22.2 mm (0.814 in)
Automatic gearbox (a) = 124.7 mm (4.90 in)

Fig. 1.24 Vibration damper location hole in crankshaft gear (Sec 35)

36 Engine dismantling – general

Refer to Part A, Section 7 of this Chapter.

37 Ancillary components – removal and refitting

Refer to Part A, Section 8 of this Chapter, with the following exceptions:

Oil filter cartridge (Section 56 of this Chapter)
Engine mountings (Section 57 of this Chapter)

Fig. 1.22 Engine and gearbox lateral adjustment (Sec 35)

Manual gearbox (c) = 394.4 ± 1 mm (15.52 ± 0.04 in)
Automatic gearbox (c) = 223.6 ± 1 mm (8.80 ± 0.04 in)

the engine mountings
e engine is correctly
essary loosen the
e mountings.
the location
nd contact
orrosion
que.

53

Camshaft

Woodruff key

Shim

Tappet

Oil seal

Valve cotters

Inner valve spring

Outer valve spring

Spring seat

Valve stem seal

Valve guide

Cylinder head

Valves

Fig. 1.25 Cylinder head and camshaft components (Sec 38)

38 Camshaft and tappets – removal

Note: *If the engine is still in the car, first carry out the following operations:*

    (a) Disconnect the battery negative lead
    (b) Remove the air cleaner and fuel pump on carburettor models (Chapter 3)
    (c) Disconnect all relevant wiring, cables and hoses
    (d) Remove the distributor (Chapter 4)
    (e) Remove the upper radiator cowl
    (f) Disconnect the drivebelts from the crankshaft pulley
    (g) Where fitted, remove the power steering pump leaving the hoses connected (Chapter 11)

1   Unscrew the nuts and lift off the valve cover, together with the reinforcement strips and gaskets. Note the location of the HT lead holder.
2   Unscrew the nuts and bolts and remove the timing belt cover(s). The engine has two covers, and an Allen key is required – the lower cover need not be removed.
3   Using a socket on the crankshaft pulley bolt (temporarily refit the bolt and damper if removed during engine removal), turn the engine so that the piston in No 1 cylinder is at TDC (top dead centre) on its compression stroke. The notch in the crankshaft pulley must be in line with the pointer on the oil pump housing – alternatively the 'O' mark (TDC) on the flywheel/driveplate must be aligned with the pointer in the bellhousing aperture. Both No 1 cylinder valves must be closed (ie cam peaks away from the tappets) and the indentation on the rear of the camshaft gear in line with the upper surface of the valve cover gasket (temporarily refit the gasket and valve cover, if necessary), see Figures 1.26, 1.27 and 1.28.
4   Loosen the water pump mounting and adjustment bolts, using an Allen key where necessary, and rotate the pump clockwise to release the tension on the timing belt.
5   Remove the timing belt from the camshaft gear and move it to one side.
6   Unscrew the centre bolt from the camshaft gear while holding the gear stationary with a bar through one of the holes or using a wide-bladed screwdriver.
7   Withdraw the gear from the camshaft and extract the Woodruff key.
8   Check that each bearing cap has its number stamped on it; if not, make an identifying mark to ensure that each cap is put back where it was originally. Note that the caps are offset and can only be fitted one way round (Fig. 1.29).
9   *It is important that the camshaft is removed exactly as described so that there is no danger of it becoming distorted.* Loosen one of the nuts on bearing cap No 2 about two turns and then loosen the diagonally opposite nut on bearing cap No 4 about two turns. Repeat

Fig. 1.27 Alignment of TDC marks on crankshaft pulley and oil pump housing (Sec 38)

Fig. 1.28 The TDC indentation on rear face of camshaft gear aligned with upper surface of valve cover gasket (Sec 38)

Fig. 1.29 Numerical order of camshaft bearing caps – check they are marked accordingly before removing (Sec 38)

Fig. 1.26 Alignment of TDC marks on flywheel/driveplate (Sec 38)

38.10 Removing a camshaft bearing cap

38.11A Removing a tappet (cam follower)

38.11B Keep tappets in correct order after removal

the operations on the other nut of bearing cap No 2 and bearing cap No 4. Continue the sequence until the nuts are free, then remove them. Loosen and remove the nuts of bearing caps Nos 1 and 3 using a similar diagonal sequence.

10 Lift the bearing caps off (photo) and lift the camshaft out. Discard the oil seal.

11 Withdraw each tappet (cam follower) in turn (photo) and mark its position (1 to 10 numbering from the timing belt end of the engine) using adhesive tape or a box with divisions (photo). Take care to keep the adjustment shims with their respective tappets.

39 Cylinder head – removal

Note: *If the engine is still in the car, first carry out the following operations:*

   (a) Disconnect the battery negative lead
   (b) Drain the cooling system (Chapter 2)
   (c) Remove the inlet and exhaust manifolds (Chapter 3)
   (d) Remove the distributor, HT leads and spark plugs (Chapter 4)
   (e) Disconnect the drivebelts from the crankshaft pulley
   (f) Disconnect the relevant wiring, cables and hoses
   (g) Where fitted, remove the power steering pump, leaving the hoses connected (Chapter 11)

1 Follow paragraphs 1 to 7 inclusive of Section 38.

2 Unbolt and remove the timing belt rear cover – note that the water pump pivot bolt must be removed and three of the oil pump bolts. Note the location of the spacers.

3 Using a splined socket unscrew the cylinder head bolts a turn at a time in reverse order to that shown in Fig. 1.32.

4 With all the bolts removed, lift the cylinder head from the block. If it is stuck, tap it free with a wooden mallet. *Do not insert a lever into the gasket joint.*

5 Remove the cylinder head gasket.

40 Valves – removal and renovation

1 Remove the camshaft and tappets, as described in Section 38, and the cylinder head as described in Section 39.

2 Follow the procedure given in Part A, Section 11 – inlet valves are 2-4-5-7-9 and exhaust valves are 1-3-6-8-10, numbered from the timing belt end of the engine.

41 Cylinder head – examination and renovation

   Refer to Part A, Section 12 of this Chapter.

42 Camshaft and bearings – examination and renovation

1 Refer to Part A, Section 13, of this Chapter.

2 Check that the oil spray jets located in the top of the cylinder head direct the spray at 90° to the camshaft (Fig. 1.31).

43 Valves – refitting

   Refer to Part A, Section 14 of this Chapter.

44 Cylinder head – refitting

1 Check that the top of the block is perfectly clean, then locate a new gasket on it with the part number or TOP marking facing upward.

2 Check that the cylinder head face is perfectly clean. Insert two long rods, or pieces of dowel into the cylinder head bolt holes at opposite ends of the block, to position the gasket and to give a location for fitting the cylinder head (photo). Lower the head on to the block, remove the guide dowels and insert the bolts and washers. Do not use jointing compound on the cylinder head joint.

Reinforcement

Cap

Cylinder head cover

Cylinder head bolts

Gaskets

Woodruff key

Cylinder head

Cylinder head gasket

Fig. 1.30 Cylinder head and associated components (carburettor engine) (Sec 39)

Fig. 1.31 Correct position of oil spray jets (arrowed) in the cylinder head (Sec 42)

44.2 Guide rod positions when fitting the cylinder head

Fig. 1.32 Cylinder head bolt tightening sequence (Sec 44)

3 Tighten the bolts using the sequence shown in Fig. 1.32 in the four stages given in the Specifications to the specified torque.
4 Locate the timing belt rear cover on the front of the cylinder head and block and tighten the retaining bolts and studs, as applicable. Refit the spacers. Leave the water pump pivot bolt loose.
5 Fit the Woodruff key in its groove and locate the gear on the end of the camshaft.
6 Fit the centre bolt and spacer and tighten the bolt to the specified torque while holding the gear stationary with a bar through one of the holes, or using a wide-bladed screwdriver.
7 Turn the camshaft gear and align the rear indentation with the upper surface of the valve cover gasket (temporarily locate the gasket on the head).
8 Check that No 1 piston is at TDC with the 'O' mark on the flywheel aligned with the pointer in the bellhousing aperture. The notch in the crankshaft pulley will also be in line with the pointer on the oil pump housing.
9 Locate the timing belt on the crankshaft, camshaft and water pump gears, turn the water pump anti-clockwise to pre-tension the belt, then check that the TDC timing marks are still aligned.
10 Use a screwdriver, as shown in Fig. 1.33, to turn the water pump anti-clockwise and tension the timing belt until it can just be twisted 90° with the thumb and index finger midway between the camshaft and water pump gears. Tighten the water pump mounting and adjustment bolts when the adjustment is correct (Fig. 1.34).
11 Refit the timing belt cover(s) and tighten the nuts and bolts.
12 Refit the valve cover and reinforcement strips, together with the HT lead holder, new gaskets and seals, and tighten the nuts.
13 If the engine is in the car, reverse the preliminary procedures given in Section 39.

Fig. 1.33 Using a screwdriver to turn the water pump when tensioning the timing belt (Sec 44)

Fig. 1.34 Timing belt tension check method (Sec 44)

45 Camshaft and tappets – refitting

1 Fit the bucket tappets in their original positions – the adjustment shims on the top of the tappets must be fitted so that the lettering on them is downwards. Lubricate the tappets and the camshaft journals.
2 Lay the camshaft into the lower half of its bearings so that the lowest point of the cams of No 1 cylinder are towards the tappets, then fit the bearing caps in their original positions, making sure that they are the right way round before fitting them over the studs.
3 Fit the nuts to bearing caps Nos 2 and 4 and tighten them in diagonal sequence until the camshaft fully enters its bearings.
4 Fit the nuts to bearing caps 1 and 3, then tighten all the nuts to the specified torque in diagonal sequence.
5 Smear a little oil onto the sealing lip and outer edge of the camshaft oil seal, then locate it open end first in the cylinder head and No 1 camshaft bearing cap.
6 Using a metal tube drive the seal squarely into the cylinder head until flush with the front of the cylinder head – *do not drive it in further otherwise it will block the oil return hole.*
7 Follow paragraph 5 to 11 inclusive of Section 44.
8 Check and, if necessary, adjust the valve clearances, as described in Section 46, with the engine cold.
9 Refit the valve cover and reinforcement strips, together with the HT lead holder, new gaskets and seals, and tighten the nuts.
10 If the engine is in the car, reverse the preliminary procedures given in Section 38.

46 Valve clearances – checking and adjustment

Refer to Part A, Section 17 of this Chapter. The procedure is identical to that for the four-cylinder engine with the following exceptions:

(a) It is not necessary to remove the timing cover
(b) From the timing belt end of the engine inlet valves are numbered 2-4-5-7-9, and exhaust valves 1-3-6-8-10

47 Timing belt and gears – removal and refitting

Note: *If the engine is still in the car, first carry out the following operations:*

(a) *Disconnect the battery negative lead*
(b) *Where fitted, remove the power steering pump bearing and the hoses connected (Chapter 11)*
(c) *Remove the alternator drivebelt (Chapter 10) and, if fitted the air conditioning compressor drivebelt (Chapter 12)*
(d) *Remove the lower radiator grille and number plate*

1   Using VW tool 2084 lock the vibration damper on the front of the crankshaft stationary, then loosen the centre bolt. The bolt is tightened to a high torque and it is recommended that the tool is used if at all possible. However, it may be possible to loosen the bolt while holding the starter ring gear stationary using a wide-bladed screwdriver or the method shown (photo).

2   Follow paragraphs 2 to 7 inclusive of Section 38 (remove both timing covers).

3   Unscrew the centre bolt and withdraw the vibration damper, together with the crankshaft gear and timing belt.

4   Separate the vibration damper from the crankshaft gear by removing the bolts using an Allen key, then reinserting two diagonally opposite bolts on a few threads and tapping them through the damper.

5   **Do not** *turn the crankshaft with the timing belt removed.*

6   If necessary, unbolt and remove the timing belt rear cover – note that the water pump pivot bolt must be removed and, three of the oil pump bolts. Note the location of the spacers.

7   Commence refitting by locating the timing belt rear cover on the front of the cylinder head and block and tighten the retaining bolts and studs, as applicable. Refit the spacers. Leave the water pump pivot bolt loose.

8   Reassemble the vibration damper to the crankshaft gear, then insert and tighten the bolts.

9   Align the key on the crankshaft gear with the slot in the crankshaft, then locate the timing belt on the crankshaft gear and fit the gear to the crankshaft (photo). Take care not to trap the belt between the gear and the oil pump housing.

10 Coat the threads of the centre bolt with an anti-corrosion compound, then insert the bolt and tighten it while holding the crankshaft stationary.

11 Follow paragraphs 4 to 11 inclusive of Section 44.

12 If the engine is in the car, reverse the preliminary procedures at the beginning of this Section.

48 Flywheel/driveplate – removal and refitting

1   The procedure is as given in Part A, Section 19 of this Chapter. However the retaining bolts may not be offset so the flywheel/driveplate and crankshaft should be marked in relation to each other before separation (photo).

2   When refitting a driveplate note that the raised pip must face the torque converter. If a replacement driveplate is to be fitted, its position must be checked and adjusted if necessary. The distance from the rear face of the block to the torque converter *mounting* face on the driveplate (Fig. 1.35) must be between 17.2 and 18.8 mm (0.667 and 0.740 in). If necessary, remove the driveplate and fit a spacer behind it to achieve the correct dimension.

47.1 One method of locking the starter ring gear

48.1 Centre punch alignment marks (arrowed) on the crankshaft and flywheel

47.9 Fitting the crankshaft gear and vibration damper to the crankshaft – note location key

Fig. 1.35 Torque converter-to-cylinder block dimension checking faces – measure in two places for average (Sec 48)

3   A new flywheel or driveplate will need to have the ignition timing
index mark scribed on its periphery in the centre of the TDC 'O' mark
as shown in Figure 1.36.

4   New flywheel/driveplate bolts must be used when refitting. Two
bolt types have been used, the later type being identified by a
shouldered head (see Figure 1.37). Both early and late models must be
fitted with the later type bolts irrespective of which type were fitted
previously. Note that the later bolt torque wrench setting differs from
that of the earlier type (without the shoulder), see Specifications.

**Fig. 1.36 Ignition timing mark position on flywheel/driveplate
(Sec 48)**

Fig. 1.37 Flywheel/driveplate retaining bolt types (Sec 48)

49 Sump – removal

Refer to Part A, Section 21 of this Chapter.

50 Crankshaft oil seals – renewal

Front oil seal

1   Remove the timing belt and crankshaft gear, as described in
Section 47.

2   If an extractor tool is available the seal may be renewed without
removing the oil pump, otherwise refer to Section 51. It is also
recommended that VW tool 2080 together with a guide sleeve be
used to install the new seal. Dip the seal in engine oil before fitting,
and if the old seal has scored the crankshaft, position the new seal on
the unworn surface.

3   Refit the crankshaft gear and timing belt, as described in Section
47.

Rear oil seal

4   Remove the flywheel or driveplate, as described in Section 48.

5   If an extractor tool is available the seal may be renewed without
removing the housing, otherwise unbolt and remove the housing
(including the two sump bolts) and remove the gasket (photo). If the
sump gasket is damaged while removing the housing it will be
necessary to remove the sump and fit a new gasket. However, refit the
sump *after* fitting the housing.

6   Drive the old seal out of the housing, then dip the new seal in
engine oil and, drive it into the housing with a block of wood or a
socket, until flush. Make sure that the closed end of the seal is facing
outwards.

7   Fit the housing together with a new gasket and tighten the bolts
evenly in diagonal sequence.

8   Refit the flywheel or driveplate, as described in Section 48.

50.5 Removing the crankshaft rear oil seal and housing

51 Oil pump – removal, examination and refitting

1   Remove the timing belt and crankshaft gear, as described in
Section 47.

2   Remove the sump, with reference to Section 49.

3   Remove the dipstick.

4   Remove the two bolts securing the oil intake pipe stay to the
crankcase (photo). Knock back the tabs of the lockplate on the intake
pipe flange (photo), remove the bolts and the intake pipe.

5   Remove the bolts securing the oil pump (photo) and take off the
oil pump and gasket (photo).

6   Remove the countersunk screws securing the pump backplate and
lift the backplate off, exposing the gears (photo).

7   Check that there is a mark on the exposed face of the gears and
if not, make a mark to show which side of the gears is towards the
engine before removing them.

8   Unscrew the pressure relief valve and remove the plug, sealing
ring, spring and plunger (photo).

9   Clean all the parts thoroughly and examine the pump casing and
backplate for signs of wear or scoring. Examine the pressure relief
valve plunger and its seating for damage and wear and check that the
spring is not damaged or distorted. Check the gears for damage and
wear. New gears may be fitted, but they must be fitted as a pair.

10 Prise out the oil seal from the front of the pump. Oil the lip of the
new seal, enter the seal with its closed face outwards and use a block
of wood to tap the seal in flush. If there is any scoring on the
crankshaft in the area on which the lip of the seal bears, the seal may
be pushed to the bottom of its recess so that the lip bears on an
undamaged part of the crankshaft.

51.4A Oil pump intake pipe

51.4B Oil pump intake pipe flange

51.5A Oil pump installed

51.5B Removing the oil pump

51.6 Oil pump with backplate removed

51.8 Removing the oil pressure relief valve

Fig. 1.38 Timing belt and oil pump components (Sec 51)

11 Reassemble the pump by fitting the gears and the backplate. The inner gear has its slotted end towards the crankshaft and although the outer gear can be fitted either way round, it should be fitted the same way round as it was before removal. Some gears have a triangle stamped on them and this mark should be towards the front.

12 Refit the oil pump, together with a new gasket, making sure that the slot on the inner gear engages the dog on the crankshaft.

13 Insert the bolts and tighten them in diagonal sequence to the specified torque.

14 Fit the oil intake pipe, together with a new gasket, tighten the bolts, and bend the lockplate tabs onto the flange.

15 Refit the dipstick, sump (Section 49), and timing belt and crankshaft gear (Section 47).

52 Pistons and connecting rods – removal and dismantling

Refer to Part A, Section 24 of this Chapter. Removal of the cylinder head is described in Section 39, and the timing belt in Section 47. Instead of removing the oil pump, remove the sump, as described in Section 49, then unbolt the oil intake pipe, as described in Section 51.

Square ring

Shouldered ring

Piston rings

Double chamfered ring with
expander spring

Piston pin

Circlip

Piston

Conrod

Bore

Bearing shell

Conrod cap

Fig. 1.39 Cylinder block connecting rod and piston assembly
components – 1.9 litre engine (Sec 52)

Fig. 1.40 Connecting rod orientation showing cylinder number (with cast marks [arrowed] facing pulley end) (Sec 52)

55.3A Removing No. 4 main bearing cap

53 Pistons and cylinder bores – examination

Refer to Part A, Section 25 of this Chapter.

54 Pistons and connecting rods – reassembly and refitting

Refer to Part A, Section 26 of this Chapter but note that new nuts should always be used for the big-end bolts and that the threads should be lightly lubricated with engine oil. With the pistons fitted, refit the oil intake pipe, together with a new gasket, tighten the bolts, and bend the lockplate tabs onto the flange bolts. Refitting of the sump is described in Section 49, the timing belt in Section 47, and the cylinder head in Section 44.

55 Crankshaft – removal, examination and refitting

1   With the engine removed from the car, remove the pistons and connecting rods, as described in Section 52. Keep the big-end bearings with their matching connecting rods to ensure correct refitting.
2   Remove the oil pump (Section 51) and rear oil seal complete with housing (Section 50).
3   Follow the procedure in Part A, Section 27, of this Chapter, paragraphs 4 to 13 inclusive (photos) but note the following exceptions:

   (a) The flanged main bearing shells are fitted to main bearing No 4 (from the front of the engine)
   (b) The needle roller bearing in the rear of the crankshaft must be pressed in to a depth of 5.5 mm (0.217 in) below the face of the flange

4   Fit the oil pump and rear oil seal housing complete with new seals, as described in Sections 51 and 50 respectively.
5   Refit the pistons and connecting rods, as described in Section 54.

56 Oil filter – removal and refitting

1   Place a suitable container beneath the right-hand side of the engine.

55.3B Removing the crankshaft

2   Unscrew the filter cartridge and discard it – it will be necessary to use a filter strap, although if this is not available drive a long screwdriver through the cartridge.
3   Clean the mating faces of the new oil filter and block, and smear a little engine oil on the filter seal.
4   Screw on the cartridge and seal, and tighten it by hand only.

57 Engine mountings – removal and refitting

Refer to Part A, Section 29 of this Chapter. When refitting the mountings, check the engine alignment as described in Section 35.

Part C

58 Fault diagnosis – engine

Symptom	Reason(s)
Engine fails to start	Discharged battery Loose battery connection Loose or broken ignition leads Moisture on spark plugs, distributor cap, or HT leads Incorrect spark plug gap Cracked distributor cap or rotor Dirt or water in carburettor (as applicable) Empty fuel tank Faulty fuel pump Faulty starter motor Low cylinder compression
Engine idles erratically	Inlet manifold air leak Leaking cylinder head gasket Worn camshaft lobes Faulty fuel pump Incorrect valve clearances Loose crankcase ventilation hoses Idling adjustments incorrect Uneven cylinder compressions
Engine misfires	Spark plug gaps incorrect Faulty coil, or transistorised ignition component (as applicable) Dirt or water in carburettor Burnt out valve Leaking cylinder head gasket Distributor cap cracked Incorrect valve clearances Uneven cylinder compressions Idling adjustments incorrect
Engine stalls	Idling adjustments incorrect Inlet manifold air leak Ignition timing incorrect
Excessive oil consumption	Worn pistons and cylinder bores Valve guides and valve stem seals worn Oil leaking from crankshaft oil seals, valve cover gasket etc
Engine backfires	Idling adjustments incorrect Ignition timing incorrect Incorrect valve clearances Inlet manifold air leak Sticking valve
Engine lacks power	Incorrect ignition timing Incorrect spark plug gap Low cylinder compression Excessive carbon build up in engine Air filter choked

Chapter 2 Cooling system

For modifications, and information applicable to later models, see Supplement at end of manual

Contents

Specifications

System type .... Pressurized radiator and expansion tank (integral on some models), belt driven water pump, thermostatically controlled electric cooling fan

System coolant capacity (including heater)
1.6 and 1.8 litre engine up to August 1983 .... 5.4 litre (9.5 Imp pint)
1.6 and 1.8 litre engine from August 1983 .... 6.0 litre (10.5 Imp pint)
1.9 and 2.0 litre engine .... 8.0 litre (14.1 Imp pint)

Antifreeze
Type .... Ethylene glycol, with corrosion inhibitor (Duckhams Universal Antifreeze and Summer Coolant)

Concentration for protection down to: **Percent antifreeze by volume**
    -25°C (-14°F) 40
    -30°C (-22°F) 45
    -35°C (-31°F) 50

Filler cap opening pressure
1.6 and 1.8 litre engine .... 1.2 to 1.5 bar (17.4 to 21.7 lbf/in^2)
1.9 and 2.0 litre engine .... 1.2 to 1.35 bar (17.4 to 19.5 lbf/in^2)

Thermostat
Starts to open:
    1.6 and 1.8 litre engine .... 85°C (185°F)
    1.9 and 2.0 litre engine .... 87°C (188°F)
Fully open:
    1.6 and 1.8 litre engine .... 105°C (221°F)
    1.9 and 2.0 litre engine .... 102°C (216°F)
Stroke (minimum):
    1.6 and 1.8 litre engine .... 7.0 mm (0.276 in)
    1.9 and 2.0 litre engine .... 8.0 mm (0.315 in)

Electric cooling fan thermo-switch operating temperatures
Switches on (all engines) .... 93° to 98°C (199° to 208°F)
Switches off (all engines) .... 88° to 93°C (190° to 199°F)

Torque wrench settings

	Nm	lbf ft
Radiator mountings	10	7
Radiator cowl fasteners	10	7
Electric thermo-switch for fan	25	18
Water pump to block	20	14
Water pump to housing (1.6 and 1.8 litre)	10	7
Water pump pulley (1.6 and 1.8 litre)	20	14
Thermostat housing	10	7
Temperature sender unit (1.9 litre)	10	7
Coolant connector housing to cylinder head:		
1.6, 1.8 and 2.0 litre	10	7
1.9 litre	20	14
Coolant pipe mountings:		
1.6 and 1.8 litre (transmission-to-engine bolts)	55	40
1.9 and 2.0 litre	20	14
Electric cooling fan mounting	10	7
Cylinder head rear outlet (heat exchanger) – 1.6 and 1.8 litre	10	7
ATF cooler (automatic transmission)	40	28

1 General description and maintenance

The cooling system is of pressurized type and includes a front (four-cylinder) or side (five-cylinder) mounted radiator, a water pump driven by an external V-belt on four-cylinder engines or by the timing belt on five-cylinder engines, and an electric cooling fan.

All 1.9, 2.0 litre and later 1.6 and 1.8 litre (from August 1983) models have a separate expansion tank. The cooling system thermostat is located in the water pump housing on four-cylinder models, and in the inlet on the left-hand side of the cylinder block on five-cylinder models.

The system functions as follows. With the engine cold, the thermostat is shut and the water pump forces the water through the internal passages then via the bypass hose (and heater circuit if turned on) over the thermostat capsule and to the water pump inlet again. This circulation of water cools the cylinder bores, combustion surfaces and valve seats. However, when the coolant reaches the predetermined temperature, the thermostat begins to open. The coolant now circulates through the top hose to the top of the radiator. As it passes through the radiator matrix it is cooled by the inrush of air when the car is in forward motion, supplemented by the action of the electric cooling fan when necessary. Finally the coolant is returned to the water pump via the bottom hose and through the open thermostat.

The electric cooling fan is controlled by a thermo-switch located in the bottom of the radiator. Water temperature is monitored by a sender unit in the cylinder head.

Note: *the electric cooling fan will operate when the temperature*

Fig. 2.1 Cooling system hose circuits – 1.6 litre engine (Sec 1)

1   *Radiator*
2   *Water pump and thermostat housing*
3   *Intake manifold*
4   *Carburettor automatic choke*
5   *Heater*
6   *Heater valve*
7   *Cylinder block and head*
8   *Coolant hose*
9   *Thermo-switch*

Note: *Later models also have an expansion tank (not shown)*

Fig. 2.2 Cooling system hose circuits – 1.8 litre engine (Sec 1)

1   Radiator
2   Water pump and thermostat
3   Expansion element
4   Automatic choke cover
5   Heater
6   ATF cooler (automatic transmission only)
7   Cylinder block and head
8   Coolant hose
9   Heater valve
10 Triple thermo-switch

Note: *Later models also have an expansion tank (not shown)*

of the coolant in the radiator reaches the predetermined level even if the ignition is switched off. Therefore extreme caution should be exercised when working in the vicinity of the fan blades.

The cooling system must be regularly checked as part of the vehicle's routine maintenance. A weekly check must be made to ensure that the coolant level is correct in the radiator or expansion tank. If a sudden drop in the coolant level occurs, further investigation of the system is necessary to locate the cause and effect any repairs which may be necessary.

Periodically check the system hoses and connections for signs of leakage, deterioration and security.

2   Cooling system – draining

1   It is preferable to drain the cooling system when the engine is cold. If this is not possible, place a cloth over the filler cap and turn it slowly in an anti-clockwise direction until the pressure starts to escape – leave it in this position until all pressure has dissipated.
2   Remove the filler cap.
3   Set the heater controls on the facia to the WARM setting so that the heater control valve is open.
4   Position a suitable container beneath the bottom hose.
5   On four-cylinder engines loosen the clips and disconnect the bottom hose and heater/inlet manifold return hoses from the water pump housing. Drain the coolant into the container.
6   On five-cylinder engines unscrew the bolt retaining the heater return pipe to the cylinder block, then loosen the clip and pull the pipe from the hose. Also loosen the clip and disconnect the hose from the bottom of the radiator. Drain the coolant into the container (Fig. 2.3).
7   Where applicable, on four-cylinder engines loosen the vent screw located on the cylinder head outlet housing.

Fig. 2.3 Radiator bottom hose connection (five-cylinder) (Sec 2)

3   Cooling system – flushing

1   After some time the radiator and engine waterways may become restricted or even blocked with scale or sediment. When this occurs the coolant will appear rusty and dark in colour and the system should then be flushed. In severe cases, reverse flushing may also be required.
2   Drain the cooling system, as described in Section 2.
3   Disconnect the top hose from the radiator, insert a hose in the radiator and allow water to circulate through the matrix and out of the bottom of the radiator until it runs clear.

4   Insert the hose in the expansion tank (where fitted) and allow the water to run through the supply hose.
5   In severe cases of contamination remove the radiator, invert it, and flush it with water until it runs clear.
6   To flush the engine and heater, insert a hose in the top hose and allow the water to circulate through the system until it runs clear from the return hose.
7   The use of chemical cleaners should only be necessary as a last resort, and the regular renewal of antifreeze should prevent the contamination of the system (refer to Section 5).

4   Cooling system – filling

1   Reconnect all hoses and check that the heater controls are set to WARM. Refit the radiator plug, if applicable.
2   Pour coolant into the radiator or expansion tank until full (photo).
3   Screw on the filler cap and run the engine at a fast idling speed for a few minutes.
4   Stop the engine and check the coolant level. Top up if necessary, and refit the filler cap.
5   Run the engine to normal operating temperature then allow it to cool. On models with an expansion tank the coolant level must reach the tip of the arrow with the engine cold or be a little higher when the engine is warm. On models without an expansion tank, remove the radiator cap with the engine cold and check that the coolant reaches the upper level mark; top up if necessary, and refit the cap (Fig. 2.4).

4.2 Topping up the cooling system through radiator filler neck

Fig. 2.4 Expansion tank coolant level mark (five-cylinder) (Sec 4)

5   Antifreeze mixture

1   The cooling system is filled at the factory with an antifreeze mixture which contains a corrosion inhibitor. The antifreeze mixture prevents freezing, raises the boiling point of the coolant and so delays the tendency of the coolant to boil, while the corrosion inhibitor reduces corrosion and the formation of scale. For these reasons the cooling system should be filled with antifreeze all the year round.
2   Any good quality antifreeze is suitable, if it is of the ethylene glycol type and also contains a corrosion inhibitor. Do not use an antifreeze preparation based on methanol, because these mixtures have a shorter life and methanol has the disadvantage of being inflammable and evaporates quickly.
3   The concentration of antifreeze should be adjusted to give the required level of protection selected from the table given in the Specifications.
4   When topping-up the cooling system always use the same mixture of water and antifreeze which the system contains. Topping-up using water only will gradually reduce the antifreeze concentration and lower the level of protection against both freezing and boiling.
5   At the beginning of the winter season, check the coolant for antifreeze concentration and add pure antifreeze if necessary.
6   Antifreeze mixture should not be left in the system for longer than its manufacturers' recommendation, which does not usually exceed three years. At the end of this time drain the system and refill with fresh mixture.

6   Radiator – removal, inspection, cleaning and refitting

1   Disconnect the battery negative lead.
2   Drain the cooling system, as described in Section 2.

Four-cylinder engines
3   Remove the front grille referring to Chapter 12 for details.
4   Loosen the hose clips and detach the top and bottom hoses from the radiator (photo).
5   Disconnect the wiring from the electric cooling fan and the fan thermo-switch on the left-hand side of the radiator.
6   Unscrew the two upper radiator retaining bracket bolts and lift the brackets from their slotted locations in the top of the radiator (photo).
7   Unscrew and remove the single screw securing the radiator on the right-hand side (from the front).
8   Lift the radiator from the lower mountings then move it to one side and lift it from the engine compartment, complete with the electric cooling fan and cowling (photo).
9   If necessary, unbolt the cooling fan and cowling from the radiator, then unscrew the nuts and separate the fan and motor from the cowling.

Five-cylinder engines
10   Loosen the clips and disconnect the radiator top and bottom hoses.
11   Disconnect the expansion tank vent hose from the radiator.
12   Disconnect the wiring from the electric cooling fan and the thermo-switch.
13   Remove the nuts and washers from the upper mountings and also unbolt the upper mounting bracket.
14   Unscrew the remaining mounting nut or cowl screws, as applicable, and lift out the radiator complete with the electric cooling fan and cowling.
15   If necessary, unbolt the cooling fan and cowling from the radiator, then unscrew the nuts and separate the fan and motor from the cowling.

All models
16   Radiator repair is best left to a specialist, although minor leaks can be stopped using a proprietary coolant additive. Clear the radiator matrix of flies and small leaves with a soft brush or by hosing.
17   Reverse flush the radiator, as described in Section 3, and renew the hoses and clips if they are damaged or have deteriorated.
18   Refitting is a reversal of removal, but fill the cooling system, as described in Section 4. If the thermo-switch is removed, fit a new sealing washer when refitting it.

6.4 Radiator top hose connection (four-cylinder)

6.6 Prise free radiator upper retaining bolt caps, then remove bolts (four-cylinder)

6.8 Lifting out the radiator (four-cylinder)

Radiator cap

Radiator

Upper hose

Washer

Thermo-switch for fan

Lower hose

Radiator fan

Cowl

Fig. 2.5 Radiator and associated components (four-cylinder)
(Sec 6)

Lock clip

Fan

Lock washer

Fan motor

Radiator cowl

Seal

Thermoswitch for electric fan

Cap

Expansion tank

Fig. 2.6 Radiator and associated components (five-cylinder)
(Sec 6)

Thermoswitch

Sender or
Thermoswitch for
coolant temperature

Gasket

Connection

Upper hose

to heat exchanger

from heat exchanger

Water pump

Sealing ring

Gasket

Gasket

Coolant pipe

Thermostat

Lower hose

7 Thermostat – removal, testing and refitting

1   On four-cylinder engines the thermostat is located in the bottom
of the water pump housing, but on five-cylinder engines it is located
behind the water pump on the left-hand side of the cylinder block
(photo).
2   To remove the thermostat first drain the cooling system, as
described in Section 2.
3   Unbolt and remove the thermostat cover, and remove the sealing
ring (photo).
4   Prise the thermostat from its housing.
5   To test whether the unit is serviceable, suspend it with a piece of
string in a container of water. Gradually heat the water and note the
temperatures at which the thermostat starts to open and is fully open.
Remove the thermostat from the water and check that it is fully closed
when cold. Renew the thermostat if it fails to operate in accordance
with the information given in the Specifications.
6   Clean the thermostat housing and cover faces, and locate a new
sealing ring on the cover.
7   Locate the thermostat in the housing – on four-cylinder engines
the arrow on the crosspiece must point away from the engine (photo),

Supply hose

Return hose

Sealing ring

ATF-cooler

Fig. 2.7 Water pump, thermostat and cooling system hoses (four-
cylinder) (Sec 7)

7.1 Thermostat housing at rear of water pump (four-cylinder)

7.3 Removing the thermostat cover (four-cylinder)

7.7 Thermostat in position showing arrow (A) for fitting direction and sealing ring (B) (four-cylinder)

Gasket

Thermostat

B

Thermoswitch for automatic choke
Thermoswitch for intake manifold preheater

Seal

Seal

Water pump

Coolant pipe

Seal

A

Seal

Temperature sender unit

To heat exchanger

20 Nm

Coolant pipe

to heat exchanger

Fig. 2.8 Water pump, thermostat and cooling system hoses (five-cylinder) (Sec 7)

A   2.0 litre   B   1.9 litre

Fig. 2.9 Thermostat orientation (five-cylinder) (Sec 7)

8.5 Water pump removal (four-cylinder). Note sealing ring position (arrowed)

but on five-cylinder engines the arrow must point downwards (Fig. 2.9).

8   Fit the thermostat cover and tighten the bolts evenly.

9   Fill the cooling system, as described in Section 4.

8   Water pump – removal and refitting

1   Drain the cooling system, as described in Section 2.

2   On models equipped with power steering, remove the pump leaving the hoses connected and place it to one side, with reference to Chapter 11.

Four-cylinder engines

3   Loosen the clips and disconnect the hoses from the rear of the water pump housing. (See photo 7.1).

4   Unscrew the nut and remove the special bolt retaining the lower timing cover to the water pump assembly.

5   Unbolt the water pump assembly from the cylinder block and remove the sealing ring (photo).

6   Unscrew the bolts and remove the water pump from its housing using a mallet to break the seal. Remove the gasket (photo).

Five-cylinder engines

7   Using an Allen key where necessary, unscrew the nuts and withdraw the timing cover.

8   Set the engine on TDC compression No 1 cylinder, and unbolt the timing belt rear cover from the oil pump, with reference to Chapter 1.

9   Loosen the water pump mounting and adjustment bolts, again using an Allen key where necessary, and rotate the pump to release the tension on the timing belt.

10   Unscrew and remove the bolts noting the location of the stay, where applicable (photo).

11   Withdraw the water pump from the cylinder block and remove the sealing ring (photo). *Do not move the crankshaft or camshaft with the timing belt slack.*

All models

12   If the water pump is faulty, renew it, as individual components are not available. Clean the mating faces of the water pump, cylinder block, and pump housing (four-cylinder engines).

13   Refitting is a reversal of removal, but use a new sealing ring and gasket as applicable. On five-cylinder engines tension the timing belt, as described in Chapter 1. At the same time check that the crankshaft and camshaft are still on TDC No 1 cylinder. Fill the cooling system, as described in Section 4. Tension the alternator/power-assisted steering pump drivebelts, as applicable, with reference to Chapters 10 and 11 respectively.

9   Cooling fan thermo-switch – testing, removal and refitting

1   If the thermo-switch located in the bottom of the radiator develops a fault, it is most likely to fail open circuit. This will cause the fan motor to remain stationary even though the coolant reaches the operating temperature.

8.6 Unscrew securing bolts to separate water pump from its housing (four-cylinder)

8.10 Water pump and mounting bolts (five-cylinder)

8.11 Removing the water pump (five-cylinder)

2   To test the thermo-switch for an open circuit fault, disconnect the wiring and connect a length of wire or suitable metal object between the two wires. The fan should operate (even without the ignition switched on) in which case the thermo-switch is proved faulty and must be renewed.

3   To remove the thermo-switch first drain the cooling system, as described in Section 2.

4   Disconnect the battery negative lead.

5   Disconnect the wiring, then unscrew the thermo-switch from the radiator and remove the sealing washer.

6   To check the operating temperature of the thermo-switch, suspend it in a pan of water so that only the screwed end of the switch is immersed and the electrical contacts are clear of the water. Either connect an ohmmeter between the switch terminals, or connect up a torch battery and bulb in series with the switch. With a thermometer placed in the pan, heat the water and note the temperature at which the switch contacts close, so that the ohmmeter reads zero, or the bulb lights. Allow the water to cool and note the temperature at which the switch contacts open. Discard the switch and fit a new one if the operating temperatures are not within the specified limits.

7   Refitting is a reversal of removal, but always fit a new sealing washer. Fill the cooling system, as described in Section 4.

10 Coolant temperature sender unit – removal and refitting

1   The temperature sender unit is located at the rear of the cylinder head (photo). To remove it, first drain half of the cooling system, with reference to Section 2.

2   Disconnect the wiring and unscrew the sender unit from the connector or cylinder head, as applicable. Remove the sealing washer(s).

3   Refitting is a reversal of removal, but always renew the washer(s). Top up the cooling system, with reference to Section 4.

11 Heater valve – removal and refitting

1   Drain the cooling system as described in Section 2.

2   Unhook and detach the control rod from the control unit operating lever and disconnect the cable retainer from the body (photo).

3   Unscrew the inlet and outlet hose clips and detach the hoses. The unit can now be withdrawn.

4   Refitting is a reversal of the removal procedure. If necessary adjust the heater control as described in Chapter 12, Section 37.

10.1 Coolant temperature sender unit location (arrowed) at the rear of the cylinder head (four-cylinder)

11.2 Heater control valve and connections

12.1 Position of core plugs in the cylinder block (four-cylinder)

12 Fault diagnosis – cooling system

Symptom	Reason(s)
Overheating	Low coolant level
	Faulty pressure cap
	Thermostat sticking shut
	Drivebelt broken (four-cylinder)
	Open circuit thermo-switch
	Faulty cooling fan motor
	Clogged radiator matrix
	Retarded ignition timing
Slow warm-up	Thermostat sticking open
	Short circuit thermo-switch
Coolant loss	Deteriorated hose
	Leaking water pump or cooling system joints
	Blown cylinder head gasket
	Leaking radiator
	Leaking core plugs (photo)

Chapter 3
Fuel and exhaust systems

For modifications, and information applicable to later models, see Supplement at end of manual

Contents

Specifications

Part A: Carburettor and associated fuel system components

Air cleaner type	Renewable paper element; automatic air temperature control on some models

Fuel pump

Type	Mechanical, diaphragm, operated by eccentric on intermediate shaft (four-cylinder) or camshaft (five cylinder)
Operating pressure:	
1.6 and 1.8 litre engine	0.2 to 0.25 bar (2.9 to 3.6 lbf/in^2)
1.9 litre engine	0.35 to 0.40 bar (5.1 to 5.8 lbf/in^2)

Fuel tank capacity	60 litres (13.2 Imp gallons)

Fuel octane requirement (minimum)

1.6 litre	91 RON
1.8 and 1.9 litre	98 RON

Carburettor 1.6 litre – 1B3

Type	Single choke downdraught, automatic choke	
	Manual gearbox	**Automatic gearbox**
Choke valve gap:		
Initial	2.05 to 2.35 mm (or 1.85 to 2.15 mm*)	2.25 to 2.55 mm
Final	3.35 to 3.65 mm (or 4.15 to 4.45 mm*)	3.15 to 3.45 mm (or 4.15 to 4.45 mm*)
Fast idle speed	3700 to 4100 rpm	3500 to 3900 rpm
Choke cover number	253 (or 234*)	213
Idle speed	900 to 1000 rpm	900 to 1000 rpm
CO content	0.5 to 1.5%	0.5 to 1.5%
Venturi	26 mm	26 mm
Main jet	x125	x122.5
Air correction jet with emulsion tube	100	100
Idle fuel/air jet	50/130	50/130
Auxiliary fuel/air jet	37.5/130	37.5/130
Float needle valve	1.75 (or 2.0*)	1.75 (or 2.0*)
Enrichment jet	102.5 (or 110*)	102.5 (or 110*)
Pump injection tube	0.40	0.50 (or 0.55*)
Pump injection capacity (slow)	0.75 to 1.05 cc/stroke	0.75 to 1.05 cc/stroke

Models pre October 1981

Carburettor 1.6 litre – 2B5

Type	Twin progressive choke downdraught automatic choke			
	Manual gearbox		**Automatic transmission**	
Choke valve gap:				
Initial	1.65 to 1.95 mm		1.65 to 1.95 mm	
Final	3.75 to 4.05 mm		3.55 to 3.85 mm	
Fast idle speed	3350 to 3450 rpm		3550 to 3650 rpm	
Choke cover number	232		232	
Idle speed	900 to 1000 rpm		900 to 1000 rpm	
CO content	0.5 to 1.5%		0.5 to 1.5%	
	Stage 1	**Stage 2**	**Stage 1**	**Stage 2**
Venturi	24 mm	28 mm	24 mm	28 mm
Main jet	x117.5	x125	x117.5	x125
Air correction jet with emulsion tube	135	92.5	135	92.5
Idle fuel/air jet	52.5/135	40/125	52.5/135	40/125
Auxiliary fuel/air jet	42.5/130	–	42.5/130	–
Idle air jet for progression reserve	–	180	–	180
Idle fuel jet for progression reserve	–	130	–	100
Float needle valve	2.0	2.0	2.0	2.0
Float setting	27.0 to 29.0 mm	29.0 to 31.0 mm	27.0 to 29.0 mm	29.0 to 31.0 mm
Enrichment valve	65	–	65	–
Pump injection tube (vertical/horizontal)	0.4/0.4 mm	–	0.4/0.4 mm	–
Injection capacity	0.85 to 1.15 cc/stroke	–	0.75 to 1.05 cc/stroke	–

Carburettor 1.6 litre – 2E2

Type	Twin progressive choke downdraught, automatic choke	
Choke valve gap:		
Manual gearbox:		
Initial	2.15 to 2.45 mm	
Final	4.55 to 4.85 mm	
Automatic transmission:		
Initial	2.55 to 2.85 mm	
Final	5.55 to 5.85 mm	
Fast idle speed	2800 to 3200 rpm	
Choke cover number	258	
Idle speed	700 to 800 rpm	
CO content	0.5 to 1.5%	

	Stage 1	Stage 2
Venturi diameter	22 mm	26 mm
Main jet	x107.5	x127.5
Air correction jet with emulsion tube	80	105
Idle fuel jet	42.5	–
Full load enrichment valve	–	0.7
Pump injection tube:		
Manual gearbox	0.35	–
Automatic transmission	0.5	–
Pump injection capacity (slow)	0.8 to 1.2 cc/stroke	

Carburettor 1.8 litre – 2E2

Type	Twin progressive choke downdraught, automatic choke	
Choke valve gap:		
Initial	1.65 to 1.95 mm	
Final:		
Manual gearbox	3.85 to 4.15 mm	
Automatic transmission	3.75 to 4.05 mm	
Fast idle speed	2800 to 3200 rpm	
Choke cover number	258	
Idle speed	700 to 800 rpm	
CO content	0.5 to 1.5%	

	Stage 1	Stage 2
Venturi diameter	22 mm	26 mm
Main jet	x105	x120
Air correction jet with emulsion tube	100	100
Idle fuel/air jet	40	–
Full load enrichment valve	–	1.25
Pump injection tube	0.35	–
Pump injection capacity (slow)	0.95 to 1.25 cc/stroke	

Carburettor 1.9 litre – 2B5 (pre August 1982)

Type	Twin progressive choke downdraught, automatic choke	
Choke valve gap:		
Manual gearbox	3.45 to 3.75 mm	
Automatic transmission	3.25 to 3.55 mm	
Fast idle speed:		
Manual gearbox	3500 to 3700 rpm	
Automatic transmission	3600 to 3800 rpm	
Idle speed (all transmissions)	750 to 800 rpm	
CO content	0.8 to 1.2%	

	Stage 1	Stage 2
Venturi	24 mm	28 mm
Main jet	x115	x122.5
Air correction jet with emulsion tube	135	115
Idle fuel/air jet	42.5/125	40/125
Auxiliary fuel/air jet	45/125	–
Idle air for progression reserve	–	205
Idle fuel jet for progression reserve	–	95
Float needle valve	2.0	2.0
Float setting	27.0 to 29.0 mm	29.0 to 31.0 mm
Enrichment valve	100	–
Pump injection tube (vertical/horizontal)	0.4/0.55 mm	–
Injection capacity	1.35 to 1.65 cc/stroke	–

Carburettor 1.9 litre – 2B5 (from August 1982)

Choke valve gap:		
Manual gearbox	3.90 to 4.20 mm	
Automatic transmission	3.70 to 4.00 mm	
Fast idle speed:		
Manual gearbox	3500 to 3700 rpm	
Automatic transmission	3600 to 3800 rpm	
Idle speed (all transmissions)	750 to 800 rpm	
CO content	0.8 to 1.2%	

	Stage 1	Stage 2
Venturi	24 mm	28 mm
Main jet	x117.5	x125
Air correction jet with emulsion tube	135	115
Idle fuel/air jet	45/130	40/130
Auxiliary fuel/air jet	42.5/130	–
Idle air jet for progression reverse	–	205
Idle fuel jet for progression reserve	–	95
Float needle diameter	2.0	2.0
Pump injection tube diameter	2 x 04	0.55
Enrichment valve	85	–
Float setting	27 to 29	29 to 31
Injection capacity (slow)	1.35 to 1.65 cc/stroke	–

Torque wrench settings

	Nm	lbf ft
Fuel tank mounting	25	18
Fuel pump	20	15
Non-return valve (1.9 litre)	20	15
Carburettor – 1B3 and 2E2	7	5
Carburettor – 2B5	10	7
Carburettor cover screws	5	4
Automatic choke cover	5	4
Automatic choke centre bolt	10	7
Carburettor throttle housing (2B5)	10	7
Carburettor bypass air cut-off valve	5	4
Inlet manifold	25	18
Inlet manifold preheater	10	7
Exhaust manifold:		
1.6 and 1.8 litre	25	18
1.9 litre	20	15
Exhaust downpipe to manifold	30	22
Exhaust system pipe joint clamp(s)	25	18

Part B: Fuel injection system

Type .... Continuous fuel injection system (CIS)

System pressure .... 4.7 to 5.4 bar (68 to 78 lbf/in²)

Warm up regulator heater coil resistance .... 16 to 22 ohm

Idle speed .... 920 ± 20 rpm

Fuel tank capacity .... As Part A

Fuel octane requirement (minimum) .... 91 RON

CO content .... 1 ± 0.2%

Torque wrench settings

	Nm	lbf ft
Thermo-time switch	30	22
Auxiliary air valve	10	7
Throttle housing	20	14
Cold start valve	10	7
Warm-up valve	10	7
Metering unit	35	25
Fuel distributor	35	25
Non-return valve	25	18
Fuel line to distributor	10	7
Fuel line to warm-up valve	20	14
Distributor/non-return valve banjo bolts	25	18
Warm-up valve/distributor line banjo bolt	10	7
Inlet manifold	25	18
Exhaust manifold	20	14

Part A: Carburettor and associated fuel system components

1 General description

The fuel system consists of a rear mounted fuel tank, a mechanical diaphragm fuel pump and a downdraught carburettor.

The air cleaner has a renewable paper element and incorporates an automatic temperature control.

A conventional exhaust system is used on all models, being sectionised for ease of replacement.

Carburetor

Return line (blue)

Bracket

Fuel reservoir

T-piece

Filter in pressure line
only in vehicles with 2B5 carburetor

A

Pump

Sealing flange

Filter

Sealing ring

Suction line (black)

Fuel pump

B

Fuel filter

Seal

Non-return valve

Sealing flange

Fuel filter in line to carburetter

B

Supply line

Return line

To carburetter

Fig. 3.1 Typical fuel system components (Sec 1)

A   1.6 and 1.8 litre

B   1.9 litre

Vacuum switch for
gearchange indicator
(Only with manual gearbox)

Solenoid changeover valve
Only with air conditioner

Air conditioner connection

To econometer

To brake servo

Check valve
Position: white connection
to brake servo

Pulldown unit

Air cleaner
Temperature regulator

1B3 carburetor

Vacuum reservoir

Vacuum unit advance

Vacuum connections	Colour
A	Black
B	Light green
C	Natural
D	Pink
E	White
F	Grey

Fig. 3.2 Fuel system vacuum lines and components – 1B3 carburettor (Sec 1)

To brake servo

Air conditioner connection

Vacuum reservoir

Solenoid changeover
valve (Only with air
conditioner)

Vacuum switch for
gearchange indicator
(Manual gearbox only)

Check valve
Position: white connection
to brake servo

Vacuum unit
Advance

Vacuum unit
for Stage II

Vacuum unit
Retard

2B5 carburetor

To econometer

Air cleaner
Temperature regulator

Pulldown unit

Fig. 3.3 Fuel system vacuum lines and components – 2B5 carburettor on the 1.6 litre engine (Sec 1)

82

To econometer

Vacuum retard unit

To air conditioner

Non-return valve

Vacuum advance unit

Vacuum reservoir

Non-return valve
Black connection goes
to vacuum reservoir

Vacuum unit for stage II

Vacuum switch for
gearshift indicator

To brake servo

Thermopneumatic valve
for stage II

Pulldown unit

Automatic choke

Temperature regulator
(single-action regulator)

Vacuum unit

Fig. 3.4 Fuel system vacuum lines and components – 2B5 carburettor on the 1.9 litre engine (Sec 1)

−.−.−.−.−.− for air conditioner only

Vacuum reservoir

Vacuum switch for gear-change indicator (Manual gearbox only)

To econometer

To brake servo

Check valve
Position: white connection to brake servo

B

C

A

Vacuum unit – advance

Pulldown unit

B

Vacuum unit Stage II

2E2 carburetor

E

D

A

F

B

A

Temperature regulator

G

Temperature-time valve

Three-point unit

Idling/overrun control valve

Air cleaner

Control box

Vacuum connections	Colour
A	Black
B	Light green
C	Natural
D	Brown
E	Yellow
F	Blue
G	White

Fig. 3.5 Fuel system vacuum lines and components – 2E2 carburettor models pre August 1983 (Sec 1)

2   Fuel and exhaust system – routine maintenance

The following routine maintenance procedures are required for the fuel and exhaust system and must be carried out at the specified intervals given at the start of this Manual. It should be noted that the intervals quoted are those for a vehicle used in normal operating conditions. If a vehicle is used in adverse conditions, such as continuous city driving or in a hot dusty climate, then it is advisable to shorten the maintenance intervals.

Fuel system general: Inspect the fuel system lines, hoses and connections at regular intervals for security and condition. In addition also check the associated vacuum hoses and connections. Occasionally lubricate the accelerator control linkages.

Fuel system adjustments: Check and if necessary adjust the engine idling speed and where possible the exhaust CO content (having first checked ignition timing as described in Chapter 4).

Air cleaner: Renew the air cleaner element as described in Section 3.

Fuel filter: Renew the fuel filter as described in Section 7.

Exhaust system: Inspect the exhaust system for signs of joint leaks, excessive corrosion and general security. Repair if necessary (Section 16).

3   Air cleaner element – renewal and cleaning

1   A dirty air cleaner element will cause a loss of performance and an increase in fuel consumption. A new element should be fitted at the specified intervals and the element should be cleaned every twelve months or more frequently under dusty conditions.

2   Release the spring clips securing the air cleaner lid and remove the lid (photo).

3   Cover the carburettor entry port to prevent any dirt entering it when the element is lifted out, and remove the element. Wipe the inside of the air cleaner with a moist rag to remove all dust and dirt and then remove the covering from the entry port, (photo).

4   If cleaning the element, place well away from the vehicle, then tap the air cleaner element to remove dust and dirt. If necessary use a soft brush to clean the outside or blow air at very low pressure from the inside surface towards the outside.

5   Refit the element, clean the cover and put it in place, then clip the cover down, ensuring that the two arrows are aligned.

4   Air cleaner – removal and refitting

1   Remove the element, as described in Section 3

2   Unscrew the nut(s) securing the air cleaner body and remove the adaptor or retaining ring (photos).

3.3 Lifting out the air cleaner element

4.2A Unscrew the retaining nuts and ...

3.2 One of the air cleaner lid retaining clips

4.2B ... remove the retaining ring to allow removal of air cleaner body

3 Note the location of all hoses and tubes, then disconnect them and withdraw the air cleaner body from the carburettor. Remove the sealing ring.

4 Refit in the reverse order of removal ensuring that all hose connections are securely made.

5 Automatic air temperature control – general

1 The air cleaner intake incorporates an automatic temperature control which is operated by vacuum. A flap within the air intake directs warm air from the exhaust manifold, or cold air from the front of the vehicle.

2 To check the control first detach the cold air intake hose from the air cleaner unit and position a mirror at the intake aperture entrance so that the movement of the control flap can be observed.

3 Now detach the hose from the control unit regulator (thermostat) on the underside of the air cleaner unit.

4 By applying suction to the end of this hose, it should operate the control flap. If the control flap fails to operate, check the vacuum hoses for security and condition. Move the regulator flap manually to ensure that it operates freely (Figure 3.6).

5 To check the temperature regulator (thermostat unit) in the air cleaner body make the above mentioned checks then with the engine cold, start it and allow it to run at idle speed. Detach the hose from the vacuum unit on the intake and check that vacuum is present by placing a finger over the end of the hose. Also check that the regulator flap closes off the warm air intake.

6 Reconnect the vacuum hose and check that the regulator flap fully opens.

7 The position of the regulator flap is controlled by the thermostat in accordance with the ambient temperature within the air cleaner.

8 A further thermostat check can be made on 1.6 and 1.8 models with the engine warmed up and running at idle speed. Check that the regulator flap is fully open, then detach the thermostat/carburettor hose at the carburettor. The regulator flap must resume its initial position with 20 seconds. If defective the thermostat or control valve regulator unit must be renewed.

Fig. 3.6 Air cleaner with element removed (1.6 and 1.8 litre engines) (Sec 5)

A   Thermostat   C   Vacuum unit
B   Intake connection (with regulator flap)

6 Mechanical fuel pump – testing, removal and refitting

1 The fuel pump is located on the left-hand side of the engine and is operated by an eccentric on the intermediate shaft (four-cylinder engines) or camshaft (five-cylinder engines).

2 If the pump is suspected of malfunctioning, it can be checked in the following way. Disconnect the pump delivery pipe (to filter), position a rag or container beneath the pump delivery pipe connection

and disconnect the high tension lead from the ignition coil to prevent the engine firing and the possibility of electrical sparks.

3 With an assistant operating the starter for a few seconds check that the pump is delivering regular spurts of fuel. If satisfactory, refit the pump delivery hose, tighten the clamps, then reconnect the high tension lead to the ignition coil.

4 If the fuel pump is to be removed, first disconnect the battery earth lead.

5 *Ensure that the car is in a well ventilated place and that there is no danger of ignition from sparks or naked flames. Never work on any part of a fuel system when the car is over an inspection pit.*

6 Unclamp and disconnect the fuel lines from the pump. Remove the two securing bolts and lift the pump, flange and gasket off, (photo).

6.6 Fuel pump removal (four-cylinder engine)

7 The pump is not repairable and must be renewed if defective.

8 Refit the pump using a new gasket in contact with the cylinder block, followed by the flange, sealing ring, and pump. When offering up the pump to the engine, ensure that its lever, or plunger fits correctly against the cam, not under it. Bolt the pump in place and attach the suction (fuel inlet) pipe, which is the pipe from the fuel filter, to the pipe on the cover of the pump.

7 Fuel line filter – renewal

1 A disposable fuel line filter is fitted in the fuel line between the fuel pump and the carburettor on 1.9 litre models or the fuel tank and the fuel pump on 1.6 and 1.8 litre models.

Fig. 3.7 Fuel line filter on 1.6 and 1.8 litre engines (Sec 7)

2   The fuel filter on the 1.9 litre models does not require renewal during routine maintenance as it is only fitted to collect any particles in the system that may have been left during manufacture. If renewing the fuel line at any time, this filter can then be omitted.
3   To renew the filter unit on the 1.6 and 1.8 litre models disconnect the fuel lines, which are secured with clips. When detaching the fuel lines have the new filter unit ready for immediate fitting to minimise fuel leakage from the disconnected lines. The arrow marking on the filter must face towards the pump.
4   On completion check that the fuel line hoses are secure and that there are no signs of fuel leakage from the connections on restarting the vehicle.

8   Fuel reservoir – removal and refitting

1   The fuel reservoir unit is fitted on 1.6 and 1.8 litre models only and is located between the fuel pump and the carburettor.
2   To remove the reservoir, disconnect the three line hoses and plug them to prevent leakage.
3   Remove the support bracket retaining screws and lift away the reservoir.
4   Refit in the reverse order to removal and then check for any signs of leakage on completion. It should be noted that the reservoir on models fitted with the 1B3 carburettor is manufactured in plastic, whilst on 2E2 carburettor models it is manufactured in metal.

9.4 Fuel tank sender unit and connections (carburettor engine)

1   *Suction line*   3   *Return line*
2   *Breather line*   4   *Wiring connector*

Fig. 3.8 Fuel reservoir (steel type) showing connections (Sec 8)

A   *To carburettor (not marked)*
B   *From fuel pump (arrow mark)*   C   *To fuel tank (marked R)*

9.7 Fuel filler pipe connecting hose

9   Fuel tank – removal, servicing and refitting

Note: *For safety reasons the fuel tank must always be removed in a well ventilated area.*
1   Disconnect the battery negative lead.
2   Remove the fuel tank filler cap.
3   Remove the luggage compartment floor covering and the circular cover from the floor which protects the fuel tank sender unit and connections.
4   Detach the fuel suction and return lines and also the breather line from the sender unit (photo).
5   Pull free and disconnect the sender unit wiring connector.
6   Jack up the rear of the vehicle and support it on safety stands. Chock the front wheels.
7   Working under the right-hand side wheel arch at the rear, loosen off the connecting hose (filler pipe to tank) retaining clips and detach the connecting hose (photo).

8   Support the tank underneath, making allowance for any fuel remaining in it, and then unscrew the tank retaining strap nuts (Figure 3.9).
9   With the straps removed, carefully lower the tank to the point where the large breather line can be disconnected from its connector at the top of the tank. Lower and remove the tank.
10 If the tank is contaminated with sediment or water, remove the gauge sender unit, as described in Section 10 and swill the tank out with clean fuel. If the tank is damaged or leaks, it should be repaired by specialists, or alternatively renewed. **Note:** *Do not, under any circumstances, solder or weld a fuel tank, for safety reasons.*
11 Refitting is a reversal of removal.

10 Fuel gauge sender unit and gravity valve – removal and refitting

Note: *For safety reasons the fuel gauge sender unit must always be removed in a well ventilated area.*
1   Disconnect the battery negative lead.
2   Remove the floor covering the luggage compartment.

Fuel gauge sender

Cap

Washer

Retaining ring

Rubber housing

Cover

Filter pipe
witch check valve

Union nut

Return line (blue)

Small breather pipe

Suction line (black)

Large breather pipe

Hose

Protective tube

Suction cage

Boot

Sealing ring

Clip

Fuel tank

Clamping strap

Fig. 3.9 Fuel tank and associated components (Sec 9)

3   Disconnect the wiring from the fuel gauge sender unit.
4   Release the clips and detach the fuel feed, return and breather hoses from their connections on the top of the sender unit.
5   Unscrew the sender unit union nut and carefully lift out the sender unit.

6   Refitting is a reversal of removal, but use a new sealing ring and smear it with a little glycerine. Ensure that the fuel lines and breather hose connections are correctly made, and are secure. When tightening the union nut ensure that the fuel/breather hose connecting unions face towards the front as shown in photo 9.4.

11.2 Disconnecting the throttle cable at the carburettor

Fig. 3.10 Accelerator cable adjustment clip – manual gearbox models (Sec 11)

11 Accelerator cable – removal, refitting and adjustment

Note: *On automatic transmission models refer also to Chapter 7, Figs 7.20 and 7.21.*
1   Remove the air cleaner, as described in Section 14.
2   Disconnect the cable from the carburettor (photo), automatic transmission and accelerator pedal, as applicable, then withdraw the cable. Refitting is a reversal of removal, but make sure that the cable is not kinked. Adjust as follows.

Adjustment – manual gearbox models
3   On 1.6 and 1.8 litre models have an assistant fully depress the accelerator pedal then check that the throttle lever on the carburettor is in the fully open position. If not, reposition the clip shown in Fig. 3.10.
4   On 1.9 litre models, disconnect the cable from the throttle lever at the carburettor then set the accelerator pedal to the idle position so that the distance from the stop on the floor to the pedal is 60.0 mm (2.36 in). With the throttle lever in its idling position, reconnect the cable and take up the slack in the cable. Insert the clip in the nearest groove to the bracket.
5   To check the adjustment on 1.9 litre models, fully depress the accelerator pedal and check that the distance between the throttle lever and stop is no more than 1.0 mm (0.04 in).

Adjustment – 1.9 litre engine with automatic transmission
6   Run the engine to normal operating temperature to ensure that the choke is fully open, then remove the air cleaner (Section 4).
7   Extract the lock clips from the pull and pushrod balljoints and detach them from the rocker linkage (Figure 3.11).
8   Actuate the throttle and rotate the automatic choke fast idle cam so that it is clear of the limit screw (Figure 3.12).
9   Loosen off the ball socket locknut then press the rocker lever against the stop. Rotate the balljoint on the rod and position it so that, when pressed down onto the balljoint, it is not strained in any way, then retighten the locknut.
10 Working inside the car, unscrew and remove the accelerator pedal stop and spacer.
11 Make up a distance piece as shown in Fig. 3.13 using a 135 mm (5.32 in) M8 bolt, and screw it into the pedal stop nut, but do not allow the bolt to touch the accelerator pedal rod.
12 Unscrew and loosen off the locknut on the pushrod (Figure 3.14).
13 Loosen off the accelerator pedal cable adjuster nut and locknut, (Figure 3.15).
14 Fit the pushrod ball onto the rocker lever and lock the balljoint.
15 Pivot the gearbox operating lever rearwards to the idle position, then rotate the adjustment nut on the pedal cable so that the cable is engaged without strain whilst leaving the accelerator pedal plate in contact with the bolt (Figure 3.16).
16 Support the gearbox operating lever in the idle position and

Fig. 3.11 Disengage the push/pull rods from the rocker linkage (Sec 11)

Fig. 3.12 Automatic choke showing fast idle cam (a) and limit screw (b) (Sec 11)

retighten the pushrod clamp nut. The bolt can then be removed from underneath the accelerator pedal and the pedal stop and spacer refitted (Figure 3.17).

17 Check that the throttle opens fully when the accelerator pedal is pressed down to its point of resistance without operating the kickdown. Hold in this position and check that the compensator spring on the pushrod is not compressed and clearance (a) in Figure 3.18 is as specified.

18 Fully depress the accelerator pedal so that it contacts the pedal stop to compress the compensator spring.

19 When adjusted correctly the throttle must be closed at idle and the gearbox operating lever must be on the stop.

Fig. 3.13 Distance piece required, set nuts at distance (a) (Sec 11)

a = 119 mm (4.68 in)

Fig. 3.14 Pushrod and clamp screw (Sec 11)

Fig. 3.15 Accelerator cable adjuster and locknut (Sec 11)

Fig. 3.16 Gearbox operating lever – move in direction of arrow to idle position (Sec 11)

Fig. 3.17 Hold lever in idle position and tighten pushrod clamp screw (Sec 11)

Fig. 3.18 Check clearance (a) as given below (Sec 11)

Full throttle (a) must equal 13.5 mm (0.53 in)
Past full throttle (a) must equal 10.5 mm (0.41 in) – compensator spring compressed

Adjustment – 1.6 litre engine with automatic transmission

20 Proceed as described in paragraph 6.

21 Check that the throttle is fully released (closed for normal idle) and that the fast idle speed adjusting screw does not contact with the automatic choke notched disc, but if it does rotate the disc accordingly to correct it.

22 Loosen off the knurled adjuster nut (Figure 3.19).

23 Loosen off the cable to support bracket locknuts at the inlet manifold and pull the outer cable towards the centre of the engine to take up any play. Do not allow the throttle to open (or the gearbox operating lever).

24 Hand tighten the carburettor side nut against the support bracket and then tighten the engine side lock nut against the opposing side of the support bracket to secure.

25 At the gearbox end, detach the operating lever return spring then get an assistant to fully depress the accelerator pedal against the stop (kickdown position). At the gearbox depress the operating lever in the direction of the arrow (Figure 3.19) to its stop kickdown position and simultaneously rotate the knurled adjuster nut to take up any play in the cable, then tighten the locknut against the underside of the bracket. Refit the operating lever return spring.

26 Check that the throttle lever is at its idling position and the gearbox operating lever is also at its idle (no throttle) position when the accelerator pedal is fully released.

27 Depress the accelerator pedal to the point where pressure is felt and the throttle is fully open, but without operating the kickdown, then check that the throttle lever is contacting the throttle stop with the kickdown spring uncompressed.

28 Now fully depress the accelerator pedal to the kickdown stop position and check that the gearbox operating lever is in contact with its stop and that the kickdown spring is compressed the specified amount shown in Figure 3.20.

Adjustment: 1.6 litre with 2E2 carburettor (with overrun cut-off) and automatic transmission, also the 1.8 litre engine with automatic transmission

29 Proceed as described in paragraph 6.

30 Loosen off the knurled cable adjuster nut on the side of the transmission.

31 Loosen off the cable nut at the cable locating bracket at the carburettor end.

32 Referring to Figure 3.21, pivot the warm up lever to the point where the throttle valve operating pin is no longer in contact. Retain the lever in this position by wedging the connecting lever with a screwdriver as shown.

33 Detach the vacuum hoses from the three-way vacuum connector and then connect up a vacuum pump as shown and seal off and plug connection B (Figure 3.22).

Fig. 3.20 Accelerator cable adjustment check at kickdown position (Sec 11)

A = 10 to 11 mm (0.40 to 0.43 in)

Fig. 3.21 1.6 and 1.8 litre models with automatic transmission – accelerator cable showing 2E2 carburettor connections (Sec 11)

A Warm-up lever	C Connecting lever
B Throttle valve operating pin	D Screwdriver position

Fig. 3.19 Accelerator pedal cable adjusting nut (A), locknut (C) and operating lever kickdown position direction (B) (Sec 11)

Fig. 3.22 Connect up vacuum pump as shown to (A) and seal off connection (B) (Sec 11)

Fig. 3.23 Kickdown spring should compress 8 mm (0.314 in) when measured at gap (a) (Sec 11)

34 If available use the special Volkswagen vacuum pump shown together with its special tool reference number (VAG 1390).
35 Apply vacuum with the pump so that the diaphragm pushrod is retained in the overrun condition with a gap between the cold idle speed adjusting screw and the diaphragm pushrod.
36 Pull the outer cable away from the carburettor to take up the play ensuring that both the throttle and gearbox operating lever remain in the overrun (closed) position.
37 Hand tighten the adjuster nut (1) then tighten the cable locknut on the opposing (carburettor) side of the support bracket to secure.

38 Proceed as described in paragraphs 25, 26, 27 and 28, but referring to Figure 3.23 to check the kickdown spring adjustment.

All models
39 Refit the air cleaner as described in Section 4.

12 Carburettor – removal and refitting

1 Disconnect the battery negative lead.
2 Remove the air cleaner, as described in Section 3.
3 Drain half of the coolant from the cooling system, with reference to Chapter 2.
4 Disconnect the coolant hoses from the automatic choke.
5 As applicable, disconnect the wiring from the automatic choke and fuel cut-off solenoid.
6 Disconnect the accelerator cable.
7 Disconnect the fuel and vacuum hoses.
8 Unscrew the through-bolts or nuts, and lift the carburettor from the inlet manifold. Remove the insulating flange gasket.
9 Refitting is a reversal of removal, but clean the mating faces of the carburettor and inlet manifold and always fit a new gasket. Tighten the mounting bolts evenly to the specified torque.

13 Carburettor – dismantling, servicing and reassembly

1 With the carburettor removed from the inlet manifold as described in the previous Section, wash it externally with a suitable solvent and allow to dry.
2 Dismantle and reassemble the carburettor, with reference to Figs. 3.24, 3.25 and 3.26, having first obtained a repair set of gaskets. Before dismantling the automatic choke, note the position of the cover in relation to the carburettor cover. See accompanying photos for dismantling of the 1B3 carburettor.

13.2A The 1B3 carburettor cleaned for dismantling

13.2B Unscrew the retaining bolts ...

13.2C ... and remove the upper body

13.2D Upper section inverted for inspection/further dismantling as necessary

13.2E Injection tube removal

13.2F Always renew the gasket on reassembly

Carburetor top part

Vacuum reservoir

Choke valve gap

Idle fuel/air jet

Auxiliary fuel/air jet

5 Nm

Enrichment tube

Pulldown unit

Adjusting screw

Fuel supply
connection

Check valve

Main jet

5 Nm

Gasket

Automatic choke cover

Float

Pin

Float needle

Plug

Fig. 3.24A Exploded view of the 1B3 carburettor (top part) (Sec 13)

Bearing ring

Pump piston

Piston seal

Injection tube

Carburetor bottom part

Part throttle enrichment jet

To the pulldown unit

Connection for temperature regulator in air cleaner

Idle adjusting screw

Adjusting screw

Part load air passage heating

Part throttle enrichment valve

CO adjusting screw

Bypass air cutoff valve

Fig. 3.24B Exploded view of the 1B3 carburettor (bottom part) (Sec 13)

3   Before removing the respective jets note their locations and note that the air correction jet on all carburettor types cannot be removed, (Figures 3.27, 3.28, 3.29 and 3.30).

4   When dismantled clean the various components with petrol and blow dry with an air line. Do not probe or clean out the jets and apertures with wire or any other similar implement as this will damage the machined surfaces.

5   Inspect the various components for signs of wear and damage and renew any parts where necessary.

6   The following checks and adjustments should be made during the assembly of each carburettor type. Do not overtighten the jets and fastenings.

1B3 carburettor

7   To check the fuel cut-off valve, apply 12 volts to the terminal and earth the body. With the valve pin depressed approximately 3 to 4 mm (0.12 to 0.16 in), the core must be pulled in.

8   When inserting the accelerator pump piston seal in the 1B3 carburettor, press it towards the opposite side of the vent drilling. The piston retaining ring must be pressed flush into the carburettor body.

9   When reassembling the float unit, locate the needle with the forced opening to the float. The float setting is preset and is not adjustable for position.

10   The choke pulldown unit can only be accurately tested using a vacuum tester and this is a task best entrusted to your VW dealer.

11   When refitting the enrichment tube check that its setting clearance, (a) in Figure 3.31, which is measured between the upper choke valve face and the bottom end of the tube is as specified.

12   The thermo-switches may be checked with an ohmmeter as shown in Figure 3.32.

2B5 carburettor

13   To adjust the float setting to the specified requirement, invert the cover and check that the float setting for stage 1 and stage 2 floats are as specified in Figure 3.33.

14   Check the fuel cut-off valve as described in paragraph 7. Note that the needle valve spring tension pin must not be depressed. If adjustment is necessary, bend the float arm tab.

15   Check and if necessary adjust the stage 2 locking lever clearance by opening the choke valve fully whilst simultaneously closing the throttle valve to normal idle position. Check that the choke idle cam adjuster screw is not in contact, then measure the locking lever clearance as shown in Figure 3.34. Bend the arm to suit if adjustment is necessary.

16   The thermo-switches can be checked with an ohmmeter as shown in Figure 3.32.

2E2 carburettor

17   When refitting the injection tube it must be correctly positioned so that fuel is sprayed in line with the recess, shown in Figure 3.35.

All models

18   When the carburettor is reassembled and refitted, refer to Section 14 for the necessary adjustments.

Fig. 3.25A Exploded view of the 2B5 carburettor (top part) (Sec 13)

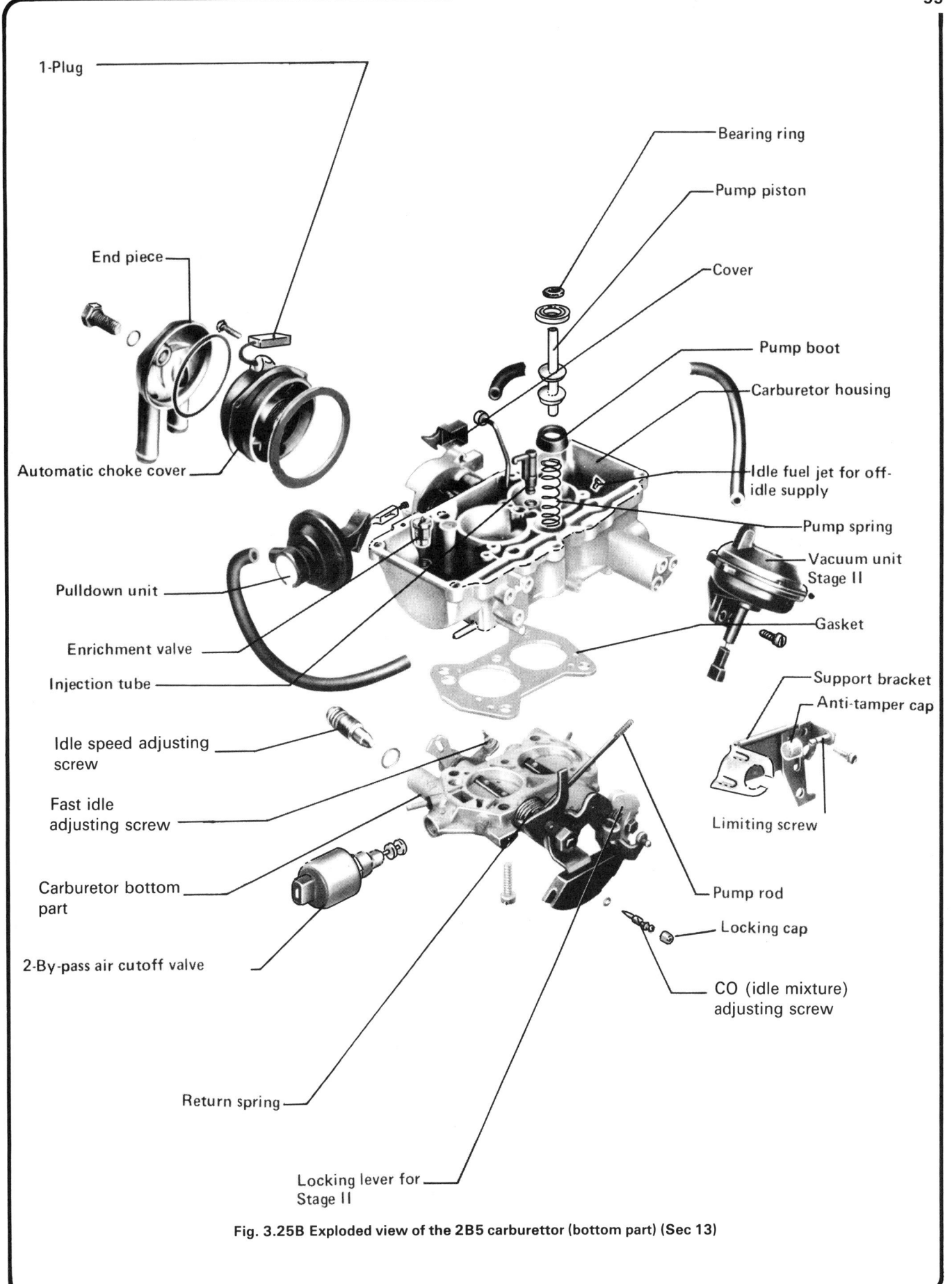

1-Plug

End piece

Bearing ring

Pump piston

Cover

Pump boot

Carburetor housing

Automatic choke cover

Idle fuel jet for off-idle supply

Pump spring

Pulldown unit

Vacuum unit Stage II

Enrichment valve

Gasket

Injection tube

Support bracket

Anti-tamper cap

Idle speed adjusting screw

Fast idle adjusting screw

Limiting screw

Carburetor bottom part

Pump rod

2-By-pass air cutoff valve

Locking cap

CO (idle mixture) adjusting screw

Return spring

Locking lever for Stage II

Fig. 3.25B Exploded view of the 2B5 carburettor (bottom part) (Sec 13)

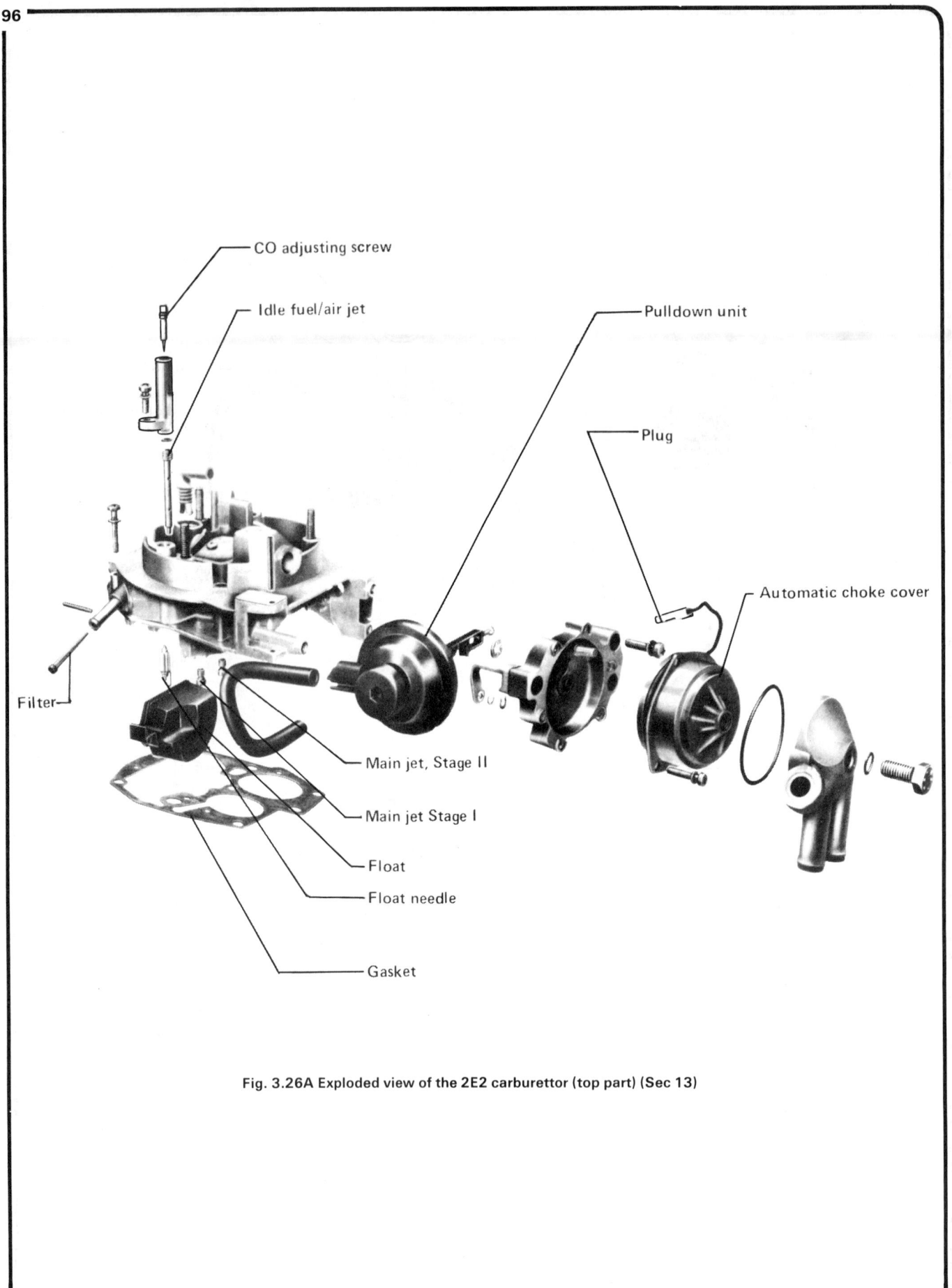

CO adjusting screw

Idle fuel/air jet

Pulldown unit

Plug

Automatic choke cover

Filter

Main jet, Stage II

Main jet Stage I

Float

Float needle

Gasket

Fig. 3.26A Exploded view of the 2E2 carburettor (top part) (Sec 13)

Temperature-time valve

Idling/overruncontrol valve

Control valve for idling speed

Part load enrichment valve

Injection tube

Limiting screw for basic
throttle valve setting

Three-point unit

Poppet valve

Accelerator pump

Vacuum unit Stage II

Expansion element

Adjusting screw

Part load air passage heating

Fig. 3.26B Exploded view of the 2E2 carburettor (bottom part) (Sec 13)

Fig. 3.27 1B3 carburettor upper body showing jet locations
(Sec 13)

3 2 1

Fig. 3.28 2B5 carburettor upper body showing jet locations
(Sec 13)

1 Idle fuel/air jet
2 Air correction jet and emulsion
   tube (do not remove)
3 Auxiliary fuel/air jet

1/2 Auxiliary fuel/air jet
3 Air correction jet and emulsion
   tube (do not remove) – Stage 1
4 Idle fuel/air jet – Stage 1

5 Idle fuel/air jet – Stage 2
6 Air correction jet and emulsion
   tube (do not remove) – Stage 2
7 Idle air jet (off/idle supply)

Fig. 3.29 2E2 carburettor upper body showing jet locations (top side) (Sec 13)

1 Idle fuel/air jet (beneath CO adjustment screw guide tube)
2 Air correction jet and emulsion tube (do not remove) – Stage 1
3 Air correction jet and emulsion tube (do not remove) – Stage 2

Fig. 3.30 2E2 carburettor upper body showing jet locations (bottom side) (Sec 13)

1 Main jet (stage 1)   3 Full load enrichment feed pipe
2 Main jet (Stage 2)   4 Progression feed pipe (stage 2)

Fig. 3.31 Enrichment tube alignment – 2B3 carburettor from October 1981 (Sec 13)

$a = 1.0 \pm 0.03$ mm $(0.04 \pm 0.001$ in)

Fig. 3.32 Checking automatic choke (I) and manifold preheater (II) thermo-switches (Sec 13)

I Below 30°C (86°F) – zero ohm   II Below 50°C (122°F) – zero ohm
   Above 40°C (104°F) – infinity   Above 55°C (131°F) – infinity

Note: Where the thermo-switches are individual the automatic choke thermo-switch is coloured red

Fig. 3.33 2B5 carburettor – float settings (Sec 13)

Stage I a = 28 ± 1 mm (1,10 ± 0.04 in)
Stage II a = 30 ± 1 mm (1.18 ± 0.04 in)

Fig. 3.34 2B5 carburettor – locking lever clearance for Stage 2 (Sec 13)

A = 1.00 ± 0.2 mm (0.039 ± 0.007 in)
B = 1.20 ± 0.2 mm (0.047 ± 0.007 in)

Fig. 3.35 2E2 carburettor – injection tube direction (Sec 13)

Fig. 3.36 1B3 carburettor – idle mixture adjusting screw location
(Sec 14)

14 Carburettor adjustments

Idling speed (1B3 carburettor)
1   Run the engine to normal operating temperature and switch off all electrical components.
2   Disconnect the crankcase ventilation hose at the air cleaner and plug the hose.
3   Make sure that the automatic choke is fully open otherwise the throttle valve linkage may still be on the fast idle cam.
4   On models with automatic transmission it is important that the accelerator cable adjustment is correct as described in Section 11.
5   Connect a tachometer to the engine, then start the engine and let it idle. Check that the idling speed is as given in the Specifications – note that the radiator fan must not be running. If necessary, turn the idling adjusting screw in or out until the idling speed is correct (photo).
6   The idle mixture adjustment screw is covered with a tamperproof cap which must be removed in order to adjust the mixture. However first make sure that current regulations permit its removal (Figure 3.36).
7   If an exhaust gas analyser is available, connect it to the exhaust system, then run the engine at idling speed and adjust the mixture screw to give the specified CO content percentage. Turn the mixture screw clockwise to weaken the mixture and anti-clockwise to enrich the mixture. Alternatively as a temporary measure adjust the mixture screw to give the highest engine speed, then readjust the idling speed if necessary.

8   After making the adjustment, fit a new tamperproof cap, and reconnect the crankcase ventilation hose.

Fast idling speed (1B3 carburettor)
9   With the engine at normal operating temperature and switched off, connect a tachometer and remove the air cleaner.
10 Fully open the throttle valve, then turn the fast idle cam and release the throttle valve so that the adjustment screw is positioned on the highest part of the cam (Figure 3.37).
11 Without touching the accelerator pedal, start the engine and check that the fast idling speed is as given in the Specifications. If not, turn the adjustment screw on the linkage as necessary. If a tamperproof cap is fitted renew it after making the adjustment.

Fig. 3.37 1B3 carburettor showing the idle cam (A) adjusting
screw (B) for the fast idle setting (Sec 14)

Choke pull-down system (1B3 carburettor)
12 Remove the air cleaner cover, as described in Section 3.
13 Half open the throttle valve then completely close the choke valve.
14 Without touching the accelerator pedal, start the engine.
15 Close the choke valve by hand and check that resistance is felt over the final 4 mm (0.16 in) of travel. If no resistance is felt there may be a leak in the vacuum connections or the pull-down diaphragm may be broken.
16 Further checking of the system requires the use of a vacuum pump and a gauge, therefore this work should be entrusted to your VW dealer.

14.5 Idle speed adjustment – 1B3 carburettor

Fig. 3.38 Choke valve gap check using drill shank (1), adjust using socket-head bolt (2) (Sec 14)

Choke valve gap (1B3 carburettor)
17 The choke valve gap measurement and adjustment points are shown in Fig. 3.38 for reference purposes only; the use of a vacuum tester and gauge is required, so this task is best left to a VW dealer.

Throttle valve basic setting (1B3 carburettor)
18 This setting is made during manufacture and will not normally require adjustment. However, if the setting has been disturbed proceed as follows.
19 First run the engine to normal operating temperature.
20 Remove the air cleaner, as described in Section 3.
21 Disconnect the vacuum advance hose at the carburettor and connect a vacuum gauge.
22 Run the engine at idling speed, then turn the idle limiting screw on the lever until vacuum is indicated on the gauge. Turn the screw out until the vacuum drops to zero, then turn it out a further quarter turn, (Figure 3.39).
23 After making the adjustment, adjust the idling speed as described in paragraphs 1 to 8.

Electric bypass air heating element (1B3 carburettor)
24 Disconnect the wiring from the fuel cut-off solenoid and thermoswitch, and connect a test lamp to the heating element wire and the battery positive terminal.
25 If the lamp lights up, the heater element is in good working order.

Accelerator pump (1B3 carburettor)
26 Hold the carburettor over a funnel and measuring glass.
27 Turn the fast idle cam so that the adjusting screw is off the cam. Hold the cam in this position during the following procedure.
28 Fully open the throttle ten times, allowing at least three seconds per stroke. Divide the total quantity by ten and check that the resultant injection capacity is as given in the Specifications. If not, refer to Fig. 3.40 and loosen the cross-head screw, turn the cam plate as required, and tighten the screw.
29 If difficulty is experienced in making the adjustment, check the pump seal and make sure that the return check valve and injection tube are clear.

Automatic choke (1B3 carburettor)
30 The line on the cover must be in alignment with the dot on the automatic choke body.

Inlet manifold preheater (1B3 carburettor)
31 Using an ohmmeter as shown in Fig. 3.41 check that the resistance of the preheater is between 0.25 and 0.50 ohms. If not, renew the unit.

Fig. 3.40 Accelerator pump adjustment on the 1B3 carburettor (Sec 14)

a   Locking screw   b   Cam plate

Fig. 3.39 Idle limiting screw (C) – 1B3 carburettor (Sec 14)

Fig. 3.41 Checking the inlet manifold preheater resistance (Sec 14)

Automatic choke (2B5 carburettor)
32 The line on the cover must be in alignment with the dot on the automatic choke body.

Idling speed (2B5 carburettor)
33 The procedure is identical to that described in paragraphs 1 to 8 inclusive.

Fast idling speed (2B5 carburettor)
34 The procedure is as given in paragraphs 9 to 11 inclusive. However, access to the adjustment screw is difficult when it is on the highest part of the cam, so it is necessary to move the cam in order to turn the screw. After making the adjustment, seal the screw with a spot of paint or fit a new tamperproof cap, as necessary.

Choke valve gap (2B5 carburettor)
35 To check and adjust the choke valve gap necessitates the use of a vacuum tester and gauge, and in view of this it is a task best entrusted to your VW dealer.

Choke pull-down system (2B5 carburettor)
36 The procedure is identical to that described in paragraphs 12 to 16 inclusive.

Accelerator pump (2B5 carburettor)
37 The procedure is identical to that described in paragraphs 26 to 29 inclusive. Refer to Figure 3.42 for adjustment.

Fig. 3.42 Accelerator pump adjustment nut (a) on the 2B5 carburettor (Sec 14)

Stage 1 throttle valve basic setting (2B5 carburettor)
38 This setting is made during manufacture and will not normally require adjustment. However, if the setting has been disturbed proceed as follows. First run the engine to normal operating temperature.
39 Remove the air cleaner, as decribed in Section 3.
40 Make sure that the fast idle adjusting screw is not contacting the fast idle linkage.
41 Unscrew the basic throttle setting screw until it no longer contacts the linkage, (Figure 3.43).
42 Open and close the throttle quickly, then turn the setting screw until it just contacts the linkage. From this position screw it in a further quarter turn.
43 Fit a tamperproof cap if necessary, then adjust the idling speed, as described in paragraph 33.

Stage 2 throttle valve basic setting (2B5 carburettor)
44 This setting is made during manufacture and will not normally require adjustment. However, if the setting has been disturbed proceed as follows. First remove the carburettor.
45 With the Stage 1 throttle valve in the idling position, unscrew the Stage 2 basic throttle setting screw until it no longer contacts the stop (Figure 3.44).
46 Disconnect the vacuum unit pullrod then turn the setting screw

Fig. 3.43 Stage I throttle valve basic setting limit screw (A) and anti-tamper cap (B) – 2B5 carburettor (Sec 14)

Fig. 3.44 Stage II throttle valve basic setting limit screw (a) and stop (b) – 2B5 carburettor (Sec 14)

until it just contacts the stop while lightly pressing the throttle lever shut. From this position screw it in a further quarter turn.
47 Fit a new tamperproof cap if necessary, then reconnect the vacuum unit pullrod.
48 Adjust the idling speed, as described in paragraph 33.

Idling speed (2E2 carburettor)
49 The procedure is basically the same as that described in paragraphs 1 to 8 inclusive, but note the following.

(a) Check that the fast idle adjustment screw (B in Fig. 3.45) is just making contact with the diaphragm pushrod (A)
(b) The idle speed and mixture (CO) adjustment screws are indicated in Fig. 3.46.

Fast idling speed (2E2 carburettor)
50 With the engine at normal operating temperature and switched off, connect a tachometer and remove the air cleaner. Plug off the temperature regulator vacuum hose.
51 Detach the Y-piece from the vacuum hose and plug the hose, (Figure 3.47).
52 Connect up a tachometer to the engine. Start and run the engine and check that the fast idle speed is as given in the Specifications, if not turn the adjustment screw on the linkage as necessary (Fig. 3.45). On completion apply sealant to the screw threads to lock it in position.

Choke pull-down system (2E2 carburettor)
53 The procedure is identical to that described in paragraphs 12 to 16 inclusive.

Fig. 3.45 Diaphragm pushrod (A) and fast idle adjustment screw (B) — 2E2 carburettor (Sec 14)

Fig. 3.46 Mixture (CO) adjustment screw (B) and control valve/ idle speed adjustment screw (A) — 2E2 carburettor (Sec 14)

Fig. 3.47 Disconnect and plug vacuum hose (1) for fast idle speed adjustment — 2E2 carburettor (Sec 14)

Choke valve gap (2E2 carburettor)
54 To check and adjust the choke valve gap necessitates the use of a vacuum tester and gauge and in view of this it is a task best entrusted to your VW dealer.

Stage 1 throttle valve basic setting (2E2 carburettor)
55 Proceed as described in Section 11, paragraphs 32 to 35 inclusive. Loosen off the limiting screw to give a clearance between it and the stop, then screw it in so that it just touches the stop. From this point screw it in a further quarter turn. Secure screw with locking compound (Figure 3.48).

Fig. 3.48 Stage I throttle valve setting limiting screw (A) and stop (B) — 2E2 carburettor (Sec 14)

Stage 2 throttle valve basic setting (2E2 carburettor)
56 This is made during manufacture and will not normally require adjustment. However if the setting has been disturbed proceed as follows. First remove the carburettor (Section 12).
57 Referring to Figure 3.49, open the throttle valve and hold in this position by inserting a wooden rod or similar implement between the valve and the venturi.
58 Using a rubber band as shown, pre-tension the Stage 2 throttle valve locking lever, then unscrew the limiting screw to provide a clearance between the stop and limiting screw.
59 Now turn the limiting screw in so that it is just in contact with the stop. The limiting screw stop point can be assessed by inserting a piece of thin paper between the screw and stop, moving the paper as the limiting screw is tightened. With the stop point reached turn the screw in a further quarter of a turn then secure it with locking compound. Close both throttle valves then measure the locking lever clearances, A and B in Figure 3.50. If the clearances are not as specified, bend the arm as necessary.

Accelerator pump (2E2 carburettor)
60 To make this check the carburettor must be removed and you will need a vacuum pump and an M8 x 20 mm bolt.
61 Detach the vacuum hoses from the three point unit then connect up the vacuum pump to the three point unit at A shown in Figure 3.22 and plug connection B. Apply vacuum with the pump to hold the diaphragm pushrod in the overrun/cut-off position and give a clearance between the fast idle speed and diaphragm pushrod.
62 Pivot up the warm up lever to the point where the throttle valve control pin has clearance and insert the M8 x 20 mm bolt as shown to hold the warm up lever in this position (Figure 3.51).
63 Hold the carburettor over a funnel and measuring glass then slowly open the throttle valve lever fully five times allowing at least three seconds per stroke. Divide the total quantity by five and check the resultant injection capacity against that given in the Specifications.
64 If adjustment is necessary, refer to Figure 3.52, loosen off screw A and rotate the cam plate B in the required direction to increase or

Fig. 3.49 Throttle valve basic setting showing rod to hold valve open (arrowed), lock lever (1), limiting screw (2) and stop (3) (Sec 14)

Fig. 3.50 Lock lever clearance with throttle valves closed – 2E2 carburettor (Sec 14)

A   0.40 ± 0.1 mm (0.015 ± 0.004 in)
B   0.15 ± 0.1 mm (0.006 ± 0.004 in)

Fig. 3.51 Accelerator pump adjustment check showing warm-up lever (A), lever (B) and bolt (C) – 2E2 carburettor (Sec 14)

Fig. 3.52 2E2 carburettor showing accelerator pump adjustment points (Sec 14)

A   Screw   B   Cam plate

decrease the injection capacity. On completion retighten the screw and seal in position with locking compound.

65 The accelerator pump injection capacity can also be checked with the carburettor in position in the vehicle, but as specialised equipment is required this is a task best entrusted to your VW dealer.

Three point unit (2E2 carburettor)

66 To check the unit for satisfactory operation you will need a vacuum pump. Detach the vacuum hoses from the unit and attach the vacuum pump to connection 1 in Figure 3.53. Apply vacuum to pull the diaphragm pushrod to the idle point and then measure the amount of rod protrusion, (a) in Figure 3.53, which must be as specified.

67 To check the overrun cut-off point, plug off the vacuum connection, B in Figure 3.22, then apply increased vacuum with the vacuum pump. This should cause the diaphragm pushrod to move to the overrun/cut-off point.

68 Measure the rod protrusion as in paragraph 66. This should be about 10 mm. Hold in this position for a minimum period of one minute. If the rod protrusion is incorrect, or it will not hold for the specified period, then the diaphragm or three point unit probably leak. They are therefore in need of renewal.

Fig. 3.53 2E2 carburettor ready for three-point unit check (Sec 14)

Pushrod to idle point a = 15 mm (0.60 in)   *For item 1 refer to text*

Idle/overrun control valve (2E2 carburettor)
69 To check this, specialised test equipment is required and it should therefore be entrusted to your VW dealer.

Temperature time valve (2E2 carburettor)
70 To check this, specialised test equipment is required and it should therefore be entrusted to your VW dealer.

Automatic choke (2E2 carburettor)
71 The line on the cover must be in alignment with the dot on the

automatic choke body (photo).

15 Inlet and exhaust manifolds – removal and refitting

1   Remove the air cleaner unit as described in Section 4.
2   Remove the carburettor as described in Section 12.
3   Disconnect the servo unit vacuum hose.
4   Disconnect and detach the coolant hose at the inlet manifold (photo).

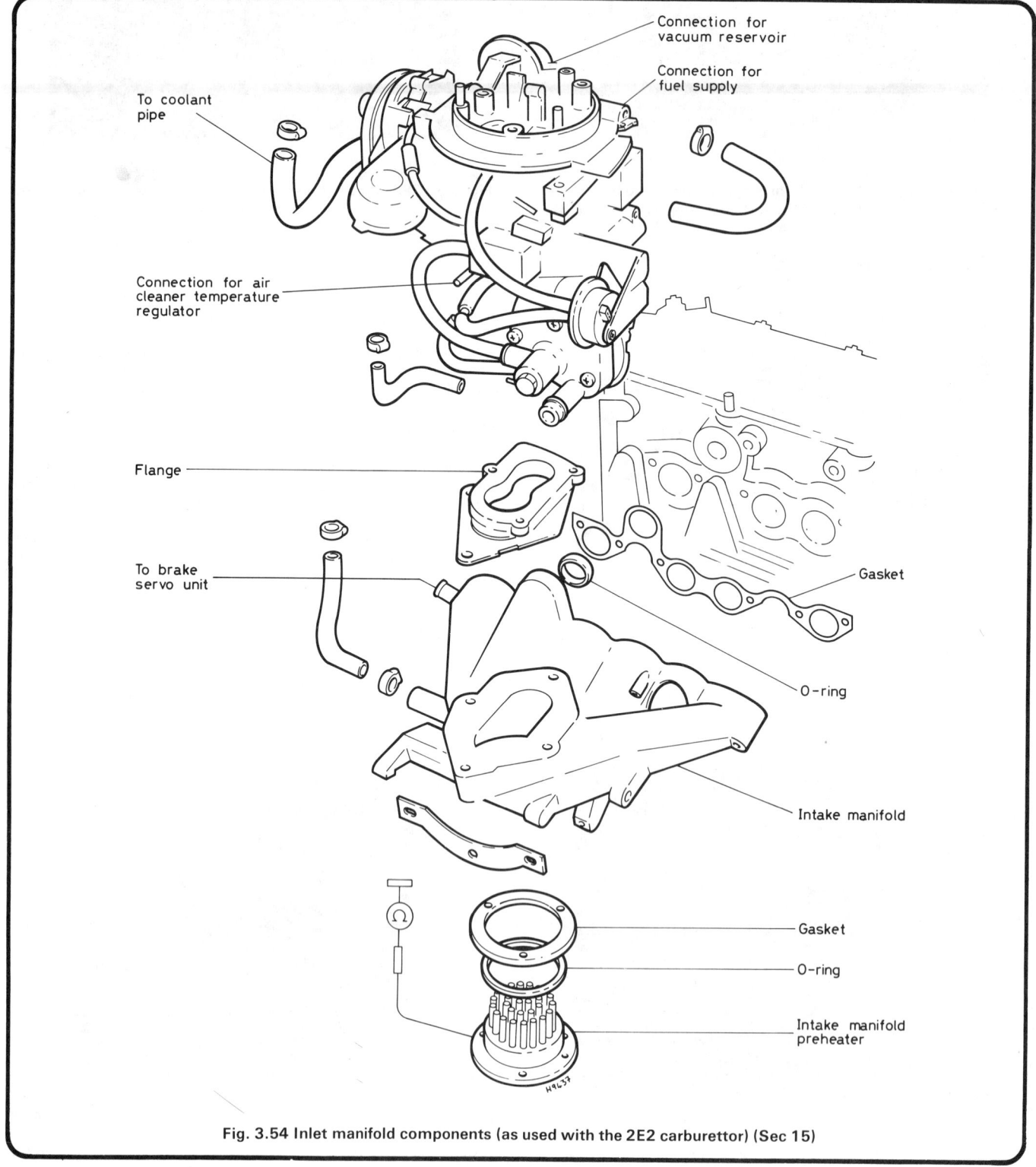

Fig. 3.54 Inlet manifold components (as used with the 2E2 carburettor) (Sec 15)

14.71 Automatic choke cover alignment on the 2E2 carburettor

15.4 Inlet and exhaust manifolds shown with carburettor removed. Note coolant hose connections to inlet manifold

16.5 Exhaust front pipe to manifold connection – always renew gasket

5   Disconnect the inlet manifold preheater lead from the base of the inlet manifold (Figure 3.54).
6   Unbolt and detach the exhaust stabilizer bracket.
7   Unscrew and remove the six Allen screws and detach the manifold.
8   Undo the six nuts securing the exhaust manifold to the down pipe and separate the two.
9   Remove the exhaust manifold to cylinder head nuts (with flat washers) and withdraw the manifold.
10   Refit in the reverse order to removal. Ensure that the mating faces are clean and use new gaskets when assembling.
11   Where given, tighten the fastenings to the specified torque wrench setting.
12   On completion check that the inlet manifold preheater cable is securely connected and located so that it will not fray against adjacent components.

16   Exhaust system – removal and refitting

1   The exhaust systems are shown in Figs. 3.55 and 3.56.

2   Before doing any dismantling work on the exhaust system, wait until the system has cooled down and then saturate the fixing bolts and joints with a proprietary anti-corrosion fluid.
3   When refitting the system new nuts and bolts should be used, and it may be found easier to cut through the old bolts with a hacksaw, rather than unscrew them.
4   When renewing any part of the exhaust system, it is usually easier to undo the manifold-to-front pipe joint and remove the complete system from the car, then separate the various pieces of the system, or cut out the defective part, using a hacksaw.
5   Refit the system a piece at a time, starting with the front pipe. Use a new joint gasket and note that it has a flanged side, the flanged side should face towards the exhaust pipe (photo).
6   Smear all the joints with a proprietary exhaust sealing compound before assembly. This makes it easier to slide the pieces to align them and ensures that the joints will be gas tight. Leave all bolts loose (photo).
7   Run the engine until the exhaust system is at normal temperature and then, with the engine running at idling speed, tighten all the mounting bolts and clips, starting at the manifold and working towards the rear silencer. *Take care to avoid touching any part of the system with bare hands because of the danger of painful burns.*
8   When the bolts and clips are tightened, it is important to ensure that there is no strain on any part of the system.

16.6A Typical pipe joint and clamp – use sealing compound when assembling joint

16.6B Exhaust system mounting strap must be in good condition and correctly located

Manifold

Gasket

Gasket

Front pipe

Bracket on gearbox

Front silencer

Intermediate pipe

Loops

Loops

Main silencer

Fig. 3.55 Exhaust system components – four-cylinder engines (Sec 16)

Exhaust manifold

Warm air deflector plate

Gasket

Gasket

Front exhaust pipe

Front exhaust pipe

Seal

Front silencer

Centre silencer

Rubber mounts
— centre silencer

Rubber mounts —
main silencer

Rear silencer

Fig. 3.56 Exhaust system components – five-cylinder engines (Sec 16)

Part B: Fuel injection system

17 Fuel injection system – general description

1   Although the fuel injection system is known as the 'K-Jetronic', it is not an electronically controlled system. The principle of the system is very simple and there are no specialised electronic components. There is an electrically driven fuel pump and there are electrical sensor and switches, but these are no different from those in general use on cars.

2   The following paragraphs describe the system and its various elements. Later Sections describe the tests which can be carried out to ascertain whether a particular unit is functioning correctly, but dismantling and repair procedures of units are not generally given because repairs are not possible.

3   The system measures the amount of air entering the engine and determines the amount of fuel which needs to be mixed with the air to give the correct combustion mixture for the particular conditions of engine operation. The fuel is sprayed continuously by an injection nozzle to the inlet port of each cylinder (photo). This fuel and air is drawn into the cylinder when the inlet valves open.

17.3 Injection nozzle, fuel line connection and seal

Airflow meter

4   This measures the volume of air entering the engine and relies on the principle that a circular disc, when placed in a funnel through which a current of air is passing, will rise until the weight of the disc is equal to the force on its lower surface which the air creates. If the volume of air is increased, and the plate were to remain in the same place, the rate of flow of air through the gap between the cone and the plate would increase and the force on the plate would increase.

5   If the plate is free to move, then as the force on the plate increases, the plate rises in the cone and the area between the edge of the plate and the edge of the cone increases, until the rate of air flow and hence the force on the plate, becomes the same as it was at the former lower flow rate and smaller cone area. Thus the height of the plate is a measure of the volume of air entering the engine.

6   The air flow meter consists of an air funnel with a sensor plate mounted on a lever which is supported at its fulcrum. The weight of the air flow sensor plate and its lever are balanced by a counterweight and the upward force on the sensor plate is opposed by a plunger. The plunger, which moves up and down as a result of the variations in air flow, is surrounded by a sleeve having vertical slots in it. The vertical movement of the plunger uncovers a greater or lesser length of the slots, which meters the fuel to the injection valves.

7   The sides of the air funnel are not a pure cone because optimum operation of the engine requires a different air/fuel ratio under different conditions such as idling, part load and full load. By making parts of

the funnel steeper than the basic shape, a richer mixture can be provided for, at idling and full load. By making the funnel flatter than the basic shape, a leaner mixture can be provided.

Fuel supply

8   Fuel is pumped continuously while the engine is running by a roller cell pump running at constant speed; excess fuel is returned to the tank. The fuel pump is operated when the ignition switch is in the START position, but once the starter is released a switch connected to the air plate prevents the pump from operating unless the engine is running.

9   The fuel line to the fuel supply valve incorporates a filter and also a fuel accumulator. The function of the accumulator is to maintain pressure in the fuel system after the engine has been switched off and so give good hot re-starting.

10   Associated with the fuel accumulator is a pressure regulator which is an integral part of the fuel metering device. When the engine is switched off, the pressure regulator lets the pressure to the injection valves fall rapidly to cut off the fuel flow through them and so prevent the engine from 'dieseling' or 'running on'. The valve closes at just below the opening pressure of the injector valves and this pressure is then maintained by the pressure accumulator.

Fuel distributor

11   The fuel distributor is mounted on the air metering device and is controlled by the vertical movement of the air flow sensor plate. It consists of a spool valve which moves vertically in a sleeve, the sleeve having as many vertical slots around its circumference as there are cylinders on the engine.

12   The spool valve is adjusted to hydraulic pressure on the upper end and this balances the pressure on the air plate which is applied to the bottom of the valve by a plunger. As the spool valve rises and falls, it uncovers a greater or lesser length of metering slot and so controls the volume of fuel fed to each injector.

13   Each metering slot has a differential pressure valve, which ensures that the difference in pressure between the two sides of the slot is always the same. Because the drop in pressure across the metering slot is unaffected by the length of slot exposed, the amount of fuel flowing depends only on the exposed area of the slots.

Cold start valve

14   The cold start valve is mounted in the intake manifold and sprays additional fuel into the manifold during cold starting. The valve is solenoid operated and is controlled by a thermo-time switch in the engine cooling system. The thermo-time switch is actuated for a period which depends upon coolant temperature, the period decreasing with rise in coolant temperature. If the coolant temperature is high enough for the engine not to need additional fuel for starting, the switch does not operate.

Pressure surge switch

15   The pressure surge switch is fitted to later models and aids throttle response at low engine temperatures (below 35°C) by causing a momentary injection of fuel from the cold start valve when the throttle is opened. The pressure surge switch operates in conjunction with throttle switch and the thermo-time switch.

Compensation units

16   For cold starting and during warming up, additional devices are required to adjust the fuel supply to the different fuel requirements of the engine under these conditions.

Warm-up regulator (valve)

17   While warming up, the engine needs a richer mixture to compensate for fuel which condenses on the cold walls of the inlet manifold and cylinder walls. It also needs more fuel to compensate for power lost because of increased friction losses and increased oil drag in a cold engine. The mixture is made richer during warming up by the warm-up regulator. This is a pressure regulator which lowers the pressure applied to the control plunger of the fuel regulator during warm-up. This reduced pressure causes the air flow plate to rise higher than it would do otherwise, thus uncovering a greater length of metering slot and making the mixture richer.

18   The valve is operated by a bi-metallic strip which is heated by an electric heater. When the engine is cold the bi-metallic strip presses

Fig. 3.57 Fuel injection system vacuum circuit and components (Sec 17)

against the delivery valve spring to reduce the pressure on the diaphragm and enlarge the discharge cross-section. This increase in cross-section results in a lowering of the pressure fed to the control plunger.

19 When the engine is started, the electrical heater of the bi-metallic strip is switched ON. As the strip warms it rises gradually until it ultimately rises free of the control spring plate and the valve spring becomes fully effective to give normal control pressure.

Auxiliary air device

20 Compensation for power lost by greater friction is compensated for by feeding a larger volume of fuel/air mixture to the engine than is supplied by the normal opening of the throttle. The auxiliary air device bypasses the throttle with a channel having a variable aperture valve in it. The aperture is varied by a pivoted plate controlled by a spring and a bi-metallic strip.

21 During cold starting the channel is open and increases the volume of air passing to the engine, but as the bi-metallic strip bends it allows a control spring to pull the plate over the aperture until at normal operating temperature the aperture is closed. The heating of the bi-metallic strip is similar to that of the warm-up regulator described above.

18 Maintenance, adjustments and precautions – fuel injection system

1 Due to the complexity of the fuel injection system, any work should be limited to the operations described in this Chapter. Other adjustments and system checks are beyond the scope of most readers and should be left to your VW dealer.

2 The mixture setting is pre-set during production of the car and should not normally require adjustment. If new components of the system have been fitted however, the mixture can be adjusted after reference to Section 25.

3 The only adjustment which may be needed is to vary the engine idle speed by means of the screw mounted in the throttle housing. Use the screw to set the engine speed to that specified when the engine is at the normal operating temperature.

4 Routine servicing of the fuel injection system consists of checking the system components for condition and security, and renewing the air cleaner element at the specified intervals (see Routine Maintenance).

5 Check the system vacuum components for condition and security, these being shown in Figure 3.57.

6 In the event of a malfunction in the system, reference should be made to the Fault Diagnosis Section at the end of this Chapter, but first make a basic check of the system hoses, connections, fuses and relays for any obvious and immediately visible defects.

7 If any part of the system has to be disconnected or removed for any reason, particular care must be taken to ensure that no dirt is allowed to enter the system.

8 The system is normally pressurised, irrespective of engine temperature, and care must therefore be taken when disconnecting fuel lines; the ignition must also be off and the battery disconnected.

9 Removal, refitting and adjustment of the accelerator cable is similar to that for the 1.9 litre manual gearbox models described in Section 11, except that the throttle lever is located in the throttle housing instead of the carburettor.

10 Removal and refitting of the fuel tank is similar to that for carburettor engine models, as described in Section 9, but it is suggested that the fuel pump and fuel level sender unit are first removed, as described in Section 23.

11 Maintenance and servicing of the exhaust system is as described in Sections 2 and 16. Removal and refitting of the exhaust manifold is similar to that described in Section 15, after removal of the inlet manifold (Section 22).

19 Air cleaner element (fuel injection system) – removal, cleaning/renewal and refitting

1 Release the spring clips securing the air cleaner cover and separate the cover from the air flow meter (Figure 3.58).

2 Withdraw the element from the housing.

3 If cleaning the element, place well away from the vehicle then tap the air cleaner element to remove dust and dirt. If necessary use a soft brush to clean the outside or blow air at a very low pressure from the inside surface towards the outside.

4 Wipe clean the inside of the cover.

5 Refit the element and secure the cover by pressing the clips.

Air cleaner housing, upper section

Filter element

Rubber bearing

Air cleaner housing

Connecting pipe for warm air intake

Warm air deflector plate

Connecting pipe for cold air intake, inside

Bracket

Thermostat

Warm air hose

Connecting pipe for cold air intake, outside

Adaptor

Cold air hose

Fig. 3.58 Air cleaner and associated components (fuel injection system) (Sec 19)

20 Air cleaner (fuel injection system) – removal and refitting

1   Remove the element as described in the previous Section.
2   Disconnect the cold air and warm air intake hoses from the air cleaner body then detach and remove the air cleaner body (Figure 3.58).
3   Refit in the reverse order of removal.

21 Air cleaner air intake thermostat (fuel injection system) – removal, testing and refitting

1   Unscrew the three retaining screws and withdraw the thermostat unit from the air cleaner body.
2   To test the thermostat, immerse it in water, the temperature of which must initially be below 30°C (86°F). At this temperature the valve flap must pivot to the left (A in Figure 3.59).
3   When the water temperature is increased to above 38°C (100°F), the intake flap should move to the closed position (B in Figure 3.59).
4   If defective the thermostat can be removed and renewed. Referring to Figure 3.60, detach the flap from the retainer at A then press the flap upwards away from retainer B and withdraw the thermostat.
5   Refit in the reverse order to removal.

22 Inlet manifold (fuel injection system) – removal and refitting

1   Disconnnect the battery earth lead.
2   Unbolt and detach the throttle valve housing from the manifold (Figure 3.61).

Fig. 3.59 Air intake thermostat (fuel injection system) (Sec 21)

Position A below 30°C (86°F)   *Position B above 38°C (100°F)*

Fig. 3.60 Dismantling air intake thermostat – refer to text for procedure (fuel injection system) (Sec 21)

Idle adjusting screw

Gasket

Cold start valve

Gasket

Throttle

Seal

Suction pump

Gasket

To warm-up valve

To brake servo

Auxiliary air valve

Thermotime switch

Fig. 3.61 Inlet manifold and associated components (fuel injection system) (Sec 22)

3   Unbolt and detach the cold start valve unit together with its gasket.
4   Detach the auxiliary air valve, the brake servo hose, suction pump hose, warm-up valve hose and crankcase ventilation hose from the manifold.
5   Remove the retaining bolts and withdraw the manifold from the cylinder head.
6   Refitting is a reversal of the removal procedure, but make sure that the mating faces are clean and always fit new gaskets.

23 Fuel pump (fuel injection system) – removal, testing and refitting

1   The fuel pump is located in the fuel tank and access to it (and the fuel level sender unit) is gained after removing the luggage compartment floor covering and cover (Figure 3.62)

2   It is a sealed unit and the brushes and commutator are not accessible for servicing. The only replacement part available is the gravity check valve on the fuel outlet.
3   Before removing the pump, *first ensure that the car is in a well ventilated place and that there is no danger of ignition from sparks or naked flames. Never work on any part of a fuel system when the car is over an inspection pit.*
4   Disconnect the battery leads and then disconnect the wires multi-connector from the pump.
5   Thoroughly clean all dirt away from the fuel pipe unions on the pump.
6   Detach the vent line and attach a suitable spare hose to its connector. Remove the fuel filler cap then blow into the temporary vent hose. Little or no resistance must be felt.
7   To remove the fuel pump together with the sender and gravity valve units, first detach the fuel supply hose, return hose and vent hose the positions of which are shown in Figure 3.63.
8   Loosen off the large union nut and withdraw the sender unit from the tank.

Fig. 3.62 Fuel tank and associated components (fuel injection system) (Sec 23)

Fig. 3.63 Fuel tank sender unit connections (fuel injection system) (Sec 23)

1 *Supply (suction) line*
2 *Return line*
3 *Vent line*
4 *Wiring connector*

Fig. 3.64 Sender unit orientation – align arrow marks (to front) (Sec 23)

9 Undo the pump bracket in the tank and withdraw the fuel pump unit from the tank.
10 Refitting is a reversal of the removal procedure. When refitting the sender unit align its reference mark with the corresponding mark to the front (Figure 3.64).

24 Idle speed (fuel injection system)– adjustment

1 Run the engine until the oil temperature is at least 60°C (140°F).
2 Check the ignition timing (Chapter 4), adjusting it if necessary. Leave the wiring disconnected from the idle stabilizer, where applicable.
3 The main headlights should be turned ON. Disconnect and plug the crankcase breather hose from the valve cover.
4 Remove the locking cap from the adjustment screw on the throttle assembly and turn the screw to achieve the idle speed given in the Specifications. The adjustments should be made only when the electric radiator fan is stationary (Figure 3.65).

Fig. 3.65 Idle speed adjustment screw (fuel injection system) (Sec 24)

5 After making the adjustment, refit the locking cap over the adjustment screw, and reconnect the wiring to the idle stabilizer, where applicable.

25 Idle mixture (fuel injection system) – adjustment

1 The idle CO adjustment screw alters the height of the fuel metering distributor plunger relative to the air control plate of the air flow meter.
2 The screw is accessible by removing the locking plug from between the air duct scoop and the fuel metering distributor on the air flow meter casing.
3 Although a special tool is recommended for this adjustment, it can be made using a long, thin screwdriver, (Figure 3.66).
4 Ensure that the engine is running under the same conditions as those necessary for adjusting the idling speed (see previous Section) and that the idling speed is correct.
5 Connect an exhaust gas analyser to the tailpipe as directed by the equipment manufacturer, and read the CO level.
6 Turn the adjusting screw clockwise to raise the percentage of CO and anti-clockwise to lower it. It is important that the adjustment is made without pressing down on the adjusting screw, because this will move the air flow sensor plate and affect the adjustment.
7 Remove the tool, accelerate the engine briefly and re-check. If the tool is not removed before the engine is accelerated there is a danger of the tool becoming jammed and getting bent.

Fig. 3.66 Mixture adjustment screw with special tool number shown (fuel injection system) (Sec 24)

Fig. 3.67 Fuel filter and fuel accumulator with associated
components (fuel injection system) (Sec 26)

26 Fuel filter (fuel injection system) – removal and refitting

1   Disconnect the battery earth lead.
2   Relieve the system pressure as described in Section 28, paragraphs 2 and 3.
3   Position a suitable container beneath the filter pipe connections and disconnect the fuel inlet and outlet pipes from the filter (Figure 3.67).
4   Loosen the filter clamp bracket screw and withdraw the filter.
5   Refit in the reverse order of removal. On completion restart the engine and check the pipe connections for any signs of leaks.

27 Fuel accumulator (fuel injection system) – removal and refitting

1   Proceed as described in paragraphs 1 and 2 in the previous Section.
2   Disconnect the fuel pipes from the fuel accumulator and catch the small amount of fuel which will be released.
3   Detach and remove the fuel accumulator from its support bracket.
4   Refitting is a reversal of removal. Check for leaks on completion with the engine restarted.

28 Fuel metering distributor – removal and refitting

1   Disconnect the battery terminals.
2   *Ensure that the vehicle is in a well ventilated space and that there are no naked flames or other possible sources of ignition.*
3   While holding a rag over the joint to prevent fuel from being sprayed out, loosen the control pressure line from the warm-up valve. The control pressure line is the one connected to the large union of the valve.
4   Mark each fuel line, and its port on the fuel distributor. Carefully clean all dirt from around the fuel unions and distributor ports and then disconnect the fuel lines.
5   Unscrew and remove the connection of the pressure control line to the fuel metering distributor.
6   Remove the locking plug from the CO adjusting screw, then remove the screws securing the fuel metering distributor (Figure 3.68).
7   Lift off the fuel metering distributor, taking care that the metering plunger does not fall out. If the plunger does fall out accidentally, clean it in fuel and then re-insert it with its chamfered end downwards (Figure 3.69).

Fig. 3.68 Fuel metering distributor retaining screws (fuel injection system) (Sec 28)

Fig. 3.69 Fuel distributor removal ensuring plunger is retained in position (fuel injection system) (Sec 28)

8   Before refitting the metering distributor, ensure that the plunger moves up and down freely. If the plunger sticks, the distributor must be renewed, because the plunger cannot be repaired or replaced separately.
9   Refit the distributor, using a new sealing ring, and after tightening the screws, lock them with paint.
10   Refit the fuel lines and the cap of the CO adjusting screw and tighten the union on the warm-up valve.

29 Air flow meter – removal and refitting

1   Remove the fuel lines from the distributor, as described in paragraphs 1 to 5 of the previous Section.
2   Loosen the clamps at the air cleaner and throttle assembly ends of the air scoop and take off the air scoop (Figure 3.70).
3   Remove the bolts securing the air flow meter to the air cleaner and lift off the air flow meter and fuel metering distributor (Figure 3.71 and photo).
4   The fuel metering plunger should be prevented from falling out when the fuel metering distributor is removed from the air flow meter (see previous Section).
5   Refitting is the reverse of removing, but it is necessary to use a new gasket between the air flow meter and the air cleaner.

29.3 Air flow meter and fuel distributor unit (inverted)

Fig. 3.70 Air scoop retaining clips (arrowed) (fuel injection system) (Sec 29)

Fig. 3.71 Air flow meter retaining bolts (arrowed) (fuel injection system) (Sec 29)

Fig. 3.72 Pressure relief valve components (fuel injection system) (Sec 30)

30 Pressure relief valve – removal, servicing and refitting

1   Release the pressure in the fuel system, as described in paragraphs 1 to 3 of Section 28.
2   Unscrew the non-return valve plug and remove the plug and its sealing washer.
3   Take out the O-ring, shims, plunger and O-ring in that order (Figure 3.72).
4   When refitting the assembly, use new O-rings and ensure that all the shims which were removed are refitted.

31 Thermo-time switch – checking

1   The thermo-time switch energises the cold start valve for a short time on starting and the time for which the valve is switched on depends upon the engine temperature.
2   This check must only be carried out when the coolant temperature is below 30°C (86°F).

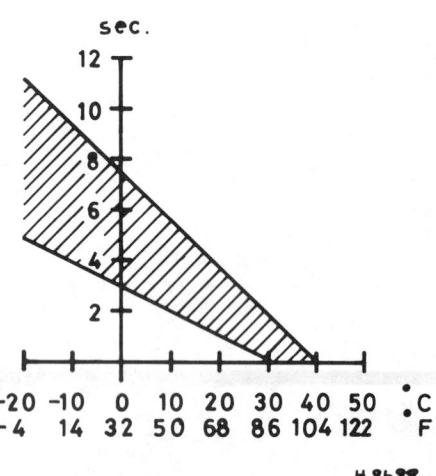

Fig. 3.73 Thermo-time switch graph (switch-on time) (fuel injection system) (Sec 31)

32.4 Cold start valve and attachments

3   Pull the connector off the cold start valve and connect a test lamp across the contacts of the connector.
4   Pull the high tension lead off the centre of the distributor and connect the lead to earth.
5   Operate the starter for 10 seconds and note the interval before the test lamp lights and the period for which it remains alight. Reference to the graph will show that at a coolant temperature of 30°C (86°F) the lamp should light immediately and stay on for two seconds (Figure 3.73).
6   Refit the high tension lead onto the distributor, and reconnect the lead to the cold start valve.

32 Cold start valve – checking

1   Ensure that the coolant temperature is below 30°C (86°F) and that the car battery is fully charged.
2   Pull the high tension lead off the centre of the distributor and connect the lead to earth.
3   Pull the connectors off the warm-up valve and the auxiliary air unit.
4   Remove the two bolts securing the cold start valve to the inlet manifold and remove the valve, taking care not to damage the gasket (photo).
5   With fuel line and electrical connections connected to the valve, hold the valve over a glass jar and operate the starter for 10 seconds. The cold start valve should produce an even cone of spray during the time the thermo-time switch is ON.
6   After completing the checks refit the valve and reconnect the leads that were disturbed.

33.1 Warm-up regulator (shown with fuel lines detached)

33 Warm-up regulator – checking

1   With the engine cold, pull the connectors off the warm-up valve and the auxiliary air unit (photo).
2   Connect a voltmeter across the terminals of the warm-up valve connector and operate the starter. The voltage across the terminals should be a minimum of 11.5 volts.
3   Switch the ignition OFF and connect an ohmmeter across the terminals of the warm-up valve. If the meter does not indicate a resistance of about 20 ohms, the heater coil is defective and a new valve must be fitted (Figure 3.74).

34 Air flow sensor lever and control plunger – checking

1   For the correct mixture to be supplied to the engine it is essential

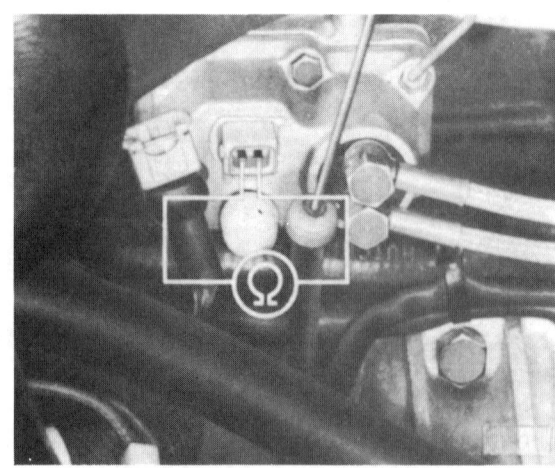

Fig. 3.74 Warm-up regulator heater coil resistance check (fuel injection system) (Sec 33)

34.2 Top view of the air flow sensor plate

34.6 Air flow sensor plate adjustment clip (arrowed)

that the sensor plate is central in the venturi and that its height is correct. First run the engine for a period of about one minute.
2 Loosen the hose clips at each end of the air scoop and remove the scoop. If the sensor plate appears to be off-centre, loosen its centre screw and carefully run a 0.10 mm (0.004 in) feeler gauge round the edge of the plate to centralise it, then re-tighten the bolt (photo).
3 Raise the air flow sensor plate and then quickly move it to its rest position. No resistance should be felt on the downward movement; if there is resistance the air flow meter is defective and a new one must be fitted.
4 If the sensor plate can be moved downwards easily, but has a strong resistance to upward movement, the control plunger is sticking. Remove the fuel distributor (Section 28) and clean the control plunger in fuel. If this does not cure the problem, a new fuel distributor must be fitted.
5 Release the pressure on the fuel distributor, as described in Section 28 and then check the rest position of the air flow sensor plate. The upper edge of the plate should be flush with the bottom edge of the air cone. It is permissible for the plate to be lower than the edge by not more than 0.5 mm (0.020 in), but if higher, or lower than the permissible limit, the plate must be adjusted (Figure 3.75).

6 Adjust the height of the plate by lifting it and bending the wire clips attaching the plate to the balance arm, but take care not to scratch or damage the surface of the air cone (photo).
7 After making the adjustment, tighten the warm-up valve union and check the idle speed and CO content.

35 Auxiliary air valve – checking

1 To carry out this test the engine coolant temperature must be below 30°C (86°F).
2 Detach the auxiliary air valve electrical plug and ensure that the contacts in the plug connector are in good condition.
3 Connect up a voltmeter across the contacts as shown (Figure 3.76), start the engine and run at idle speed. The voltage reading must be a minimum of 11.6V.
4 Leave the engine running at idle speed and pinch the air intake duct to auxiliary air valve hose together. The engine speed should drop.
5 When the engine is warmed up to its normal operating temperature, reconnect the auxiliary valve plug then pinch the hose together again. This time the engine speed should remain unaltered.

Fig. 3.75 Sensor plate position requirement (fuel injection system) (Sec 34)

Fig. 3.76 Auxiliary air valve check (fuel injection system) (Sec 35)

Part C: Fault diagnosis

36 Fault diagnosis – fuel system (carburettor models)

Note: *High fuel consumption and poor performance are not necessarily due to carburettor faults. Make sure that the ignition system is properly adjusted, that the brakes are not binding and that the engine is in good mechanical condition before tampering with the carburettor.*

Symptom	Reason(s)
Fuel consumption excessive	Air cleaner choked, giving rich mixture Leak from tank, pump or fuel lines Float chamber flooding due to incorrect level or worn needle valve Carburettor incorrectly adjusted Idle speed too high Choke faulty (sticks on) Excessively worn carburettor
Lack of power, stalling or difficult starting	Faulty fuel pump Leak on suction side of pump or in fuel line Intake manifold or carburettor flange gaskets leaking Carburettor incorrectly adjusted Faulty choke Emission control system defect
Poor or erratic idling	Weak mixture (screw tampered with) Leak in intake manifold Leak in distributor vacuum pipe Leak in crankcase extractor hose Leak in brake servo hose

37 Fault diagnosis – fuel system (fuel injection models)

Before assuming that a malfunction is caused by the fuel system, check the items mentioned in the special note at the start of the previous Section.

Symptom	Reason(s)
Engine will not start (cold)	Fuel pump faulty Auxiliary air device not opening Start valve not operating Start valve leak Sensor plate rest position incorrect Sensor plate and/or control plunger sticking Vacuum system leak Fuel system leak Thermotime switch remains open
Engine will not start (hot)	Faulty fuel pump Warm control pressure low Sensor plate rest position incorrect Sensor plate and/or control plunger sticking Vacuum system leak Fuel system leak Leaky injector valve(s) or low opening pressure Incorrect mixture adjustment
Engine difficult to start (cold)	Cold control pressure incorrect Auxiliary air device not opening Faulty start valve Sensor plate rest position faulty Sensor plate and/or control plunger sticking Fuel system leak Thermotime switch not closing
Engine difficult to start (hot)	Warm control pressure too high or too low Auxiliary air device faulty Sensor plate/control plunger faulty Fuel or vacuum leak in system Leaky injector valve(s) or low opening pressure Incorrect mixture adjustment

Symptom	Reason(s)
Rough idling (during warm-up period)	Incorrect cold control pressure Auxiliary air device not closing (or opening) Start valve leak Fuel or vacuum leak in system Leaky injector valve(s), or low opening pressure
Rough idling (engine warm)	Warm control pressure incorrect Auxiliary air device not closing Start valve leaking Sensor plate and/or control plunger sticking Fuel or vacuum leak in system Injector(s) leaking or low opening pressure Incorrect mixture adjustment
Engine backfiring into intake manifold	Warm control pressure high Vacuum system leak
Engine backfiring into exhaust manifold	Warm control pressure high Start valve leak Fuel system leak Incorrect mixture adjustment
Engine misfires (on road)	Fuel system leak
Engine 'runs on'	Sensor plate and or control plunger sticking Injector valve(s) leaking or low opening pressure
Excessive petrol consumption	Fuel system leak Mixture adjustment incorrect Low warm control pressure
High CO level at idle	Low warm control pressure Mixture adjustment incorrect Fuel system leak Sensor plate and/or control plunger sticking Start valve leak
Low CO level at idle	High warm control pressure Mixture adjustment incorrect Start valve leak Vacuum system leak
Idle speed adjustment difficult (too high)	Auxiliary air device not closing

Chapter 4 Ignition system

For modifications, and information applicable to later models, see Supplement at end of manual

Contents

Specifications

System type .... 12 volt battery with transistorized coil ignition (TCI)

Distributor

Rotor rotation .... Clockwise

Firing order:

Four-cylinder	1-3-4-2 (No 1 at timing belt end)
Five-cylinder	1-2-4-5-3 (No 1 at timing belt end)

1.6 litre engine

Engine type

	WV, YN	YP	DT
Ignition timing – before TDC	$9° \pm 1°$ at 900 to 1000 rpm	$0 \pm 1°$ at 900 to 1000 rpm	$18° \pm 1°$ at 700 to 800 rpm
Vacuum hose connection for timing check	Off	On	On

1.8 litre engine

Engine type

	DS
Ignition timing – before TDC	$18° \pm 1°$ at 700 to 800 rpm
Vacuum hose position for timing check	On

1.9 litre engine

Engine type

	WN
Ignition timing – before TDC	$TDC \pm 1°$ at 800 to 850 rpm
Vacuum hose position for timing check	On

2.0 litre engine

Engine type

	JS
Ignition timing – before TDC	$18°$ at 800 to 900 rpm
Vacuum hose position for timing check	On

Coil

Primary resistance .... 0.52 to 0.76 ohm
Secondary resistance .... 2400 to 3500 ohm

Spark plugs

Type:

1.6 litre engine	Bosch W7D, W7DC, W8D
	Beru 14-7D, 14-8D, 14-7DU/RS 35
	Champion N7YC
	NGK BP6-E
1.8 litre engine	Bosch W6 DO
	Beru 14-6DU
	Champion N79Y
1.9 litre engine	Bosch W5D
	Beru 14-5D
	Champion N7YC
2.0 litre engine	Bosch W6 DO
	Beru 14-6 DU
	Champion N79Y

Spark plug electrode gap:

1.6 litre engine	0.6 to 0.8 mm (0.023 to 0.031 in)
1.8 litre engine	0.8 to 0.9 mm (0.031 to 0.035 in)
1.9 litre engine	0.6 to 0.8 mm (0.023 to 0.031 in)
2.0 litre engine	0.8 to 0.9 mm (0.031 to 0.035 in)

Torque wrench settings

	Nm	lbf ft
Spark plugs	20	15
Distributor clamp bolt:		
Four-cylinder	25	18
Five-cylinder	15	11

1 General description

The ignition system consists of the battery, coil, distributor and spark plugs. All models covered by this manual have a transistorised ignition system incorporating a magnetic sensor and control unit. On some models a digital idle stabilizer (DIS) unit is incorporated into the system and its function is to stabilise the idle speed by advancing the ignition at low engine speeds (600 to 800 rpm).

The transistorised system functions in a similar manner to a conventional system, but the contact points and condenser are replaced by a magnetic sensor in the distributor and a control unit

Fig. 4.1 Main components of the ignition system (Sec 1)

mounted separately. As the distributor driveshaft rotates, the magnetic impulses are fed to the control unit which switches the primary circuit on and off. No condenser is necessary as the circuit is switched electronically with semiconductor components.

The ignition advance is controlled mechanically by centrifugal weights and by a vacuum capsule mounted on the side of the distributor.

To prevent damage to the system or personal injury observe the precautions given in Section 6.

2 Ignition system – routine maintenance

The following routine maintenance procedures must be carried out at the specified intervals given at the start of this manual.

1   Remove, clean and reset the spark plugs. Reset the electrode gap before refitting (see Section 11).
2   Clean and inspect the ignition system HT and LT lead connections. Renew if defective in any way.
3   Remove the spark plugs and renew them at the specified intervals with a set of the recommended types.
4   Check and if necessary adjust the ignition timing as described in Section 9.

3 Distributor – removal and refitting

1   Pull the high tension connection from the centre of the ignition coil and remove the caps from the spark plugs.
2   Release the two spring clips securing the distributor cap, then remove the distributor cap with the ignition harness attached. On models with metal screening round the top of the distributor, it is necessary to remove the screw from the bonding strap before the cap can be taken off. Do not allow the metal cover clip to fall inwards as the rotor or trigger wheel may be damaged (photo).
3   Disconnect the control unit lead multi-plug. On some later models it is necessary to release the wire retaining clip to detach the multi-plug (Fig. 4.2).
4   Note the exact position of the rotor arm, so that the distributor can be fitted with the rotor arm in the same position, and also put mating marks on the distributor mounting flange and base. By marking these positions and also ensuring that the crankshaft is not moved while the distributor is off, the distributor can be refitted without upsetting the ignition timing.
5   Pull the vacuum pipe(s) from the vacuum control unit, marking the position of the pipes if there is more than one.
6   Remove the bolt and washer from the distributor clamp plate and take the clamp plate off. Remove the distributor and gasket (photos).
7   When refitting the distributor always renew the gasket (photo). Provided the crankshaft has not been moved, turn the rotor arm to such a position that when the distributor is fully installed and the gears mesh, the rotor will turn and take up the position which it held before removal. On the four-cylinder engine if the distributor will not seat fully, withdraw the unit and use pliers to turn the oil pump driveshaft slightly, then try again.
8   Fit the clamp plate and washer, then fit the bolt and tighten it.

3.2 Distributor cap screen bonding (earth) strap – arrowed (five-cylinder engine)

Fig. 4.2 Press wire retaining clip (arrow) to release wire connector – later models (Sec 3)

9   Fit the distributor cap and clip it in place, then reconnect the high and low tension wires.
10   If the engine has been the subject of overhaul, the crankshaft has been rotated or a new distributor is being fitted, then the procedure for installing the distributor will differ according to engine capacity; refer to Section 8 of this Chapter.

3.6A Distributor clamp and bolt (four-cylinder engine)

3.6B Distributor removal (four-cylinder engine)

3.7 Distributor gasket (four-cylinder engine)

Are your plugs trying to tell you something?

Normal.
Grey-brown deposits, lightly coated core nose. Plugs ideally suited to engine, and engine in good condition.

Heavy Deposits.
A build up of crusty deposits, light-grey sandy colour in appearance.
Fault: Often caused by worn valve guides, excessive use of upper cylinder lubricant, or idling for long periods.

Lead Glazing.
Plug insulator firing tip appears yellow or green/yellow and shiny in appearance.
Fault: Often caused by incorrect carburation, excessive idling followed by sharp acceleration. Also check ignition timing.

Carbon fouling.
Dry, black, sooty deposits.
Fault: over-rich fuel mixture.
Check: carburettor mixture settings, float level, choke operation, air filter.

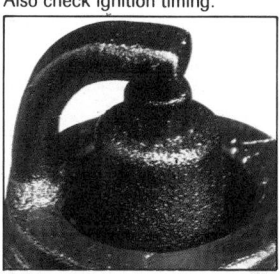

Oil fouling.
Wet, oily deposits. Fault: worn bores/piston rings or valve guides; sometimes occurs (temporarily) during running-in period.

Overheating.
Electrodes have glazed appearance, core nose very white – few deposits. Fault: plug overheating. Check: plug value, ignition timing, fuel octane rating (too low) and fuel mixture (too weak).

Electrode damage.
Electrodes burned away; core nose has burned, glazed appearance. Fault: pre-ignition. Check: for correct heat range and as for 'overheating'.

Split core nose.
(May appear initially as a crack). Fault: detonation or wrong gap-setting technique. Check: ignition timing, cooling system, fuel mixture (too weak).

WHY DOUBLE COPPER IS BETTER FOR YOUR ENGINE.

Unique Trapezoidal Copper Cored Earth Electrode — 50% Larger Spark Area — Copper Cored Centre Electrode

Champion Double Copper plugs are the first in the world to have copper core in both centre <u>and</u> earth electrode. This innovative design means that they run cooler by up to 100°C – giving greater efficiency and longer life. These double copper cores transfer heat away from the tip of the plug faster and more efficiently. Therefore, Double Copper runs at cooler temperatures than conventional plugs giving improved acceleration response and high speed performance with no fear of pre-ignition.

Champion Double Copper plugs also feature a unique trapezoidal earth electrode giving a 50% increase in spark area. This, together with the double copper cores, offers greatly reduced electrode wear, so the spark stays stronger for longer.

 FASTER COLD STARTING

 FOR UNLEADED OR LEADED FUEL

 ELECTRODES UP TO 100°C COOLER

 BETTER ACCELERATION RESPONSE

 LOWER EMISSIONS

 50% BIGGER SPARK AREA

 THE LONGER LIFE PLUG

Plug Tips/Hot and Cold.
Spark plugs must operate within well-defined temperature limits to avoid cold fouling at one extreme and overheating at the other.
Champion and the car manufacturers work out the best plugs for an engine to give optimum performance under all conditions, from freezing cold starts to sustained high speed motorway cruising.
Plugs are often referred to as hot or cold. With Champion, the higher the number on its body, the hotter the plug, and the lower the number the cooler the plug. For the correct plug for your car refer to the specifications at the beginning of this chapter.

Plug Cleaning
Modern plug design and materials mean that Champion no longer recommends periodic plug cleaning. Certainly don't clean your plugs with a wire brush as this can cause metal conductive paths across the nose of the insulator so impairing its performance and resulting in loss of acceleration and reduced m.p.g.
However, if plugs are removed, always carefully clean the area where the plug seats in the cylinder head as grit and dirt can sometimes cause gas leakage.
Also wipe any traces of oil or grease from plug leads as this may lead to arcing.

DOUBLE COPPER

Screening

Earth wire

Distributor cap

Distributor rotor

Brush and spring

Plug connector

Dust cap

Pin

Spring washer (s)

Washer(s)

Circlip

Trigger wheel

Bracket

Connecting plug

Retaining knob

Connecting piece

Hall sender

Washer

Base plate

Distributor

Vacuum unit

Clamp

Washer

Fig. 4.3 Exploded view of the distributor (four-cylinder type shown) (Sec 4)

4.2 Removing the dust cap (four-cylinder engine)

4.3 Distributor driveshaft and trigger wheel (four-cylinder engine)

4 Distributor – dismantling, inspection and reassembly

Note: *Before commencing work check that spare parts are individually available for the distributor.*

1 Wipe clean the exterior of the distributor.
2 Pull the rotor arm off the driveshaft, then lift off the dust cap (photo). Do not allow the cap retaining clips to touch the trigger wheel.
3 Mark the trigger wheel in relation to the driveshaft, then prise out the retainer and withdraw the wheel, together with the locating pin (Figure 4.4 and photo).
4 Remove the retainer and washers, noting their location.
5 Remove the screws and withdraw the vacuum unit and packing after disconnecting the operating arm.
6 Remove the retainer and washer from the baseplate and also remove the screw securing the socket to the side of the distributor. Withdraw the magnetic pick-up and socket together.
7 Remove the screws and lift out the baseplate followed by the washer.
8 Clean all the components and examine them for wear and damage.
9 Inspect the inside of the distributor cap for signs of burning, or tracking. Make sure that the small carbon brush in the centre of the distributor cap is in good condition and can move up and down freely under the influence of its spring.
10 Check that the rotor arm is not damaged. Use an ohmmeter to measure the resistance between the brass contact in the centre of the rotor arm and the brass contact at the edge of the arm. The measured value of resistance should be between 600 and 1400 ohms on the 1.6 and 1.8 models or 1000 ohms on 1.9 and 2.0 models.
11 Suck on the pipe connection to the vacuum diaphragm and check that the operating rod of the diaphragm unit moves. Retain the diaphragm under vacuum to check that the diaphragm is not perforated.
12 Reassemble the distributor in reverse order of dismantling, but smear a little grease on the bearing surface of the baseplate.

Fig. 4.5 Thermo-pneumatic valve location (1) (later four-cylinder models) (Sec 5)

2   Check valve

Fig. 4.4 Prising free the trigger wheel. If distorted it must be renewed (Sec 4)

5 Thermo-pneumatic valve and check valve – checking

1 Later four-cylinder models fitted with automatic transmission have a thermo-pneumatic valve and check valve fitted. They are located in the vacuum line between the distributor and the carburettor. Their function is to improve acceleration when the engine coolant temperature is below 46°C (113°F) by maintaining the vacuum within the vacuum unit.
2 The thermo-pneumatic valve can be tested for satisfactory

operation by blowing through it. At temperatures below 30°C (86°F) the valve must be closed while at temperatures over 46°C (118°F) it must be open.

3   To check the efficiency of the check valve, blow through the white connection first to see if the valve is open. Blow through the valve from the black connection and check that the valve is shut.

4   Renew the valve(s) if found to be defective. When reconnecting, the white connection of the check valve must face towards the vacuum advance unit on the distributor.

6   Transistorised coil ignition system – precautions

1   To prevent personal injury and damage to the ignition system, the following precautions must be observed when working on the ignition system.

2   Do not attempt to disconnect any plug lead or touch any of the high tension cables when the engine is running, or being turned by the starter motor.

3   Ensure that the ignition is turned OFF before disconnecting any of the ignition wiring.

4   Ensure that the ignition is switched OFF before connecting or disconnecting any ignition testing equipment such as a timing light.

5   Do not connect a suppression condenser or test lamp to the coil negative terminal (1).

6   Do not connect any test appliance or stroboscopic lamp requiring a 12 volt supply to the coil positive terminal (15).

7   If the HT cable is disconnected from the distributor (terminal 4), the cable must immediately be connected to earth and remain earthed if the engine is to be rotated by the starter motor, for example if a compression test is to be done.

8   If a high current boost charger is used, the charger output voltage must not exceed 16.5 volts and the time must not exceed one minute.

9   The ignition coil of a transistorised system must never be replaced by the ignition coil from a contact breaker type ignition system.

10 If an electric arc welder is to be used on any part of the vehicle, the car battery must be disconnected while welding is being done.

11 If a stationary engine is heated to above 80°C (176°F) such as may happen after paint drying, or steam cleaning, the engine must not be started until it has cooled.

12 Ensure that the ignition is switched OFF when the car is washed.

7   Transistorised coil ignition system – testing

Digital Idle Stabilizer (DIS)

1   The DIS is fitted in the circuit between the Hall generator in the distributor and the control unit. It operates at engine speeds between 600 and 840 rpm and effectively advances the ignition in order to increase the engine speed to the correct idling speed. Not all models are fitted with the DIS.

2   To check the DIS, VW garages use an electronic tester connected to the flywheel TDC sensor unit. However, a timing light may be used just as effectively. Connect the timing light then start the engine and allow it to idle. Note the ignition timing.

3   Switch on all the electrical equipment including the heated rear window and main headlights, then check that the ignition timing has advanced. If not, the DIS unit is faulty.

Control unit

4   First check that the ignition coil and DIS are in order.

5   Disconnect the multi-plug from the control unit and measure the voltage between contacts 4 and 2 with the ignition switched on (Fig. 4.6). Note that on early models the control unit is located on the bulkhead, but on later models it is behind the glove compartment. If the voltage is not approximately the same as battery voltage, check the wiring for possible breakage.

6   Switch off the ignition and reconnect the multi-plug.

7   Disconnect the multi-plug from the distributor and connect a voltmeter across the coil primary terminals. With the ignition switched on at least 2 volts must register, falling to zero after approximately 1 to 2 seconds. If this does not occur, renew the control unit and coil.

8   Connect a wire briefly between the centre terminal of the distributor multi-plug and earth. The voltage should rise to at least 5 volts, otherwise the control unit should be renewed (Figure 4.7).

Fig. 4.6 Checking the voltage at the control unit multi-plug (Sec 7)

Fig. 4.7 Checking the voltage at the distributor multi-plug (Sec 7)

9   Switch off the ignition and connect a voltmeter across the outer terminals of the distributor multi-plug. Switch on the ignition and check that 5 volts is registered. If not, check the wiring for possible breakage.

Hall Generator

10 First check the ignition coil, DIS, and control unit. The following test should be made within ambient temperature extremes of 0° and 40°C (32° and 104°F).

11 Disconnect the central HT lead from the distributor cap and earth it with a bridging wire.

12 Pull back the rubber grommet on the control unit and connect a voltmeter across terminals 6 and 3 (Fig. 4.8).

13 Switch on the ignition, then turn the engine slowly in the normal direction using a spanner on the crankshaft pulley bolt.

14 On 1.6 and 1.8 litre models the voltage should alternate between 0 and 2 volts.

15 On 1.9 litre and 2.0 litre models the voltage should alternate between 0 to 0.7 volts, and 1.8 volts to battery voltage; if required, the distributor cap can be removed – with a full air gap 0 to 0.7 volts should register, but when the trigger wheel covers the air gap 1.8 volts to battery voltage should register.

16 If the results are not as given in paragraph 14 or 15 the Hall generator is faulty.

Fig. 4.8 Checking the voltage at the control unit multi-plug terminals 6 and 3 (Sec 7)

Fig. 4.9 TDC timing mark location on the rear of the camshaft gear on four-cylinder engines (Sec 8)

8 Ignition timing – basic setting

1   If the distributor has been removed and the ignition timing disturbed, it will be necessary to reset the timing using the following static method before setting it dynamically, as described in Section 9.

Four-cylinder engines

2   Turn the engine using a spanner on the crankshaft pulley bolt until the TDC mark (0) on the flywheel or driveplate is aligned with the pointer in the timing aperture (photo), which is located next to the distributor.
3   Check that the mark on the rear of the camshaft gear is aligned with the cylinder head cover, as shown in Fig. 4.9. If the mark is on the opposite side of the cylinder head, turn the crankshaft forward one complete revolution, and again align the TDC mark.
4   Turn the oil pump shaft so that its lug is parallel with the crankshaft (Figure 4.10).
5   With the distributor cap removed turn the rotor arm so that the centre of the metal contact is aligned with the mark on the rim of the distributor body (photo).
6   Hold the distributor over its recess in the cylinder block with the vacuum unit slightly clockwise of the position shown in Fig. 4.11.

Fig. 4.10 Oil pump shaft lug position when fitting distributor (Sec 8)

8.2 TDC (top dead centre) timing marks aligned on the four-cylinder engine

8.5 Align the rotor arm metal contact with the TDC mark (arrowed) on the distributor body rim (four-cylinder engine)

7   Insert the distributor fully. As the drivegear meshes with the intermediate shaft, the rotor will turn slightly anti-clockwise and the body can be realigned with the rotor arm to take up the final positions shown in Fig. 4.11. A certain amount of trial and error may be required for this. If the distributor cannot be fully inserted into its mounting hole, slightly reposition the oil pump driveshaft lug. Turn the distributor body until the original body-to-cylinder head marks are in alignment – then clamp the distributor in position.

Five-cylinder engines

8   Turn the engine using a spanner on the crankshaft pulley bolt until the TDC mark (O) is aligned with the lug in the timing aperture in the flywheel or driveplate housing (Figure 4.12).
9   Check that the mark on the rear of the camshaft gear is aligned with the upper edge of the valve cover gasket. If the mark is on the opposite side of the cylinder head, turn the crankshaft forward one complete revolution and again align the TDC mark, (Figure 4.13).
10 With the distributor cap removed, turn the rotor arm so that the centre of the metal contact is aligned with the mark on the rim of the distributor body (Figure 4.14).
11 Hold the distributor over the location aperture in the rear of the cylinder head with the vacuum unit facing downward.
12 Insert the distributor fully. As the drivegear meshes with the camshaft, the rotor will turn slightly anti-clockwise, and the body can then be realigned with the rotor arm so that the vacuum unit faces slightly to the right (Figure 4.15).
13 Fit the clamp and tighten the bolt.

Fig. 4.13 TDC timing mark location on the rear of the camshaft gear on five-cylinder engines (Sec 8)

Fig. 4.14 Set distributor arm contact in line with mark on distributor body prior to fitting (five-cylinder engines) (Sec 8)

Fig. 4.11 Distributor is fitted with rotor arm pointing towards cylinder No 1 firing point (Sec 8)

Fig. 4.12 Aligning TDC timing marks on the five-cylinder engine (Sec 8)

Fig. 4.15 Distributor fitted position with rotor arm at TDC on No 1 cylinder (five-cylinder engines) (Sec 8)

9 Ignition timing – dynamic setting

1 Check and if necessary adjust the idle speed and idle mixture setting as described in Chapter 3.
2 Where a digital idle stabilizer is fitted, both plugs must be disconnected from the unit and the plugs connected together. Switch the engine off. (Figures 4.16 and 4.17).
3 Before making the dynamic timing check, the distributor vacuum unit hose on some 1.6 litre engine models must be detached, see Specifications.
4 When checking the ignition timing, the engine must be at normal operating temperature with the choke fully open, but with the radiator cooling fan stationary.
5 The ignition timing may be checked using a digital tester connected to the TDC sensor in the flywheel or driveplate housing. However, as this equipment is not normally available to the home mechanic, the following method describes the use of a timing light.
6 Connect the timing light to the engine in accordance with the manufacturer's instructions.
7 Run the engine at idling speed and direct the timing light through

9.7 Flywheel dynamic timing mark aligned with pointer on bellhousing (four-cylinder engine)

Fig. 4.16 Plug connections to the digital idle stabilizer (DIS) (Sec 9)

the timing aperture in the flywheel or driveplate housing. The mark on the flywheel or driveplate should appear in line with the pointer or reference edge on the housing. If adjustment is necessary, loosen the clamp bolt and turn the distributor body until the correct position is achieved, then tighten the bolt (photo).
8 Gradually increase the engine speed and check that the ignition advances – the centrifugal advance can be checked by pinching the vacuum hoses, and an indication of the vacuum advance can be obtained by releasing the hoses and noting that a different advance occurs.
9 Switch off the engine and remove the timing light. Reconnect the vacuum hose and digital idle stabilizer plugs, as applicable.

10 Ignition coil – testing

1 It is rare for an ignition coil to fail, but if there is reason to suspect it, use an ohmmeter to measure the resistance of the primary and secondary circuits.
2 Measure the primary resistance between the terminals 1 and 15 and the secondary resistance between the centre HT terminal and terminal 1. The correct resistance values are given in the Specifications (Figures 4.18 and 4.19).

Fig. 4.17 Connect the DIS plugs together (arrowed) when making ignition timing checks (Sec 9)

Fig. 4.18 Coil terminals for primary resistance check (Sec 10)

Fig. 4.19 Coil terminals for secondary resistance check (Sec 10)

11 Spark plugs and HT leads – general

1   The correct functioning of the spark plugs is vital for the correct running and efficiency of the engine. The spark plugs should be renewed every 10 000 miles (15 000 km). However, if misfiring or bad starting is experienced in the service period, they must be removed, cleaned and regapped.
2   The condition of the spark plugs will also tell much about the overall condition of the engine.
3   If the insulator nose of the spark plug is clean and white, with no deposits, this is indicative of a weak mixture, or too hot a plug. (A hot plug transfers heat away from the electrode slowly – a cold plug transfers it away quickly).
4   If the tip and insulator nose is covered with hard black-looking deposits, then this is indicative that the mixture is too rich. Should the plug be black and oily, then it is likely that the engine is fairly worn, as well as the mixture being too rich.
5   If the insulator nose is covered with light tan to greyish brown deposits, then the mixture is correct and it is likely that the engine is in good condition.
6   If there are any traces of long brown tapering stains on the outside of the white portion of the plug, then the plug will have to be renewed, as this shows that there is a faulty joint between the plug body and the insulator, and compression is being lost.
7   Plugs should be cleaned by a sand blasting machine, which will free them from carbon more thoroughly than cleaning by hand. The machine will also test the condition of the plugs under compression. Any plug that fails to spark at the recommended pressure should be renewed.
8   The spark plug gap is of considerable important, as, if it is too large or too small, the size of the spark and its efficiency will be seriously impaired. The spark plug gap should be set to the figure given in the Specifications at the beginning of this Chapter.
9   To set it, measure the gap with a feeler gauge, and then bend open, or close the *outer* plug electrode until the correct gap is achieved. The centre electrode should *never* be bent as this may crack the insulation and cause plug failure, if nothing worse.
10   Always tighten the spark plugs to the specified torque.
11   Periodically the spark plug leads should be wiped clean and checked for security to the spark plugs.

12 Fault diagnosis – ignition system

1   There are two distinct symptoms of ignition faults. Either the engine will not start or fire, or it starts with difficulty and does not run normally.
2   If the starter motor spins the engine satisfactorily, there is adequate fuel and yet the engine will not start, the fault is likely to be on the LT side.
3   If the engine starts, but does not run satisfactorily, it is more likely to be an HT fault.

Engine fails to start
4   If the starter motor spins the engine satisfactorily, but the engine does not start, first check that the fuel supply to the engine is in order, with reference to Chapter 3.
5   Check for broken or disconnected wires to the coil and distributor and for damp distributor cap and HT leads.
6   Refer to Section 7 and carry out the test procedures described.

Engine starts, but misfires
7   Bad starting and intermittent misfiring can be an LT fault, such as poor connection of the coil or the distributor LT leads.
8   If these are satisfactory look for signs of tracking and burning inside the distributor cap, then check the plug leads, plug caps and plug insulators for signs of damage.
9   If the engine misfires regularly, it indicates that the fault is on one particular cylinder.

Chapter 5 Clutch

For modifications, and information applicable to later models, see Supplement at end of manual

Contents

Specifications

Type .... Single dry plate and diaphragm spring cover, cable operation

Driven plate
Diameter .... 190 mm (7.48 in), 200 mm (7.87 in), 210 mm (8.26 in) or 215 mm (8.46 in)

Pressure plate
Maximum distortion (inner edge to outer edge) .... 0.3 mm (0.012 in)
Diaphragm spring finger maximum scoring depth .... 0.3 mm (0.012 in)

Cable free play (at clutch pedal) .... 15 mm (0.6 in)

Torque wrench settings

	Nm	lbf ft
Pressure plate (clutch cover) bolts	25	18
Clutch release lever pinch bolt	25	18
Release shaft retaining bolt	15	11
Release bearing guide sleeve	15	11

1 General description

The clutch is of single dry plate type with a diaphragm spring cover, and actuation is by cable.

The clutch cover is bolted to the rear face of the flywheel, and the driven plate is located between the cover pressure plate and the flywheel friction surface. The driven plate hub is splined to the gearbox input shaft and is free to slide along the splines. Friction lining material is riveted to each side of the driven plate, and the driven plate hub incorporates cushioning springs to absorb transmission shocks and ensure a smooth take-up of drive.

When the clutch pedal is depressed, the cable moves the release lever, and the release bearing is forced onto the diaphragm spring fingers. As the centre of the spring is pushed in, the outer part of the spring moves out and releases the pressure plate from the driven plate. Drive then ceases to be transmitted to the gearbox.

When the clutch pedal is released, the diaphragm spring forces the pressure plate into contact with the friction linings on the driven plate and at the same time pushes the driven plate along the input shaft splines into engagement with the flywheel. The driven plate is now firmly sandwiched between the pressure plate and the flywheel and so the drive is taken up.

As the friction linings wear, the pressure plate moves closer to the flywheel and the release cable free play is reduced. Periodic adjustment must therefore be carried out, as described in Section 2. No other routine maintenance is required on the clutch system.

2 Clutch – adjustment

1 The clutch should be checked and, if necessary, adjusted every 10 000 miles (15 000 km).
2 To check the adjustment measure the free play at the clutch pedal. If it is not as given in the Specifications, the cable must be adjusted as follows.

**Fig. 5.1 Clutch cable adjuster location (arrowed) – type 014/1
(four-speed) and 013 (five-speed) gearboxes (Sec 2)**

2.3 Clutch cable and release arm (four-cylinder models)

**Fig. 5.2 Clutch cable adjuster location (arrowed) – type 093 (five-
speed) gearbox (Sec 2)**

3   On models fitted with the 014 type gearbox (four-speed) and
013 type gearbox (five-speed), loosen off the locknuts at the gearbox
end of the cable, reposition the outer cable to give the required free
play, then retighten the locknuts (photo).
4   On models fitted with the 093 gearbox (five-speed), extract the
adjuster clip from the cable guide and reposition the outer cable
accordingly to provide the correct free play, then refit the adjuster clip
into position in the appropriate cable groove (Fig. 5.2).
5   On all models fully depress the clutch pedal several times, then
recheck the adjustment. Where applicable, lightly grease the adjuster
threads to prevent rusting.

3   Clutch cable – renewal

1   Disconnect the battery negative lead.
2   Slacken off the cable adjustment by loosening the locknut(s) and
turning the ferrule or extracting the spring clip (as applicable).
3   Release the outer cable from the gearbox bracket and unhook the
inner cable from the release arm (photo).
4   Working inside the car, unhook the inner cable from the top of the
clutch pedal.
5   Withdraw the clutch cable through the bulkhead into the engine
compartment.
6   Fit the new cable using a reversal of the removal procedure, and
finally adjust the cable as described in Section 2.

3.3 Clutch cable ferrule end fitting (014 and 013 type gearbox)

4   Clutch pedal – removal and refitting

1   The clutch and brake pedals share a common bracket assembly
and pivot shaft.
2   Disconnect the battery negative lead.
3   Unhook the inner cable from the top of the clutch pedal, with
reference to Section 3.
4   On five-cylinder engine models an over-centre return spring is
fitted at the top of the pedal. Disconnect it by extracting the circlip and
withdrawing the pivot pin (Fig. 5.3).
5   Extract the clip from the end of the pivot shaft and slide off the
clutch pedal.
6   Clean the pedal and shaft, then temporarily refit the pedal and
check the bushes for wear. If necessary, the bushes can be pressed or
driven out and new bushes fitted.
7   The inner bush is of plastic and the outer bush is rubber. To fit the
bushes just dip the rubber bush in soapy water and press it into the
pedal, then similarly press the plastic bush in from the shouldered side
of the pedal until flush.
8   Refitting is a reversal of removal, but first lubricate the pivot shaft
with a little grease. Finally check the cable free play and, if necessary,
adjust it as described in Section 2.

Clutch cable

Pedal bracket

Over-centre spring

Bearing pin

Lock clip

Circlip

Stop

Bushes

Clutch pedal

Clutch pedal

Fig. 5.3 Clutch pedal and support bracket components (Sec 4)

5 Clutch − removal, inspection and refitting

1 Access to the clutch is obtained either by removing the engine (Chapter 1) or by removing the gearbox (Chapter 6). If the clutch requires attention and the engine is not in need of a major overhaul, it is preferable to gain access to the clutch by removing the gearbox, provided that either a pit is available, or the car can be put on ramps to give a good ground clearance (photo).

2 Put a mark on the rim of the clutch pressure plate cover and a corresponding mark on the flywheel so that the clutch can be refitted in exactly the same position.

3 Slacken the clutch cover retaining bolts a turn at a time, working in diagonal pairs round the casing. When all the bolts have been loosened enough to release the tension of the diaphragm spring, remove the bolts and lift off the clutch cover and the friction plate (photo).

4 Clean the parts with a damp cloth, ensuring that the dust is not inhaled. *Because the dust produced by the wearing of the clutch facing may contain asbestos, which is dangerous to health, parts should not be blown clean or brushed to remove dust.*

5 Examine the fingers of the diaphragm spring for signs of wear, or scoring. If the depth of any scoring exceeds 0.3 mm (0.012 in), a new cover assembly must be fitted (Fig. 5.4).

5.1 Engine and gearbox separation gives access to the clutch unit

5.3 Removing the clutch cover and friction plate

Fig. 5.5 Examine pressure plate for wear and distortion (Sec 5)

Fig. 5.4 Examine the clutch diaphragm spring ends at points arrowed (Sec 5)

Fig. 5.6 Clutch friction plate run-out check method (Sec 5)

6   Lay the clutch cover on its diaphragm spring end, place a steel straight edge diagonally across the pressure plate and test for distortion of the plate (Fig. 5.5). If a 0.3 mm (0.012 in) feeler gauge can be inserted in any gap beneath the straight edge, the clutch cover must be discarded and a new one fitted. The check for distortion should be made at several points round the plate.

7   Check that the pressure plate is not badly scored, and shows no signs of cracking, or burning. Note that the retaining bolts should be renewed on reassembly.

8   Inspect the friction plate and fit a new plate if the surface of the friction material left is approaching the level of the rivets. Discard the plate if the friction material has become impregnated with oil, or shows signs of breaking into shreds (Fig. 5.6).

9   Examine the friction plate splined hub for signs of damage, or wear. Check that when the hub is on the gearbox input shaft, the hub slides smoothly along the shaft and that the radial clearance between the gearbox shaft and clutch hub is small.

10   If there is reason to suspect that the clutch hub is not running true, it should be checked by mounting the hub between centres and checking it with a dial gauge. Unless you have the proper equipment, get your local dealer to make this check.

11   Do not re-use any part which is suspect. Having gone to the trouble of dismantling the clutch, it is well worth ensuring that when reassembled it will operate satisfactorily for a long time. Check the flywheel for scoring and tiny cracks caused by overheating; refinish or renew as necessary (see Chapter 1).

12   Ensure that all the parts are clean, free of oil and grease and are in a satisfactory condition before reassembling.

13   Fit the friction plate so that the torsion spring cages are towards the pressure plate, (photo).

14   Fit the clutch cover to the flywheel ensuring (where applicable) that the marks made before dismantling are lined up, and insert all bolts finger tight to hold the cover in position.

15   Centralise the friction plate either by using a proprietary tool, or by making up a similar tool to hold the friction plate concentric with the hole in the end of the crankshaft (photo). If the clutch cover is tightened without the friction plate being centralised, it will be impossible to refit the gearbox as the input shaft will not pass through the driven plate hub and engage the spigot bearing.

16   With the centraliser holding the clutch friction plate in position, tighten all the clutch cover bolts a turn at a time in diagonal sequence until the specified torque is achieved. Remove the centering tool and smear the hub splines with molybdenum disulphide grease.

17   Check the release bearing in the front of the gearbox for wear and smooth operation, and if necessary renew it, with reference to Section 6.

18   Refit the engine or gearbox with reference to Chapters 1 or 6.

6   Release bearing and mechanism – removal and refitting

1   To remove the release bearing, either lift the release arm to disengage the forks from the spring clips, or extract the clips from each

5.13 Locating a new friction plate into position

5.15 Centralising the clutch friction plate using a proprietary tool

Bolt
(Secures release shaft, gearbox 013 only)

Return spring

Rubber bush

Axial guide
(for release shaft, gearbox 093 only)

Plastic guide sleeve
Do not grease

Circlip

Clutch lever

Bush

Clutch cable

Release shaft

Retaining spring

Clutch cable

Retaining clip

Release bearing

Fig. 5.7 Clutch release mechanism components shown with the two operating cable types available according to gearbox type
(Sec 6)

6.1A Clutch release bearing and release shaft

6.1B Showing the release bearing clips location

6.2 Clutch release lever

6.3 Release shaft retaining bolt location on four-cylinder models

6.4 Unhooking the release shaft return spring

6.5 Removing the release shaft flanged bush

side of the bearing, noting how they are fitted (photos). The bearing can then be withdrawn from the guide sleeve.

2   Mark the release lever in relation to the shaft then unscrew the clamp bolt and withdraw the lever (photo).

3   On four-speed (014) and five-speed 013 gearbox models, unscrew and remove the release shaft bolt from the rear of the bellhousing. The bolt engages in the end of the release shaft (photo).

4   Note the position of the return spring on the release shaft then unhook it from the release shaft fork, (photo and Fig. 5.8).

5   Extract the circlip from the splined end of the release shaft and prise out the rubber bush (where fitted) and the flanged bush (photo).

6   Turn the release shaft so that the forks are free of the guide sleeve, then remove the inner end from the bush and withdraw the shaft from inside the bellhousing (photo).

7   Clean the release bearing with a dry cloth. Do not wash the bearing in solvent, because this will cause its lubricant to be washed out. If the bearing is noisy, or has excessive wear, discard it and obtain a new one.

Fig. 5.8 Clutch release mechanism return spring location on the 093 gearbox type (Sec 6)

6.6 Removing the release shaft

8   Inspect the release shaft and its bushes for wear. Do not remove the inner bush unless a new one has to be fitted. If a new inner bush is required, the old one will need a special extractor to remove it.

9   Before refitting the release shaft, coat the bearing surfaces with molybdenum disulphide grease and ensure that the return spring is fitted to the shaft.

10   Refitting is a reversal of removal. However, on four-speed 014 and five-speed models fitted with the 013 gearbox, press in the release

Fig. 5.9 Insert the dowel bolt and press in the release shaft to compress the rubber bush to 18 mm (0.7 in) – 013 gearbox only (Sec 6)

6.10A Checking the release shaft rubber bush dimension

Fig. 5.10 Release lever fitting dimension (Sec 6)

013 gearbox type – 169 mm (6.65 in)
093 gearbox type – 193 mm (7.6 in)
014 gearbox type – 169 mm (6.65 in)

shaft until the rubber bush is compressed to approximately 18 mm (0.7 in) (photo) before inserting and tightening the dowel bolt. If a new release lever is being fitted, position it on the splined shaft as shown in Fig. 5.10 (photo). Coat all bearing surfaces with high melting point grease, except for the plastic guide sleeve.

6.10B Checking the release lever fitted dimension

Fault diagnosis appears overleaf

7   Fault diagnosis – clutch

Symptom	Reason(s)
Judder when taking up drive	Oil or grease contamination of friction linings Loose or worn engine/gearbox mountings Worn friction linings Worn driven plate or input shaft splines
Clutch slip	Incorrect adjustment Friction linings worn or contaminated with oil Weak diaphragm spring
Clutch drag (failure to disengage)	Incorrect adjustment Driven plate sticking on input shaft splines Driven plate sticking to flywheel Input shaft spigot bearing seized
Noise evident on depressing clutch pedal	Dry or worn release bearing Input shaft spigot bearing dry or worn

Chapter 6 Manual gearbox and final drive

For modifications, and information applicable to later models, see Supplement at end of manual

Contents

Specifications

Type .... Four or five forward speeds and reverse. Synchromesh on all forward speeds with integral final drive

Identification
Gearbox code number:

014/1	Four-speed gearbox fitted up to July 1983
014/11	Four-speed gearbox fitted from August 1983
013	Five-speed gearbox fitted to four-cylinder models
093	Five-speed gearbox fitted to five-cylinder models

Ratios

Gearbox 014/1 and 014/11

Gearbox code letters

	MY/IM	2T	4V	5V	8M	UT
Final drive	4.11:1	4.11:1	4.11:1	4.11:1	4.11:1	4.11:1
1st	3.45:1	3.45:1	3.45:1	3.45:1	3.45:1	3.45:1
2nd	1.94:1	1.79:1	1.94:1	1.94:1	1.78:1	1.79:1
3rd	1.29:1	1.13:1	1.28:1	1.28:1	1.28:1	1.065:1
4th	0.91:1	0.83:1	0.91:1	0.88:1	0.90:1	0.77:1
Reverse	3.17:1	3.17:1	3.17:1	3.17:1	3.17:1	3.17:1

Gearbox 013

	QJ	QJ*	3M	2P	9G	2N	8G
Final drive	4.11:1	4.11:1	4.11:1	4.11:1	4.11:1	4.11:1	4.11:1
1st	3.45:1	3.45:1	3.45:1	3.45:1	3.45:1	3.45:1	3.45:1
2nd	1.94:1	1.94:1	1.94:1	1.94:1	1.94:1	1.78:1	1.78:1
3rd	1.29:1	1.28:1	1.28:1	1.28:1	1.28:1	1.13:1	1.13:1
4th	0.90:1	0.90:1	0.90:1	0.96:1	0.90:1	0.82:1	0.82:1
5th	0.68:1	0.73:1	0.73:1	0.80:1	0.73:1	0.68:1	0.68:1
Reverse	3.17:1	3.16:1	3.16:1	3.16:1	3.16:1	3.16:1	3.16:1

*From September 1983

Gearbox 093

	VW and 2V
Final drive	4.90:1
1st	2.85:1
2nd	1.52:1
3rd	0.96:1
4th	0.70:1
5th	0.53:1
Reverse	3.17:1

Gearbox lubrication
Lubricant type .... Hypoid gear oil, viscosity SAE 80 or SAE 80W/90, to API-GL4 (Duckhams Hypoid 80)

Oil capacity:

Gearbox 014	1.7 litre (3.0 Imp pint)
Gearbox 013	2.0 litre (3.5 Imp pint)
Gearbox 093	2.4 litre (4.1 Imp pint)

Synchro ring to cone clearance

All models	New clearance	Wear limit
1st and 2nd	1.1 to 1.7 mm (0.04 to 0.06 in)	0.5 mm (0.02 in)
3rd and 4th	1.35 to 1.9 mm (0.05 to 0.07 in)	0.5 mm (0.02 in)
5th (013 and 093)	1.1 to 1.7 mm (0.04 to 0.06 in)	0.5 mm (0.02 in)
4th gear axial clearance — all models (maximum)	0.10 to 0.40 mm (0.004 to 0.015 in)	
4th gear thrust washers available — all models except 014/11 gearbox	3.47 mm (0.136 in) 3.57 mm (0.141 in) 3.67 mm (0.144 in)	
4th gear circlips available — (014/11 gearbox) and internal spline gear circlips available — (013 and 093 gearbox)	2.35 mm (0.0925 in) 2.38 mm (0.0937 in) 2.41 mm (0.0948 in) 2.44 mm (0.0960 in) 2.47 mm (0.0972 in)	

Torque wrench settings

	Nm	lbf ft
Gearbox to engine bolts	55	41
Driveshafts to gearbox	45	33
Drive flange to gearbox:		
014	20	15
013 and 093	25	18
Subframe to body	70	51
Front gearbox support to gearbox	25	18
Bonded rubber mount to body	110	80
Bonded rubber mount to gearbox	25	18
Gearbox mounting to gearbox (093)	40	30
Coupling to steering (093)	45	33
Filler and drain plugs	25	18
Reverse relay lever bolt	35	26
Reverse light switch (014)	30	22
Pinion nut	100	74
Input shaft bolt	45	33

1 General description

Either a four- or five-speed gearbox is fitted according to model, and there are two variations of each gearbox, as listed in the Specifications (Figures 6.1 and 6.2).

The gearbox is bolted to the rear of the engine in conventional manner, but because of the front wheel drive configuration, drive is transmitted to a differential unit located at the front of the gearbox and then through the driveshafts to the front wheels. All forward gears incorporate synchromesh engagement, and reverse gear is obtained by engaging a spur type idler gear with the 1st/2nd synchro sleeve on the output shaft and a spur gear on the input shaft.

Gearshift is by means of a floor mounted lever, and a single rod

Fig. 6.1 Four-speed manual gearbox showing identification mark location (A) (Sec 1)

Fig. 6.2 Five-speed manual gearbox showing identification mark location (A) (Sec 1)

and linkage clamped to the selector rod which protrudes from the rear of the gearbox. The selector rod incorporates a finger which engages the other selector rod in the bearing carrier.

When overhauling the gearbox, due consideration should be given to the costs involved, since it is often more economic to obtain a service exchange or good secondhand gearbox rather than fit new parts to the existing gearbox. Repairs to the differential are not covered, as the special instrumentation required is not normally available to the home mechanic.

2 Routine maintenance – gearbox

The manual gearbox requires the minimum amount of mainten-ance, only the following checks need be made at the specified intervals given at the front of this manual (see Routine Maintenance).
1   *Check gearbox for signs of oil leaks:* If possible run the vehicle over an inspection pit or raise and support it on safety stands to make this (and the following) check. Inspect the gearbox casing for any signs of serious oil leaks. Oil leakage from the transmission will necessitate further investigation and if serious must be remedied without delay. A very minor leak may be permissible providing regular checks are made to ensure that the leak does not get any worse and to ensure that the gearbox oil level is maintained. Do not confuse gearbox oil leaks with engine oil leaks which may have sprayed onto the gearbox casing.
2   *Check the gearbox oil level.* The vehicle must be parked level for this check. Remove the oil level/filler plug from the side of the gearbox and check that the oil level is up to the base of the filler orifice. If not, top up with the specified grade of oil and refit the plug (photo).

3 Gearbox – removal and refitting

Note: *If necessary, the engine and gearbox on four-cylinder models can be removed together as described in Chapter 1, and the gearbox then separated on the bench. However, this Section describes the removal of the gearbox leaving the engine in situ.*
1   Position the front of the car over an inspection pit or on car ramps and apply the handbrake firmly.
2   Disconnect the battery negative lead.
3   Unscrew and remove the upper bolts attaching the gearbox to the engine, noting the location of any brackets.

2.2 Topping up the gearbox oil level

4   Working underneath the vehicle, disconnect the reverse light switch, gear shift and econometer lead wires and release the cable clip(s).
5   Unscrew the nut and disconnect the speedometer cable from the differential cover or gearbox casing (as applicable).
6   Detach the clutch cable from the gearbox with reference to Chapter 5.
7   Remove the front exhaust downpipe from the manifold and exhaust system with reference to Chapter 3 (photo).
8   *On five-cylinder models only*, remove the air cleaner (Chapter 3), and also support the front of the engine with a hoist or bar similar to that shown in Figure 6.3.
9   Disconnect the driveshafts from the drive flanges with reference to Chapter 8 and tie them to one side.
10   *On four-cylinder models only*, unbolt and remove the centre engine mounting bracket (Figure 6.4).

3.7 Exhaust to transmission bracket location

Fig. 6.5 Detach the steering tie-rod bracket – five-cylinder models (Sec 3)

Fig. 6.3 Support bar required for gearbox removal on five-cylinder models – typical (Sec 3)

Fig. 6.4 Unbolt the central engine mounting bracket – four-cylinder models (Sec 3)

11 Unbolt and remove the gearbox front cover.
12 Remove the starter motor, as described in Chapter 10.
13 *On five-cylinder models only,* disconnect the steering tie-rod bracket from the steering gear with reference to Chapter 11 (Figure 6.5).
14 Support the gearbox with a trolley jack or stand.
15 Unscrew the lockbolt securing the selector adaptor to the selector rod on the rear of the gearbox (photo). On four-speed gearboxes it may be necessary to first remove the locking wire.
16 Press the support rod from the balljoint and withdraw the adaptor from the selector lever (photo).
17 Unscrew and remove the lower bolts attaching the gearbox to the engine.
18 Loosen the bolt securing the gearbox stay to the underbody (photo). Unscrew and remove the stay inner bolt and pivot the stay from the gearbox.
19 Unbolt the bonded rubber mounting from the gearbox.
20 *On four-cylinder models only,* unbolt and remove the front gearbox support bracket.
21 With the help of an assistant withdraw the gearbox from the engine, making sure that the input shaft does not hang on the clutch. Lower the gearbox to the ground.
22 Refitting is a reversal of removal, but lightly lubricate the splines of the input shaft with molybdenum disulphide powder or paste and make sure that the engine/gearbox mountings are free of strain; if necessary refer to Chapter 1 for the correct alignment procedure. Where applicable secure the selector adaptor lockbolt with new locking wire. Adjust the gear lever and linkage as described in Section 11 or 21. Check and, if necessary, top up the oil level.

---

4   Gearbox (014) – dismantling into major assemblies

1   Remove the gearbox drain plug, drain out the oil and refit the plug. Clean away external dirt from the gearbox casing.
2   Remove the bolts from the gearshift housing. If necessary give the housing a light tap to separate it from the gear housing and then manoeuvre the gearshift housing off the gear housing. Remove the shim and gasket (Figure 6.6).
3   Carefully pull the 3rd/4th gear selector rod out of the casing until the small interlock plunger can be removed. Be careful not to pull the shaft out further than is absolutely necessary because the locking keys of the synchro-hub may fall out (Figure 6.7).
4   Having removed the plunger, push the shaft back in to its neutral position. If the locking keys of the synchro-hub have fallen out it will not be possible to push the rod back in and the alternative method of removing the pinion nut will have to be used after removing the bearing carrier. This involves gripping the 4th gear in a soft-jawed vice, then unscrewing the pinion nut.

3.15 Remove the adaptor to selector (shift) rod lockbolt (arrowed)

3.16 Disconnect the support rod and selector rod

3.18 Gearbox mounting and stay

Fig. 6.6 Gearshift housing and bearing carrier retaining bolts – 014 gearbox (Sec 4)

1   M8 x 75 (with washer)   3   M8 x 46 (without washer)
2   M8 x 45 (with washer)

Fig. 6.7 Withdraw 3rd/4th selector shaft (3) to expose interlock plunger (white arrow) – 014 gearbox (Sec 4)

5   Pull the upper selector rod out to engage reverse gear and the lower one out to engage first gear. By engaging the two gears at once the shafts will be locked and the pinion nut can be undone. Remove the inner race, on the 014/1 gearbox.
6   Remove the circlip and thrust washer from the end of the input shaft.
7   If available, use the special puller to remove the input shaft bearing from the gear carrier housing, while supporting the front end of the input shaft with a bar bolted to the final drive housing. If not available, it will be necessary to remove the input shaft and pinion shaft simultaneously later (Figure 6.8). On gearboxes fitted with a Combi (double taper roller) bearing it is first necessary to lever off the plastic cage using a small screwdriver as a lever.

Fig. 6.8 Bar for supporting the input shaft during dismantling procedure – 014 gearbox (Sec 4)

8   Where applicable, remove the gearshift/fuel consumption indicator switch.
9   Remove the bolts securing the bearing carrier and detach the bearing carrier with the input shaft and pinion shaft from the final drive housing.
10   Drive the dowel pins back until they are flush with the joint face. Clamp the gearbox in a soft-jawed vice. Support the free end of the 3rd/4th gear selector shaft by jamming a block of hardwood under it and drive the roll-pin out of the selector shaft. If the free end of the shaft is not supported while the pin is driven out, the bore for the shaft in the gear carrier may be damaged.
11   Pull out the 3rd/4th gear selector shaft until the 3rd/4th gear selector fork can be removed, and then push the shaft back to its neutral position.

Selector fork for 3rd and 4th gears

Input shaft

Input shaft ball or combi bearing

Selector fork for 1st and 2nd gears

Selector shaft for 1st and 2nd gears

Pinion (output shaft)

Shim

Thrust washer

Circlip

Reverse gear shaft

Operating dog for 1st and 2nd gear selector shaft

Gasket

Small interlock plunger

Bolt M 8 x 45

Dowel pins

Bearing carrier

Reverse gear
(• Chamfered side of teeth face gearbox housing)

Front gearbox support

Bolt M 8 x 46

Gearshift housing

Bolt M 8 x 45

Bracket
(• Exhaust pipe mounting)

Bolt M 8 x 46

Bolt M 8 x 75

1st inner race
(• For pinion bearing)

Pinion nut

Shim

Rear gearbox support

Fig. 6.9 Exploded view of the bearing carrier and gearshift housing and associated components (Sec 4)

Fig. 6.10 Remove reverse gearshaft (arrowed) (Sec 4)

12 Remove the input shaft assembly.

13 Drive out the reverse gear shaft and remove reverse gear and its selector segment (if fitted) (Figure 6.10).

14 Drive out the roll-pin from the 1st/2nd gear operating dog and remove the dog from the selector shaft.

15 Using a soft-faced hammer, or a hammer and drift, drive the pinion shaft out of its bearing. While doing this check that the 1st/2nd gear selector shaft does not become jammed, and if necessary tap the shaft lightly to free it. Recover the taper-roller bearing race when the shaft is removed on 014/11 gearboxes.

16 Dismantle the gearbox housing as follows. First insert a suitable rod through one of the bolt holes of a coupling flange, so that the rod is against one of the cover ribs and so prevents the flange from rotating. Then remove the bolt from the centre of the flange. Repeat the operation on the other coupling flange and then use two levers to prise out the flanged shafts. Mark each shaft as it is removed to ensure that it is fitted to its correct side of the gearbox housing.

17 Remove the ten bolts from the differential cover, remove the cover, and take out the differential (Figure 6.11).

5 Input shaft (014) – dismantling and reassembly

1   Both the four- and five-speed gearbox types have many fundamentally similar components, the input shaft on all models being almost identical. The rear end of the 014 input shaft is of course shorter, not having to accommodate the 5th gear, neither does it incorporate the inner race of the rear roller bearing.

2   The dismantling and reassembly of the 014 input shaft is therefore as described in Section 14 for the 013 and 093 input shaft, and reference should therefore be made to that Section for the relevant details. The photo sequences given in that Section can also be used, any important differences between gearbox types being noted in the relevant photo caption. Other minor differences may be apparent, but should not affect the procedure described.

3   The modification notes given in paragraphs 1 and 19 of Section 14 are also applicable to the 014/11 gearbox.

4   The details given in paragraph 7 of Section 14 are not applicable to the four-speed gearbox.

5   An exploded diagram showing the component parts of the 014 gearbox input shaft is shown in Figure 6.12.

Gearbox housing

Switch
(for shift and consumption indicator)

Gasket

Oil filler plug

Oil drain plug

Differential

Final drive cover

Bolt

Flanged shaft

Bolt

**Fig. 6.11 Gearbox housing and differential components –
014 gearbox (Sec 4)**

Circlip
(Only on gearboxes up to assembly)
date 21 06 3

4th gear thrust washer
(Only on gearboxes up to assembly)
date 21 06 3

4th gear needle roller bearing

Circlip
(Only on gear boxes from assembly)
date 22 06 3

Locking key

Synchro hub

Operating sleeve

Spring

3rd gear synchroniser ring

3rd speed gear

4th speed gear

4th gear synchroniser ring

Circlip

3rd and 4th gear operating sleeve/synchro unit

3rd gear needle roller bearing

Fig. 6.12 Input shaft components on the 014 gearbox (Sec 5)

Gearbox housing

Needle roller bearing

Input shaft

Bearing case

Thrust ball race

Combi bearing

Thrust washer

Locking ring

Pinion nut

1st inner race/ball bearing

Ball bearing

Bearing carrier

2nd inner race/ball bearing

Shim

1st gear needle bearing

1st speed gear

1st gear synchro ring

1st/2nd gear synchro sleeve and hub

2nd gear needle bearing

Circlip

Pinion

Roller bearing

Roller bearing outer race

Pinion nut

Inner race/double taper roller bearing

Outer race/double taper roller bearing

Adjustment shim

Inner race/double taper roller bearing

Needle roller bearing for 1st speed gear

Locking key

Synchro hub

Sleeve

Spring

2nd gear synchro ring

2nd speed gear

3rd speed gear
(wide shoulder goes towards 4th gear)

4th speed gear
(wide shoulder goes towards pinion head)

Pin

Gearbox housing

Fig. 6.13 Pinion shaft components on the 014 gearbox with inset showing later (014/II) pinion shaft rear bearing assembly (Sec 6)

6 Pinion shaft (014) – dismantling and reassembly

1   The dismantling and reassembly procedure for the 014 gearbox pinion shaft is identical to that described for the 013 and 093 five-speed gearbox types in Section 15. The rear end of the 014 pinion shaft is shorter not having to accommodate the 5th gear and the rear bearing (in the bearing carrier) also differs. In the 014/1 gearbox it is a ball bearing (with shim) type whilst in the 014/11 gearbox it is a double taper roller bearing type.
2   Note that when refitting the 1st/2nd synchroniser the external teeth of the operating sleeve must face towards the pinion end (ie the opposite way round to the 013 and 093 gearbox).
3   With the above mentioned exceptions, the photos used to illustrate Section 15 can be used as a reference when assembling the 014 gearbox pinion shaft. An exploded diagram of the 014 pinion shaft is shown in Figure 6.13.

7 Gearbox/final drive housing (014) – servicing

1   The procedure is identical to that described for the 013 and 093 gearbox given in Section 16, but note that the 014 gearbox pinion bearing outer track is secured in the same manner as the 013 gearbox (by a pin), the removal of which is described in paragraph 3 of that Section.
2   Because of the close similarities, the photos shown in Section 16 for the 013 gearbox type can also be used for reference when servicing the 014 gearbox types. Figure 6.14 shows the housing and components.

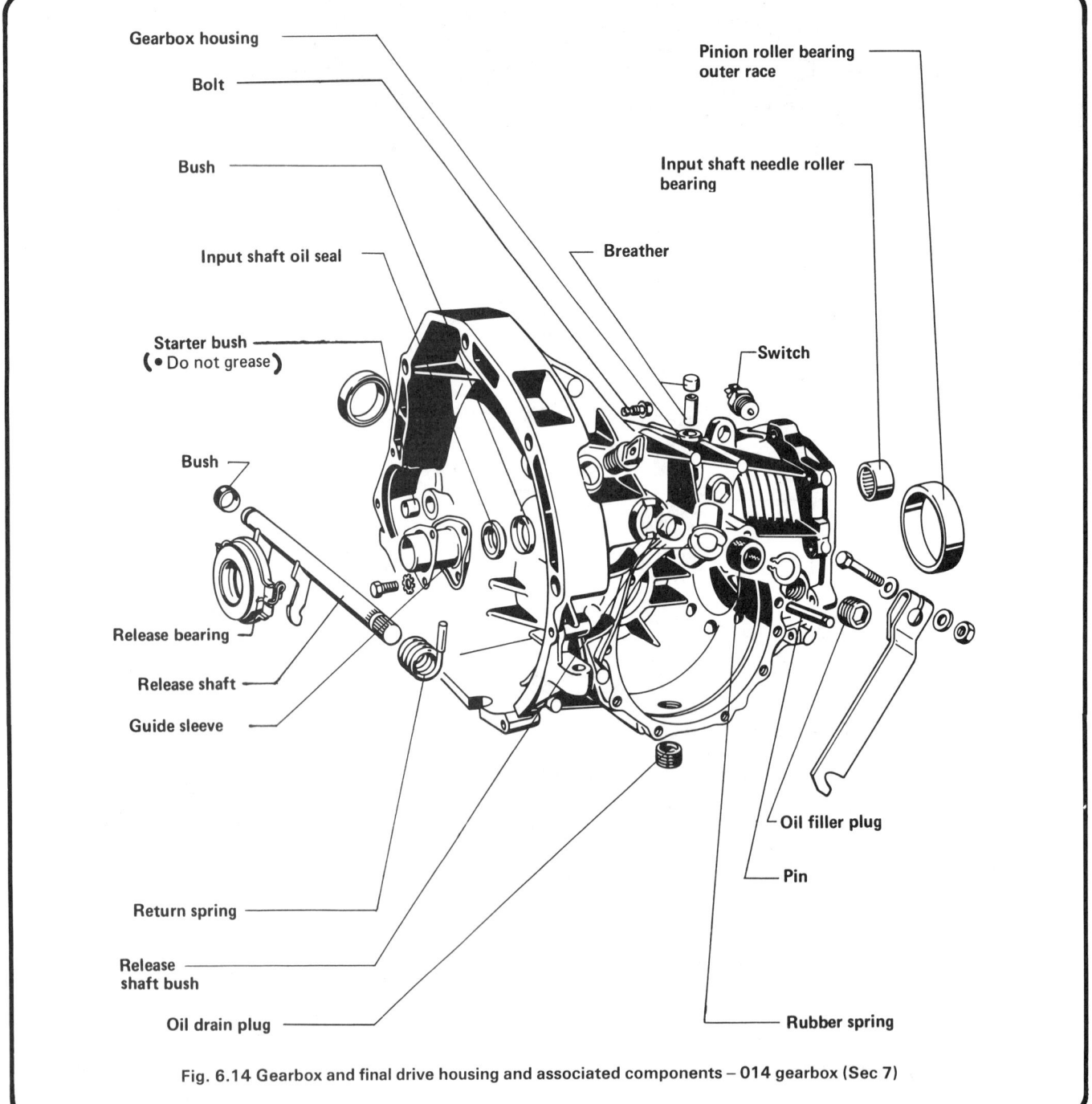

Fig. 6.14 Gearbox and final drive housing and associated components – 014 gearbox (Sec 7)

Plug,

Guide sleeve

Reverse gear detent

Outer race for roller bearing

Reverse gear selector shaft

Relay lever

Pin

Bearing carrier

Plug

Gear detent

Interlock plunger

Small interlock plunger

Spring

Guide sleeve

3rd/4th gear selector shaft

Fig. 6.15 Bearing carrier on 014/II gearbox – gearbox 014/I components similar, but ball-bearing fitted (Sec 8)

8   Bearing/gear carrier (014) – servicing

1   The procedure is identical to that described for the 013 and 093 gearbox types given in Section 17, with the following exceptions.

Pinion bearing removal

2   The outer track of the bearing can be driven out of the case using a suitable drift, but the fitting of a new bearing and determining the correct thickness of shim needs to be done by a VW dealer.

Selector rod detents – removal and refitting

3   Unscrew the pivot bolt and remove the reverse relay lever. Remove the pin from the reverse selector rod and pull the rod from the bearing carrier (Figure 6.15).

4   Pull the 3rd/4th gear selector rod out of the bearing carrier, taking care to recover the small interlock plunger within the rod (Figure 6.16).

5   To remove the detent plug at the top of the bearing carrier cut a 6 mm thread in the plug, screw a bolt into the plug and pull the bolt to extract the plug. With the plug removed, the spring and the detent can be removed (Figure 6.17).

6   The two detents in the side of the box are removed by driving in their plugs until the plugs can be removed from the gear selector rod bores. The detent, spring and sleeves can then be shaken out, together with the large interlock plungers.

7   Models produced from 1984 on have a guide sleeve fitted in the detent bores. The guide sleeves can be removed by making up a suitable wire hook which when engaged with the base edge of the sleeve can pull it out (Figure 6.18).

8   Refitting is the reverse of removal. The correct position of the detents and interlock plungers is shown in Figure 6.16. When refitting the relay lever, adjust it as described in Section 17, paragraph 9.

Fig. 6.16 Cross-section diagram of the selector rod detents on the 014/II gearbox (Sec 8)

Fig. 6.17 Detent plug removal method using 6 mm bolt – 014 gearbox (Sec 8)

Fig. 6.18 Detent sleeve extraction method – 014/II gearbox (Sec 8)

9 Gearshift housing (014) – servicing

1   Pull out the selector rod and spring (Figure 6.19).
2   Before removing the rear bush, lever out the rear oil seal, and then use a long drift to tap out the bush from the front end of the housing.
3   Enter the new bush squarely into the rear of the housing and tap it home flush with the end of the casting, using a block of wood. In order to drive the new bush in fully, rub the outside diameter of the *old* bush with a piece of emery cloth to reduce its diameter enough to make it an easy fit in the casting, then use this bush as a drift.
4   Fit a new oil seal, with the open end of the seal inwards, and using a block of hardwood against the seal, drive it in until its face is flush with the end of the casting.
5   The procedure for removing and fitting the front bush is similar, except that there is no oil seal and it is necessary to note which way round the bush is fitted.
6   Lubricate the bushes and smear the lip of the oil seal with gear oil before refitting the selector rod.
7   Refit the selector rod and spring as described in the following Section.

10 Gearbox (014) – reassembly

1   If the selector rods have been removed from the bearing carrier, check that they have been inserted correctly and that the interlock plungers are in their proper places.
2   Fit the pinion assembly and the 1st/2nd gear selector fork into the bearing carrier.
3   Using a suitable piece of tubing as a drift, tap the outer part of the taper-roller bearing (014/11), or the outer part of the ball-bearing inner race (014/1) on to the end of the shaft, but while doing this make frequent checks to ensure that the 1st/2nd gear selector shaft has not jammed. If it has jammed, tap it lightly to free it.
4   Fit the 1st/2nd gear operating dog on the shift rod, line up its hole with the hole in the shift rod, then drive in the roll-pin (Figure 6.20).
5   Fit reverse gear and segment into the bearing carrier and then drive in the reverse gear shaft.
6   Fit the input shaft assembly loosely into the box without its bearing.
7   Pull back the 3rd/4th gear selector rod until the 3rd/4th gear selector fork can be fitted into the groove in the synchro-hub sleeve. Push the selector rod back to its neutral position and line up the hole in the selector rod with the hole in the fork. Support the free end of the shaft in the same way as when removing the selector fork and drive in the roll-pin.

Fig. 6.19 Gearshift housing components on the 014 gearbox (Sec 9)

8   Fit a new gasket to the gearbox housing and fit the bearing carrier, with the input and pinion shaft assemblies, to the gearbox housing. Line up the holes and drive in the dowel pin. Insert and tighten the bolts (see Figure 6.6).

9   Fit the input shaft ball bearing squarely on to the end of its shaft, ensuring that the closed side of the bearing cage is towards the bearing carrier. Using a suitable tube, or a block of hardwood, drive the bearing in, taking care to see that it stays square to the shaft while also supporting the shaft on a block of wood.

10   Fit the thrust washer and circlip on top of the input shaft bearing.

11   Pull back the two selector rods until 1st and reverse gears are both engaged and the shafts are locked together. Fit the pinion shaft nut, tighten it to the specified torque and lock the nut to the shaft. Move the selector shafts back to their neutral position and check that both shafts are able to rotate freely.

12   The next operation requires great care if unnecessary work is to be avoided. Very carefully pull out the 3rd/4th selector rod just enough for the small interlock plunger to be inserted. Smear grease on to the plunger, insert it into the hole and push the selector rod back in. If the rod is pulled out too far, the locking keys of the synchro-hub can come out and the gear assembly will have to be separated from the gearbox housing so that the locking keys can be re-inserted into the synchro-hub.

13   The procedure for reassembling the gearshift housing to the bearing carrier now differs according to gearbox type. Where the pinion bearing is a Combi (double taper roller) type, proceed as detailed in paragraphs 18 to 21 inclusive. Where the pinion bearing is a ball type, proceed as follows in paragraphs 14 to 17 inclusive.

14   When refitting the gearshift housing to the bearing carrier, use a new gasket; because the thickness of gasket influences the position of the pinion, the correct thickness must be fitted. If no parts of the bearing carrier have been renewed, measure the thickness of the old gasket, which will be either 0.30 or 0.40 mm (0.012 or 0.016 in) and use a new gasket of the same thickness.

15   If a new input shaft bearing has been fitted, measure the amount by which the outer race projects from the end face of the bearing carrier (a) (Figure 6.21). If this is between 0.20 and 0.26 mm (0.008 and 0.010 in) use a 0.30 mm (0.012 in) thick gasket. If the projection is between 0.27 and 0.32 mm (0.011 and 0.013 in), use a 0.40 mm (0.016 in) thick gasket.

16   When refitting the gearshift housing, first ensure that the shim is in place in the housing recess, with the recess in the shim towards the spring. If no parts of the bearing carrier have been renewed and assuming that the original gearshift housing is being refitted, the original shim can be re-used.

17   If a new pinion bearing or gearshift housing are being used then it will be necessary to assess the pinion shaft end shim requirement. To do this, measure the amount by which the pinion bearing outer race projects from the endface of the bearing carrier (b) and then measure the recessed depth of the shim contact face within the gearshift housing (from its outer contact face c). The shim thickness required is calculated by applying the formula $a + c - b$. For example, if $a = 0.30$

Fig. 6.21 Measuring the input shaft bearing projection on the 014 gearbox (Sec 10)

Fig. 6.22 Sectional view showing measurement points for assessing pinion bearing shim thickness (ball bearing type 014 gearbox) (Sec 10)

a   Input shaft bearing protrusion
b   Pinion bearing protrusion
c   Seat depth in gearshift housing
d   Gasket thickness
s   Shim thickness

mm, $c = 2.58$ mm and $b = 2.42$ mm the shim thickness required will be *0.46 mm*. Shims are available in thicknesses ranging from 0.40 mm to 0.75 mm. Continue reassembly from paragraph 22 onwards.

18   When refitting the gearshift housing to the bearing carrier, use a new gasket; on later models fitted with the taper roller (Combi) bearing at the rear end of the pinion shaft, the gasket thickness used will be 0.40 mm, no alternative being used.

19   If the original bearing carrier, pinion and output shaft bearings and gearshift housing are being re-used then the original shims can be refitted during assembly. If however any of these items have been renewed then it will be necessary to assess the shim thickness requirement for both the pinion and input shaft bearings.

Fig. 6.20 Insert the 1st/2nd operating dog roll pin – 014/I gearbox (Sec 10)

Fig. 6.23 Sectional view showing measurement points for assessing pinion and input shaft bearing shim requirements (later Combi bearing type 014 gearbox) (Sec 10)

a	Input shaft bearing protrusion
b	Pinion bearing protrusion
c	Seat depth in gearshift housing
d	Seat depth in gearshift housing

e	Thickness of gasket
s	Thickness of shim
v	Thickness of shim

20 Referring to Figure 6.23, measure the amount that the pinion bearing protrudes at its outer race from the endface of the bearing carrier (b), then measure the bearing recess depth in the gearshift housing (c). Now use the formula $c - b + 0.3$ mm to assess the pinion bearing shim requirement. Shims are available in thicknesses ranging from 0.15 to 1.40 mm in increments of 0.05 mm.

21 To assess the output bearing shim requirement, repeat the measuring procedure in paragraph 20 but use the formula $d - a$. Output bearing shims are available in thicknesses of 1.55 mm to 1.70 mm in increments of 0.05 mm. As an example if $a = 7.8$ mm, and $d = 9.0$ mm the shim requirement V will be 1.55 mm.

22 Position the selected shim(s) into position in the gearshift housing recess(es).

23 The spring clip is now located onto the gearshift housing. Fit the spring by first putting it over the internal selector lever. Compress the spring and slide it with the internal selector lever into the housing so that the end of the spring rests against the end of the housing and the shim. Move the spring and the selector lever into the housing as far as they will go, and turn the selector lever so that the spring and selector lever are as shown in Figure 6.24.

24 Check that the new gasket is correctly positioned then insert the selector lever finger into the slots in the selector rods and push the gearshift housing into place. Select the retaining bolts referring to Figure 6.6 and smear their threads with sealant prior to fitting. Insert and tighten the bolts to the specified torque wrench setting.

25 Lower the differential into the final drive housing with the crownwheel teeth facing inward.

26 If the final drive cover is sealed by means of an O-ring, fit the O-ring and locate the cover onto the housing. Where no O-ring is used, smear the final drive cover mating face with a suitable sealant before fitting. Insert the retaining bolts and tighen them evenly in a diagonal sequence to the specified torque wrench setting.

27 Insert the drive flanges into each side of the differential and tighten the bolts while holding the flanges stationary with a rod through one of the bolt holes.

28 Fill the gearbox with oil to the correct level.

11 Gearshift lever (014) — removal, refitting and adjustment

1   The adjustment of the gearshift linkage requires a special tool, so if the linkage is undone, it is very important to mark the position of the shift rod in the shift finger before separating them.

2   Put a mark to show how far the shift rod is inserted into the clamp, and also mark a horizontal line on both the shift finger and the shift rod so that they can be reconnected without any rotational change.

3   Release the bolt on the clamp and separate the shift rod from the shift finger.

4   From inside the car, remove the nuts and washers securing the lever housing to the car floor and remove the gear lever assembly and shift rod.

5   To separate the shift rod from the gear lever, undo and remove the shift rod clevis bolt.

6   After refitting the gear lever, by reversing the removal operations, the basic setting of the linkage should be tested by engaging 1st gear and then moving the gear lever as far to the left as it will go. Release the lever and measure the distance which it springs back on its own. This should be between 5 and 10 mm (0.20 and 0.39 in). If this basic adjustment is incorrect, it is unlikely that all the gears can be engaged. The gear lever will either have to be set up using a special VW gauge, or the adjustment can be made by a lengthy process of trial and error.

7   Check that the centralizing holes of the housing and lever bearing plate are aligned when tightening the securing bolts (Figure 6.26).

12 Gearshift linkage (014) — dismantling and reassembly

1   The gearshift linkage consists of two principal parts, the shift rod coupling assembly and the lever assembly.

Gear lever assembly

2   Remove the gear lever as described in Section 11.

3   Dismantle the assembly by unscrewing the gear knob, removing the circlip from the gear lever and lifting off the washer and spring. The

Fig. 6.24 Fitted position of the selector lever spring in the 014 gearshift housing (Sec 10)

1	Housing
2	Spring clip
3	Internal selector shaft

4	Reverse gear selector shaft
5	1st/2nd selector shaft
6	3rd/4th selector shaft

Housing

Retaining ring

Rubber guide

Upper ball half

Compression spring

Shell

Lower ball half

Gearshift knob

Lock ring

Lever bearing

Gear lever

Lever housing

Stop pad

Reverse stop

Fig. 6.25 Exploded view of the 014 gearshift lever components (Secs 11 and 12)

12.3 Location of gear lever, circlip, washer and spring

Fig. 6.26 Holes in lever housing and bearing plate must align
(Secs 11 and 12)

gear lever can then be pulled down out of the lever bearing assembly
(photo).
4   Before separating the lever bearing assembly from the lever
housing, mark round the lever bearing plate with a scriber so that it
can be returned to exactly the same position, then remove the two
screws and washer from the plate (Figure 6.26).

5   Do not dismantle the bearing unless it is necessary to grease it.
Push the rubber guide and locking ring (if fitted) down out of the
housing plate, then prise the plastic shells apart and remove the ball
halves and spring — the shells can then be removed from the rubber
guide.
6   When reassembling have the rubber guide with its shouldered end

Shift rod coupling complete

Shift rod

Shift finger

Clip

Side plate, right

Support

Side plate, left

Self-locking nut

Self-locking bolt

Bush

Self-locking nut

Adaptor

Fig. 6.27 Exploded view of the 014 gearshift linkage components (Secs 11 and 12)

uppermost and press the two shells into it. Press the lower ball half
into the shells, then the spring and finally press in the upper ball half,
pushing the shells slightly apart if necessary.
7 After assembling the parts into the rubber guide, push the
assembly up into the lever bearing plate together with the locking ring,
where fitted.
8 When inserting the lever into the bearing, note that the lever is
cranked to the left, and when refitting the lever bearing plate to the
housing, take care to line up the plate with the scribed mark made
before dismantling.

Shift rod coupling
9 To dismantle the shift rod coupling, remove the bolt from the end
of the support rod. Mark the position of the adaptor on the gearbox
selector lever, then remove the wire from the bolt (where applicable),
loosen the bolt and remove the shift rod coupling assembly.
10 Prise the ball coupling of the support off its mounting on the side
plate. Remove the bolt which clamps the two side plates together and
extract the shift finger and its bushes.
11 When reassembling the shift rod coupling, note that the adaptor
should be fitted so that the hole for the clamp bolt is towards the front
and the groove for the clamp bolt on the shift finger is on the left-hand
side. Make sure that the holes in the two side plates are exactly in line,
so that the coupling is assembled without any strain.
12 All the joints and friction surfaces of the shift rod coupling should
be lubricated with multi-purpose grease and after refitting the
assembly to the gearbox, the clamp bolt should be tightened and then
locked with soft iron wire (where applicable).

13 Gearbox (013 and 093) – dismantling into major assemblies

Note: *Photo sequence shows 013 unit – some components of the
093 unit may differ slightly from those shown.*
1 Remove the drain plug, drain the oil and refit the plug (photo).
Clean away external dirt from the gearbox casing.
2 Pierce the cover plate with a screwdriver and prise it out – a new
plate must be obtained for the reassembly procedure.

13.3A Gear indicator switch location

13.3B Reverse lamp switch location and wiring connections

13.1 Location of the drain plug

13.5 Removing a drive flange

3 Remove the reverse lamp switch wiring and unscrew the switch.
Also unscrew the gear indicator switch (photos).
4 Remove the clutch release bearing and shaft, as described in
Chapter 5.
5 Unscrew the drive flange centre bolts while holding the flange
stationary with a rod inserted through a bolt hole. Mark each flange
side for side, then withdraw them from the differential (photo).

Gear train

Reversing light switch

Drive flange

Gasket

Dowel pins

Gearbox housing

Final drive cover

Oil filler plug

Dowel sleeve

Hex head bolt,

Oil drain plug

Input shaft

Hex head bolt M 8 x 35
with washer

Differential

Spring pin

Selector fork for 3rd
and 4th gear

Reverse gear

Selector rod for 1st and
2nd gear

Selector fork for 1st
and 2nd gear

Output shaft/
pinion

Fig. 6.28A Exploded view of the 013 and 093 gearbox (Sec 13)

Spring pin

5th gear selector fork

5th speed driving gear with operating sleeve/synchro hub

5th gear synchro ring

5th gear needle bearings

5th gear clutch member

Cylinder roller bearing inner race

Gasket

Thrust washer

Pinion nut

5th speed driven gear

Socket head bolt,

Gearshift housing

Cover plate

Selector rod for 3rd and 4th gear

Reverse gear shaft

Small interlock plunger

1st inner race for pinion roller bearing

Bearing carrier

Fig. 6.28B Exploded view of the 013 and 093 gearbox (Sec 13) (continued)

13.6A Removing the differential cover ...

13.6B ... and differential (013 gearbox)

13.6C Right-hand side view of the differential (013 gearbox)

13.6D Left-hand side view of the differential (013 gearbox)

13.7 Using a nut splitter to hold the input shaft stationary

6   On the 013 gearbox, unbolt and remove the differential cover and lift out the differential (photos). Although it is possible to remove the differential from the 093 gearbox at this stage, there is a likelihood of damage to the crownwheel and pinion teeth, and it is therefore recommended that the differential be removed after dismantling the remainder of the gearbox.

7   Unscrew the bolt from the end of the input shaft and remove the thick washer. The input shaft must be held stationary in order to unscrew the bolt – we used a nut splitter and a block of wood (photo), but it is possible to make up a tool similar to that shown in Figure 6.29 using an old clutch driven plate.

8   Using an Allen key, unscrew the bolts from the gearshift housing, noting the location of the bracket and bolts (Figure 6.30 or 6.31 as applicable) (photo).

9   Pull the gearshift housing from the gear carrier and remove the gasket (photo). If the bearing is tight on the end of the input shaft a puller will be required.

10   Using a pin punch drive the roll pin from the 1st/2nd selector dog and turn the dog anti-clockwise (photo).

11   Pull out the notched selector rod to engage 3rd gear, then turn the main selector rod anti-clockwise and extract it from the gear carrier (photo).

12   Remove the 1st/2nd selector dog and move the 3rd/4th selector rod to neutral (photo).

13   Using a pin punch, drive the roll pin from the 5th gear selector fork while supporting the selector rod with a block of wood to prevent damage to the bore in the bearing carrier (photo).

14   Engage 5th gear by moving the synchro sleeve and 1st gear by pulling out the 1st/2nd selector rod. Both the input and pinion shafts are now locked to enable the nut to be unscrewed from the pinion shaft. After removing the nut return the gears to neutral.

15   Unscrew the bolts securing the gear carrier to the final drive housing, noting the location of the mounting and exhaust brackets (photos).

Fig. 6.29 Tool for holding the input shaft stationary on 013 and 093 gearboxes (Sec 13)

16   Remove the gear carrier and gasket, and if necessary knock out the dowel pins (photo). To prevent unnecessary damage to the oil seal wrap adhesive tape around the input shaft splines before removing the gear carrier.

17   Using a puller beneath the 5th gear, pull off the 5th gear and synchro unit, 5th gear clutch member, and 5th selector fork. It may be possible to lever off these items, but this will depend on how tight the clutch member is on the input shaft.

Fig. 6.30 Gearshift housing and bearing carrier retaining bolt positions and identification for the 013 gearbox (Sec 13)

1   Socket-head bolt and washer (M8 x 55)
2   Socket-head bolt (no washer) (M8 x 58)
3   Hex. head bolt and washer (M8 x 45)
4   Hex. head bolt (no washer) (M8 x 46)

Fig. 6.31 Gearshift housing and bearing carrier retaining bolt positions and identification for the 093 gearbox (Sec 13)

1   Socket-head bolt and washer (M8 x 55)
2   Hex. head bolt and washer (M8 x 45)

13.8 Mounting bracket location on the gearbox housing

13.9 Removing the gearshift housing

13.10 Removing the 1st/2nd selector dog roll pin

13.11 Removing the main selector rod

13.12 Removing the 1st/2nd selector dog

13.13 Removing the 5th gear selector fork roll pin

13.15A Mounting bracket location on the gear carrier

13.15B Exhaust mounting bracket location on the gear carrier

13.16 Removing the gear carrier

13.18 5th gear and synchro unit with the splined clutch member

13.19 Removing the 5th gear needle roller bearings

13.21 Removing the 5th gear thrust washer

13.22 Removing the 3rd/4th selector fork roll pin

13.23A Removing the 3rd/4th selector rod (arrowed)

13.23B Interlock plunger location in the 3rd/4th selector rod

18 Separate the clutch member and synchro ring from the 5th gear and synchro unit (photo).

19 Remove the 5th gear needle roller bearings from the input shaft (photo).

20 Using a puller remove the 5th driven gear from the pinion shaft.

21 Lever off the 5th gear thrust washer and inner race (photo). If the inner race is tight use a puller.

22 Using a pin punch, drive the roll pin from the 3rd/4th selector fork while supporting the selector rod with a block of wood to prevent damage to the bore in the bearing carrier (photo).

23 Pull the 3rd/4th selector rod out of the gear carrier. Remove the small interlock plunger from the rod and put it in a safe place (photo).

24 The pinion shaft must now be pushed through the tapered roller bearing inner race approximately 6 to 8 mm (0.24 to 0.32 in) to allow clearance for the input shaft to be removed. To do this support the

gear carrier and use a press, or alternatively use a plate (photo) and long bolts inserted into the bearing outer race retaining ring. If the latter method is used remove each bolt and insert the long bolts separately to prevent the ring from dropping.

25 Remove the input shaft together with the 3rd/4th selector fork from the gear carrier (photo).

26 Set the selector rods to neutral.

27 Using a soft metal drift, drive out the reverse gear shaft and remove the reverse gear (photo).

28 Remove the pinion shaft together with 1st/2nd selector rod and fork (photos).

29 Recover the interlock plungers from the gear carrier and put them in a safe place.

30 Remove the differential on the 093 gearbox, as necessary (see paragraph 6).

13.24 Home-made plate for removing the pinion shaft

13.25 Removing the input shaft with 3rd/4th selector fork

13.27 Removing the reverse gear shaft

13.28A Removing the pinion shaft with the 1st/2nd selector rod and fork

13.28B The pinion (upper) and input shaft assemblies removed for inspection and shown in their gear meshed positions

Circlip

Bearing carrier

Cylinder roller bearing

Gearshift housing

Inner race/cylinder roller bearing

Ball bearing

Input shaft

Circlip

Baffle plate

Spring

5th gear synchro hub

Operating sleeve

5th gear synchro ring

Locking key

3rd gear

3rd gear synchro ring

5th speed driving gear (with synchro hub)

3rd gear needle bearing

3rd/4th gear operating sleeve/synchro hub

5th speed driving gear with operating sleeve and synchro hub

Thrust washer

Operating sleeve

4th gear needle bearing

Locking key

Synchro hub

Spring

5th gear needle bearing

Circlip for synchro hub

Circlip

4th gear synchro ring

4th gear

Thrust washer for 4th gear

Needle bearing for input shaft

Gearbox housing

Fig. 6.32 Input shaft components on 013 and 093 gearboxes (Sec 14)

14.1A Removing the input shaft circlip ...

14.1B ... and thrust washer (earlier models only)

14.2 Removing the 4th gear and needle roller bearing

14.4A Withdraw the circlip ...

14.4B ... and remove the 3rd/4th synchroniser

14.4C Using a puller to remove the 3rd/4th synchroniser

14.5A Removing 3rd gear ...

14.5B ... and the split needle roller bearing

14.8 Input shaft dismantled for inspection

14 Input shaft (013 and 093) – dismantling and reassembly

1   Remove the circlip from the end of the shaft and on earlier models withdraw the thrust washer (photos). Refer to paragraph 19 for modification note on later models.

2   Lift off the 4th gearwheel with its needle roller bearing (photo). If the bearing is removed from the gear, put a paint mark on the bearing and the gear so that the bearing is not turned end-to-end on reassembling.

3   Remove the 4th gear synchro-ring.

4   Remove the circlip retaining the synchro-hub and take the hub off the shaft. It may be possible to hold the 3rd gearwheel and tap the shaft out of the synchro hub, or it may be necessary to have the hub pressed off (photos).

5   Remove the 3rd gear synchro-ring, the 3rd gearwheel and its needle roller bearing (photos).

6   Mark the gear and bearing so that the bearing is not turned end-for-end on reassembly.

7   To remove the inner race of the cylinder roller bearing from the rear end of the shaft, insert a clamp/puller beneath it and drive out the input shaft using a soft drift. Figure 6.33 illustrates the bearing removal using a suitable separator clamp/puller and press. A long metal tube can be used to fit the race on reassembly.

8   Clean the respective components and inspect them for signs of damage or excessive wear. Gearbox components are very expensive, and if any gears or shafts are required it may be more economic to fit an exchange gearbox (photo).

9   Check the synchroniser rings for wear by positioning them onto their gear cones and measure the clearance (a) shown in Figure 6.34. If worn beyond the limit specified they must be renewed.

10 Commence reassembly by lubricating the 3rd gear needle roller bearing with gear oil, then fit the bearing onto the shaft, ensuring that the bearing is the same way up as it was before removal.

11 Fit the 3rd gearwheel.

12 If the synchroniser has been dismantled, look for mating marks etched on the outer edge. If so, the hub must be assembled with these marks in line. Later models do not have mating marks and do not need to be reassembled in a particular position.

13 Fit the three locking keys into the hub before fitting the sleeve and then retain the keys with the springs, positioning the springs as shown in Figure 6.35 with the angled end of the spring fitted into the hollow of the locking key.

14 Note that the splines on the bore of the synchro-hub are chamfered at one end. The chamfered end of the hub inner splines must fit into the shaft first, facing 3rd gear. The hub also has an additional groove at one end (Figure 6.36) and this groove faces 4th gear.

Fig. 6.33 Method of removing the roller bearing inner race from the input shaft (Sec 14)

Fig. 6.34 Synchro-ring wear gap (a) (Sec 14)

Fig. 6.35 Correct fitting of synchro springs (Sec 14)

Fig. 6.36 Synchro-hub groove (white arrow) and chamfer (black arrow) (Sec 14)

Fig. 6.37 Check 4th gear axial clearance (Sec 14)

Fig. 6.38 4th gear retaining clips position (arrowed) on later models (Sec 14)

15 Press the synchroniser on to the mainshaft, first turning the 3rd gear synchro-ring so that the grooves on it are aligned with the synchroniser locking keys.

16 Insert the circlip on top of the synchro-hub and then press the synchroniser back against the circlip. This increases the gap between the synchroniser and 3rd gear which ensures better lubrication of the 3rd gear bearing.

17 Fit the 4th gear synchro-ring, aligning the grooves in it with the synchroniser locking keys, then check its clearance using a feeler gauge as shown in Figure 6.34.

18 On earlier models (pre June 1983), fit 4th gear and its bearing, first lubricating the bearing with gear oil, then fit the thrust washer and the circlip. Measure the axial clearance between 4th gear and the thrust washer. This clearance should be at least 0.10 mm (0.004 in), but less than 0.40 mm (0.016 in). If it exceeds the upper limit, a thicker thrust washer must be fitted and these are available in three thicknesses, 3.47 mm (0.136 in), 3.57 mm (0.141 in) and 3.67 mm (0.144 in) (Figure 6.37).

19 From June 1983 the input shaft of both the 013 and 093 gearboxes was modified, the 4th speed gear being secured by a circlip alone with no thrust washer being fitted between the gear and the circlip. The circlip location groove in the shaft is repositioned and the thrust washer location shoulder on the shaft deleted (Figure 6.38). If the later shaft is being fitted to replace the early type it is important that the later type circlip is fitted as it differs dimensionally from the early type.

15 Pinion shaft (013 and 093) – dismantling and reassembly

1 The depth of the pinion's engagement with the crownwheel is adjusted during manufacture to the optimum position for quiet running and long life. When components affecting the pinion engagement are changed, adjustments must be made to regain this optimum position. Before the pinion shaft is dismantled or replacement items fitted, the position of the pinion must be established by measurement. Because this requires the use of specialist measuring equipment the work should be entrusted to your VW dealer. The components which affect the pinion engagement are the gearbox casing, the bearing carrier, the pinion bearings and the 1st gear needle roller bearing. The crownwheel and pinion must be renewed as a matched pair and the pinion engagement adjusted to the figure etched onto the crownwheel – a job for your VW dealer.

2 Using a suitable puller, remove the bearing race and 1st gear, then remove the needle roller bearing and sleeve, keeping them identified for position (photos).

3 Lift off the 1st gear synchro-ring.

4 Using a puller with its legs placed beneath the 2nd gearwheel, draw off the gear and the 1st/2nd gear synchroniser assembly. Remove the 2nd gear synchro-ring.

5 Lift off the 2nd gear needle roller bearing and mark it to ensure correct refitting.

6 The 3rd speed and 4th speed gears are pressed and shrunk on to the shaft, and if they need to be removed, the work should be entrusted to a VW dealer. However, it may be possible to remove them with a suitable puller after removal of the selective circlip and heating in boiling water.

7 Clean the respective components and inspect them for signs of damage or excessive wear. Gearbox components are expensive to replace and if any gears or shafts are in need of renewal it may be more economic to fit an exchange gearbox.

15.2A From the pinion shaft remove the bearing ...

15.2B ... 1st gear ...

15.2C ... needle roller bearing ...

15.2D ... and bearing sleeve

15.9A Pinion shaft ready for fitting ...

15.9B ... the roller bearing ...

8   Check the synchroniser rings for wear by positioning them onto their gear cone and measure the clearance (a) shown in Figure 6.34. If worn beyond the specified limit they must be renewed, but note the advice given in paragraph 16 regarding the 1st gear synchro-ring.
9   Commence assembly by ensuring that the shaft is free of oil and grease then locate the roller bearing onto the shaft fitting it flush against the pinion (photo).

10 To refit the 3rd and 4th speed gears they will need to be pre-heated as described for removal (paragraph 6). Fit the 4th speed gear first followed by the 3rd speed gear and in each case the wide shouldered gear face must be fitted towards the pinion. If necessary use a suitable puller to locate the gears on the shaft (photos).
11 If new gears or pinion shaft have been fitted you will need to select the correct circlip. To do this, measure the play between the 3rd

15.10A ... 4th gear, ...

15.10B ... using a puller, ...

15.10C ... and 3rd gear

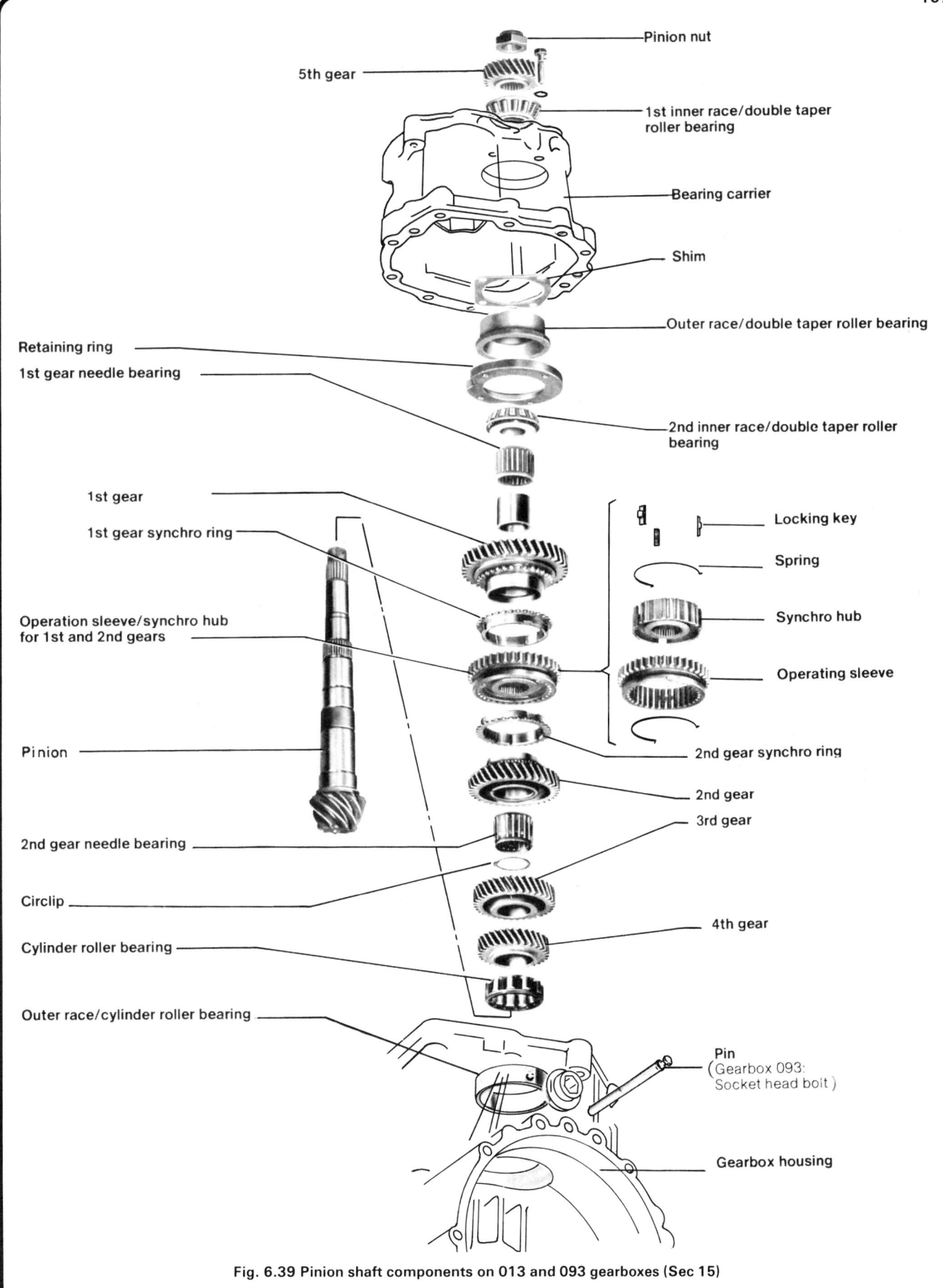

Fig. 6.39 Pinion shaft components on 013 and 093 gearboxes (Sec 15)

15.11 Check for size of circlip required ...

15.13A Locate the needle bearing and 2nd gear ...

gear and the circlip groove shoulder in the shaft as shown using a set of feeler gauges (photo). Where the play measured is under 1.6 mm (0.629 in) fit a 1.5 mm (0.059 in) thick circlip but if over this amount use a 1.6 mm (0.629 in) thick circlip.

12 Check that the selective circlip is fully engaged in its groove on the shaft when fitted (photo).

13 Lubricate the 2nd gear needle roller bearing with gear oil and fit it to the shaft. Locate the 2nd gearwheel onto its bearing, then place the synchro-ring on the gear (photos).

14 If the synchroniser assembly has been dismantled, it must be reassembled in the following way. The sleeve and the hub may have matching marks, if so they must be assembled with these marks lined up. Fit the three locking keys into their slots and secure the keys with the retaining springs. The springs should be spaced 120° apart and the angled end of the springs should be engaged in the hollow of a locking key. If there are no matching marks on the hub and sleeve the two parts need not be assembled in any particular position, except that the grooves on the hub splines must face the 1st gear (Figure 6.40).

15 Fit the synchroniser assembly to the shaft ensuring that the groove in the synchro hub faces towards 1st gear, with the external teeth of the operating sleeve away from the pinion end. Before pressing the hub down fully, turn the 2nd gear synchro-ring so that the slots in it

15.13B ... then fit the synchro ring

15.12 ... and engage selected circlip into groove against 3rd gear

Fig. 6.40 Correct fitment of 1st/2nd synchro springs (Sec 15)

are aligned with the locking keys in the synchroniser assembly (photos).

16 Fit the 1st gear synchro-ring, lining up its slots with the locking keys in the synchroniser assembly. Later models have a modified synchro-ring with a tooth missing at three points (Figure 6.41). The

15.15A Fitting the 1st/2nd synchroniser (**Caution** – Fit as shown for the 013 gearbox and opposite way round on the 014 gearbox)

15.15B 1st/2nd synchroniser correctly installed (013 gearbox)

Fig. 6.41 Identification of modified synchro-ring for 1st gear (Sec 15)

tooth angle on these synchro-rings was altered from 120° to 110° to improve the engagement of 1st gear. This type of ring must only be used on 1st gear, and if the 1st gear ring is being renewed, the 120° type having the full number of teeth should be fitted, as the modified ring is not available as a spare part.

17 Fit the 1st gear bearing sleeve, then lubricate the needle roller bearing with gear oil and fit it over the sleeve (photo).

18 Fit the 1st gearwheel then press on the second inner race of the tapered roller bearing. Use a tube to drive the bearing into position if necessary (photo).

15.17 Fitting 1st gear synchro ring and needle roller bearing

15.18 Fitting the bearing to the pinion shaft

16 Gearbox/final drive housing (013 and 093) – servicing

1 The removal and refitting of the clutch release mechanism fitted in the gearbox housing is described in Chapter 5.

Input shaft needle bearing

2 Using a drift, or piece of hardwood dowel of suitable size, drive the bearing out from the clutch bellhousing end of the casing. Fit the new bearing so that the lettering on the bearing faces the drift used for installation. Enter the bearing into the bore squarely from the gearbox

Gearbox housing

Input shaft oil seal

Guide sleeve

Starter bush

Release shaft

Release shaft bush

Release bearing

Return spring

Bush (013 only)

Shim

Outer race/taper roller bearing

Outer race/taper roller bearing

Shim

Magnet

Needle bearing for input shaft

Outer race/cylinder roller bearing

Hex head bolt (013 only)

Breather

Oil filler plug

Pin (gearbox 013) Socket head bolt (gearbox 093)

Rubber bush (013 only)

Clutch lever

Oil drain plug

Speedo drive

Final drive cover

Drive flange oil seal

Fig. 6.42 Gearbox/final drive housing – 013 and 093 gearboxes (Sec 16)

16.2 Location of input shaft needle roller bearing (A) and pinion shaft taper roller bearing outer race (B) in the final drive housing

Fig. 6.43 Pinion bearing securing bolt location on the 093 gearbox (Sec 16)

side of the casing, and using a drift, or a piece of hardwood, knock it in until it is flush with the face of the casting (photo).

Pinion bearing outer track – 013 gearbox
3   The outer track of the pinion bearing is secured by a pin which engages a depression in the outer circumference of the bearing (photo). Grip the grooved end of the pin and pull it out at least $\frac{1}{8}$ in (3.2 mm) so that the other end is clear of the bearing. Using a suitable drift, tap the outer race out of the end of the casing. When fitting a new outer track, line up the depression in the outer track with the pin, and then drive the track in flush with the face of the casting before tapping home the pin (the grooves marking on the end face of the bearing track should face towards the fitting tool).

16.3 Removing the pinion shaft bearing outer race retaining pin (013 gearbox). **Note**: the 093 gearbox pinion shaft bearing outer race is secured by means of a socket-head bolt

Pinion bearing outer track – 093 gearbox
4   The pinion bearing outer track on the 093 gearbox is secured by a socket-head bolt which must be removed with an Allen key before the outer track can be drifted out of the housing. When fitting the outer track into the housing, line up the depression in the outer track with the location bolt hole, then drive or press the outer track into position

so that the depression and bolt hole are aligned. Refit and tighten the socket head bolt to the specified torque wrench setting (Figure 6.43).

Driveshaft flange oil seals
5   The driveshaft oil seals in the gearbox housing and in the final drive cover may be prised out with a large screwdriver (photo).
6   Fit new seals with the lips of the seal inwards (photo). Take care to enter the seal squarely into the housing and drive it in fully using a hammer and a block of wood.
7   After fitting the seal, smear its lips with gear oil and fill the space between the lips with multi-purpose grease.

16.5 Prising out a driveshaft flange oil seal

16.6 Installing a driveshaft flange oil seal

16.9 Removing the clutch release bearing guide sleeve and plate

Input shaft oil seal
8   Remove the clutch release bearing as described in Chapter 5.
9   Remove the three bolts attaching the guide sleeve to the housing and remove the guide sleeve and plate (photo).
10   Use a hooked lever to remove the oil seal, or prise it out with a short lever (photo). If the bush is also to be removed, this must be driven out towards the bellhousing using a piece of tubing of suitable diameter, which is long enough to extend into the gearbox housing. To renew the oil seal only, it is not necessary to dismantle the gearbox housing.
11   Drive the bush into the housing until the flat end of the bush seats against the bottom of the recess.
12   If the oil seal is being fitted with the input shaft in position, slide a piece of plastic sleeving over the splines of the input shaft, or wrap plastic tape round them before sliding the seal over the shaft. This will prevent the splines from damaging the seal. Fit the seal with its flat face outwards and oil the lips with gear oil before fitting it. Drive the seal in flush, using a hammer and a block of wood.
13   Fit the guide sleeve and plate and re-insert and tighten the fixing bolts. If the guide sleeve is plastic, it should be kept free from grease.

16.10 Input shaft oil seal location in the final drive casing

Starter bush
14   The starter bush is located in the bellhousing and if worn should be renewed. If an internal expanding removal tool is not available, it may be possible to force out the bush under hydraulic action by filling the bush with heavy grease then driving a tight fitting dowel rod into the bush.
15   Drive the new starter bush into the bellhousing until flush.

17 Bearing/gear carrier (013 and 093) – servicing

Note: *The photo sequence shown illustrates the 013 unit – some of the 093 gearbox bearing/gear carrier components may differ slightly from those shown.*
1   If the bearing carrier is being renewed, the meshing of the crownwheel and pinion is affected. To ensure correct meshing, the pinion projection will need to be measured by a VW dealer before and after the new carrier is fitted. They can then advise on the appropriate thickness of shim and gasket to be fitted between the new gear carrier and the gearbox housing to regain the original pinion projection.

Pinion bearing renewal
2   Unscrew the four bolts and remove the bearing outer race retaining ring, noting the location of the cut-outs (photos).
3   Using a metal tube, drive the outer race from the bearing carrier and remove the shim (photo).
4   Refitting is a reversal of the removal procedure, but it will be necessary for a VW dealer to determine the correct thickness of shim to fit behind the race.

Selector rod detents – removal and refitting
5   Before removing the reverse relay lever, unscrew and remove the detent from the side of the bearing carrier. The relay lever is operated by a pin in the 5th/reverse selector rod (photos).
6   To remove the detent plugs, cut a 6 mm thread in the plugs, screw a bolt into each plug in turn and pull the bolt to extract the plug. With the plugs removed, the springs and detents can be extracted.
7   The internal selector lever bush can be removed and refitted using a suitable drift. When refitting the bush, drive it in flush to the carrier mating face.
8   Refitting of the detents, springs and plugs is a reversal of the removal procedure. The correct positions of the detents and interlock plungers is shown in Figure 6.45.
9   When refitting the relay lever adjust it as follows. Temporarily install the reverse gear and shaft, followed by the relay lever. Insert the bolt and washer and pressing the relay lever in the direction indicated (arrow in Figure 6.46) screw the bolt in so that it is touching the relay

Plug

Guide sleeve

Spring

Gear detent

Bush for internal selector lever

Relay lever

Shim

Outer race/taper roller bearing

Interlock plunger

Small interlock plunger

Circlip

Cylinder roller bearing

Bearing carrier

Retaining ring

Selector rod for 5th and reverse gears

Fig. 6.44 Gear carrier components on 013 and 093 gearboxes (Sec 17)

17.2A Remove the four bolts ...

17.2B ... and the pinion bearing outer race retaining ring

17.3 Pinion bearing outer race and shim

17.5A Removing the reverse detent from the bearing carrier

17.5B Location of the reverse relay lever and 5th/reverse selector rod in the bearing carrier

17.6 Selector rod detents in the bearing carrier

Fig. 6.45 Cross-section diagram of the selector rod detents on 013 and 093 gearboxes (Sec 17)

Input shaft bearing — renewal

10 Extract the circlip then, using a metal tube, drive the bearing into the bearing carrier.
11 To fit the new bearing, first fit the circlip then, using the metal tube on the outer track, drive the bearing into the carrier until it contacts the circlip.

18 Gearshift housing (013 and 093) — servicing

Note: *Photo sequence shows 013 unit — some components of the 093 unit may differ slightly from those shown.*

Selector oil seal — renewal

1 Prise out the oil seal with a screwdriver (photo).
2 Insert the new oil seal and drive it in until flush using a block of wood, making sure that it is kept square to the housing.
3 Fill the space between the oil seal lips with multi-purpose grease.

18.1 Main selector rod oil seal in the gearshift housing

Fig. 6.46 Press relay lever in direction indicated by arrow (Sec 17)

Selector bush — renewal

4 Remove the oil seal and, using a suitable metal tube, drive the bush into the gearshift housing.
5 Drive the new bush into the housing from the same direction, then fit a new oil seal.

Input shaft ball-bearing — removal and refitting

6 Prise out the baffle plate from inside the gearshift housing. As the plate is peened into position it may be necessary to use a round file to remove the peening first.
7 Extract the circlip and, using a soft metal drift on the outer track, drive the bearing into the housing to remove it (photo).
8 Drive the bearing fully into the housing using the metal tube on the outer track, then fit the circlip.
9 Press in the baffle plate and peen over the housing shoulder in three places to secure (photo).

19 Fifth gear components (013 and 093) — servicing

1 Examine the 5th gear and 5th driven gear for wear and damage and renew them, as necessary.
2 If it is required to dismantle the synchroniser, first mark the sleeve and gear hub in relation to each other, then slide off the sleeve and remove the keys and springs.
3 When reassembling the synchroniser observe the mating marks. The selector fork groove on the sleeve must be towards the 5th gear.

lever and correctly aligned with the lever bolt hole. Now press the lever towards the bolt and unscrew the bolt until the start of the thread is heard to engage, then torque tighten the bolt to the amount specified. To check that the relay mechanism engages freely in all directions select reverse gear a few times and if satisfactory remove the reverse gear and shaft as this is necessary to enable later fitting of the selector rods.

Seal

Bush for internal selector lever

Magnet

Pin

Switch for gearshift indicator/econometer

Gearshift housing

Ball bearing

Circlip

Baffle plate

Fig. 6.47 Gearshift housing components on 013 and 093 gearboxes (Sec 18)

18.7 Outer view of the input shaft bearing in the gearshift housing

18.9 The three points (arrowed) requiring peening to secure the input shaft bearing baffle plate

With the keys inserted, locate the inner spring in one of the keys, then use a screwdriver to position the spring under the other keys. Fit the outer spring in a different key with the free end facing the opposite direction to the inner spring.
4   Check the synchro ring for wear as described in Section 14 by fitting it on the clutch member.

20 Gearbox (013 and 093) – reassembly

Note: *Photo sequence shows 013 unit – some components of the 093 unit may differ slightly from those shown.*
1   On the 093 gearbox lower the differential into the final drive housing and fit the cover together with a new O-ring, where applicable. Insert and tighten the cover bolts in diagonal sequence to the specified torque. If required, the differential may be fitted on the 013 gearbox at this stage (see paragraph 28).
2   With the gear carrier on the bench, fit the interlock plungers in their correct positions as shown in Figure 6.45. If the selector detents have been removed they can be fitted later. If a pen magnet is available the interlock plungers may be fitted as the work proceeds (photo).
3   Engage the 1st/2nd selector fork and rod with the 1st/2nd synchro sleeve on the pinion shaft, then lower them simultaneously into the gear carrier casing.
4   With the gear carrier on its side, insert the reverse gear shaft and at the same time locate the reverse gear between the relay lever jaws (photo). Drive in the shaft until flush.
5   Engage the 3rd/4th selector fork with the 3rd/4th synchro sleeve on the input shaft, then lower them into the gear carrier and into engagement with the pinion shaft gears. Take care to keep the synchro sleeves central in their hubs otherwise the keys may fall out.
6   Insert the small interlock plunger in the 3rd/4th selector rod and retain it with grease. Make sure that the interlock plungers are in position then insert the 3rd/4th selector rod into the gear carrier and through the selector fork.
7   Align the holes, then drive the roll pin into the fork end rod while supporting the rod with a block of wood.

8   Support the front ends of the shafts, then fit the tapered roller bearing inner race on the pinion shaft and drive it on using a metal tube until it contacts the outer race (photos).
9   Locate the 5th gear thrust washer on the input shaft, then drive on the 5th gear inner race using a metal tube (photo). The inner race can if necessary be pre-heated to 120°C (248°F) to ease the installation.
10 Locate the 5th driven gear on the pinion shaft and drive it fully onto the splines using a metal tube (photo). The gear may be pre-heated as the race in paragraph 9 to ease installation.
11 Locate the 5th gear needle roller bearings on the input shaft and lubricate them with gear oil.
12 Engage the 5th selector fork with the synchro sleeve on the 5th gear and synchro unit, then locate the assembly over the input shaft and 5th/reverse selector rod (photo).
13 Fit the 5th synchro-ring to the synchroniser, making sure that the slots are aligned with the keys (photo).
14 Fit the clutch member and drive it fully onto the splines using a metal tube (photo). The member can if necessary be pre-heated to 120°C (248°F) to ease the installation.
15 Locate a new gasket on the final drive housing (photo).
16 To prevent damage to the oil seal, wrap adhesive tape around the input shaft splines (photo). Lower the gear carrier onto the final drive housing and insert the bolts, together with the mounting bracket.
17 Drive in the dowel pins until flush, then tighten the bolts in diagonal sequence to the specified torque. Remove the adhesive tape.
18 Engage 5th gear by moving the synchro sleeve (ie leaving the 5th/reverse selector rod in neutral) and 1st gear by pulling out the 1st/2nd selector rod. Both the input and pinion shafts are now locked.
19 Fit and tighten the pinion shaft nut to the specified torque, and lock by punching the collar onto the shaft flat (photos). After tightening the nut, return the gears to neutral.
20 Align the holes, then drive the roll pin into the 5th gear selector fork and rod while supporting the rod with a block of wood.
21 Locate the 1st/2nd selector dog on its rod near its final position, but do not fit the roll pin at this stage.
22 Pull out the notched selector rod to engage 3rd gear, then insert the main selector rod by engaging the ends of the springs over the

20.2 Using a pen magnet to insert an interlock plunger

20.4 Fitting the reverse gear shaft and reverse gear

20.8A Locate the bearing on the pinion shaft ...

20.8B ... then drive it on with a metal tube

20.9 Installing the 5th gear inner race

20.10 Install the 5th driven gear

20.12 Installing the 5th gear and synchro unit together with its selector fork

20.13 Fitting the 5th gear synchro ring

20.14 Fitting the 5th gear clutch member

20.15 Locate a new gasket onto the final drive housing

20.16 Wrap adhesive tape around the input shaft splines to prevent damage to the oil seal

20.19A Fit the pinion shaft nut and ...

20.19B ... tighten to the specified torque ...

20.19C ... then secure by peening nut collar onto flat of shaft

20.22A Engage 3rd gear and fit the main selector rod ...

20.22B ... then engage neutral

20.26 Tighten the input shaft bolt

20.27 Fit a new cover plate to the gearshift housing

3rd/4th selector rod, locating the finger in the notch, and pushing the main selector rod into the bush. When fitted, push the 3rd/4th selector rod into neutral (photos).

23 Align the holes, then drive the roll pin into the 1st/2nd selector dog and rod while supporting the rod with a block of wood.

24 Locate a new gasket on the gear carrier, then lower the gearshift housing into position. If necessary, gently tap the inner race of the ball-bearing to locate it on the end of the input shaft.

25 Insert the bolts together with the brackets, having first applied sealing compound to the bolt threads. Using an Allen key, tighten the bolts in diagonal sequence.

26 Insert the bolt and thick washer in the end of the input shaft, and tighten to the specified torque while holding the shaft stationary using the method described in Section 13 paragraph 7 (photo).

27 Clean the recess then press in a new cover plate (photo).

28 If not fitted yet, lower the differential into the final drive housing. Clean the cover and housing mating faces and apply a little sealing compound to them. Locate the cover on the housing, then insert and tighten the bolts in diagonal sequence to the specified torque. Note that the magnet on the cover should be positioned at the bottom (photo).

29 Insert the drive flanges into each side of the differential, and tighten the bolts while holding the flanges stationary with a rod through one of the bolt holes (photo).

30 Refit the clutch release bearing and shaft, as described in Chapter 5.

31 Insert and tighten the reverse lamp switch and gear indicator switch (if applicable) and clip the wiring into position.

20.29 Tighten the drive flange bolt

32 Refill the gearbox with the recommended quality and quantity of oil.

21 Gearshift lever (013 and 093) – removal, refitting and adjustment

1 The procedure is basically the same as that described for the 014 gearbox in Section 11. However, after checking the return distance in 1st gear, engage 5th gear and move the gear lever to the right as far as possible. After releasing the gear lever, it should spring back 5 to 10 mm (0.20 to 0.39 in).

2 The return movement from both 1st and 5th gears should be approximately the same, but if not, slight adjustment can be made by moving the gear lever bearing plate sideways within the elongated holes. If this is insufficient, it will be necessary to either use a special VW gauge, or attempt a lengthy process of trial and error repositioning the shift rod on the shift finger.

3 If the reverse stop in the gear lever housing is disturbed, first set it to the basic position which is fully pressed down. If reverse gear cannot be engaged, move the stop up as required and secure it by tightening the bolts.

22 Gearshift linkage (013 and 093) – dismantling and reassembly

The procedure is identical to that for the 014 gearbox described in Section 12. However, the bottom of the gear lever is not cranked and can therefore be fitted either way round.

20.28 The magnet on the differential cover must be at the bottom of the gearbox

23 Fault diagnosis – manual gearbox and final drive

Symptom	Reason(s)
Ineffective synchromesh	Worn synchro rings
Jumps out of gear	Weak or broken detent spring
	Worn selector forks or dogs
	Weak synchro springs
	Worn synchro unit or gears
	Worn bearings or gears
Noisy operation	Worn bearings or gears
Difficult engagement of gears	Worn selector components
	Worn synchro units
	Clutch fault
	Gearbox input shaft spigot bearing seized in end of crankshaft
	Incorrect gearshift adjustment

Chapter 7 Automatic transmission and final drive

For modifications, and information applicable to later models, see Supplement at end of manual

Contents

Specifications

Type .... Three-speed planetary gearbox with hydrodynamic torque converter, final drive differential located between torque converter and gearbox

Identification code number
089 .... 1.6 and 1.8 litre engine models
087 .... 1.9 and 2.0 litre engine models

Application – code numbers/letters
089/KF (up to October 1982) .... Fitted to 1.6 litre engine models
089/KAD (from October 1982) .... Fitted to 1.8 litre engine models
089/KAL (from August 1983) .... Fitted to 1.6 litre engine models
089/KAH (from August 1983) .... Fitted to 1.6 and 1.8 litre engine models
087/RR (up to October 1982) .... Fitted to 1.9 litre engine models
087/RBA (October to December 1982) .... Fitted to 1.9 litre engine models
087/RBD (from December 1982) .... Fitted to 2.0 litre engine models

Ratios (089)

	089/KF	089/KAD	089/KAL	089/KAH
Final drive	3.73 : 1	3.25 to 1	3.42 to 1	3.25 to 1
1st	2.55 to 1	2.71 to 1	2.71 to 1	2.71 to 1
2nd	1.45 to 1	1.50 to 1	1.50 to 1	1.50 to 1
3rd	1.00 to 1	1.00 to 1	1.00 to 1	1.00 to 1
Reverse	2.46 to 1	2.43 to 1	2.43 to 1	2.43 to 1

Ratios (087)

	087/RR	087/RBA	087/RBD	087/RBH
Final drive	3.45 to 1	3.25 to 1	3.25 to 1	3.45 to 1
1st	2.55 to 1	2.71 to 1	2.71 to 1	2.71 to 1
2nd	1.45 to 1	1.50 to 1	1.50 to 1	1.50 to 1
3rd	1.00 to 1	1.00 to 1	1.00 to 1	1.00 to 1
Reverse	2.46 to 1	2.43 to 1	2.45 to 1	2.45 to 1

Lubrication
Transmission fluid type/specification .... Dexron type ATF (Duckhams D-Matic)
Final drive oil type/specification .... Hypoid gear oil, viscosity SAE 90, to API-GL5, MIL-L-2105B (Duckhams Hypoid 90S)

Lubricant capacity

	Total	Service
089 and 087 gearbox	6 litre (10.6 Imp pt)	3 litre (5.3 Imp pt)
089 final drive	0.75 litre (1.3 Imp pt)	
087 final drive	1.0 litre (1.8 Imp pt)	

Torque converter

	089	087
Maximum diameter of bush	34.25 mm (1.35 in)	34.12 mm (1.34 in)
Maximum out-of-round of bush	0.03 mm (0.001 in)	0.03 mm (0.001 in)

Torque wrench settings

	Nm	lbf ft
Torque converter to driveplate	30	22
Gearbox to engine	55	41
Mounting to body	40	30
Mounting to gearbox	55	41
Gearbox to final drive housing	30	22
Oil pan	20	15
Strainer cover	3	2
Selector cable clamp nut	8	6
Selector bracket nuts	15	11

1 General description

The automatic transmission consists of three main assemblies, these being being the torque converter, which is directly coupled to the engine; the final drive unit which incorporates the differential assembly; and the planetary gearbox with its hydraulically operated multi-disc clutches and brake bands. The gearbox also houses a rear mounted oil pump, which is coupled to the torque converter impeller, and this pump supplies automatic transmission fluid to the planetary gears, hydraulic controls and torque converter. The fluid performs a triple function by lubricating the moving parts, cooling the automatic transmission system and providing a torque transfer medium. The final drive lubrication is separate from the transmission lubrication system, unlike the manual gearbox where the final drive shares a common lubrication system.

The torque converter is a sealed unit which cannot be dismantled. It is bolted to the crankshaft driveplate and replaces the clutch found on an engine with manual transmission.

The gearbox is of the planetary type with epicyclic gear trains operated by brakes and clutches through a hydraulic control system. The correct gear is selected by a combination of three control signals; a manual valve operated by the gearshift cable, a manual valve operated by the accelerator pedal, and a governor to control hydraulic pressure. The gearshift cable and selector lever allow the driver to select a specific gear and override the automatic control, if desired.

087 ... ...

Fig. 7.1 The 087 type automatic transmission unit showing identification mark location (Sec 1)

Fig. 7.2 The 089 type automatic transmission unit showing identification mark location (Sec 1)

The accelerator control determines the correct gear for the desired rate of acceleration, and the governor determines the correct gear in relation to engine speed.

Because of the need for special test equipment, the complexity of some of the parts and the need for scrupulous cleanliness when servicing automatic transmissions, the amount which the owner can do is limited, but those operations which can reasonably be carried out are detailed in the following Sections. Repairs to the final drive differential are also not recommended.

The automatic transmission has three forward speeds and one reverse, controlled by a six position lever with the following positions:

P	Park
R	Reverse
N	Neutral
D	Drive
2	Low
1	Low

The selector lever has a push button which must be depressed when selecting the following positions:

From	P to R
	R to P
	N to R
	2 to 1

The selector lever can be moved freely between all other positions. If the lever is set to positions D or 2, the automatic transmission changes gears automatically.

Position D

This position is for normal driving, and once selected the three forward gears engage automatically throughout the speed range from zero to top speed.

Position 2

With the lever in this position, the two lower gears will engage automatically, but the highest gear will not engage. For this reason position 2 should only be selected when the speed of the car is below 70 mph (110 kph). Selecting Position 2 will make use of the engine's braking effect and the actual change can be made without letting up the accelerator pedal.

Position 1

This position is rarely needed but can be used for ascending or descending steep hills. The transmission remains in the lowest gear and Position 1 should only be selected when the car speed is below 40 mph (64 kph).

Reverse

Reverse must only be selected when the car is absolutely stationary and with the engine running at idling speed.

Park

In the park position the transmission is locked mechanically by the engagement of a pawl. This position must only be selected when the car is absolutely stationary, otherwise the transmission will be damaged.

2 Automatic transmission – precautions and maintenance

1 If the car is being towed, the ignition key must be inserted so that the steering wheel is not locked and the gear selector must be in *Neutral*. Because the lubrication of the transmission is limited when the engine is not running, the car must not be towed for more than 30 miles (48 km), or at a speed greater than 30 mph (48 kph) unless the front wheels of the car are lifted clear of the road.

2 Routine maintenance consists of checking the final drive oil level and the automatic transmission fluid level every 10 000 miles (15 000 km) or 12 months, whichever occurs first. When checking the final drive oil level, if the level is found to be too high, fluid may be leaking from the gearbox or hydraulic circuit. It is advisable to check the automatic transmission fluid at periodic intervals between those specified above to ensure that the correct level is maintained.

3 Checking the automatic transmission fluid level should be carried out with the engine warm and running at idling speed with the selector

lever in *Neutral* and the handbrake applied. Withdraw the dipstick and wipe it with a piece of clean, lint-free rag. It is important that the rag is both clean and lint-free, because even a tiny speck of dirt can damage or cause a malfunction of the transmission. The level of fluid is satisfactory anywhere between the two marks on the dipstick, but either too high, or too low a level must be avoided. The difference between the marks is equivalent to 0.4 litre (0.7 Imp pt). If necessary, top up the level through the dipstick tube using the specified fluid – see *'Recommended lubricants and fluids'* at the beginning of this manual.

4   The automatic transmission fluid must be drained and renewed at 30 000 miles (45 000 km) or every three years, whichever occurs first, see Section 3. Note that the final drive oil does not need changing.

3   Automatic transmission fluid – draining and refilling

1   This job should not be attempted unless clean, dust free conditions can be achieved.
2   With the car standing on level ground, place a container of at least six pints capacity beneath the oil pan of the transmission. For working room beneath the car, jack it up and support it with axle stands, or use car ramps.
3   Unscrew the union nut securing the dipstick tube to the oil pan, pull out the tube and allow the fluid to drain out. **Note:** *Do not drive or tow the vehicle when there is no oil in the transmission!*
4   Remove the retaining screws and withdraw the oil pan. Remove the gasket (Figure 7.3).
5   Remove the screws and withdraw the cover, strainer, and gasket.
6   Clean the pan and strainer with methylated spirit and allow to dry.
7   Refit the strainer, cover and pan in reverse order using new gaskets and tightening the screws to the specified torque.
8   Insert the dipstick and tighten the union nut.
9   Wipe round the top of the dipstick tube, then remove the dipstick.
10   With the car on level ground, fill the transmission with the correct quantity and grade of fluid, using a clean funnel if necessary.
11   Start the engine and with the handbrake applied, select every gear position once. With the engine idling and the transmission in *Neutral*, check the level of the fluid on the dipstick, and if necessary top up to the lower mark.
12   Road test the vehicle until the engine is at normal temperature, then again check the fluid level and top up if necessary. The amount of fluid which must be added to raise the level from the lower mark to the upper mark on the dipstick is about half a pint (0.4 litre). Do not overfill the transmission, because an excess of fluid will upset its operation and any excess fluid will have to be drained.

4   Automatic transmission type 089 – removal and refitting

1   Position the car over an inspection pit or on car ramps. Apply the handbrake.
2   Disconnect the battery negative lead.
3   Support the front of the engine using a hoist or support bar. Fig. 7.4 shows the VW tool specially designed for the job, but it should be relatively easy to make a support bar yourself along similar lines, if you have decided not to use a hoist.
4   Unscrew and remove the upper engine-to-transmission securing bolts.
5   Unscrew and remove the front engine support to the front body member.
6   Remove the starter motor as described in Chapter 10.
7   Unscrew the three torque converter-to-driveplate bolts while holding the starter ring gear stationary with a screwdriver. It will be necessary to rotate the engine to position the bolts in the starter aperture, using a socket on the crankshaft pulley bolt (Figure 7.5).
8   Detach and remove the converter cover plate.
9   Unscrew the nut and disconnect the speedometer cable from the transmission. Also release the cable from the clip on the dipstick tube, where applicable.
10   Disconnect the driveshafts from the transmission, with reference to Chapter 8. For additional working room it is necessary to remove one or both driveshafts, or alternatively tie them to one side.
11   Index mark the relative positions of the left-hand steering balljoint and wishbone (suspension arm), then detach the balljoint and fit a suitable spacer plate to them as shown in Figure 7.6.
12   Unbolt and disconnect the exhaust pipe location bracket from the

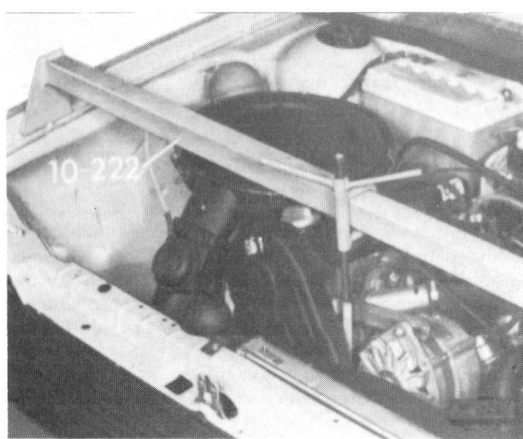

Fig. 7.4 Using a special bar to support the front of the engine – typical (Sec 4)

Fig. 7.3 Automatic transmission oil pan and strainer components (Sec 3)

Fig. 7.5 A torque converter to driveplate bolt viewed through the starter motor aperture (Sec 4) transmission. For additional working area, unbolt and remove the front exhaust pipe with reference to Chapter 3.

13 Unbolt and remove the selector lever cable bracket, Figure 7.7.

14 Unhook the return spring then withdraw the selector lever cable securing clip and detach the cable.

15 Disconnect the pedal cable support bracket from the transmission then detach the pedal cable.

16 Unscrew the retaining bolt and remove the bonded rubber mounting (Figure 7.8).

Fig. 7.6 Mark relative positions and detach the balljoint from the suspension wishbone and fit spacer plate (Sec 4)

Fig. 7.7 Selector lever cable bracket (Sec 4)

Fig. 7.8 Bonded rubber mounting and retaining bolt (arrowed) (Sec 4)

17 Raise the engine using the support bar so that the gearbox is slightly lowered allowing easier removal and subsequent refitting.

18 Unscrew the two retaining bolts, withdraw the throttle bracket and detach the cable (Figure 7.9).

19 Position a trolley jack or suitable support under the transmission to take its weight. Locate a flat piece of wood between the jack saddle and transmission oil pan to spread the load and prevent damage to the pan.

20 Unscrew and remove the lower engine-to-transmission retaining bolts.

21 With the help of an assistant, withdraw the transmission from the engine, making sure that the torque converter remains fully engaged with the transmission splines.

22 Lower the transmission and remove it from under the car.

Fig. 7.9 Throttle cable and bracket securing bolts (arrowed) (Sec 4)

Fig. 7.10 Diagram showing correctly seated torque converter (Sec 4)

a = 10 mm (0.4 in)

23 Refitting is a reversal of removal, but make sure that the torque converter is correctly fitted. If the pump shaft is correctly engaged, the boss of the torque converter will be about 10 mm (0.4 in) from the open end of the bellhousing (Fig. 7.10). If the boss of the torque converter is found to be flush with the open end of the bellhousing (Fig. 7.11) it is likely that the pump shaft has pulled out of the pump driveplate splines. *The pump driveplate will be destroyed if the gearbox is bolted to the engine with the pump shaft in this position.* Refill the cooling system with reference to Chapter 2. Reconnect the driveshafts with reference to Chapter 8 and the starter with reference to Chapter 10. If necessary adjust the accelerator and selector cables as described in Sections 10 and 11.

Fig. 7.11 Diagram showing incorrectly seated torque converter with pump shaft disengaged from pump driveplate splines (A) (Sec 4)

Fig. 7.13 Front subframe mounting bolts (Sec 5)

hoses are securely located and top up the cooling system as described in Chapter 3.

5 Automatic transmission type 087 – removal and refitting

1   Proceed as described in paragraphs 1 to 4 in the previous Section.
2   Drain the cooling system as described in Chapter 2 then disconnect the hoses from the oil (ATF) cooler.
3   Unscrew and remove the engine support bolts.
4   Disconnect the accelerator cable support bracket from the transmission then detach the accelerator cable.
5   Disconnect and remove the throttle pushrod.
6   Disconnect the automatic transmission fluid filler tube from the oil pan.
7   Unbolt and disconnect the selector lever cable bracket.
8   Unhook the return spring, detach the selector lever cable retainer and disconnect the cable.
9   Remove the right-hand side deflector plate.
10 Proceed as described in paragraphs 6, 7, 9 and 10 in the previous Section.
11 Unscrew the hose clips then pull free the hoses from the ATF cooler connections shown in Figure 7.12.
12 Unscrew and remove the front subframe bolts (Figure 7.13).
13 Remove the retaining bolts and detach the bonded rubber transmission mounting (see Figure 7.8).
14 Proceed as described in paragraphs 19 to 22 in the previous Section to remove the transmission.
15 Refit the transmission in the reverse order of removal, referring to paragraphs 23 and 24 in the previous Section.
16 In addition, on completion check that the transmission oil cooler

6 Torque converter – checking and draining

1   The torque converter is a welded unit and if it is faulty the complete unit must be replaced. Only the bush can be renewed.
2   Examine the bush for signs of scoring and wear. To check for wear requires an internal micrometer or dial gauge; if one is available measure the bore diameter to see if it exceeds the wear limit given in the Specifications.
3   To remove the bush requires a commercial extractor and a slide hammer. After fitting a new bush, its diameter must be between the limits given; if not the bush must be removed and another one fitted. For this reason the job is really one for a VW agent.
4   Check that the cooling vanes on the converter are secure.
5   Fit the turbine shaft into the converter and check that the turbine turns freely.
6   If the fluid was dirty when drained from the oil pan, drain the fluid from the torque converter before the automatic transmission is refitted.
7   Have ready a container of about half a gallon (2 litres) capacity, a washing-up liquid bottle and a piece of plastic tubing of not more than 8 mm (0.32 in) outside diameter.
8   Put the torque converter on the bench and support it so that it is angled slightly.
9   Cut one end of the plastic tube at an angle so that the end of the tube will not be blocked if it comes against a flat surface and push this end into the torque converter hub until it touches the bottom.
10 Connect the spout of the washing up liquid bottle to the other end of the tube, hold the bottle below the level of the torque converter and squeeze the bottle. As the bottle expands again, fluid will be sucked into it; as soon as the fluid begins to syphon, pull the tube end off the bottle and rest the tube end in the larger container. Syphon as much fluid as possible from the torque converter. On reassembly and installation, the converter will fill with fluid as soon as the engine is started.

7 Automatic transmission – dismantling and reassembly

1   The gearbox may be separated from the final drive housing and the governor may be removed, but dismantling of the gearbox is not recommended, owing to the number of specialised tools and repair techniques required.
2   With the gearbox on the bench, pull out the torque converter if not already removed.
3   Unscrew and remove the fluid filler pipe if the fluid has been drained.
4   Remove the four nuts and washers which secure the gearbox to the final drive housing and prise away the gearbox. Remove the sealing ring, gasket and the shim (Figure 7.16).

Fig. 7.12 Coolant hoses location on the oil cooler (Sec 5)

Fig. 7.14 Checking the torque converter bush internal diameter with a dial gauge (Sec 6)

Fig. 7.15 Syphoning fluid from the torque converter (Sec 6)

ATF pump shaft

Turbine shaft

O ring

Gasket

Governor

Final drive

Torque converter oil seal

Torque converter

Oil filler tube

Gearbox

Shim

Fig. 7.16 The final drive housing separated from the transmission – 087 transmission shown (Sec 7)

Fig. 7.17 Sealing rings (arrowed) must be seated correctly on the turbine shaft (Sec 7)

5   With the gearbox removed, the turbine shaft and pump shaft can be pulled out and examined. When examining the turbine shaft, check that the sealing rings (Fig. 7.17) are seated properly.

6   Both the pump shaft and the turbine shaft are available in various lengths, so it is important to take the old shaft when obtaining a new one.

7   When reassembling be sure to refit the shim to the front of the gearbox and use a new gasket and sealing ring. Make sure that the pump shaft is inserted properly (see Section 4).

8   Final drive housing – servicing

1   The removal and dismantling of the differential and final drive assembly is not recommended, owing to the number of specialised tools and repair techniques required.

2   Removal of the driveshaft flanges and renewal of the oil seals is similar to the procedure used for the manual gearbox described in Chapter 6.

3   The torque converter oil seal may be renewed as follows. Using the access holes in the side of the final drive housing, drive off the old seal with a hammer and chisel (Fig. 7.18). Fit a new seal over the boss, taking care to keep the seal square, and then carefully drive it on fully with a hammer and metal tube. Note that the seal is made of very soft material and should *not* be cleaned with liquid solvents.

Fig. 7.18 Removing the torque converter oil seal from the final drive housing (Sec 8)

9   Governor – removal, overhaul and refitting

1   The governor assembly is attached to the final drive housing by two bolts with spring and plain washers. Remove the bolts and washers and withdraw the governor assembly and cover.

2   Remove the two bolts which pass through the assembly and remove the governor shaft, the balance weight, transfer plate and filter (if fitted).

3   If the thrust plate is scored, fit a new one.

4   If the governor shaft is worn, a new shaft can be fitted, but the balance weight must not be changed.

5   Remove the circlip from the end of the pin and remove the centrifugal weight, the valve, the spring and the spring cup.

6   Clean all the parts thoroughly and lubricate them with transmission fluid before reassembly.

7   When fitting the transfer plate make sure that it is fitted in the position shown in Fig. 7.19. As the filter is no longer fitted to new units, discard it where applicable.

8   When refitting the governor, ensure that the ring seal inside the cover is in place and in good condition.

Fig. 7.19 Exploded view of the governor (Sec 9)

10 Accelerator pedal and linkage – adjustment

1   The accelerator linkage must be adjusted so that the operating lever on the gearbox is at its idle position when the throttle is closed. If the adjustment is incorrect the shaft speeds will be too high when the throttle is partially open and the main pressure will be too high when the engine is idling.

089 transmission

2   Run the engine to normal operating temperature to ensure that the choke is fully open. Remove the air cleaner unit as described in Chapter 3.
3   Check that the throttle valve is closed and in its idling position.
4   Loosen both locknuts at the cable bracket on the engine, then pull the cable ferrule away from the engine to eliminate all play and tighten the locknuts in this position.
5   Working inside the car, unscrew and remove the accelerator pedal stop and spacer.
6   Make up a distance piece as shown in Fig. 7.21 using a 135 mm (5.32 in) M8 bolt with two nuts fitted and locked in the position shown in Figure 7.22.
7   Screw the distance piece bolt into the accelerator pedal stop nut (E in Figure 7.20).
8   Loosen the locknut on the accelerator pedal cable bracket on the transmission, and turn the knurled adjuster so that the bottom of the accelerator pedal just contacts the distance piece – do not confuse the pedal rod with the bottom of the pedal. Check that the lever on the transmission is still in its idle position.
9   Remove the distance piece and refit the pedal stop, spacer and switch, as applicable.

10   Check the adjustment by depressing the accelerator pedal to the full throttle position (ie until resistance is felt). The throttle valve at the engine must be fully open without the cable kickdown spring being compressed. Now depress the accelerator pedal fully onto the stop – the kickdown spring must be compressed by 8 mm (0.31 in) on models with the 2E2 carburettor or 10 to 11 mm (0.40 to 0.43 in) on other models and the lever on the transmission must contact the kickdown stop.

087 transmission

11   Run the engine to normal operating temperature to ensure that the choke is fully open. Remove the air cleaner unit as described in Chapter 3.
12   Check that the ball and socket linkage rod is not seized.
13   Referring to Figure 7.21, remove the pushrod ball socket retainer and disconnect the pushrod from the relay lever.
14   Check that the throttle valve lever is in the idle position (against the stop), then adjust the threaded end of the pullrod (A) so that the connecting lever touches the stop on the relay lever bracket, (arrowed).
15   Loosen off the clamp bolt on the transmission end of the pushrod (B) then reconnect and secure the pushrod to the relay lever.
16   Move the operating lever (transmission end) to its throttle closed position and the carburettor throttle lever to the idle position and then retighten the clamp bolt on the pushrod.
17   Working within the vehicle, unscrew and remove the pedal stop and packing.
18   Make up a distance piece as shown in Figure 7.22 using a 130 mm (5.1 in) M8 bolt with two nuts set and locked together at distance (a). Screw the distance bolt into position in the pedal stop nut.
19   Loosen the locknut on the accelerator pedal cable bracket on the transmission, and turn the knurled adjuster so that the bottom of the

Fig. 7.20 Accelerator pedal and linkage on the 089 transmission (Sec 10)

A   Cable to carburettor linkage and adjuster locknuts (1 and 2)
B   Accelerator pedal cable and adjuster nut (3)
C   Operating lever

D   Spring
E   Distance piece bolt location

Fig. 7.21 Accelerator pedal and linkage on the 087 transmission (Sec 10)

A	Pullrod adjuster	D	Pedal cable adjuster nut	2	Throttle valve lever	5	Pushrod
B	Pushrod adjuster screw	E	Distance piece bolt location	3	Lever	6	Relay bracket
C	Spring	1	Pullrod	4	Pushrod lever	7	Operating lever

A   Pullrod adjuster
B   Pushrod adjuster screw
C   Spring

D   Pedal cable adjuster nut
E   Distance piece bolt location
1   Pullrod

2   Throttle valve lever
3   Lever
4   Pushrod lever

5   Pushrod
6   Relay bracket
7   Operating lever

Fig. 7.22 Distance piece made from bolt required for accelerator/pedal linkage adjustment according to transmission type (Sec 10)

089 transmission: bolt length 135 mm (5.3 in) with nuts set at distance (a) to = 124 mm (4.8 in)
087 transmission: bolt length 130 mm (5.1 in) with nuts set at distance (a) to = 119 mm (4.6 in)

accelerator pedal just contacts the distance piece – do not confuse the pedal rod with the bottom of the pedal. Check that the lever on the transmission is still in its idle position.
20 Remove the distance piece and refit the pedal stop and spacer.
21 Check the adjustment by depressing the accelerator pedal to the full throttle position (ie until resistance is felt). The throttle valve at the

engine must be fully open. Now depress the accelerator pedal fully onto the stop – the transmission lever must contact the kickdown stop.

11 Selector lever and cable – removal, refitting and adjustment

1 Disconnect the battery negative lead.
2 Remove the grub screw and detach the knob from the selector lever (Figure 7.23).
3 Prise off the cover together with the blanking strip or brushes.
4 Remove the screws and withdraw the console.
5 Disconnect the wiring from the starter inhibitor switch and selector illumination bulb.
6 Unscrew the cable clamp nut, and also unscrew the nut from the floor bracket. Pull the cable clear.
7 Unscrew the nuts and remove the bracket and lever assembly from the floor.
8 Unbolt the cable bracket from the transmission, then extract the circlip and remove the cable end from the lever. Withdraw the cable from under the car.
9 Refitting is a reversal of removal, but before fitting the console

Fig. 7.23 Selector lever and cable components for 087 and 089
automatic transmissions (Sec 11)

Grub screw

Cover

Console

Grub screw

Contact bridge

Contact plate

Selector cable

Cable clamp

Bracket

O ring

Boot

Circlip

adjust the cable as follows. Move the selector lever fully forwards to the P (park) position. Loosen the cable clamp nut, then move the lever on the transmission fully rearwards to the P (park) position. Tighten the cable clamp nut to the specified torque. Lightly lubricate the selector lever and cable pivots with engine oil.

12 Inhibitor switch – removal, refitting and adjustment

1   Disconnect the battery earth lead.

2   Remove the grub screw and detach the knob from the selector lever.
3   Prise off the cover together with the blanking strip or brushes.
4   Remove the screws and withdraw the console.
5   Disconnect the wiring from the starter inhibitor switch then remove the screws and withdraw the switch.
6   Refitting is a reversal of removal, but before fitting the console check that it is only possible to start the engine with the selector lever in positions N (neutral) or P (park). If necessary, reposition the switch within the elongated screw holes.

13 Fault diagnosis – automatic transmission and final drive

Symptom	Reason(s)
No drive in any gear	Fluid level too low
Erratic drive in forward gears	Fluid level too low Dirty filter
Gear changes at above normal speed	Accelerator linkage adjustment incorrect Dirt in governor
Gear changes at below normal speeds	Dirt in governor
Gear engagement jerky	Idle speed too high
Gear engagement delayed on upshift	Fluid level too low Accelerator linkage adjustment incorrect
Kickdown does not operate	Accelerator linkage adjustment incorrect
Fluid dirty or discoloured	Brake bands and clutches wearing
Parking lock not effective	Selector lever out of adjustment Parking lock defective

Chapter 8 Driveshafts

Contents

Specifications

Type ....
Double constant velocity (CV) joint, tubular driveshafts except on automatic transmission models where the right-hand driveshaft is solid

Shaft length

	Right-hand	Left-hand
Manual gearbox 014 and 013	530 mm (20.866 in)	530 mm (20.866 in)
Manual gearbox 093 (pre January 1983)	498.5 mm (19.625 in)	544.1 mm (21.421 in)
Manual gearbox 093 (from January 1983)	496.0 mm (19.53 in)	541.6 mm (21.32 in)
Automatic gearbox 089	492.2 mm (19.38 in)	589.5 mm (23.21 in)
Automatic gearbox 087	483.9 mm (19.05 in)	583.0 mm (22.95 in)
Automatic gearbox 087	476.7 mm (18.77 in)	574.5 mm (22.62 in)

CV joint lubricant ....
VAG G6 grease

Torque wrench settings

	Nm	lbf ft
Inner CV joint to flange	45	33
Driveshaft nut	230	170

---

1 General description and maintenance

Drive is transmitted from the splined final drive differential gears and drive flanges to the inner constant velocity (CV) joints. The driveshafts are either tubular or solid, as given in the Specifications, and are splined at each end to the CV joint hubs. The outer CV joints incorporate splined shafts which are attached to the front wheel hubs.

The driveshaft joints are sealed and require no maintenance apart from checking the rubber boots at the specified routine maintenance intervals for any sign of leakage or damage, in which case they must be renewed.

If the joints are suspected of excessive wear, noticeable when changing from acceleration to overrun and vice versa, the shafts should be removed and the joints dismantled to inspect for wear or damage, and overhauled or renewed as necessary.

2 Driveshafts – removal and refitting

1 Prise the hub cap from the centre of the roadwheel.
2 Unscrew the driveshaft nut. *This is tightened to a very high torque and no attempt to loosen it must be made unless the full weight of the car is on the roadwheels.*
3 Loosen the four bolts securing the roadwheel.
4 Jack the car and support the car securely on stands, or wood blocks.
5 Remove the roadwheel.

6 Using a socket wrench, remove the bolts from the inner driveshaft coupling and separate the driveshaft from the gearbox drive flange. Note the location of the bolt lock plates (photos).

2.6A Driveshaft inner joint coupling bolts (arrowed)

2.6B Removing the bolts and lock plates from the driveshaft inner joint coupling

Fig. 8.1 Disconnect the front suspension balljoint from the suspension wishbone arm (Sec 2)

7   On manual transmission models it is necessary to disconnect the right-hand side front suspension balljoint from the suspension wishbone. On automatic transmission models it will be necessary to disconnect both the right and left-hand side balljoints from the wishbones. To do this first mark the exact position of the balljoint on the wishbone – this is important as the wheel camber setting is adjusted by moving the balljoint. Unscrew the nuts and release the balljoint.
8   Using a hub puller, press the driveshaft out of the front wheel hub, then withdraw the driveshaft.
9   Clean the splined end of the driveshaft and the wheel hub.
10 Refitting is a reversal of the removal procedure.
11 Tighten the nuts and bolts to the specified torque. If a suitable torque wrench is not available to tighten the driveshaft nut, tighten the nut firmly, then take the car to a VW agent for final tightening – the front wheel camber can also be checked at the same time.

3   Driveshafts – overhaul

1   With the driveshaft removed as described in the preceding Section, remove the two clamps on the rubber boot at the inner end of the shaft and pull the boot down the shaft and off the coupling.

Fig. 8.2 Exploded view of the driveshaft (Sec 3)

2   Remove the circlip from the end of the shaft, and using a suitable drift, remove the protective cap from the outer ring.
3   Support the inner joint, then press the driveshaft out. Remove the dished washer noting its fitted direction.
4   Remove the two clamps from the outer joint boot and pull the boot down the shaft.

Fig. 8.3 Outer CV joint removal from shaft using soft-faced hammer (Sec 3)

Fig. 8.5 Arrange hub and cage as shown to remove the balls (Sec 3)

Fig. 8.6 Align rectangular openings in cage with housing to remove (Sec 3)

5   To release the hub from the circlip, strike the inner face of the hub outer ring with a soft face mallet, (Fig. 8.3).
6   Withdraw the outer joint from the driveshaft together with the spacer and dished washer.
7   Before starting to dismantle the outer joint, mark the position of the hub in relation to the cage and housing. Because the parts are hardened this mark will either have to be done with a grinding stone, or with paint.
8   Swivel the hub and cage and take out the balls one at a time (Fig. 8.5).
9   Turn the cage until the two rectangular openings align with the housing and then remove the cage and hub (Fig. 8.6).
10 Turn the hub until one segment can be pushed into one of the rectangular openings in the cage and then swivel the hub out of the cage (Fig. 8.7). The parts of the joint make up a matched set and no individual parts can be replaced. If there is excessive play in the joint which is noticeable when changing from acceleration to overrun, or vice versa, a new joint must be fitted, but do not renew a joint because the parts have been polished by wear and the track of the balls is clearly visible.
11 When reassembling the joint, clean off all the old grease and use a new circlip, rubber boot and clips. Use only the special coupling grease, recommended by VW for packing the joint — see Specifications.
12 Press half a sachet of grease (45 g, 1.6 oz) into the joint and then fit the cage and hub into the housing, ensuring that it will be possible

Fig. 8.4 Cross-section view of the outer joint (Sec 3)

1   Circlip
2   Spacer
3   Dished washer

Fig. 8.7 Outer CV joint hub removal from cage (Sec 3)

to line up the mating marks of the hub, cage, and housing after the balls have been inserted.
13 Press the balls into the hub from alternate sides; when all six have been inserted check that the mating marks on the hub, cage and housing are aligned.
14 Fit a new circlip into the groove of the hub then squeeze the

remainder of the grease into the joint so that the total amount is 90 g (3.2 oz).

15 The inner joint is dismantled in a similar way. Pivot the hub and cage and press them out of the housing as shown in Fig. 8.8.

16 Press the balls out of the cage, then align two grooves and remove the hub from the cage (Fig. 8.9).

17 When reassembling the joint, press half of the charge of grease into each side of the joint. Note that the chamfer on the splined hub must be on the larger diameter side of the outer ring. It will be necessary to pivot the joint hub when reassembling in order to align the balls with the grooves (Fig. 8.10).

18 Check the operation of the inner joint unit when assembled by moving the hub through its full axial range by hand.

19 It is advisable to fit new rubber boots to the shaft; a defective boot will soon lead to the need to fit a new joint due to wear caused by grit entering the joint. Fit the boots to the shaft and put any residual grease into the boots.

20 Fit the dished washer to the inner end of the driveshaft and locate the protective cap on the boot. Note that the concave side of the dished washer must face the joint (Fig. 8.11). On solid driveshaft models the dished washer is splined on its inner diameter.

21 Press the inner joint onto the end of the driveshaft and secure it with a new circlip.

22 Tap the protective cap onto the outer ring.

Fig. 8.10 Reassembling the inner joint (Sec 3)

Fig. 8.8 Inner CV joint hub and cage removal (Sec 3)

Fig. 8.11 Correct location of the dished washer on the driveshaft inner end (Sec 3)

Fig. 8.9 Removing the inner joint hub from cage (arrows indicate grooves) (Sec 3)

Fig. 8.12 Check for deformity in the rubber boot on reassembly (Sec 3)

23 Locate the dished washer and spacer on the outer end of the driveshaft, and check that the retaining circlip is located in the shaft groove.

24 Using a mallet, drive the outer joint onto the driveshaft until the circlip engages the groove.

25 Fit new clamps to each end of the rubber boots, locate the boots over the joints, and tighten the clamps. If necessary the crimped type clamps can be replaced by plastic, ratchet type.

26 When the rubber boots are secured check that they are not deformed. An inward fold of the boot can be caused by a vacuum when fitting and can be relieved by lifting the small diameter (shaft end) of the boot (Fig. 8.12).

4 Fault diagnosis – driveshafts

Symptom	Reason(s)
Vibration and noise on lock	Worn driveshaft joints
Noise on taking up drive or between acceleration and overrun	Worn driveshaft joints Worn front wheel hub and driveshaft splines Loose driveshaft bolts or nut

Chapter 9 Braking system

Contents

Specifications

System type ....

Four wheel hydraulic, with discs on front, and drums on rear. Twin diagonally split hydraulic circuits with vacuum servo assistance. Self-adjusting rear brakes. Load sensitive rear brake pressure regulator on some models. Cable operated handbrake on rear wheels.

Disc brakes

Teves caliper
Disc thickness	10 mm (0.394 in)
Disc wear limit	8 mm (0.314 in)
Maximum run-out allowable	0.06 mm (0.002 in)
Pad thickness	10 mm (0.394 in)
Minimum pad thickness allowable (including backplate)	7 mm (0.276 in)

Mk II caliper
Disc thickness	12 mm (0.472 in)
Disc wear limit	10 mm (0.394 in)
Maximum run-out allowable	0.06 mm (0.002 in)
Minimum pad thickness allowable (including backplate)	7 mm (0.276 in)

Mk II caliper – 85 kW variant
Disc thickness	20 mm (0.787 in)
Disc wear limit	18 mm (0.708 in)
Maximum run-out allowable	0.06 mm (0.002 in)
Minimum pad thickness allowable (including backplate)	7 mm (0.276 in)

Drum brakes

	Four-cylinder manual gearbox models	All other models
Internal diameter	180 mm (7.087 in)	200 mm (7.874 in)
Wear limit	181 mm (7.126 in)	201 mm (7.913 in)
Drum radial run-out	0.05 mm (0.002 in)	0.05 mm (0.002 in)
Wheel cylinder diameter	14.29 mm (0.563 in)*	17.46 mm (0.688 in)
Brake lining minimum thickness	2.5 mm (0.098 in)	2.5 mm (0.098 in)

* 17.46 mm (0.688 in) on models fitted with pressure limiter

Brake master cylinder
Type ....
Brake fluid type ....

Torque wrench settings
Caliper or caliper bracket to wheel bearing housing bolts ....
Upper and lower caliper guide bolts (Mk II caliper) ....
Disc guard (splash) plate ....
Wheel bolts ....
Rear brake backplate ....
Servo to bearing bracket ....

ATE (Teves) or FAG (Schafer)
Hydraulic fluid to FMVSS 116 DOT 3 or DOT 4 (Duckhams Universal Brake and Clutch Fluid)

Nm	lbf ft
70	52
40	30
10	7
110	81
60	44
20	15

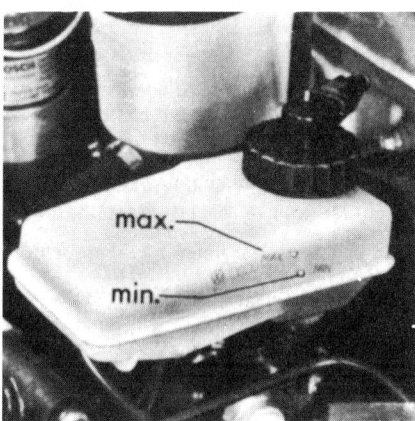

Fig. 9.1 Master cylinder fluid level to be maintained between the MAX and MIN markings (Sec 2)

1 General description

The braking system is hydraulic with servo-assistance, and there are disc brakes on the front wheels and drum brakes on the rear. The system has a tandem master cylinder which incorporates two completely independent braking circuits, each circuit operating a front wheel and the diagonally opposite rear wheel. This ensures that if one circuit fails, the car can still be brought to rest in a straight line, even though the braking distance will be greater.

Some models incorporate a brake pressure regulator, which limits the pressure applied to the rear brake cylinders to a proportion of that applied to the front, and so prevents the rear wheels from locking.

The rear brakes are self-adjusting and incorporate a wedged key which automatically adjusts the length of the brake shoe upper pushrod on each wheel.

The handbrake operates on the rear wheels only and on some models incorporates a switch which illuminates a warning light on the instrument panel – the same light also warns of low brake fluid level.

2 Maintenance – brake system

1 The brake fluid level should be checked every week – the reservoir is translucent and the fluid level should be between the MIN and MAX marks. If necessary, top up with the specified brake fluid (Figure 9.1). However, additional fluid will only be necessary if the hydraulic system is leaking, therefore the source of the leak must first be traced and rectified. Note that the level will drop slightly as the front disc pads wear, but in this case it is not necessary to top up the level.
2 Every 10 000 miles (15 000 km) or 12 months, if this occurs sooner, the hydraulic pipes and unions should be checked for chafing, leakage, cracks and corrosion. At the same time check the operation of the brake pressure regulator and check the disc pads and rear brake linings for wear. Also check the servo vacuum hose for condition and security.
3 Check the brake warning device for correct operation by switching the ignition on and releasing the handbrake. Now press the contact on the reservoir filler cap down and get an assistant to check that the handbrake and dual circuit warning lamp light up.
4 Renew the brake fluid every 2 years.

3 Disc pads – inspection and renewal

1 Pad thickness can be checked without removing the roadwheel. Turn the wheel until the brake pad is visible through one of the openings in the wheel rim.
2 With the aid of a torch to increase visibility, measure the thickness of each brake pad including its metal backplate and compare this with the minimum value given in the Specifications. A rough guide to the amount of life remaining in brake pads which are nearing their minimum is that the rate of wear is about 1 mm (0.039 in) for every 1000 km (620 miles) driving, (Figure 9.2 and 9.3).
3 If the brake pads are to be re-used, they must be refitted to the position from which they were taken. To ensure this, mark the pads before removing them.
4 First apply the handbrake, then jack up the front of the car and support it on axle stands. Remove the roadwheels.

Teves caliper
5 Extract the retaining spring, then use a punch to drive out the pad retaining pins (Figure 9.4).
6 Pull out the inner pad using a hooked instrument.
7 Press the floating caliper frame outwards to disengage the pad

Fig. 9.2 Check the disc pads for wear by measuring thickness (a) through one of the wheel rim apertures – Teves caliper (Sec 3)

Fig. 9.3 Disc pad thickness check (a) through one of the wheel rim apertures for the Mk II caliper (Sec 3)

Fig. 9.4 Remove the pad retaining pin (Teves caliper) (Sec 3)

from the projection on the caliper frame and then pull out the outer pad (Figure 9.5).

8   Using two pieces of wood, lever the piston back into the cylinder. While doing this check that brake fluid will not overflow from the reservoir, and if necessary use a flexible plastic bottle to extract some fluid. **Note**: *Brake fluid is poisonous, so no attempt should be made to siphon the fluid by mouth.*

9   Check that the piston cutaway is positioned at 20° to the horizontal (see Fig. 9.6) and, if necessary, rotate the piston as required.

Mk II caliper
10   Unhook and remove the pad retaining springs at the top and the bottom of the caliper (photo). Note that a later Mk II caliper is fitted from February 1984 in which the retaining springs are of the flat section type (Figures 9.7 and 9.8).

3.10 Early type Mk II caliper brake pad retaining spring

Fig. 9.5 Outer pad and locating projection on the Teves caliper (Sec 3)

Fig. 9.7 The later type Mk II caliper unit (Sec 3)

Fig. 9.6 Checking the piston position with a 20° gauge – arrow indicates forward rotation of disc (Sec 3)

Fig. 9.8 The later type Mk II caliper brake pads and retaining springs (Sec 3)

3.11A Unscrew the guide pins (early Mk II type shown) ...

3.11B ... and withdraw the caliper unit

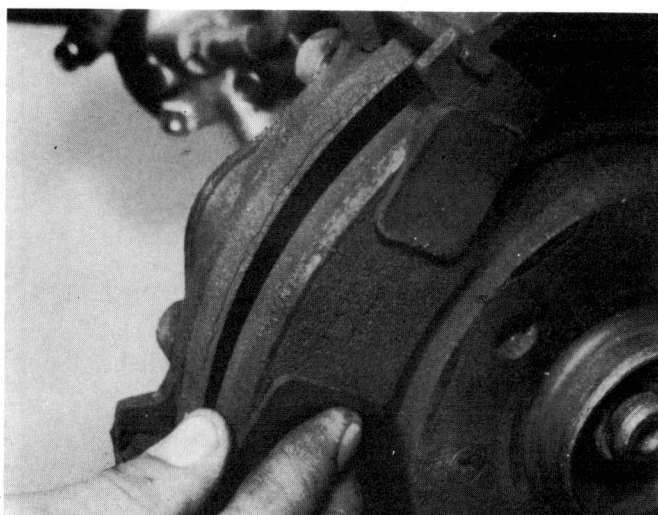

3.12 Remove the brake pads from the carrier (Mk II caliper)

11 Unscrew and remove the upper and lower caliper guide pins then withdraw the caliper unit (photos).
12 Remove the brake pads from the carrier noting fitted positions (photo).
13 Compress the piston back into the cylinder as described in paragraph 8.
14 The repair kit includes new caliper housing guide pins and these will differ according to type. The later type pins fitted to calipers from February 1984 on, consist of a socket head screw and pin guide sleeve (Figure 9.9).

Fig. 9.9 Socket-head screws and guide sleeves fitted to later Mk II calipers (Sec 3)

Teves and Mk II calipers
15 Brush the dust and dirt from the caliper, piston, disc and pads, but *do not inhale it, as it is injurious to health.* Scrape any scale or rust from the disc and pad backing plates.
16 Fitting the brake pads is a reversal of the removal procedure, but on the later Mk II type caliper locate the retaining springs onto the carrier prior to fitting the pads into position. Also on the later Mk II caliper type, as the caliper is fitted into position, simultaneously insert the guide pins (socket head screws) to ensure that the threads are in alignment. Fully fitting the caliper at this stage could mean that the retaining springs will get distorted later when fitting the pins, which in turn will give noisy braking.
17 On completion the brake pedal should be depressed firmly several times with the car stationary, so that the disc pads take up their normal running position. Also check and if necessary top up the brake fluid level in the reservoir.

4 Disc caliper – removal and refitting

1 Remove the disc pads, as described in Section 3.
2 Remove the brake fluid reservoir filler cap and tighten it down onto a piece of polythene sheeting placed over the reservoir filler hole in order to prevent the loss of fluid in the following procedure. Alternatively fit a brake hose clamp on the hydraulic hose attached to the caliper.
3 Loosen the hydraulic hose union, but do not attempt to unscrew it at this stage.

Teves caliper
4 Unscrew the two bolts securing the caliper to the suspension strut while supporting the caliper (Figure 9.10).
5 Unscrew the caliper from the hydraulic hose and plug the end of the hose.

Mk II caliper
6 The caliper unit can be removed in the same manner as that

Fig. 9.10 Teves caliper and associated components (Sec 4)

Fig. 9.11 The Mk II caliper and associated components (Sec 4)

Fig. 9.12 Exploded view of the Teves caliper (Sec 5)

described in paragraphs 10 and 11 in the previous Section. Do not allow the caliper to hang on the hydraulic hose (Figure 9.11).
7   Unscrew the caliper from the hydraulic hose and plug the end of the hose. The caliper is now free.
8   If necessary, unbolt the caliper bracket from the suspension strut.

Teves and MK II calipers
9   Refitting is a reversal of removal but the following special points concerning the caliper or caliper bracket retaining bolts should be noted.
10 New retaining bolts must always be used when refitting the caliper or caliper bracket, but note that on later models the hex-headed retaining bolts and lock washers have been superseded by flanged locking bolts (Fig. 9.13). Additionally, the bolt holes in the caliper have been provided with a 45° chamfer on their internal circumference to accept the new bolts. As only the flanged locking bolts are now supplied by VW parts stockists, it will be necessary to chamfer the bolt holes of early calipers to accept the flanged bolts. This can be done with a countersunk drill bit or suitable scraper. The earlier hex-headed bolts **must not** be used on calipers with chamfered bolt holes.
11 Ensure that all mating faces are clean when refitting and tighten the bolts and unions to the specified torque. Finally bleed the hydraulic system as described in Section 14.

5   Disc caliper — overhaul

1   Remove the caliper as described in the previous Section, then clean it externally taking care not to allow any foreign matter to enter the hydraulic hose aperture.

Teves caliper
2   Press the mounting frame off the floating frame by hand and separate the two frames.
3   Place a block of wood in the floating frame and drive out the cylinder assembly, using a soft metal drift (Figure 9.15).
4   Use a foot pump or a compressed air supply to blow the piston out of the cylinder, but support the cylinder with the piston facing downwards to avoid the risk of injury when the piston is ejected.
5   Use a blunt screwdriver to prise the seal out of the piston bore, taking great care not to scratch the bore of the cylinder.
6   Clean the caliper components thoroughly with methylated spirit and allow to dry.
7   Fit a new seal into the groove in the cylinder bore. Apply a thin coat of brake cylinder paste to the seal and to the cylinder. Then squeeze the piston into the cylinder using a vice fitted with soft jaws.
8   Rest the floating frame on the bench, then insert the brake cylinder and tap it fully into the frame.

Fig. 9.13 Brake caliper retaining bolts (Sec 4)

1   Later type flanged locking bolts   2   Early type hex-headed bolts

Fig. 9.14 Caliper chamfered bolt holes (arrowed) to accept later type flanged locking bolts (Sec 4)

Fig. 9.15 Removing the cylinder on the Teves caliper (Sec 5)

Fig. 9.17 Dust cap location on Mk II caliper piston (Sec 5)

Top — early type   *Bottom — later type*

Fig. 9.16 Installing the mounting frame on the Teves caliper
(Sec 5)

9   With the locating spring fitted to the mounting frame, press the
mounting frame onto the floating frame (Figure 9.16).
10 Set the piston cutaway 20° to the horizontal as described in
Section 3. The angle can be checked by making a simple gauge out of
card.

Mk II caliper

11 Use a foot pump, or a compressed air supply to blow the piston
out of the cylinder, but place a block of wood inside the frame to
prevent damage to the piston. Remove the dust cap.
12 Use a blunt screwdriver to prise the seal out of the piston bore,
taking great care not to scratch the bore of the cylinder.
13 Clean the caliper components thoroughly with methylated spirit
and allow to dry.
14 Fit a new seal into the groove in the cylinder bore. Apply a thin
coat of brake cylinder paste to the seal and to the cylinder.
15 Fit the dust cap on to the piston as shown in Fig 9.17, and then
offer the piston up to the cylinder and fit the sealing lip of the dust cap
into the groove of the cylinder bore, using a screwdriver. On later

models, the dust cap inner lip locates in the groove within the cylinder
housing.
16 Smear brake cylinder paste over the piston and then press the
piston into the cylinder until the outer lip of the dust cap springs into
place in the piston groove.
17 Check the guide pins, bolts and dust caps for condition and, if
necessary, renew them. The bolts are self-locking and the manufacturers recommend that they are renewed whenever they are removed.

---

6   Brake disc — examination, removal and refitting

---

1   Jack up the front of the car and support it on axle stands. Remove
the roadwheel.
2   Rotate the disc and examine it for deep scoring or grooving. Light
scoring is normal, but if excessive the disc should be removed and
renewed, or ground by a suitably qualified engineering works. Use a
micrometer in several positions to check the disc thickness.
3   To remove the brake disc first remove the caliper as described in
Section 4. However, do not disconnect the hydraulic hose — suspend
the caliper by wire from the coil spring making sure that the hydraulic
hose is not strained.
4   Remove the countersunk cross-head screw and withdraw the
brake disc from the hub.
5   Refitting is a reversal of removal, but make sure that the mating
faces of the hub and disc are clean.

Fig. 9.18 Exploded view of the Mk II caliper (Sec 5)

7.1 Brake shoe inspection aperture in rear brake backplate

7.7 Note position of brake shoes and springs prior to dismantling

7.8 Remove the rear brake shoe retaining springs

7   Rear brake shoes – inspection and renewal

1   The thickness of the rear brake linings can be checked without removing the brake drums. Remove the rubber plug which is above the handbrake cable entry on the brake backplate. Use a torch to increase visibility and check the thickness of friction material remaining on the brake shoes. If the amount remaining is close to the minimum given in the Specifications, a more thorough examination should be made by removing the brake drum (photo).
2   Chock the front wheels, then jack up the rear of the car and support it on axle stands. Remove the rear wheels and release the handbrake.
3   Remove the cap from the centre of the brake drum by tapping it on alternate sides with a screwdriver or blunt chisel.
4   Extract the split pin and remove the locking ring.
5   Unscrew the nut and remove the thrust washer (Figure 9.19).
6   Withdraw the brake drum, making sure that the outer wheel bearing does not fall out. If the brake drum binds on the shoes, insert a small screwdriver through a wheel bolt hole and lever up the wedged key in order to release the shoes.

7   Note the positon of the brake shoes and springs and mark the webs of the shoes, if necessary, to aid refitting (photo).
8   Using pliers, depress the spring retainer caps, turn them through 90° and remove them together with the springs (photo).
9   Prise the brake shoes away from the lower pivot support and then disengage the lower return spring.
10   Detach the handbrake cable from the lever.
11   Using suitable pliers, unhook the wedge spring and the upper return spring and remove the brake shoes.
12   To separate the pushrod from the brake shoe, clamp the pushrod in a vice and unhook the retaining spring (Figure 9.22). As they are separated note how the wedged key is located.
13   Brush the dust from the brake drum, brake shoes, and backplate, *but do not inhale it, as it is injurious to health.* Scrape any scale or rust from the drum.
14   Measure the brake shoe lining thickness. If worn down to the specified minimum amount, renew all four rear brake shoes.
15   Clean the brake backplate. If there are any signs of loss of grease from the rear hub bearings, the oil seal should be renewed with reference to Chapter 11. If hydraulic fluid is leaking from the wheel

Fig. 9.19 Rear brake drum and wheel bearing assembly components (Sec 7)

Fig. 9.20 Rear brake assembly components – 180 mm type (Sec 7)

Fig. 9.21 Rear brake assembly components – 200 mm type (Sec 7)

Fig. 9.22 Clamp the pushrod when separating from the brake shoe (Sec 7)

Fig. 9.23 Reconnecting the locating spring and brake shoe to the pushrod (Sec 7)

7.22 Rear brake self-adjusting wedged key and spring connection (arrowed)

8   Rear wheel cylinder – removal, overhaul and refitting

1   Remove the brake shoes, as described in Section 7.
2   Remove the brake fluid reservoir filler cap and place it to one side away from dirt and where it will not drip fluid onto the vehicle paintwork. Cover the master cylinder filler neck with a piece of clean polythene sheeting and secure by fastening in position around the filler neck with an elastic band. This will prevent excessive loss of fluid in the following procedure.
3   Loosen the brake pipe union on the rear of the wheel cylinder (photo).
4   Using an Allen key, unscrew the wheel cylinder mounting bolts.
5   Unscrew the brake pipe union and withdraw the wheel cylinder from the backplate. Plug the end of the hydraulic pipe, if necessary.
6   Clean the exterior of the wheel cylinder, taking care not to allow any foreign matter to enter the hydraulic pipe aperture.
7   Remove the rubber boots from the ends of the cylinder and extract the two pistons and the spring between them.
8   Inspect the cylinder bore for signs of scoring and corrosion and the pistons and seals for wear. If the cylinder is satisfactory a repair kit can be used; otherwise the cylinder should be discarded and a new

cylinder, it must be repaired or renewed, as described in Section 8. Do not touch the brake pedal while the shoes are removed. Position an elastic band over the wheel cylinder pistons to retain them.
16   Apply a little brake grease to the contact areas of the pushrod and handbraake lever.
17   Clamp the pushrod in a vice, then hook the tensioning spring on the pushrod and leading shoe and position the shoe slot over the pushrod (Figure 9.23).
18   Fit the wedged key between the shoe and pushrod with the lug facing towards the backplate.
19   Locate the handbrake lever on the trailing shoe in the pushrod, and fit the upper return spring.
20   Connect the handbrake cable to the handbrake lever, swivel the shoes upward and locate the top of the shoes on the wheel cylinder pistons.
21   Fit the lower return spring to the shoes, then lever the bottom of the shoes onto the bottom anchor.
22   Fit the spring to the wedged key and leading shoe as noted during dismantling (photo).
23   Fit the retaining springs and caps.
24   Press the wedged key upwards to give the maximum shoe clearance.
25   Fit the brake drum and adjust the wheel bearings, with reference to Chapter 11.
26   Depress the brake pedal once firmly in order to adjust the rear brakes.
27   Repeat the procedure on the remaining rear brake, then lower the car to the ground.
28   Check that the operation of both the foot and handbrake are satisfactory.

8.3 Brake pipe union connection to the rear wheel cylinder (arrowed) with mounting bolts above (each side of bleed nipple)

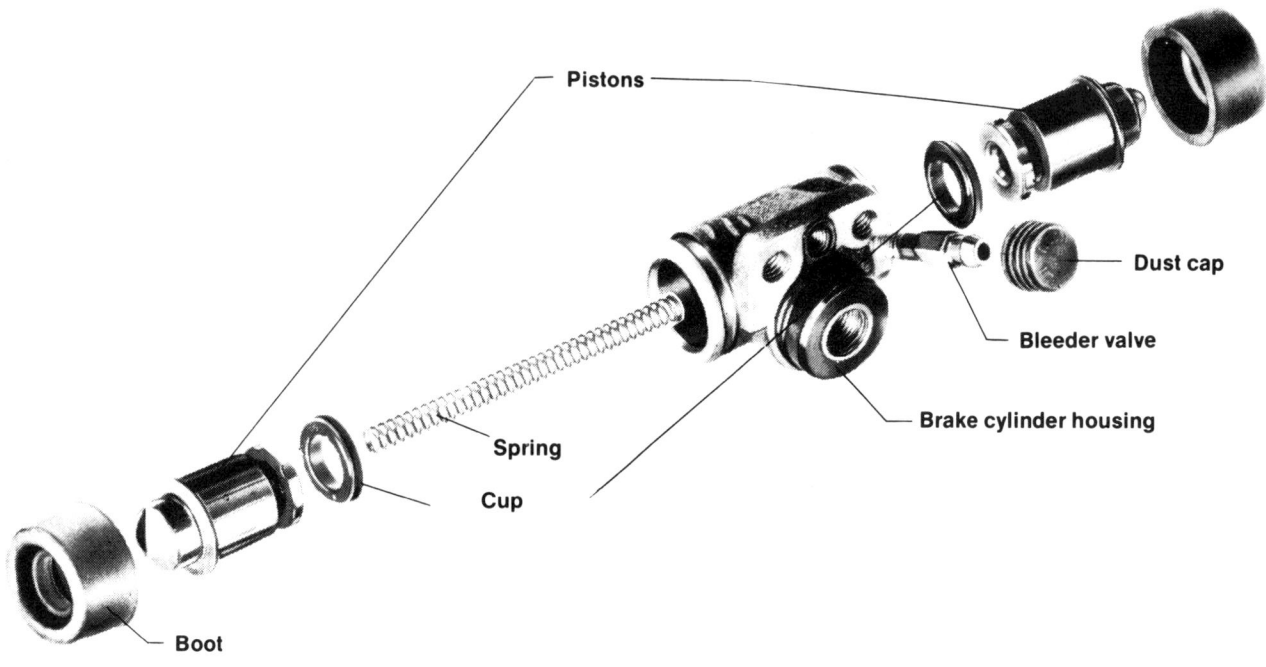

Fig. 9.24 Exploded view of the rear wheel cylinder (Sec 8)

complete assembly fitted. If servicing a cylinder, use all the parts in the repair kit. Clean all the metal parts, using methylated spirit if necessary, *but never petrol or similar solvents,* then leave the parts to dry in the air, or dry them with a lint-free cloth.

9 Apply brake cylinder paste to the seals and fit them so that their large diameter end is nearest to the end of the piston.

10 Smear brake cylinder paste on to the pistons and into the bore of the cylinder. Fit a piston into one end of the cylinder and then the spring and other piston into the other end. Take care not to force the pistons into the cylinders because this can twist the seals.

11 Locate the rubber boots over the pistons and into the grooves of the wheel cylinder.

12 Refitting is a reversal of removal, but bleed the hydraulic system as described in Section 14.

9 Brake drum – inspection and renovation

1 Whenever the brake drums are removed, they should be checked for wear and damage. Light scoring of the friction surface is normal but if it is excessive, or if the internal diameter exceeds the specified wear limit, the drum and hub assembly should be renewed.

2 After a high mileage the friction surface may become oval. Where this has occurred, it may be possible to have the surface ground true by a qualified engineering works. However, it is preferable to renew the drum and hub assembly.

10 Master cylinder – removal and refitting

1 Depress the footbrake pedal several times to dissipate the vacuum in the servo unit.

2 Remove the brake fluid reservoir filler cap and draw off the fluid using a syringe or flexible plastic bottle. Take care not to spill the fluid on the car's paintwork – if some is accidentally spilled, wash it off immediately with copious amounts of cold water (photo).

3 Refit the filler cap, but disconnect the wiring for the fluid level warning circuit.

10.2 Removing the master cylinder cap with level warning device

4 Place some rags beneath the master cylinder, then unscrew the brake pipe union nuts and pull the pipes just clear of the master cylinder. Plug the ends of the pipes or cover them with masking tape.

5 Where applicable disconnect the wiring from the brake light switch.

6 Unscrew the mounting nuts and withdraw the master cylinder from the front of the servo unit. Remove the seal (Figure 9.25).

7 Refitting is a reversal of removal, but always fit a new seal. Finally bleed the hydraulic system as described in Section 14.

Fig. 9.25 Brake master cylinder and servo unit connecting components (Sec 10)

11 Master cylinder – overhaul

Note: *A FAG (Schafer) or ATE (Teves) master cylinder will be fitted and it is important to identify which type is on your vehicle so that the correct repair kit is supplied.*

1   Empty the master cylinder and reservoir and discard the fluid.
2   Pull the reservoir off the master cylinder.
3   Remove the stop screw from the cylinder and then remove the circlip from the mouth of the bore (Figure 9.26).
4   Pull out the piston pushrod assembly, the secondary piston assembly and finally the loose spring.
5   Inspect the bore of the cylinder for signs of wear, damage and corrosion. If the cylinder is in good condition it may be re-used with a service kit, otherwise obtain a new cylinder assembly.
6   Clean all the metal parts, using methylated spirit if necessary, *but never petrol or similar solvents,* then leave the parts to dry in the air or dry them with a clean lint-free cloth. Remove the seals, but note their fitting orientation.
7   Use all the parts supplied in the repair kit and moisten all components with brake fluid before fitting them. Make sure that the correct repair kit is obtained as there are two types of master cylinder – ATE and FAG. If the repair kit supplied is a 'ready to use' kit proceed from paragraph 14.
8   Reassemble the secondary piston assembly in the following order. Fit the two piston seals at the larger diameter end of the piston. The piston seals are identified by their chamfer and groove; the sealing lips of the two seals should face away from each other. Fit the cup washer, the primary cup with its lips towards the closed end of the cylinder, the support ring and finally the conical spring.
9   While holding the master cylinder body vertically with its open end pointing downwards, feed the secondary piston assembly into the cylinder. Guide the lips of the seals into the bore carefully.
10 Fit the cup washer, primary cup, support ring, the cylindrical spring, the stop sleeve and the stroke limiting screw to the short end of the primary piston and tighten the screw firmly. To the longer end of the piston fit the metal washer, the secondary cup with its lip

towards the washer, the plastic washer, the other secondary cup, with its lip facing the same way as the first one, and finally the second metal washer.
11 Insert the primary piston assembly into the cylinder bore with the spring end first. Insert the stop screw, and if necessary move the piston so that the stop screw can be screwed in fully. After screwing in the stop screw, fit the circlip to the mouth of the cylinder bore.
12 Fit a new seal over the end of the master cylinder.
13 Lubricate the seals with brake fluid then press the reservoir into them.

Assembly with ready to use kit

14 Lubricate the cylinder bore with brake cylinder paste then with the cylinder unit mounted in a vice, detach the large end cap of the fitting sleeve containing the repair kit and extract the parts.
15 Remove the second end cap from the sleeve then push the sleeve short end in to align both ends of the sleeve.
16 Locate the fitting sleeve into the cylinder wall and then push the cylinder components into the cylinder so far as they will travel using a suitable punch or pushrod. Fit a new stop screw into the cylinder wall using a new washer, then remove the sleeve (Figure 9.27).
17 Change the position of the cylinder in the vice so that its rear end (cylinder opening) faces upwards.
18 Smear the secondary cups and piston shaft with the silicone grease supplied and then position a washer into the housing.
19 Locate the secondary cup into the fitting sleeve, then fit the cup in position on the pushrod piston shaft with the sleeve and insert into the cylinder.
20 Push the secondary cup down using the long sleeve section and pull back the short sleeve section the thickness of the cup (Figure 9.28 and 9.29).
21 Insert the plastic washer, the second cup and then the second washer. Locate circlip to secure, fit the residual pressure valves and the brake light switch.
22 Fit a new seal over the end of the master cylinder.
23 Lubricate the seals with brake fluid then press the reservoir into them to complete.

209

Cap

Plug

Master cylinder housing

Brake light switch

Pressure valves

Stop screw

Seal

Seal

Secondary piston (assembly)

Conical spring

Support ring

Primary cup

Cup washer

Intermediate piston

Piston seals

Stop sleeve

Stroke limiting screw

Push rod piston (assembly)

Support ring

Cup washer

Plastic washer

Washer

Cylindrical spring

Push rod piston

Secondary cups

Primary cup

Circlip

Fig. 9.26 Exploded view of the master cylinder (Sec 11)

Fig. 9.27 Inserting 'ready-to-use' master cylinder piston kit
(Sec 11)

Fig. 9.28 Inserting the secondary piston cap into the master
cylinder (with 'ready-to-use' kit) (Sec 11)

Fig. 9.29 Sectional view showing sealing cup locations in the
master cylinder (Sec 11)

12 Brake pressure regulator – testing and adjustment

1   The brake pressure regulator is located to the side of the rear axle, and is controlled by the up-and-down movement of the rear axle (photo).
2   To test the operation of the regulator, have an assistant depress the footbrake firmly then release it quickly. With the weight of the car on the suspension, the arm on the regulator should move, indicating that the unit is not seized (photo).
3   To test the regulator for leakage, pressure gauges must be connected to the left-hand front caliper and right-hand rear wheel cylinder. As the equipment will not normally be available to the home mechanic, this work should be entrusted to a VW dealer.

12.1 Brake pressure regulator showing pipe connections and pressure spring attachment

12.2 Brake pressure spring (A) and regulator arm (B) attachments

13 Hydraulic brake lines and hoses – removal and refitting

1   Before removing a brake line or hose, unscrew the brake fluid reservoir filler cap and seal off the reservoir filler neck with a piece of clean polythene sheeting and an elastic band to retain it. This will reduce the loss of hydraulic fluid when a line air hose is disconnected.
2   To remove a rigid brake line, unscrew the union nuts at each end, prise open the clips and withdraw the line. Refitting is a reversal of removal (photo).

13.2A Typical rigid-to-flexible brake line connections with support brackets

13.2B Grommet (arrowed) must support rigid brake line where passing through body panel

Fig. 9.30 Brake line components to front brakes (Sec 13)

1 Flexible line to caliper
2 Bracket clip
3 Master cylinder rigid
   line
4 Master cylinder rigid
   line
6 Grommet
7 Location bracket –
   rigid line
8 Location bracket – hose
9 Location bracket – hose

Fig. 9.31 Brake line components to rear brakes (Sec 13)

1   Hose bracket clip
2 and 4   Rigid line – master cylinder to pressure regulator unit
6 and 7   Rigid line – to wheel cylinder
8   Flexible hoses
9 and 10   Rigid lines – from pressure regulator
11   Rigid line clip
12   Rigid line location bracket

3   To remove a flexible brake hose, unscrew the union nut securing the rigid brake line to the end of the flexible hose while holding the end of the flexible hose stationary. Remove the clip and withdraw the hose from the bracket. Unscrew the remaining end from the component or rigid pipe according to position. Refitting is a reversal of removal, but position flexible hoses clear of adjacent steering and suspension components.
4   Bleed the hydraulic system as described in Section 14 after fitting a rigid brake line or flexible brake hose.

14 Hydraulic system – bleeding

1   If any of the hydraulic components in the braking system have been removed or disconnected, or if the fluid level in the master cylinder has been allowed to fall appreciably, it is inevitable that air will have been introduced into the system. The removal of all this air from the hydraulic system is essential if the brakes are to function correctly and the process of removing it is known as bleeding.
2   There are a number of one-man, do-it-yourself, brake bleeding kits currently available from motor accessory shops. It is recommended that one of these kits should be used wherever possible, as they greatly simplify the bleeding operation, and also reduce the risk of expelled air and fluid being drawn back into the system.
3   If one of these kits is not available then it will be necessary to gather together a clean jar and a suitable length of clear plastic tubing which is a tight fit over the bleed screw, and also to engage the help of an assistant.
4   Before commencing the bleeding operation, check that all rigid pipes and flexible hoses are in good condition and that all hydraulic unions are tight. Take great care not to allow hydraulic fluid to come into contact with the car's paintwork, otherwise the finish will be

seriously damaged. Wash off any spilled fluid immediately with cold water.
5   If hydraulic fluid has been lost from the master cylinder, due to a leak in the system, ensure that the cause is traced and rectified before proceeding further, or a serious malfunction of the braking system may occur.
6   To bleed the system, clean the area around the bleed screw at the wheel cylinder to be bled. If the hydraulic system has only been partially disconnected and suitable precautions were taken to prevent further loss of fluid, it should only be necessary to bleed that part of the system. However, if the entire system is to be bled, the following sequence must be adhered to:

(1)   Right-hand rear wheel cylinder
(2)   Left-hand rear wheel cylinder
(3)   Right-hand front caliper
(4)   Left-hand front caliper

When bleeding the rear wheel cylinders on models with a brake pressure regulator, have an assistant hold the regulator lever to the rear.
7   Remove the master cylinder filler cap and top up the reservoir. Periodically check the fluid level during the bleeding operation and top up as necessary.
8   If a one-man brake bleeding kit is being used, connect the outlet tube to the bleed screw and then open the screw half a turn. If possible position the unit so that it can be viewed from the car, then depress the brake pedal to the floor and slowly release it. The one-way valve in the kit will prevent expelled air from returning to the system at the end of each stroke. Repeat this operation until clean hydraulic fluid, free from air bubbles, can be seen coming through the tube. Now tighten the bleed screw and remove the outlet pipe.
9   If a one-man brake bleeding kit is not available, connect one end of the plastic tubing to the bleed screw and immerse the other end in the jar containing sufficient clean hydraulic fluid to keep the end of the tube submerged (photos). Open the bleed screw half a turn and have

your assistant depress the brake pedal to the floor and then slowly release it. Tighten the bleed screw at the end of each downstroke to prevent expelled air and fluid from being drawn back into the system. Repeat this operation until clean hydraulic fluid, free from air bubbles, can be seen coming through the tube. Now tighten the bleed screw and remove the plastic tube.

10 If the entire system is being bled the procedures described above should now be repeated at each wheel. Do not forget to recheck the fluid level in the master cylinder at regular intervals and top up as necessary.

11 As an alternative to the methods just described, the brake (and clutch, see Chapter 13 Supplement) may be bled using a pressure bleeding kit. The kit, which uses the air pressure from the spare tyre is available from most accessory stores.

12 By connecting a pressurised container to the master cylinder fluid reservoir, bleeding is then carried out by simply opening each bleed screw in turn and allowing the fluid to run out, rather like turning on a tap, until no air is visible in the expelled fluid.

13 By using this method, the large reserve of hydraulic fluid provides a safeguard against air being drawn into the master cylinder during bleeding which often occurs if the fluid level in the reservoir is not maintained.

14 Pressure bleeding is particularly effective when bleeding 'difficult' systems or when bleeding the complete system at time of routine fluid renewal.

15 When completed, recheck the fluid level in the master cylinder, top up if necessary, and refit the cap. Check the 'feel' of the brake pedal; this should be firm and free from any 'sponginess', which would indicate air still present in the system.

16 Discard any expelled hydraulic fluid as it is likely to be contaminated with moisture, air and dirt, which makes it unsuitable for further use.

15 Brake pedal – removal and refitting

1   The brake and clutch pedals share a common bracket assembly and pivot shaft. However, on some models the pivot shaft is fixed to the bracket and on other models it is free to move (Figure 9.32).

14.9A Bleed tube connected to a front brake caliper

14.9B Rear brake bleed nipple and dust cap

Fig. 9.32 Brake pedal and vacuum servo unit components (Sec 15)

15.2 General view of the brake and clutch pedal assembly (shown with lower trim panel removed)

2   Working inside the car, extract the clip and remove the clevis pin securing the servo pushrod or intermediate pushrod to the pedal (photo). Remove the lower panel, if necessary.

3   Extract the clip from the end of the pivot shaft, unhook the return spring (where fitted) and withdraw the pedal from the shaft. On some models it is necessary to loosen the bracket mounting nuts and move the bracket to one side.

4   Check the pedal bushes for wear. If necessary drive them out from each side and press in new bushes using a soft-jawed vice.

5   Refitting is a reversal of removal, but lubricate the pivot shaft with a little multi-purpose grease.

16 Handbrake lever – removal and refitting

1   Chock the front wheels, then jack up the rear of the car and support it on axle stands.

2   Unscrew the nut from the handbrake pullrod and remove the compensator bar (Figure 9.33).

3   Pull the rubber bellows from the underbody and off the pullrod.

4   Working inside the car, prise out the gaiter and move it up the handbrake lever.

5   Disconnect the wiring from the handbrake warning switch.

6   Unscrew the mounting bolts and withdraw the handbrake lever assembly and switch bracket.

7   Remove the central screws and withdraw the lower cover, then extract the clips, push out the clevis pin and remove the pullrod.

8   If necessary the ratchet may be dismantled by removing the clips and clevis pin or grinding off the rivet head. However, if the ratchet is known to be worn, renew the complete assembly.

9   Refitting is a reversal of removal, but lubricate the pivots and compensator bar with multi-purpose grease. Finally adjust the handbrake, as described in Section 17.

17 Handbrake – adjustment

1   Chock the front wheels, then jack up the rear of the car and support it on axle stands.

2   Fully release the handbrake lever, then firmly depress the brake pedal once.

3   Pull the handbrake lever onto the 2nd notch and check that it is just possible to turn the rear wheels by hand. If necessary, adjust the position of the nut on the end of the pullrod beneath the car. The nut is located next to the compensator bar (photo).

4   Fully release the handbrake lever and check that both rear wheels turn freely.

5   Lower the car to the ground.

Switch for handbrake indicator light

Compensator bar

Adjusting nut

Fig. 9.33 Handbrake lever and associated components (Sec 16)

17.3 Handbrake adjustment nut and compensator

18 Vacuum servo unit – description and testing

1   The vacuum servo unit is located between the brake pedal and the master cylinder and provides assistance to the driver when the brake pedal is depressed. The unit operates by vacuum from the inlet manifold.
2   The unit basically consists of a diaphragm and non-return valve. With the brake pedal released, vacuum is channelled to both sides of the diaphragm, but when the pedal is depressed, one side is opened to the atmosphere. The resultant unequal pressures are harnessed to assist in depressing the master cylinder pistons.
3   Normally, the vacuum servo unit is very reliable, but if the unit becomes faulty, it should be renewed. In the event of a failure, the hydraulic system is in no way affected, except that higher pedal pressures will be necessary.
4   To test the vacuum servo unit depress the brake pedal several times with the engine switched off to dissipate the vacuum. Apply moderate pressure to the brake pedal then start the engine. The pedal should move down slightly if the servo unit is operating correctly.
5   To test the check valve in the vacuum hose, disconnect it from the hose then blow through the valve in the direction of the arrow marking. Air should pass through the check valve. However if air is supplied in the reverse direction through the valve it should not, as the valve must be closed to airflow in that direction. Renew the valve unit if found to be defective.

19 Vacuum servo unit – removal and refitting

1   Remove the master cylinder, as described in Section 10.
2   On right-hand drive models remove the glovebox, with reference to Chapter 12.
3   Pull the vacuum hose free from the servo unit connector and where applicable, the non-return valve.

4   Working inside the vehicle detach the lower trim panel on the driver's side.
5   Disconnect the pushrod clevis from the brake pedal by releasing the clip and withdrawing the clevis pin (photo).
6   Unscrew the mounting nuts and withdraw the servo unit from the bulkhead into the engine compartment.
7   Refitting is a reversal of removal. However, on models where the clevis is adjustable check the dimension shown in Fig. 9.34 and, if necessary, loosen the locknut, reposition the clevis, and re-tighten the locknut. Lubricate the clevis pin with a little molybdenum disulphide based grease. The mounting nuts are self-locking and should always be renewed.

19.5 Servo unit pushrod to pedal attachment
    A   Clevis, pin and clip   B   Adjustment locknut

Fig. 9.34 Servo unit pushrod setting dimension (a) (Sec 19)

a = 220 mm (8.66 in)

Fault diagnosis appears overleaf

20 Fault diagnosis – braking system

Symptom	Reason(s)
Excessive pedal travel	Brake fluid leak Air in hydraulic system Faulty master cylinder
Uneven braking and pulling to one side	Disc pads or brake shoes contaminated with oil or brake fluid Seized wheel cylinder or caliper Unequal tyre pressures Loose suspension anchor point
Brake judder	Worn drums and/or discs Contaminated disc pad or brake shoe linings Loose suspension anchor point
Brake pedal feels 'spongy'	Air in hydraulic system Faulty master cylinder
Excessive effort to stop car	Faulty servo unit Seized wheel cylinder or caliper Contaminated disc pad or brake shoe linings

Chapter 10 Electrical system

For modifications, and information applicable to later models, see Supplement at end of manual

Contents

Specifications

System type .... 12 volt, negative earth

Battery
Capacity .... 36, 45, 54, or 63 Ah

Alternator
.... Motorola or Bosch
Output .... 45, 65, 75 or 90 Amp
Minimum brush length· .... 5.0 mm (0.2 in)
Drivebelt tension – drivebelt up to 1000 mm (39.3 in) long:
    New belt .... 2 mm (0.078 in)
    Used belt .... 5 mm (0.196 in)
Drivebelt tension – drivebelt over 1000 mm (39.3 in) long:
    New belt .... 10 mm (0.4 in)
    Used belt .... 15 mm (0.6 in)
Stator winding resistance:
    Bosch 45 Amp .... 0.18 to 0.20 ohm
    Bosch 65 Amp .... 0.10 to 0.11 ohm
    Bosch 75 and 90 Amp .... 0.10 ohm maximum
    Motorola 65 Amp .... 0.13 to 0.15 ohm
    Motorola 45 Amp with 6 wire ends .... 0.27 to 0.3 ohm
    Motorola 45 Amp with 3 wire ends .... 0.09 to 0.11 ohm
Diode resistance .... 50 to 80 ohm
Rotor winding resistance:
    Bosch 45 Amp .... 3.4 to 3.7 ohm
    Bosch 65 Amp .... 2.8 to 3.0 ohm
    Bosch 75 and 90 Amp .... 3.0 to 4.0 ohm
    Motorola 45 and 65 Amp .... 3.8 to 4.2 ohm

Starter motor
Type .... Pre-engaged
Commutator minimum diameter .... 33.5 mm (1.32 in)
Commutator maximum run-out .... 0.03 mm (0.001 in)
Commutator insulation undercut .... 0.5 to 0.8 mm (0.02 to 0.03 in)
Minimum brush length .... 13.0 mm (0.5 in)

Fuses (late models)*

No	Function	Rating (amp)
1	Radiator fan	30
2	Brake lights	10
3	Cigarette lighter, radio, clock, central locking and interior lights	15
4	Emergency light system	15
5	Fuel pump (electric)	15
6	Foglights (main current)	15
7	Side and tail lights − left side	10
8	Side and tail lights − right side	10
9	High beam (right) and high beam warning light	10
10	High beam (left)	10
11	Windscreen wipers, washers and headlamp washers	15
12	Coolant warning lamp, exterior mirror adjuster and sliding/tilting roof. Rear wiper/washer (Passat)	15
13	Rear window and outside mirror heating	15
14	Blower	20
15	Reverse lights, automatic transmission shift illumination	10
16	Horn (single)	15
17	Automatic choke, idle cut-off valve and electric manifold heating	10
18	Horn (dual), front seating heating, stop/start system and brake warning lamp	15
19	Indicators	10
20	Number plate light, foglights (switch current) and glovebox light	10
21	Low beam − left side	10
22	Low beam − right side	10

*For early models, see Fig. 10.26

Separate holder fuses (above fusebox)

Rear foglight	10
Electric window lifters	30

Bulbs

	Wattage
Headlamps:	
Standard	45/40
Halogen	60/55
Sidelight	4
Direction indicators	21
Stop/tail lights	21/5
Reversing lights	21
Foglamp (rear)	21
Foglamp (front)	55
Number plate light	10
Interior light	10
Ashtray and heater illumination	1.2
Instrument panel illumination	3
Instrument panel warning lights:	
All except charge and temperature warning lights	1.2
Charge and temperature warning lights	2
Glove compartment light	4
Luggage compartment light	5

1 General description

The electrical system is of 12 volt negative earth type. The battery is charged by a belt-driven alternator which incorporates a voltage regulator. The starter is of pre-engaged type incorporating four brushes, and on this type of motor a solenoid moves the drive pinion into engagement with the starter ring gear before the motor is energised.

Although repair procedures are given in this Chapter, it may well be more economical to renew worn components as complete units.

2 Electrical system − maintenance

The following routine maintenance procedures should be undertaken at the specified intervals given at the start of this manual.
1   Battery: Refer to Section 4 in this Chapter.
2   Alternator: Refer to Section 7 in this Chapter.
3   Alternator drivebelt: Check condition and adjustment of the drivebelt as described in Section 9 of this Chapter.
4   Vehicle lighting: Periodically check that all of the front and rear lights are functioning correctly. The headlights and (where applicable) the foglights should be checked for alignment as described in Section 27. Renew any defective bulbs.
5   Windscreen/rear window wipers: Check their operation (having wet the glass first) and also the condition of the wiper blade rubbers. Renew if necessary. At the same time, check that the windscreen, rear window and headlamp washers (as applicable) operate in a satisfactory manner. Check and when necessary top up the fluid reservoirs.
6   Wiring: Periodically check the wiring and connections for condition and security.

3 Battery − removal and refitting

1   The battery is located in the engine compartment just in front of the bulkhead (photo).
2   Loosen the negative terminal clamp and disconnect the lead.

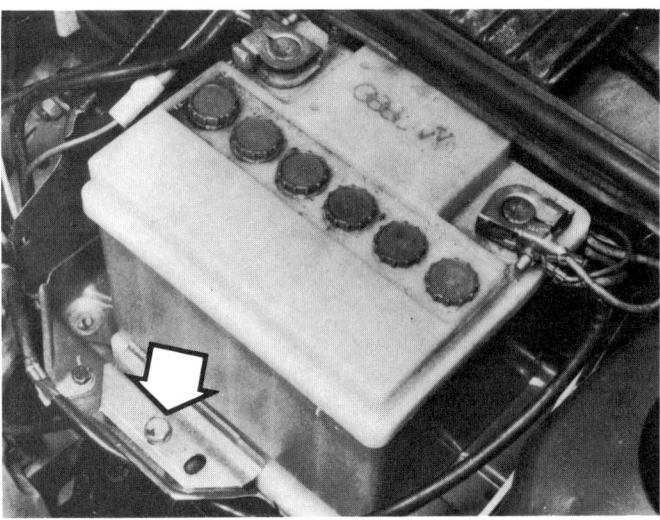

3.1 Battery location showing lead connections and retaining clamp and bolt (arrowed) at base

3   Loosen the positive terminal clamp and disconnect the lead.
4   Unscrew the bolt and remove the battery holding clamp.
5   Lift the battery from the platform, taking care not to spill any electrolyte.
6   Refitting is a reversal of removal, but make sure that the polarity is correct before connecting the leads, and do not overtighten the clamp bolts. **Note:** *The curved side of the holding clamp must contact the base of the battery.*

4   Battery – maintenance

1   Where a conventional battery is fitted, the electrolyte level of each cell should be checked every month and, if necessary, topped up with distilled or de-ionized water until the separators are just covered. On some batteries the case is translucent and incorporates minimum and maximum level marks. The check should be made more often if the car is operated in high ambient temperature conditions.
2   Where a low maintenance battery is fitted it is not necessary to check the electrolyte level.
3   Every 15 000 km (10 000 miles) or 12 months, whichever occurs first, disconnect and clean the battery terminals and leads. After refitting them, smear the exposed metal with petroleum jelly.
4   At the same time, inspect the battery clamp and platform for corrosion. If evident, remove the battery and clean the deposits away, then treat the affected metal with a proprietary anti-rust liquid and paint with the original colour.
5   When the battery is removed, for whatever reason, it is worthwhile checking it for cracks and leakage. Cracks can be caused by topping up the cells with distilled water in winter *after* instead of *before* a run. This gives the water no chance to mix with the electrolyte, so the former freezes and splits the battery case. If the battery case is fractured, it may be possible to repair it with a proprietary compound, but this depends on the material used for the case. If electrolyte has been lost from a cell, refer to Section 5 for details of adding a fresh solution.
6   If topping up the battery becomes excessive and the case is not fractured, the battery is being over-charged and the voltage regulator will have to be checked.
7   If the car covers a very small annual mileage, it is worthwhile checking the specific gravity of the electrolyte every three months to determine the state of charge of the battery. Use a hydrometer to make the check, and compare the results with the following table.

	Normal climates	Tropics
Discharged	1.120	1.080
Half charged	1.200	1.160
Fully charged	1.280	1.230

8   If the battery condition is suspect, first check the specific gravity of electrolyte in each cell. A variation of 0.040 or more between any cells indicates loss of electrolyte or deterioration of the internal plates.
9   A further test can be made using a battery heavy discharge meter. The battery should be discharged for a maximum of 15 seconds at a load of three times the ampere-hour capacity (at the 20 hour discharge rate). Alternatively connect a voltmeter across the battery terminals and spin the engine on the starter with the ignition disconnected (see Chapter 4), and the headlamps, heated rear window and heater blower switched on. If the voltmeter reading remains above 9.6 volts, the battery condition is satisfactory. If the voltmeter reading drops below 9.6 volts, and the battery has already been charged as described in Section 6, it is faulty and should be renewed.

5   Battery – electrolyte replenishment

1   If after fully charging the battery, one of the cells maintains a specific gravity which is 0.040 or more lower than the others, but the battery also maintains 9.6 volts during the heavy discharge test (Section 4), it is likely that electrolyte has been lost.
2   If a significant quantity of electrolyte has been lost through spillage, it will not suffice merely to refill with distilled water. Top up the cell with a mixture of 2 parts sulphuric acid to 5 parts distilled water (photo).

5.2 Replenishing the battery electrolyte

3   When mixing the electrolyte *never* add water to sulphuric acid – *always* pour the acid slowly onto the water in a glass container. *If water is added to sulphuric acid, it will explode!*
4   Top up each cell as required to a level 5 mm (0.20 in) above the separators or to the acid level marking on the battery casing.
5   After topping up the cell with fresh electrolyte, recharge the battery and check the hydrometer readings again.

6   Battery – charging

1   In winter when a heavy demand is placed on the battery, such as when starting from cold and using more electrical equipment, it is a good idea to occasionally have the battery fully charged from an external source at a rate of 10% of the battery capacity (ie 6.3 amp for a 63 Ah battery). It is necessary to disconnect the battery leads for charging.
2   Continue to charge the battery until no further rise in specific gravity is noted over a four hour period.

3   Alternatively, a trickle charger, charging at a rate of 1.5 amp can
be safely used overnight.
4   Special rapid 'boost' charges, which are claimed to restore the
power of the battery in 1 to 2 hours, can be dangerous unless they are
thermostatically controlled, as they can cause serious damage to the
battery plates through overheating.
5   While charging the battery, ensure that the temperature of the
electrolyte never exceeds 37.8°C (100°F) and loosen the vent caps
(where applicable).
6   If a maintenance-free battery is fitted consult your dealer when it
is necessary to recharge it from an external source as specialised
procedures are sometimes required depending on battery type.

7   Alternator – maintenance and special precautions

1   Periodically wipe away any dirt which has accumulated on the
outside of the unit, and also check that the plug is pushed firmly on the
terminals. At the same time, check the tension of the drivebelt and
adjust it if necessary as described in Section 9.
2   Take extreme care when making electrical circuit connections on
the car, otherwise damage may occur to the alternator or other
electrical components employing semi-conductors. Always make sure
that the battery leads are connected to the correct terminals. Before
using electric-arc welding equipment to repair any part of the car,
disconnect the battery leads and alternator multi-plug. Never run the
engine with the alternator multi-plug or a battery lead disconnected.

8   Alternator – removal and refitting

1   Disconnect the battery negative lead.
2   Loosen the alternator adjustment nuts or bolts and swivel the
alternator toward the engine. If difficulty is experienced, loosen the
pivot bolt.
3   Slip the drivebelt from the pulley.
4   Note the location of the wiring then disconnect it from the rear of
the alternator (photo). On some models it will first be necessary to
remove the duct cover and hose.

8.4 Alternator multi-plug (Bosch)

5   Remove the link bolt and pivot bolt, and withdraw the alternator
from the engine. If necessary, remove the upper timing cover plug in
order to remove the pivot bolt (photos).
6   If necessary, the mounting brackets may be unbolted, and on four-
cylinder engines the rubber bushes removed (Fig. 10.1). When refitting
the bracket on five-cylinder engines, the short bolt must be tightened
first.
7   Refitting is a reversal of removal, but adjust the drivebelt as
described in Section 9.

8.5A Remove upper timing cover plug ...

8.5B ... for access to alternator bolt

8.5C Alternator adjuster strap bolt removal – note spacing washer

Earth wire

Rubber mounting with bush

Bracket

Cup washer

Alternator support

Rubber mounting

Cup washer with
guide collar

Alternator

Rubber mounting
with bush

Bracket

V-belt

Socket head screw

Fig. 10.1 Alternator and mounting/adjustment components – 1.6 litre engine (Sec 8)

9   Alternator drivebelt – renewal and adjustment

1   Every 15 000 km (10 000 miles) the alternator drivebelt should be checked for condition, and re-tensioned. If there are signs of cracking or deterioration, the drivebelt should be renewed.

2   To remove the drivebelt, loosen the adjustment nuts or bolts and swivel the alternator toward the engine. If necessary loosen the pivot bolt.

3   Slip the drivebelt from the pulleys. On models fitted with power steering, it will first be necessary to remove the drivebelt in order to remove the alternator drivebelt.

4   Fit the new drivebelt over the pulleys, then lever the alternator from the engine until the specified tension is achieved using firm thumb pressure mid-way between the pulleys. Lever the alternator at the pulley end to prevent any torsional damage.

5   Tighten the adjustment nuts or bolts followed by the pivot bolts.

6   Run the engine for several minutes, then recheck the tension and adjust if necessary.

10.2A Bosch 45 Amp alternator rear end view

10.2B Removing the regulator and brush holder (Bosch 45 amp) ...

10.2C ... to check the brushes for excessive wear

Bearing

Rotor

Bearing

End plate

Spacer

Fan

Belt pulley

Regulator

Regulator/brushes

Wire clip

Housing

Terminal W

Diode plate

Screws

Stator

Fig. 10.2 Exploded view of the Bosch 45 Amp and 65 Amp alternator (Sec 10)

10 Alternator – servicing

Note: *The voltage regulator and brushes can be removed without removing the alternator. However, the following complete dismantling procedure assumes that the alternator is on the bench.*
1   Clean the exterior of the alternator.

Bosch 45A and 65A

2   Remove the screws and withdraw the voltage regulator and brushes. If the brushes are worn below the specified minimum length, they cannot be renewed individually, only in unit with the regulator unit (photos).
3   Mark the end housings and stator in relation to each other (Fig. 10.2).
4   Grip the pulley in a vice then unscrew the nut and withdraw the washer, pulley and fan, together with any spacers. Prise out the key.
5   Unscrew the through-bolts and tap off the front housing, together with the rotor.
6   Using a mallet or puller, remove the rotor from the front housing and remove the spacers.
7   Remove the screws and retaining plate. Drive the bearing from the front housing with a soft metal drift.
8   Using a suitable puller, remove the bearing from the slip ring end of the rotor, but take care not to damage the slip rings.
9   Carefully separate the stator from the rear housing without straining the three wires. Identify each wire for location, then unsolder them using the minimum of heat to avoid damage to the diodes. Long nosed pliers may be used as a heat sink, as shown in Fig. 10.3.
10   Remove the screws and separate the diode plate from the rear housing.
11   Remove the wave washer from the rear housing (if fitted).
12   Check the stator windings for a short to ground by connecting an ohmmeter or test bulb between each wire and the outer ring. Check that the internal resistance between the wires is as given in the Specifications using an ohmmeter between wires 1 and 2, then 1 and 3, and 2 and 3 – the numbering of the wires is of no importance, (Fig. 10.4).
13   Using the ohmmeter check that the resistance of each diode is as given in the Specifications when the ohmmeter is connected across the diode in one direction. Reverse the wires and check that there is now no resistance.
14   Check the rotor windings for a short to ground by connecting an ohmmeter or test bulb between each slip ring and the winding core (Fig. 10.5). Check that the internal resistance of the winding is as given in the Specifications using an ohmmeter between the two slip rings.
15   Clean all the components and obtain new bearings, brushes etc, as required.
16   Reassembly is a reversal of dismantling, but when fitting the

Fig. 10.4 Check the stator winding for a short circuit (Sec 10)

Fig. 10.5 Check the rotor windings for a short circuit (Sec 10)

bearing to the front housing, drive it in using a metal tube *on the outer race* making sure that the open end of the bearing faces the rotor. When fitting the rear bearing to the rotor, drive it on using a metal tube *on the inner race,* making sure that the open end of the bearing faces the rear housing.

Bosch 75A and 90A

17   The procedure is identical to that described in paragraphs 2 to 16 with the following exceptions.

   (a)   A suppressor condenser is attached to the rear housing and can be removed by unscrewing the single retaining screw and disconnecting the lead.
   (b)   The diode plate has two terminals protruding through the rear housing, and there are two wave washers and a plain washer in the rear housing.
   (c)   The front (drive end) ball bearing must be fitted with the casing side towards the bearing housing. The rear bearing may be installed either way round as both sides are closed.

Fig. 10.3 Using pliers as a heat sink when unsoldering the stator wires (Sec 10)

Fig. 10.6 Exploded view of the Bosch 75 and 90 Amp alternators (Sec 10)

Motorola 45A and 65A

18 Remove the screws and lift the voltage regulator from the rear housing. Note the location of the wires, then disconnect them and withdraw the regulator.

19 Remove the screws and withdraw the brush holder and brushes. If the brushes are worn below the specified minimum length renew the brush holder and brushes as a complete unit (Fig. 10.8).

20 Mark the end housings and stator in relation to each other.

21 Grip the pulley in a vice, then unscrew the nut and withdraw the washer, pulley and fan, together with any spacers. Prise out the key.

22 Unscrew the through-bolts and nuts, and tap off the front housing, together with the rotor.

23 On the 45A alternator remove the three screws securing the three bearing retaining plates to the front housing.

24 On the 65A alternator, remove the three screws securing the one-piece bearing retaining plate to the front housing.

25 Using a mallet or puller, remove the rotor and bearing from the front housing.

Fig. 10.7 Exploded view of the Motorola 45 Amp alternator (Sec 10)

**Fig. 10.8 Check dimension (a) for brush minimum length –
Motorola alternator (Sec 10)**

26 Using a suitable puller, remove the bearings from each end of the rotor, together with the retaining plate and spacer. Take care not to damage the slip rings.

27 On the 45A alternator unclip and remove the cover from the rear housing. On the 65A model, remove the screws and withdraw the cover from the rear housing.

28 Identify the stator wires for location, then unsolder them from the diode plate using the minimum of heat to avoid damage to the diodes, (Fig. 10.10). Long nosed pliers may be used as a heat sink in a similar manner to that shown in Fig. 10.3.

29 Remove the stator from the rear housing.

30 On the 65A alternator, unsolder the D+ wire from the diode plate using the procedure described in paragraph 28. Note the wire location, then remove the screws and withdraw the diode plate.

31 Remove the O-ring from the rear housing.

32 Check the stator, diodes, and rotor, as described in paragraphs 12, 13 and 14.

33 Clean all the components and obtain new bearings, brushes etc, as required.

Bearing

Rotor

Wire clip

Cover

Diode plate

Bearing

Regulator

D+ connecting plate

Brush holder

End plate

Housing

O-Ring

Belt pulley

Stator

Fig. 10.9 Exploded view of the Motorola 65 Amp alternator (Sec 10)

Fig. 10.10 Stator wire connections on the Motorola alternator (Sec 10)

1   B+
2   D+ for warning lamp
3   B+ suppression condenser
4   Earth
5   To regulator

Fig. 10.11 Voltage regulator wire terminals on the Motorola 45 Amp alternator (Sec 10)

1   Green wire DF
2   Red wire D+
3   Black wire Earth

Fig. 10.12 Voltage regulator connections on the Motorola 65 Amp alternator (Sec 10)

1   Green wire DF
2   Red wire D+

34 Reassembly is a reversal of dismantling, but lubricate the rear housing O-ring with multi-purpose grease before fitting.
35 Check that the voltage regulator wiring connections are correct and securely made (Figs. 10.11 and 10.12).

11 Starter motor – testing in the car

1   If the starter motor fails to respond when the starter switch is operated, first check that the fault is not external to the starter motor.
2   Connect a test lamp between chassis earth and the large terminal on the starter solenoid, terminal 30. This terminal is connected directly to the battery and the test lamp should light whether or not the ignition switch is operated (Fig. 10.13 or 10.14).
3   Remove the test lamp connection from the large terminal (30) and transfer it to the smaller terminal (50) on the solenoid. The lamp should light only when the starter switch is in its *Start* position.
4   If both these tests are satisfactory the fault is in the starter motor.
5   If the starter motor is heard to operate, but the engine fails to start, check the battery terminals, the starter motor leads and the engine-to-body earth strap for cleanliness and tightness.

Fig. 10.13 Starter motor solenoid connections (Sec 11)

1   Terminal 30 (from the battery)
2   Terminal 15a (to coil on vehicles with series resistance or resistance wire only)
3   Terminal 50 (from ignition/starter switch)
4   Field winding connection

Fig. 10.14 Alternative starter motor solenoid connections on some models (Sec 11)

1   Terminal 30 (from battery)
2   Terminal 50 (from ignition switch)
3   Field winding connection

12 Starter motor – removal and refitting

1   Disconnect the battery negative lead.
2   Note the location of the wires on the starter solenoid, then disconnect them by removing the nut and screws, as applicable (photo).
3   Unscrew the mounting bolts and withdraw the starter motor (photo).
4   Refitting is a reversal of removal, but make sure that the mating faces are clean and tighten the mounting bolts to the specified torque.

13 Starter motor – overhaul

1   Mark the housings and mounting bracket (where fitted) in relation to each other.

2   Remove the nuts and washers and withdraw the end mounting bracket (where fitted).
3   Unscrew the through-bolts and remove them (photo).
4   Remove the screws and withdraw the small end cover and gasket, then extract the circlip and remove the shims. Note the exact number of shims, as they determine the shaft endfloat. Withdraw the bearing housing (photos).
5   Lift the brush springs and extract the field winding brushes (photo).
6   Note the position of the brush holder plate in relation to the field winding housing, then withdraw the plate from the armature.
7   Unscrew the nut and disconnect the field wire from the solenoid.
8   Remove the field winding housing from the armature.
9   Unscrew the three bolts and remove the solenoid from the drive end housing. Unhook the core from the lever.
10 Unscrew and remove the lever pivot bolt and prise out the lever cover pad.

12.2 Wiring connections to starter motor solenoid

12.3 Starter motor mounting bolts (A) and front mounting bracket (B)

13.3 Unscrew and remove the through-bolts

13.4A Remove the end cover (arrowed) ...

13.4B ... the circlip ...

13.4C ... and shims

13.4D Withdraw the bearing housing

13.5 Lift spring to extract the brushes from the holders

Stop ring

Pinion drive

Armature

Snap ring

Intermediate bearing

Solenoid

Carbon brushes

Bearing housing

Housing

Support plate

Brush holder plate

Bearing bush

Fig. 10.15 Exploded view of the 0.8 and 1.7 kW starter motor (Sec 13)

Bearing bush

Snap ring

Armature

Stop ring

Pinion drive

Housing

Carbon brushes

Solenoid

Brush holder plate

Bearing bush

Fig. 10.16 Exploded view of the 1.1 kW starter motor (Sec 13)

11 Remove the armature from the drive end housing and disengage the lever from the pinion drive.

12 Using a metal tube, drive the stop ring off the circlip, then extract the circlip and pull off the stop ring.

13 Withdraw the pinion drive from the armature.

14 Clean all the components in paraffin and wipe dry, then examine them for wear and damage. Check the pinion drive for damaged teeth and make sure that the one-way clutch only rotates in one direction. If the shaft bushes are worn they can be removed using a soft metal drift and new bushes installed. However, the new bushes must first be soaked in hot oil for approximately five minutes. Clean the commutator with a rag moistened with a suitable solvent. Minor scoring can be removed with fine glasspaper, but deep scoring will necessitate the commutator being skimmed in a lathe and then being undercut. Commutator refinishing is a job which is best left to a specialist.

15 Measure the length of the brushes. If less than the minimum given in Specifications, fit new brushes. Crush the old brushes to free the copper braid and file the excess solder off the braid. Fit new brushes to the braid and hold the braid with a pair of flat nosed pliers below the

carbon brush, to prevent solder from flowing down the braid. Solder the brushes on using radio quality solder and a heavy duty soldering iron of at least 250 watt rating. Check that the brushes move freely in their holders and if necessary dress the brushes with a fine file.

16 Reassembly is a reversal of the dismantling procedure, but note the following. To fit the brush assembly over the commutator, either hook the brush springs on to the edge of the brush holder, or bend pieces of wire to hold the springs off the brushes until the brush assembly has been fitted. As soon as this has been done, release the brush springs and position them so that they bear on the centres of the brushes. Apply a little molybdenum disulphide grease to the splines of the pinion drive. Fit a new circlip to the pinion end of the shaft and ensure that the circlip groove is not damaged. Any burrs on the edges of the groove should be removed with a fine file. During reassembly apply sealing compound to the points indicated in Figs. 10.17 and 10.18.

14 Automatic stop/start system (ASS) – general

This system is fitted as optional equipment to manual gearbox models only and is a fuel economy device. Activated by a control switch the system automatically switches off the engine when the vehicle is stationary in heavy traffic delays.

Two system types have been fitted, an early system used up to October 1983 and a late system type used from that date. On the early system the restart switches are mounted on the accelerator and clutch pedal assemblies, whilst the later model type has the restart switch on the gearbox.

On both early and late models the control switch is mounted in the same place, to the right of the driver on the facia panel. The switch is marked SSA and incorporates an integral warning light to indicate that the switch is in the ON position and the system activated.

The system should only be used when the vehicle has reached its normal operating temperature. When activated, the system will automatically stop the engine when the vehicle speed drops below 2 kph (1.2 mph) on early models or 5 kph (3.1 mph) on later models. In addition on later models, the engine must have run at its normal idle speed for a period of at least 2 seconds.

When traffic conditions permit, the engine can be restarted by simultaneously depressing the accelerator and clutch pedals on earlier models or by depressing the clutch pedal and moving the gear lever fully to the left in neutral or engaging reverse on later models. Once the engine has restarted, the gear engagement can be made in the normal manner. If when restarted the engine stalls or for any reason stops the restart procedure should be repeated, but on later models the gear lever must be moved back into neutral within 6 seconds.

The following safety precautions should be noted when using the ASS, these being:

(a) Do not use the system when the engine temperature is below 55°C (131°F) or when the ambient temperature is very low as the engine will take longer to warm up.

(b) Do not allow the vehicle to roll when the engine is switched off, check that the handbrake is fully applied.

(c) During extended delays switch the engine off in the normal manner with the ignition key as electrical accessories will otherwise be left on and the battery run down.

(d) If leaving the vehicle for any length of time, switch off the ASS and always take the ignition key with you.

Fig. 10.17 Sealing points on the 0.8 and 1.7 kW starter motor (Sec 13)

Fig. 10.18 Sealing points on the 1.1 kW starter motor (Sec 13)

15 Automatic stop/start system components (up to 1983) – removal and refitting

The system layout and components are shown in Fig. 10.19. Should the system malfunction in any way, have the fault diagnosed by your VW dealer. The following system components may be removed and refitted.

Control unit

1 Disconnect the battery earth lead.

2 The control unit is located directly behind the radio/heater control panel and these will therefore have to be removed for access as described in Section 43.

3 Disconnect the wiring connector from the control unit then

Fig. 10.19 Automatic stop/start system components (up to 1983) (Sec 15)

15.3 Automatic stop/start system control unit (early models)

15.6 Accelerator pedal clamp bolt

remove the securing screw each side of the unit and withdraw it (photo).

4   Refit in the reverse order of removal.

Accelerator pedal switch

5   Disconnect the battery earth lead.

6   Remove the accelerator pedal. Depending on model, this is achieved by unscrewing the clamp bolt (photo) or removing the securing clip and bush and withdrawing the pedal from or with the pivot shaft as applicable.

7   Detach the wiring connector and withdraw the pedal switch. On some models it is necessary to first remove the switch retaining screws (Fig. 10.20).

8   Refit in the reverse order of removal.

Fig. 10.20 Accelerator pedal switch location and retaining screws (automatic stop/start system up to 1983) (Sec 15)

2041

Fig. 10.21 Clutch pedal switch removal showing location of VW tool 2041 (automatic stop/start system) (Sec 15)

Clutch pedal switch

9 Disconnect the battery earth lead.

10 Detach and remove the lower instrument panel trim on the driver's side.

11 Disconnect the wiring connector from the switch.

12 You will now need VW special tool number 2041 or to fabricate an equivalent tool. Push and locate the tool between the pedal bracket and the relay plate/fusebox. Secure the tool (2041) in front of the clutch pedal switch and pull the switch out of its sleeve (Fig. 10.21).

13 Refit in the reverse order of removal. A new switch must always be used when refitting and must be pushed home into its sleeve by hand with the aid of a hammer shaft. Check that the switch is fully home then reconnect the wire connector.

14 Before refitting the lower trim panel, fully depress the clutch pedal to engage the switch over the retainer.

Speed sender unit

15 Disconnect the battery earth lead.

16 Unscrew and remove the drive cable at each end of the sender unit, detach the wiring connector and withdraw the unit (photos).

17 Refit in the reverse order of removal.

15.16A Automatic stop/start system speed sender unit drive cable removal ...

15.16B ... and wiring connector removal

Diode

18 This is located under the dashboard on the driver's side.

19 Disconnect the battery earth lead, remove the lower trim panel for access, disconnect and remove the diode from the control unit wiring harness.

20 Refit in the reverse order to removal ensuring that secure connections are made.

16 Automatic stop/start system components (from 1983) – removal and refitting

The system layout and components are shown in Fig. 10.22. Should the system malfunction in any way have the fault diagnosed by your VW dealer. The following components may be removed and refitted.

234

Connector for coil

Connector for reversing light switch and gearbox switch
for gearshift and consumption indicator

Gearbox switch

Switch-off relay for rear window and oil pressure monitor

Switch unit

Connector for oil pressure switch

Connector for starter
(terminal 50)

Speed sensor

Connector for ignition switch

Main switch

Overrun control valve

Connector for thermo-time valve
for overrun cutoff

Connector for manifold preheating
(hedgehog)

Connector for instrument loom

Fig. 10.22 Automatic stop/start system layout (from 1983) (Sec 16)

Switch control unit
1 Disconnect the battery earth lead.
2 The switch is located under the dashboard on the driver's side. Unclip and remove the lower trim panel for access (Fig. 10.23).
3 Disconnect the wiring multi-connector from the switch then pull the switch from the relay plate.
4 Refit in the reverse order to removal.

Fig. 10.23 Switch control unit location – automatic stop/start system from 1983 (Sec 16)

Speed sensor unit
5 Disconnect the battery earth lead.
6 The speed sensor is located on the rear face of the speedometer. Remove the instrument panel as described in Section 19, then undo the two retaining screws and pull the sensor unit free (Fig. 10.24).
7 Refit in the reverse order to removal.

Fig. 10.24 Speed sensor location and securing screws – automatic stop/start system from 1983 (Sec 16)

Overrun control valve
8 Disconnect the battery earth lead.
9 Remove the air cleaner unit as described in Chapter 3.
10 The overrun control valve location is shown in Fig. 10.25. Pull free the connector hoses then undo and remove the two retaining screws (arrowed) and remove the unit.

Fig. 10.25 Overrun control valve location (automatic stop/start system) (Sec 16)

11 It should be noted that the valve contains a diode which is wired in parallel to the solenoid and if checking it for polarity watch the polarity.
12 Refitting is the reverse procedure to removal.

ASS switch
13 Disconnect the battery earth lead.
14 Use a thin flat blade screwdriver and carefully prise free the switch from the facia panel. When released from the panel, withdraw the switch and disconnect the wire connector.
15 Refit in reverse order of removal.

17 Fuses and relays – general

1 The fuses and relays are located behind the left-hand side of the facia (photo). Access to them is gained by removing the curved cover inside the glovebox (right-hand drive models) or storage space (left-hand drive models).
2 The fuse and relay circuits are shown on the back of the cover, together with some spare fuses. In addition, in-line fuses are fitted to

17.1 Fuses and relays location – typical

Fig. 10.26 Fuses and relay positions viewed from the passenger seat – early models (Sec 17)

Fuses		Rating	Relays and control units	
1	Dipped beam left	8A	16	Vacant
2	Dipped beam right	8A	17	Relief relay (for x contact)
3	High beam left	8A	18	Fuel pump relay
4	High beam right	8A	19	Wash/wipe intermittent facility relay
5	Heated rear window	16A	20	Emergency light relay
6	Brake lights, turn signals	8A	21	Control unit for gearchange indicator
7	Cigarette lighter, glovebox light, radio	8A	22	Dual horn relay
8	Turn signals	8A	23	Manifold pre-heating relay/glow plug relay
9	Reversing lights, horn	8A	24	Rear wiper and washer relay
10	Fresh air blower	16A	25	Fog light relay
11	Wiper motor, gearchange/consumption indicator	8A	26	Headlight washer relay
			27	Change-over relay for day driving lights
12	Number plate light, glovebox light	8A	28	Switch relay for day driving lights
13	Side light right	8A	29	Fuse box
14	Side light left	8A	30	Window lifter relay
15	Radiator fan	25A	31	Air conditioner relay

Note: *The number and location of the relays fitted may vary according to model and options fitted*

17.2 An in-line fuse

certain models, as given in the Specifications, and their location is shown in the wiring diagrams given at the end of this Manual (photo).
3   Always renew a fuse with one of identical rating, and never renew it more than once without finding the source of the trouble (usually a short circuit).
4   All relays are of the plug-in type. Relays cannot be repaired and if one is suspect, it should be removed and taken to an auto electrical workshop for testing.

18 Ignition switch/steering column lock – removal and refitting

1   Remove the steering column combination switch, as described in Section 21.
2   Prise the lockwasher from the inner column and remove the spring followed by the contact ring.
3   Using an Allen key, unscrew the clamp bolt from the steering lock housing and slide the housing from the outer column. Disconnect the multi-plug.
4   To remove the ignition switch, unscrew the cross-head screw inside the housing.
5   To remove the lock cylinder it will be necessary to drill a 3 mm (0.118 in) diameter hole in the housing at the location shown in Fig. 10.27 – the retaining pin can then be depressed and the lock cylinder removed.
6   Refitting is a reversal of removal.

19 Instrument panel cluster – removal and refitting

1   Disconnect the battery earth lead.
2   Remove the steering wheel as described in Chapter 11. Although not essential, this does allow greater freedom of access.
3   Using a flat blade tool, carefully prise free and remove the switch trim panel between the steering column and instrument cluster panel (photo).
4   Unscrew and remove the four screws retaining the dash panel insert trim and withdraw the trim (Fig. 10.28).
5   Unscrew and remove the cluster panel retaining screws.
6   Reach through the side and to the rear of the cluster panel and disconnect the speedometer drive cable by pressing the connector lugs together (photo).
7   Pivot the cluster panel forward and withdraw it sufficiently to detach the wiring multi-connectors and the vacuum hose, (photos).

Fig. 10.27 Location for drilling hole in order to remove the lock cylinder (Sec 18)

a = 12 mm (0.47 in)
b = 10 mm (0.39 in)

Fig. 10.28 Instrument panel insert trim retaining screw locations (arrowed) (Sec 19)

19.3 Switch trim panel removal

19.7B Instrument panel cluster removed

19.6 Speedometer drive cable connector

19.7A Detaching the vacuum hose from the instrument panel cluster

When fully removing the instrument cluster panel take care not to damage the printed circuit foil.

8   Refitting is a reversal of the removal sequence, but make sure that all connections are securely made and check instruments for satisfactory operation on completion.

20 Instrument panel cluster – dismantling, testing and reassembly

1   Remove the instrument panel cluster as described in Section 19.
2   Remove the relevant instrument with reference to Figs 10.29 or 10.30 but take particular care not to damage the printed circuit foil.
3   To test the voltage stabilizer connect a voltmeter between the terminals shown in Fig. 10.31 with a 12 volt supply to the remaining terminal. A constant voltage of 10 volts must be registered. If the voltage is above 10.5 volts or below 9.5 volts renew the voltage stabilizer.
4   The accuracy of the fuel gauge can be checked by draining the fuel tank and then adding exactly 5 litres of fuel. After leaving the ignition switched on for at least two minutes the fuel gauge needle should be level with the upper edge of the red reserve zone. If not, either the fuel gauge or tank unit is faulty.
5   If renewing the gearchange/consumption indicator avoid touching the back of the gauge. Removal necessitates detaching the printed circuit, the warning lamp housing and removing the retaining screw (arrowed in Fig. 10.32). Renew the diode or consumption indicator as necessary.
6   When renewing the normal type clock (which incorporates the fuel gauge) it is important to ensure the correct printed circuit connections when refitting. The connections are shown in Fig. 10.34.
7   The digital type clock is secured by two retaining screws, Fig. 10.35. When removing the clock take care not to allow the adjuster pins for the hours and minutes to fall out.
8   The warning lamp LED indicators in the lamp housing are positioned as shown in Fig. 10.36. When renewing the LEDs, each diode can be pulled free from the retainer plate, but note how one of the connector prongs is offset. This is the minus connection and it is important that they are correctly refitted. If necessary the diode holder unit can be removed by carefully levering it free from the warning lamp housing.
9   The individual circuits of the printed circuit foil can be checked for continuity using Figs. 10.37, 10.38, and 10.39 for reference.
10 If renewing the printed circuit foil it should be noted that a common type is supplied for all models. If fitting a new printed circuit foil to the dash insert on models with a normal type clock it is necessary to cut off the connector pins used for the digital clock and vice versa for models with the digital clock.

Instrument lighting bulb

Printed circuit

Gear change and consumption indicator

LEDs

Voltage stabilizer

Speedometer

Coolant temerature indicator

Warning lamp housing

Diode holder

Digital clock

Rev counter

Retaining plate

Fuel gauge

Dash panel insert

Fig. 10.29 Exploded view of instrument panel cluster unit with digital clock and gearchange/consumption indicator (Sec 20)

Dash panel insert

Voltage stabilizer

Speedometer

Clock

Gear change indicator

Warning lamp housing

Fuel gauge

Retaining plate

Instrument lighting bulb

Diode holder

LEDs

Coolant temperature gauge

Printed circuit

Fig. 10.30 Exploded view of instrument panel cluster unit with normal type clock and gearchange indicator (Sec 20)

Fig. 10.31 Voltage stabilizer test terminals (Sec 20)

Fig. 10.32 Gearchange/consumption indicator (bottom arrow)
and retaining screw (top arrow) (Sec 20)

Fig. 10.33 Gearchange/consumption indicator connections
(Sec 20)

Fig. 10.34 Normal type clock connections (Sec 20)

1 LED (plus)	4 Solenoid valve (earth)
2 LED (minus)	5 Vacuum connection
3 Solenoid valve (plus)	

1 Earth connection	2 Plus (live) connection

Fig. 10.35 Digital clock retaining screws (arrowed) (Sec 20)

Fig. 10.36 LED locations in the warning lamp housing (Sec 20)

K1 High beam (yellow)	K5 Indicators (green)
K2 Alternator (red)	K29 Glow time (yellow) – diesel
K3 Oil pressure (red)	K48 Gearchange indicator (yellow)

Fig. 10.37 Printed circuit functions with 14 pin connector (Sec 20)

1 Instrument lighting
2 Earth (terminal 31)
3 Fuel gauge (to sender)
4 Coolant temperature gauge (to sender)
5 Tachometer (terminal 1)
6 Clock
7 High beam warning light (terminal 56a)
8 Vacant
9 Oil pressure warning lamp (to switch)
10 Glow time warning lamp – diesel
11 Vacant
12 Alternator warning lamp (terminal 61)
13 Indicator warning lamp (terminal 49a)
14 Plus wire (terminal 5)

Fig. 10.38 Printed circuit functions with 6 pin connector (Sec 20)

1 Vacant
2 Vacant
3 Vacant
4 Vacant
5 LED (gearchange indicator)
6 Solenoid valve (consumption indicator)

Fig. 10.39 Printed circuit connection designations (Sec 20)

Voltage stabilizer	1	Plus (+) input	
	2	Earth (−)	
	3	Output	
Coolant temperature gauge	4	To gauge sender	
	5	Earth (−)	
	6	Output	
Fuel gauge	7	To gauge sender	
	8	To voltage stabilizer output	

Digital clock	9	Plus (+)
	10	Earth (−)
Tachometer	11	Earth (−)
	12	From ignition coil (terminal 1)
	13	To voltage stabilizer input
	14	To 6 pin connector
Gearchange/consumption indicator	15	LED earth
	16	To 6 pin connector
	17	Solenoid valve

20.11 Instrument panel cluster bulb removal

21.4A Detach the multi-plug lead connector ...

21.4B ... then remove the three retaining screws (arrowed)

11 The instrument light bulbs can be renewed by withdrawing the holder and pulling free the bulb (photo). Refit in reverse.
12 Reassembly and refitting of the instrument cluster is a reversal of the removal procedure. Check the various functions for satisfactory operation on completion.

21 Steering column combination switches – removal and refitting

1 Disconnect the battery earth lead.
2 Remove the steering wheel as described in Chapter 11.
3 Unscrew and remove the lower to upper steering column shroud screws and detach the lower cover.
4 Disconnect the multi-plug then remove the three screws and withdraw the combination switches (photos).
5 The switches are not repairable or adjustable and if defective must be renewed.
6 Refitting is a reversal of removal. If fitting an intermittent device for the windscreen wipers, locate the relay holder in place of the bridge and withdraw the wedge (Fig. 10.41).
7 Tighten the switch securing screws securely to ensure a good earth connection. Check switches for satisfactory operation on completion.

Steering wheel

Cover

Horn button

Slip ring

Wiper switch

Trim

Turn signal switch

Retaining washer

Lock cylinder

Spring

Contact ring

Ignition switch

Steering lock

Support ring

Choke knob

Column tube

Cheese head screw

Fig. 10.40 Steering column assembly components (Sec 21)

**Fig. 10.41 Wedge location in windscreen wiper switch unit
(Sec 21)**

22 Rocker switches – removal and refitting

1   Rocker switches are fitted to the lower facia panel and to the central console, their functions and positons depending on model. The function of each switch is indicated by a symbol on its face, and some switches incorporate a warning light.
2   Disconnect the battery earth lead.
3   To remove a lower facia panel switch, first carefully prise free the trim panel.
4   Reach behind the switch concerned and compress the retaining lugs whilst simultaneously pushing the switch from its aperture.
5   Disconnect the lead connector to fully remove the switch.
6   To remove the switch bulb, twist free the holder and then pull the bulb out for inspection and if necessary renewal.
7   Refitting is a reversal of removal. Check switch operation on completion.

23 Door and luggage compartment light switches – removal and refitting

1   Disconnect the battery earth lead.

Door switch
2   Open the door, unscrew the switch retaining screw and withdraw the switch (photo).
3   Disconnect the switch wire.
4   Refit in the reverse order of removal.

Luggage compartment switch
5   The luggage compartment switch location is dependent on the model and year, the two main types being shown in Fig. 10.42.

23.2 Location of door courtesy light switch

**Fig. 10.42 Luggage compartment lights and switches on the
Variant and Passat saloon (Sec 23)**

6   In each case the switch is secured by retaining screws and with these removed the switch can be withdrawn and the wiring connector detached.
7   Refit in the reverse order of removal.

Boot light switch – Santana
The switch is fitted to the underside of the boot lid adjacent to the nearside number plate light. This switch has a single screw fixing and is removed in the same manner as that described above for other models.

24 Cigarette lighter – removal and refitting

1   Detach the battery earth lead.
2   Remove the two retaining screws and withdraw the trim panel in which the lighter unit is mounted.
3   Disconnect the lead connector from the rear of the lighter unit and pull free the bulbholder (photo).
4   Compress the retaining clips and extract the lighter unit from the trim panel (photo).
5   Refit in the reverse order of removal.

25 Speedometer cable – removal and refitting

1   Disconnect the battery earth lead.
2   Refer to Section 19 and proceed as described in paragraphs 2 to 6 inclusive and disconnect the speedometer cable at the rear side of the speedometer unit.
3   Working in the engine compartment, disconnect the speedometer cable from the transmission.
4   Withdraw the speedometer cable through the bulkhead into the engine compartment.
5   Refitting is a reversal of removal.

26 Headlamps and headlamp bulbs – removal and refitting

1   To remove a bulb, open the bonnet and remove the plug and rubber cap from the rear of the headlight.
2   Press and twist the retaining ring or unhook the clip, and remove the headlamp bulb, but do not touch the glass if it is to be re-used (photos).
3   To remove the headlamp unit complete, remove the surround and

24.3 Detaching the plug connector from the cigar lighter. The illumination bulb is also shown removed

26.2A Unhook the clip ...

24.4 Cigar lighter unit removal

26.2B ... to remove headlight bulb

Adjusting screw

Protective cap

Retaining clip

Support frame

Halogen bulb

Bulb

Side light holder

Side light bulb

Adjusting screw

Cap for fog light

Fog light bulb

Adapter

Headlight insert

Fog light adjusting screw

Fog light

Fog light blank

Fig. 10.43 Combined head and foglamp unit components (Sec 26)

Fig. 10.44 Head and foglamp unit securing screw positions
(Sec 26)

Fig. 10.45 Headlamp insert retainers (1) and adjuster screw (2)
(Sec 26)

front grille, and disconnect the direction indicator wiring (where wing mounted), or foglamp wiring (where wing mounted) as applicable.

4 Undo and remove the securing screws arrowed in Fig. 10.44, and remove the combined headlamp, fog or indicator lamp unit.

5 To remove the headlamp insert, rotate the plastic retainers 90° and remove the adjustment screw (Fig. 10.45).

6 Refitting is a reversal of the removal procedure. On completion check the lights for satisfactory operation and check the head and spotlamp beam alignments as described in Section 27.

27 Headlamps – alignment

1 It is recommended that the alignment is carried out by a VW dealer using modern beam setting equipment. However, in an emergency, the following procedure will provide an acceptable light pattern.

2 Position the car on a level surface with tyres correctly inflated, approximately 10 metres (33 feet) in front of and at right-angles to a wall or garage door.

3 Draw a horizontal line on the wall or door at headlamp centre height. Draw a vertical line corresponding to the centre-line of the car, then measure off points either side of this, on the horizontal line, corresponding with the headlamp centres.

4 Switch on the main beam and check that the areas of maximum illumination coincide with the headlamp centre marks. If not, turn the adjustment screws as necessary – the upper screw controls horizontal adjustment and the lower screw height adjustment (photo).

27.4 Headlamp/foglamp adjuster screw locations

A Headlamp vertical adjuster   C Foglamp adjuster
B Headlamp horizontal adjuster

28 Lamp bulbs – renewal

Note: Lamp bulbs should always be renewed with ones of identical type and rating, as listed in the Specifications.

Front sidelights

1 Each sidelight is located in a holder which is mounted in the headlight reflector unit. Access is from the engine compartment side, so raise and support the bonnet.

2 Twist the bulbholder anti-clockwise and remove it from the headlamp (photo).

3 Push and twist the bulb to remove it.

4 Refit in reverse order and check operation.

Front direction indicators – bumper mounted

5 Remove the two screws and withdraw the lens.

6 Push and twist the bulb to remove it, (photo).

28.2 Sidelight bulb holder removal from the headlamp

28.6 Front indicator bulb removal – bumper mounted

7 The bulb can only be fitted in one position because of the offset pins. Make sure that the gasket is serviceable.

8 Check operation of indicator on completion.

Front direction indicators – wing mounted

9 Raise and support the bonnet. Pull the rubber cap from the rear of the indicator unit, press the holder lug towards the bulb and withdraw the holder.

10 Press and untwist the bulb to remove it from the holder.

11 Refit in reverse ensuring that the lug fully engages as the holder is fitted. Check the operation of the indicator on completion.

Front foglamp – bumper mounted

12 Undo the lens retaining screws and withdraw the lens. Withdraw the bulb, but do not touch it with the fingers if it is to be re-used. Refit in reverse order of removal.

Front foglamp – wing mounted

13 Open the bonnet. Rotate the cap at the rear of the lamp in an anti-clockwise direction and remove the cap (photo).

14 Unhook the bulbholder retaining clip and pivot it back out of the way. Detach the lead connector, then extract the bulb and holder. Do not touch the bulb with the fingers if it is to be re-used.

28.13 Foglight cap removal (wing mounted)

15 Refit in the reverse order ensuring that the holder locates with the lug in the reflector. Fit the cap with the TOP marking uppermost.
16 Check the light for satisfactory operation on completion. Adjust the light if necessary by turning the screw indicated in photo 27.4.

Rear lamp cluster
17 Open the tailgate. Depress the plastic clips and withdraw the bulbholder (photo).
18 Push and twist the faulty bulb to remove it (photo).
19 Refit in reverse order and check operation of all lights in cluster.

Number plate light – bumper mounted
20 Prise the light out of the bumper.
21 Lever out the clips and remove the cover.
22 Push and twist the bulb to remove it.
23 Refit in reverse and check operation on completion.

Number plate light – boot lid mounted
24 Open the boot lid and remove the light retaining screws (photo).
25 Squeeze the plastic clips and remove the bulbholder (photo).
26 Push and twist the bulb to remove it.
27 Refit in the reverse order to removal and check operation on completion.

Interior/luggage compartment light
28 Prise out the light using a screwdriver. When removing the interior light, insert the screwdriver at the opposite end to the switch.
29 Remove the festoon type bulb from the spring contacts (photo).
30 When fitting the bulb, make sure that the spring contacts are tensioned sufficiently to make good contact with the bulb.
31 Note that the luggage compartment light may be located on the rear panel or beneath the top panel, or in the Santana integral with the rear combination light on each side.

Glovebox lamp
32 Open the glovebox and prise out the switch/bulbholder.
33 Push and twist the bulb to remove it.

29 Horn – removal and refitting

1   The horns are located beneath the right-hand side of the engine compartment (photo).
2   Disconnect the battery negative lead.
3   Disconnect the wiring from the relevant horn then unbolt it from the bracket.
4   Refitting is a reversal of removal.

28.17 Rear lamp cluster removed

28.18 Rear lamp cluster bulb locations

28.24 Number plate light lens removal – boot lid mounted

28.25 Number plate light bulb and holder assembly – boot lid mounted

28.29A Interior light unit removed – front

28.29B Interior light unit removed – rear

29.1 Horn location and mounting bracket

Fig. 10.46 Wiper blade rubber removal (Sec 30)

Fig. 10.47 Engage wiper blade rubber with lugs in retaining slots (arrowed) (Sec 30)

29.5 Horn press contact removed from steering wheel spoke

5   To check the horn press contact on the steering wheel prise free the press pad from the spoke. The wires can then be disconnected from the contact plates if required (photo).
6   Refit in reverse and on completion check operation of horn.

30 Wiper blades – renewal

1   The wiper blades should be renewed when they no longer clean the windscreen effectively.
2   If the rubbers only are worn they can be renewed by pressing together the steel strips on the rubber enclosed side (using pliers) then sliding the rubber from the blade complete with strips (Fig. 10.46).
3   Press the replacement rubber into the lower blade clips then locate both strips into the first rubber groove. The strip slits must face the rubber and locate in the rubber groove lugs. Press the steel strips and the rubber together and fit the upper clips. The lugs on each side must engage with the securing slots (arrowed) in the rubber (Fig. 10.47).
4   To renew the wiper blade and rubber complete, lift the wiper blade and arm from the windscreen.
5   Depress the plastic clip and withdraw the blade from the hooked end of the arm (photo).
6   Insert the new blade, making sure that the plastic clip is engaged.

30.5 Removing a wiper blade from the wiper arm

31 Windscreen wiper motor – removal and refitting

1   Disconnect the battery negative lead.
2   Prise the pushrods off the wiper motor crank.
3   Mark the crank in relation to the motor spindle, then unscrew the nut and remove the crank from the spindle.

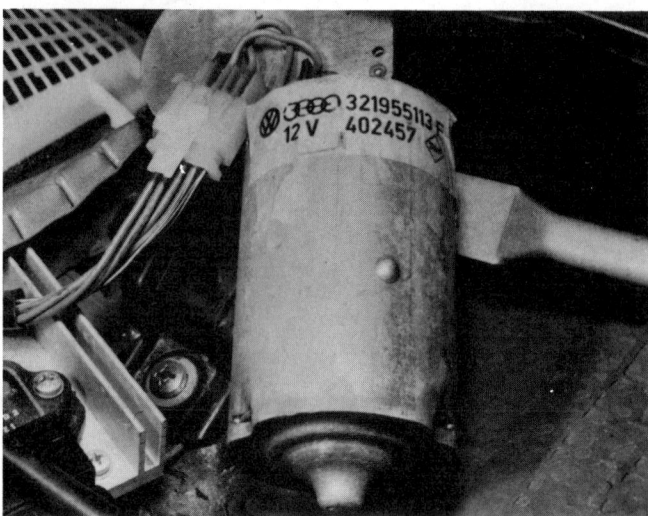

31.4 Windscreen wiper motor and lead connectors

32.1A Prise the wiper arm cover free ...

Fig. 10.48 Wiper motor crank alignment position when parked
(Sec 31)

32.1B ... and unscrew the retaining nut

4   Unbolt the wiper motor from the frame and disconnect the wiring
(photo).
5   Refitting is a reversal of removal. If a new wiper motor is being
fitted, switch on the ignition and run the motor for a short period
before switching it off. The motor is now in its parked position and the
crank should be fitted to the spindle in the position shown in Fig.
10.48.

32 Windscreen wiper arms and linkage – removal and refitting

1   Prise up the covers and unscrew the nuts securing the wiper arms
to the spindles (photo).
2   Carefully lever off the wiper arms (photo).
3   Unscrew the spindle bearing nuts and remove the rubber spacers
(photo).
4   Disconnect the battery negative lead.
5   Unscrew the wiper frame mounting bolt and withdraw the linkage
assembly, at the same time disconnecting the wiring from the motor.
6   Remove the wiper motor from the frame, with reference to
Section 31.
7   Prise the pushrods from the spindle arms (photo).

32.2 Withdraw the wiper arm

32.3 Wiper arm spindle, nut and rubber spacer

32.7 Pushrod and spindle arm joint

Park position

Wiper rubbers

Wiper motor

Wiper frame

Wiper bearing

Connecting rods

Fig. 10.49 Windscreen wiper components (Sec 32)

Fig. 10.50 Windscreen wiper arm and blade PARK settings (Sec 32)

a = 36 mm (1.4 in)   *b = 63 mm (2.5 in)*

8 If the spindle bearings are to be removed, saw off the rivets. After fitting the new bearings clinch the new rivets onto the wiper frame.

9 Refitting is a reversal of removal, but smear a little molybdenum disulphide grease in the pushrod ball sockets. Before fitting the wiper arms in their parked position, switch on the ignition and run the wiper motor for a short period before switching it off.

10 On refitting the wiper arms and blades check that their parked position is as shown in Fig. 10.50.

33 Rear wiper blade – renewal

The rear wiper blade is renewed in the same manner as that described for the windscreen in Section 30.

34 Rear wiper motor – removal and refitting

1 Disconnect the battery earth lead.

2 Raise and support the tailgate, prise free the tailgate trim clips and detach the trim panel.

3 Use a suitable screwdriver and lever the connecting rod free from the motor arm pivot (photo).

4 Detach the wiper motor wiring connector and the earth lead (photo).

Wiper blade

Jet

Pump

Container

Wiper bearing

Wiper motor

Connecting rod

Fig. 10.51 Rear window wiper components (Secs 34 and 35)

34.3 Prise free the connecting rod from the rear wiper motor arm

34.4 Rear wiper motor wiring connection and earth lead to tailgate

34.5 Rear wiper mounting bolts (arrowed)

Fig. 10.52 Rear window wiper arm and blade alignment position when parked (Sec 34)

a = 27 mm (1.06 in)

Fig. 10.53 Rear window wiper motor crank arm position when parked (Sec 34)

5   Undo the motor support frame mounting bolts and withdraw the motor and frame assembly (photo).
6   If the wiper motor is to be renewed unbolt and remove it from the support frame.
7   Refit in the reverse order to removal. If a new motor is being fitted, run the motor for a short period on completion then switch it off and check that the wiper blade rest position is as shown in Fig. 10.52. If adjustment is necessary check that the motor crank arm is positioned as shown in Fig. 10.53 with the earth connecting rivet just visible (arrowed). Adjust the crank arm or wiper arm if necessary.

35 Rear wiper arm and linkage – removal and refitting

1   To remove the wiper arm, proceed as described in Section 32, paragraphs 1 and 2.
2   Unclip and detach the rear trim panel from the tailgate.
3   Prise free and detach the connecting rod from the wiper bearing and wiper motor crank arm pivots.

35.4 Rear wiper arm bearing unit

4   Remove the retaining screws and withdraw the wiper bearing unit (photo).
5   Refit in the reverse order of removal. Lubricate the connecting rod ball sockets before fitting the rod. On completion check the wiper operation and also the wiper arm blade and arm rest position when parked (see Fig. 10.52).

36 Windscreen, rear window and headlight washer systems

1   The component parts of each system are similar, consisting of a fluid reservoir, pump unit, hoses and connections and adjustable jets. Where headlight washers are fitted, the fluid reservoir used is of larger capacity and serves both the headlights and the windscreen washer systems although each system operates independently as required (photo).

2   The systems are shown in Figs. 10.51, 10.54 and 10.55.

3   It is important not to allow the reservoirs to run dry and when topping up use a screenwash additive that contains an anti-freeze content. Do not use cooling system anti-freeze as this can damage the paintwork.

4   Should the washers of a system fail to operate check that the hoses, connections and seals are secure and in good condition also that the pump is operational.

5   If the jets become blocked, detach and clean them by applying compressed air through them, do not pick and probe the jets using wire. Failure to unblock the jets will necessitate their renewal and with the headlight washer system the pressure valves should also be renewed at the same time. Check that the jets are adjusted in accordance with the illustrations (Figs. 10.56 and 10.57).

36.1 Rear window washer reservoir and pump unit – Variant (Estate)

Fig. 10.54 Windscreen washer components and jet adjustment positions (Sec 36)

a = 434 mm (17.1 in)   b = 450 mm (17.7 in)   c = 435 mm (17.1 in)   d = 320 mm (12.5 in)

Jet

Container

Pump for
headlight washer

Pump

Jet

Pressure valve

Fig. 10.55 Headlight washer system components (Sec 36)

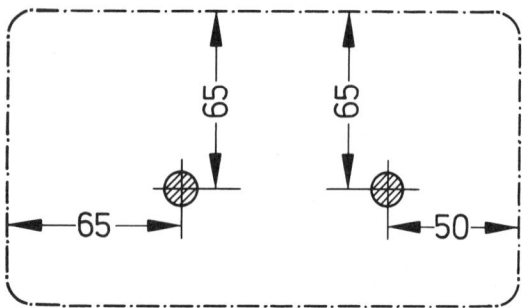

Fig. 10.56 Headlight washer jet adjustment – left side (dimensions in mm) (Sec 36)

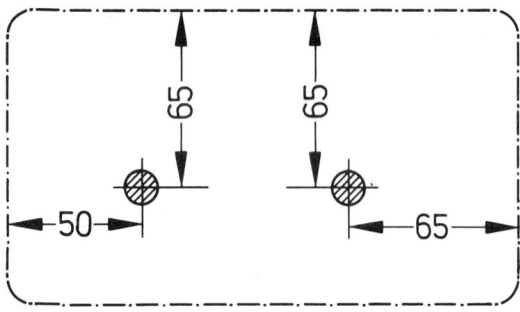

Fig. 10.57 Headlight washer jet adjustment – right side (dimensions in mm) (Sec 36)

Fig. 10.58 Cruise control system actuating controls (Sec 37)

37 Cruise control system – description and operation

This system is available on models produced from August 1983 and is designed to assist the driver on long distance and motorway driving (in ideal conditions) by holding the speed of the vehicle at a selected level. The speed level can only be set at speeds above 30 kph (19 mph) and on automatic transmission models in the driving range D or 2.

The system is not designed for use in heavy traffic conditions or in other adverse driving conditions such as on snow or ice.

The system is actuated by means of control buttons on the indicator arm, the system being brought into operation by moving the sliding button to the EIN position then when the desired cruising speed is reached the push button in the end of the stalk is pressed in briefly and released. The foot can then be removed from the accelerator pedal. Should it be necessary to further increase the programmed speed press the FIX button in until the desired speed is reached, then release it. Alternatively the speed can also be increased in the normal manner by pressing down on the accelerator pedal but using this method, when the accelerator pedal is released, the speed will again return to the programmed level originally set (Fig. 10.58).

The system will temporarily cancel when the brake or clutch pedals are depressed or when the speed drops well below the programmed level such as when climbing a hill in a high gear. The programmed speed can later be resumed by moving the slide button to the left (AUFN).

The system programme can be cancelled by moving the slide button to the right (AUS) or switching off the ignition.

Do not under any circumstances move the gear lever into neutral without operating the clutch pedal when the cruise control system is engaged or serious damage to the engine could well result!

If the system shows any malfunction at any time have it checked by your VW dealer.

38 Cruise control system components – removal and refitting

The cruise control system layout and components are shown in Fig. 10.59. The following components can be removed and refitted as described.

Switch unit

1 This unit is located behind the dash trim panel on the passenger side. Disconnect the battery earth lead, remove the trim panel for access to the switch, then detach the switch wiring connections. Remove the screws securing the switch unit and withdraw the switch (Fig. 10.60).
2 Refit in the reverse order of removal.

Speed sensor

3 The speed sensor unit is located on the rear face of the speedometer on the instrument panel. Remove the instrument panel as described in Section 19, then unscrew and remove the two retaining screws and pull the sensor unit from the speedometer (Fig. 10.24).
4 Refit in the reverse order to removal.

Indicator/CCS switch

5 The combined indicator and cruise control system (CCS) switch is removed and refitted in the same manner as that for the standard indicator switch assembly described in Section 21.

Vent valves

6 A vent valve is fitted to the brake and the clutch pedal. To gain access to one or both valves first disconnect the battery earth lead then unclip and detach the lower dash trim panel on the driver's side.
7 Detach the wiring connector from the valve and pull free the vacuum hose.
8 If available use the VW special tool, number 2041 and pull the valve unit free from its bush. Once remove the valve must be renewed as the thread will have been damaged on removal (Fig. 10.61).
9 Refit the valve by initially screwing it into its location bracket by hand. When it has started, use a 10 mm socket as shown and push the valve through the bush to the stop (Fig. 10.62).
10 The valve is adjusted by pulling the appropriate pedal back fully to the stop.

Operating element

11 Unclip or unscrew the linkage, pull off the vacuum hose and remove the unit (arrowed in Fig. 10.63) to allow removal of the element.
12 Refit in the reverse order of removal, but adjust the element linkage in the following manner.
13 Run the engine until its normal operating temperature is reached, then with the engine running at its normal idle speed turn the linkage adjuster nut to provide a bush to stop plate clearance of 0.1 to 0.3 mm (0.004 to 0.011 in).

Turn signal switch with switch for CCS

Speed sensor

Dash insert

Wiring loom

Vent valves on clutch and brake pedals

Vacuum hoses

Switch unit

Connection for tester (only for production)

Brake light switch

Linkage

Operating element

Vacuum pump

Fig. 10.59 Cruise control system components and layout (Sec 38)

Fig. 10.60 Cruise control system switch unit location and retaining screws (arrowed) (Sec 38)

Fig. 10.63 Cruise control system operating element (Sec 38)

Fig. 10.61 Cruise control system vent valve removal using VW special tool 2041 (Sec 38)

1   Clutch pedal   2   Brake pedal

Fig. 10.64 Cruise control system element adjustment linkage (Sec 38)

1   Linkage adjuster nut   2   Bush-to-stop-plate
                                          clearance

---

39 Radio – removal and refitting

1   Disconnect the battery earth lead.
2   Pull free the radio control knobs. It may be necessary on some models to depress the control knob retaining pin on the shaft (through an access hole in the knob) to enable the knobs to be withdrawn.
3   Unscrew the retaining nuts from the radio control shafts, withdraw the washers and remove the radio trim panel.
4   Remove the radio attachment screws then partially withdraw the radio to enable the respective leads to be disconnected before fully removing the unit (photo).
5   Refit in the reverse order of removal ensuring that the lead connections are securely made.

---

40 Radio aerial – removal and refitting

1   Disconnect the battery earth lead.
2   Remove the radio as described in the previous Section.
3   Detach and remove the instrument panel cluster as described in Section 19.

Fig. 10.62 Cruise control vent valve refitting using 10 mm socket (Sec 38)

1   Clutch pedal   2   Brake pedal

39.4 Radio wiring and aerial lead connections

Fig. 10.65 Front wing lining attachment points (Sec 40)

A Screws   *B Spreader clips*

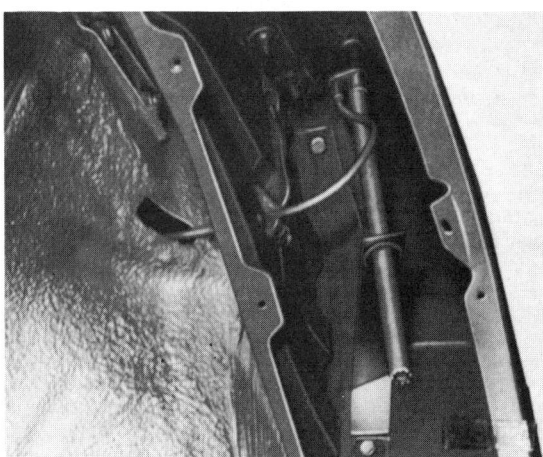

Fig. 10.66 Aerial location within inner wing housing (Sec 40)

4 Pull the aerial lead through the bulkhead towards the plenum chamber.

5 Detach and remove the wheel arch lining from under the wing panel concerned. The lining is secured by five spreader clips and three Phillips screws. To remove the clips, drive the lock pin through the clip and then pull the clip free using suitable pliers (Fig. 10.65).

6 Reach up under the wing panel and pull the aerial lead through (Fig. 10.66).

7 Remove the aerial union nut and pass the aerial down through the wing panel to withdraw it.

8 Refitting is a reversal of the removal procedure. When re-routing the lead avoid locating it near the windscreen wiper linkages and the heater and fresh air controls behind the dash panel. Refit grommets to protect the aerial where it passes through the body panel apertures.

---

41 Mobile radio equipment – interference-free installation

Aerials – selection and fitting

The choice of aerials is now very wide. It should be realised that the quality has a profound effect on radio performance, and a poor, inefficient aerial can make suppression difficult.

A wing-mounted aerial is regarded as probably the most efficient for signal collection, but a roof aerial is usually better for suppression purposes because it is away from most interference fields. Stick-on wire aerials are available for attachment to the inside of the windscreen, but are not always free from the interference field of the engine and some accessories.

Motorised automatic aerials rise when the equipment is switched on and retract at switch-off. They require more fitting space and supply leads, and can be a source of trouble.

There is no merit in choosing a very long aerial as, for example, the type about three metres in length which hooks or clips on to the rear of the car, since part of this aerial will inevitably be located in an interference field. For VHF/FM radios the best length of aerial is about one metre. Active aerials have a transistor amplifier mounted at the base and this serves to boost the received signal. The aerial rod is sometimes rather shorter than normal passive types.

A large loss of signal can occur in the aerial feeder cable, especially over the Very High Frequency (VHF) bands. The design of feeder cable is invariably in the co-axial form, ie a centre conductor surrounded by a flexible copper braid forming the outer (earth) conductor. Between the inner and outer conductors is an insulator material which can be in solid or stranded form. Apart from insulation, its purpose is to maintain the correct spacing and concentricity. Loss of signal occurs in this insulator, the loss usually being greater in a poor quality cable. The quality of cable used is reflected in the price of the aerial with the attached feeder cable.

The capacitance of the feeder should be within the range 65 to 75 picofarads (pF) approximately (95 to 100 pF for Japanese and American equipment), otherwise the adjustment of the car radio aerial trimmer may not be possible. An extension cable is necessary for a long run between aerial and receiver. If this adds capacitance in excess of the above limits, a connector containing a series capacitor will be required, or an extension which is labelled as 'capacity-compensated'.

Fitting the aerial will normally involve making a $\frac{7}{8}$ in (22 mm) diameter hole in the bodywork, but read the instructions that come with the aerial kit. Once the hole position has been selected, use a centre punch to guide the drill. Use sticky masking tape around the area for this helps with marking out and drill location, and gives protection to the paintwork should the drill slip. Three methods of making the hole are in use:

(a) Use a hole saw in the electric drill. This is, in effect, a circular hacksaw blade wrapped round a former with a centre pilot drill, (Fig. 10.67).

(b) Use a tank cutter which also has cutting teeth, but is made to shear the metal by tightening with an Allen key.

(c) The hard way of drilling out the circle is using a small drill, say $\frac{1}{8}$ in (3 mm), so that the holes overlap. The centre metal drops out and the hole is finished with round and half-round files.

Whichever method is used, the burr is removed from the body metal and paint removed from the underside. The aerial is fitted tightly ensuring that the earth fixing, usually a serrated washer, ring or clamp, is making a solid connection. *This earth connection is important in*

Fig. 10.67 Drilling the bodywork for aerial mounting (Sec 41)

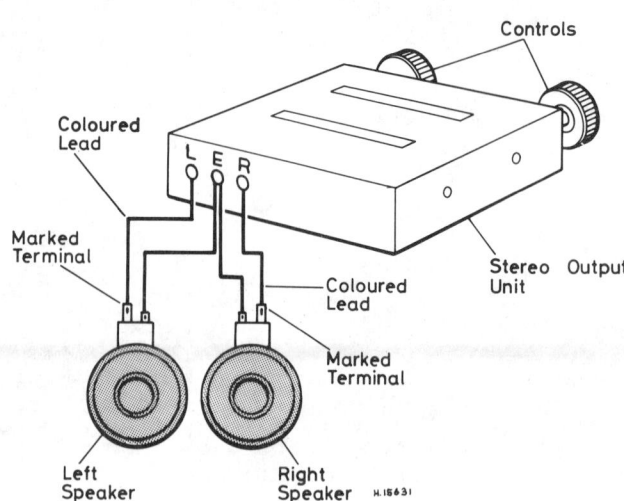

Fig. 10.69 Speaker connections must be correctly made as shown (Sec 41)

reducing interference. Cover any bare metal with primer paint and topcoat, and follow by underseal if desired.

Aerial feeder cable routing should avoid the engine compartment and areas where stress might occur, eg under the carpet where feet will be located. Roof aerials require that the headlining be pulled back and that a path is available down the door pillar. It is wise to check with the vehicle dealer whether roof aerial fitting is recommended.

Loudspeakers

Speakers should be matched to the output stage of the equipment, particularly as regards the recommended impedance. Power transistors used for driving speakers are sensitive to the loading placed on them.

Before choosing a mounting position for speakers, check whether the vehicle manufacturer has provided a location for them. Generally door-mounted speakers give good stereophonic reproduction, but not all doors are able to accept them. The next best position is the rear parcel shelf, and in this case speaker apertures can be cut into the shelf, or pod units may be mounted.

For door mounting, first remove the trim, which is often held on by 'poppers' or press studs, and then select a suitable gap in the inside

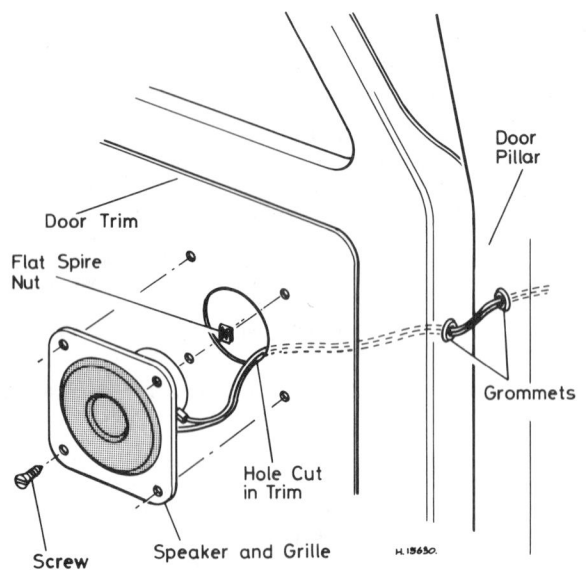

Fig. 10.68 Door-mounted speaker installation (Sec 41)

door assembly. Check that the speaker would not obstruct glass or winder mechanism by winding the window up and down. A template is often provided for marking out the trim panel hole, and then the four fixing holes must be drilled through. Mark out with chalk and cut cleanly with a sharp knife or keyhole saw. Speaker leads are then threaded through the door and door pillar, if necessary drilling 10 mm diameter holes. Fit grommets in the holes and connect to the radio or tape unit correctly. Do not omit a waterproofing cover, usually supplied with door speakers. If the speaker has to be fixed into the metal of the door itself, use self-tapping screws, and if the fixing is to the door trim use self-tapping screws and flat spire nuts, (Figs. 10.68 and 10.69).

Rear shelf mounting is somewhat simpler but it is necessary to find gaps in the metalwork underneath the parcel shelf. However, remember that the speakers should be as far apart as possible to give a good stereo effect. Pod-mounted speakers can be screwed into position through the parcel shelf material, but it is worth testing for the best position. Sometimes good results are found by reflecting sound off the rear window.

Unit installation

Many vehicles have a dash panel aperture to take a radio/audio unit, a recognised international standard being 189.5 mm x 60 mm. Alternatively a console may be a feature of the car interior design and this, mounted below the dashboard, gives more room. If neither facility is available a unit may be mounted on the underside of the parcel shelf; these are frequently non-metallic and an earth wire from the case to a good earth point is necessary. A three-sided cover in the form of a cradle is obtainable from car radio dealers and this gives a professional appearance to the installation; in this case choose a position where the controls can be reached by a driver with his seat belt on, (Fig. 10.70).

Installation of the radio/audio unit is basically the same in all cases, and consists of offering it into the aperture after removal of the knobs *(not* push buttons) and the trim plate. In some cases a special mounting plate is required to which the unit is attached. It is worthwhile supporting the rear end in cases where sag or strain may occur, and it is usually possible to use a length of perforated metal strip attached between the unit and a good support point nearby. In general it is recommended that tape equipment should be installed at or nearly horizontal.

Connections to the aerial socket are simply by the standard plug terminating the aerial downlead or its extension cable. Speakers for a stereo system must be matched and correctly connected, as outlined previously.

Fig. 10.70 Mounting component details for radio/cassette unit (Sec 41)

Note: *While all work is carried out on the power side, it is wise to disconnect the battery earth lead.* Before connection is made to the vehicle electrical system, check that the polarity of the unit is correct. Most vehicles use a negative earth system, but radio/audio units often have a reversible plug to convert the set to either + or − earth. *Incorrect connection may cause serious damage.*

The power lead is often permanently connected inside the unit and terminates with one half of an in-line fuse carrier. The other half is fitted with a suitable fuse (3 or 5 amperes) and a wire which should go to a power point in the electrical system. This may be the accessory terminal on the ignition switch, giving the advantage of power feed with ignition or with the ignition key at the 'accessory' position. Power to the unit stops when the ignition key is removed. Alternatively, the lead may be taken to a live point at the fusebox with the consequence of having to remember to switch off at the unit before leaving the vehicle.

Before switching on for initial test, be sure that the speaker connections have been made, for running without load can damage the output transistors. Switch on next and tune through the bands to ensure that all sections are working, and check the tape unit if applicable. The aerial trimmer should be adjusted to give the strongest reception on a weak signal in the medium wave band, at say 200 metres.

Interference

In general, when electric current changes abruptly, unwanted electrical noise is produced. The motor vehicle is filled with electrical devices which change electric current rapidly, the most obvious being the contact breaker.

When the spark plugs operate, the sudden pulse of spark current causes the associated wiring to radiate. Since early radio transmitters used sparks as a basis of operation, it is not surprising that the car radio will pick up ignition spark noise unless steps are taken to reduce it to acceptable levels.

Interference reaches the car radio in two ways:

(a) by conduction through the wiring.
(b) by radiation to the receiving aerial.

Initial checks presuppose that the bonnet is down and fastened, the radio unit has a good earth connection (*not* through the aerial downlead outer), no fluorescent tubes are working near the car, the aerial trimmer has been adjusted, and the vehicle is in a position to receive radio signals, ie not in a metal-clad building.

Switch on the radio and tune it to the middle of the medium wave (MW) band off-station with the volume (gain) control set fairly high. Switch on the ignition (but do not start the engine) and wait to see if irregular clicks or hash noise occurs. Tapping the facia panel may also produce the effects. If so, this will be due to the voltage stabiliser, which is an on-off thermal switch to control instrument voltage. It is located usually on the back of the instrument panel, often attached to the speedometer. Correction is by attachment of a capacitor and, if still troublesome, chokes in the supply wires, (Fig. 10.71).

Fig. 10.71 Voltage stabilizer interference suppression (Sec 41)

Switch on the engine and listen for interference on the MW band. Depending on the type of interference, the indications are as follows.

A harsh crackle that drops out abruptly at low engine speed or when the headlights are switched on is probably due to a voltage regulator.

A whine varying with engine speed is due to the alternator. Try temporarily taking off the drive belt − if the noise goes this is confirmation.

Regular ticking or crackle that varies in rate with the engine speed is due to the ignition system. With this trouble in particular and others in general, check to see if the noise is entering the receiver from the wiring or by radiation. To do this, pull out the aerial plug, (preferably shorting out the input socket or connecting a 62 pF capacitor across it). If the noise disappears it is coming in through the aerial and is *radiation noise*. If the noise persists it is reaching the receiver through the wiring and is said to be *line-borne*.

Interference from wipers, washers, heater blowers, turn-indicators, stop lamps, etc is usually taken to the receiver by wiring, and simple treatment using capacitors and possibly chokes will solve the problem. Switch on each one in turn (wet the screen first for running wipers!) and listen for possible interference with the aerial plug in place and again when removed.

Note that if most of the vehicle accessories are found to be creating interference all together, the probability is that poor aerial earthing is to blame.

Component terminal markings

Throughout the following sub-sections reference will be found to various terminal markings. These will vary depending on the manufacturer of the relevant component. If terminal markings differ from those mentioned, reference should be made to the following table, where the most commonly encountered variations are listed.

Alternator	Alternator terminal (thick lead)	Exciting winding terminal
DIN/Bosch	B+	DF
Delco Remy	+	EXC
Ducellier	+	EXC
Ford (US)	+	DF
Lucas	+	F
Marelli	+B	F

Ignition coil	Ignition switch terminal	Contact breaker terminal
DIN/Bosch	15	1
Delco Remy	+	–
Ducellier	BAT	RUP
Ford (US)	B/+	CB/–
Lucas	SW/+	–
Marelli	BAT/+B	D

Voltage regulator	Voltage input terminal	Exciting winding terminal
DIN/Bosch	B+/D+	DF
Delco Remy	BAT/+	EXC
Ducellier	BOB/BAT	EXC
Ford (US)	BAT	DF
Lucas	+/A	F
Marelli		F

Suppression methods – ignition

Suppressed HT cables are supplied as original equipment by manufacturers and will meet regulations as far as interference to neighbouring equipment is concerned. It is illegal to remove such suppression unless an alternative is provided, and this may take the form of resistive spark plug caps in conjunction with plain copper HT cable. For VHF purposes, these and 'in-line' resistors may not be effective, and resistive HT cable is preferred. Check that suppressed cables are actually fitted by observing cable identity lettering, or measuring with an ohmmeter – the value of each plug lead should be 5000 to 10 000 ohms.

A 1 microfarad capacitor connected from the LT supply side of the ignition coil to a good nearby earth point will complete basic ignition interference treatment. *NEVER fit a capacitor to the coil terminal to the contact breaker – the result would be burnt out points in a short time.*

If ignition noise persists despite the treatment above, the following sequence should be followed:

(a) Check the earthing of the ignition coil; remove paint from fixing clamp.

(b) If this does not work, lift the bonnet. Should there be no change in interference level, this may indicate that the bonnet is not electrically connected to the car body. Use a proprietary braided strap across a bonnet hinge ensuring a first class electrical connection. If, however, lifting the bonnet increases the interference, then fit resistive HT cables of a higher ohms-per-metre value (Fig. 10.72).

(c) If all these measures fail, it is probable that re-radiation from metallic components is taking place. Using a braided strap between metallic points, go round the vehicle systematically – try the following: engine to body, exhaust system to body, front suspension to engine and to body, steering column to body, gear lever to engine and to body, Bowden cable to body, metal parcel shelf to body. When an offending component is located it should be bonded with the strap permanently.

(d) As a next step, the fitting of distributor suppressors to each lead at the distributor end may help.

(e) Beyond this point is involved the possible screening of the distributor and fitting resistive spark plugs, but such advanced treatment is not usually required for vehicles with entertainment equipment.

Electronic ignition systems have built-in suppression components, but this does not relieve the need for using suppressed HT leads. In some cases it is permitted to connect a capacitor on the low tension supply side of the ignition coil, but not in every case. Makers' instructions should be followed carefully, otherwise damage to the ignition semiconductors may result.

Fig. 10.72 Braided earth strap between bonnet and body (Sec 41)

Suppression methods – generators

Alternators should be fitted with a 3 microfarad capacitor from the B+ main output terminal (thick cable) to earth. Additional suppression may be obtained by the use of a filter in the supply line to the radio receiver, (Fig. 10.73).

It is most important that:

(a) Capacitors are never connected to the field terminals of the alternator.

(b) Alternators must not be run without connection to the battery.

1000 μF 16 VOLT ELECTROLYTIC CAPACITOR   Choke   12 VOLTS +

Fig. 10.73 Line-borne interference suppression (Sec 41)

Suppression methods – voltage regulators

Alternator regulators come in three types:

(a) *Vibrating contact regulators separate from the alternator. Used extensively on continental vehicles.*
(b) *Electronic regulators separate from the alternator.*
(c) *Electronic regulators built-in to the alternator.*

In case (a) interference may be generated on the AM and FM (VHF) bands. For some cars a replacement suppressed regulator is available. Filter boxes may be used with non-suppressed regulators, (Fig. 10.74). But if not available, then for AM equipment a 2 microfarad or 3 microfarad capacitor may be mounted at the voltage terminal marked D+ or B+ of the regulator. FM bands may be treated by a feed-through capacitor of 2 or 3 microfarad, (Figs. 10.75 and 10.76).

Electronic voltage regulators are not always troublesome, but where necessary, a 1 microfarad capacitor from the regulator + terminal will help, (Fig. 10.77).

Integral electronic voltage regulators do not normally generate much interference, but when encountered this is in combination with alternator noise. A 1 microfarad or 2 microfarad capacitor from the warning lamp (IND) terminal to earth for Lucas ACR alternators and Femsa, Delco and Bosch equivalents should cure the problem, (Fig. 10.78).

Fig. 10.76 Suppression of FM interference by vibrating contact voltage regulator (alternator equipment) (Sec 41)

Fig. 10.74 Typical filter box for vibrating contact voltage regulator (alternator equipment) (Sec 41)

Fig. 10.77 Electronic voltage regulator suppression (Sec 41)

Fig. 10.75 Suppression of AM interference by vibrating contact voltage regulator (alternator equipment) (Sec 41)

Fig. 10.78 Suppression of interference from electronic voltage regulator when integral with alternator (Sec 41)

Suppression methods – other equipment

Wiper motors – Connect the wiper body to earth with a bonding strap. For all motors use a 7 ampere choke assembly inserted in the leads to the motor, (Fig. 10.79).

Heater motors – Fit 7 ampere line chokes in both leads, assisted if necessary by a 1 microfarad capacitor to earth from both leads.

Electronic tachometer – The tachometer is a possible source of ignition noise – check by disconnecting at the ignition coil CB terminal. It usually feeds from ignition coil LT pulses at the contact breaker

Fig. 10.79 Wiper motor suppression
(Sec 41)

Fig. 10.80 Use of relay to reduce horn interference (Sec 41)

terminal. A 3 ampere line choke should be fitted in the tachometer lead at the coil CB terminal.

Horn – A capacitor and choke combination is effective if the horn is directly connected to the 12 volt supply. The use of a relay is an alternative remedy, as this will reduce the length of the interference-carrying leads, (Fig. 10.80).

Electrostatic noise – Characteristics are erratic crackling at the receiver, with disappearance of symptoms in wet weather. Often shocks may be given when touching bodywork. Part of the problem is the build-up of static electricity in non-driven wheels and the acquisition of charge on the body shell. It is possible to fit spring-loaded contacts at the wheels to give good conduction between the rotary wheel parts and the vehicle frame. Changing a tyre sometimes helps – because of tyres' varying resistances. In difficult cases a trailing flex which touches the ground will cure the problem. If this is not acceptable it is worth trying conductive paint on the tyre walls, (Fig. 10.81).

Fig. 10.81 Use of spring contacts at wheels (Sec 41)

Fuel pump – Suppression requires a 1 microfarad capacitor between the supply wire to the pump and a nearby earth point. If this is insufficient a 7 ampere line choke connected in the supply wire near the pump is required.

Fluorescent tubes – Vehicles used for camping/caravanning frequently have fluorescent tube lighting. These tubes require a relatively high voltage for operation and this is provided by an inverter (a form of oscillator) which steps up the vehicle supply voltage. This can give rise to serious interference to radio reception, and the tubes themselves can contribute to this interference by the pulsating nature of the lamp discharge. In such situations it is important to mount the aerial as far away from a fluorescent tube as possible. The interference problem may be alleviated by screening the tube with fine wire turns spaced an inch (25 mm) apart and earthed to the chassis. Suitable chokes should be fitted in both supply wires close to the inverter.

Radio/cassette case breakthrough

Magnetic radiation from dashboard wiring may be sufficiently intense to break through the metal case of the radio/cassette player. Often this is due to a particular cable routed too close and shows up as ignition interference on AM and cassette play and/or alternator whine on cassette play.

The first point to check is that the clips and/or screws are fixing all parts of the radio/cassette case together properly. Assuming good earthing of the case, see if it is possible to re-route the offending cable – the chances of this are not good, however, in most cars.

Next release the radio/cassette player and locate it in different positions with temporary leads. If a point of low interference is found, then if possible fix the equipment in that area. This also confirms that local radiation is causing the trouble. If re-location is not feasible, fit the radio/cassette player back in the original position.

Alternator interference on cassette play is now caused by radiation from the main charging cable which goes from the battery to the output terminal of the alternator, usually via the + terminal of the starter motor relay. In some vehicles this cable is routed under the dashboard, so the solution is to provide a direct cable route. Detach the original cable from the alternator output terminal and make up a new cable of at least 6 mm² cross-sectional area to go from alternator to battery with the shortest possible route. *Remember – do not run the engine with the alternator disconnected from the battery.*

Ignition breakthrough on AM and/or cassette play can be a difficult problem. It is worth wrapping earthed foil round the offending cable run near the equipment, or making up a deflector plate well screwed down to a good earth. Another possibility is the use of a suitable relay to switch on the ignition coil. The relay should be mounted close to the ignition coil; with this arrangement the ignition coil primary current is not taken into the dashboard area and does not flow through the ignition switch. A suitable diode should be used since it is possible that at ignition switch-off the output from the warning lamp alternator terminal could hold the relay on, (Fig. 10.82).

Connectors for suppression components

Capacitors are usually supplied with tags on the end of the lead, while the capacitor body has a flange with a slot or hole to fit under a nut or screw with washer.

Connections to feed wires are best achieved by self-stripping connectors. These connectors employ a blade which, when squeezed down by pliers, cuts through cable insulation and makes connection to the copper conductors beneath.

Chokes sometimes come with bullet snap-in connectors fitted to the wires, and also with just bare copper wire. With connectors, suitable female cable connectors may be purchased from an auto-accessory shop together with any extra connectors required for the cable ends after being cut for the choke insertion. For chokes with bare wires, similar connectors may be employed together with insulation sleeving as required.

Fig. 10.82 Use of ignition coil relay to suppress case breakthrough
(Sec 41)

VHF/FM broadcasts

Reception of VHF/FM in an automobile is more prone to problems than the medium and long wavebands. Medium/long wave transmitters are capable of covering considerable distances, but VHF transmitters are restricted to line of sight, meaning ranges of 10 to 50 miles, depending upon the terrain, the effects of buildings and the transmitter power.

Because of the limited range it is necessary to retune on a long journey, and it may be better for those habitually travelling long distances or living in areas of poor provision of transmitters to use an AM radio working on medium/long wavebands.

When conditions are poor, interference can arise, and some of the suppression devices described previously fall off in performance at very high frequencies unless specifically designed for the VHF band. Available suppression devices include reactive HT cable, resistive distributor caps, screened plug caps, screened leads and resistive spark plugs.

For VHF/FM receiver installation the following points should be particularly noted:

(a) Earthing of the receiver chassis and the aerial mounting is important. Use a separate earthing wire at the radio, and scrape paint away at the aerial mounting.

(b) If possible, use a good quality roof aerial to obtain maximum height and distance from interference generating devices on the vehicle.

(c) Use of a high quality aerial downlead is important, since losses in cheap cable can be significant.

(d) The polarisation of FM transmissions may be horizontal, vertical, circular or slanted. Because of this the optimum mounting angle is at 45° to the vehicle roof.

Citizens' Band radio (CB)

In the UK, CB transmitter/receivers work within the 27 MHz and 934 MHz bands, using the FM mode. At present interest is concentrated on 27 MHz where the design and manufacture of equipment is less difficult. Maximum transmitted power is 4 watts, and 40 channels spaced 10 kHz apart within the range 27.60125 to 27.99125 MHz are available.

Aerials are the key to effective transmission and reception. Regulations limit the aerial length to 1.65 metres including the loading coil and any associated circuitry, so tuning the aerial is necessary to obtain optimum results. The choice of a CB aerial is dependent on whether it is to be permanently installed or removable, and the performance will hinge on correct tuning and the location point on the vehicle. Common practice is to clip the aerial to the roof gutter or to employ wing mounting where the aerial can be rapidly unscrewed. An alternative is to use the boot rim to render the aerial theftproof, but a popular solution is to use the 'magmount' – a type of mounting having

a strong magnetic base clamping to the vehicle at any point, usually the roof.

Aerial location determines the signal distribution for both transmission and reception, but it is wise to choose a point away from the engine compartment to minimise interference from vehicle electrical equipment.

The aerial is subject to considerable wind and acceleration forces. Cheaper units will whip backwards and forwards and in so doing will alter the relationship with the metal surface of the vehicle with which it forms a ground plane aerial system. The radiation pattern will change correspondingly, giving rise to break-up of both incoming and outgoing signals.

Interference problems on the vehicle carrying CB equipment fall into two categories:

(a) Interference to nearby TV and radio receivers when transmitting.

(b) Interference to CB set reception due to electrical equipment on the vehicle.

Problems of break-through to TV and radio are not frequent, but can be difficult to solve. Mostly trouble is not detected or reported because the vehicle is moving and the symptoms rapidly disappear at the TV/radio receiver, but when the CB set is used as a base station any trouble with nearby receivers will soon result in a complaint.

It must not be assumed by the CB operator that his equipment is faultless, for much depends upon the design. Harmonics (that is, multiples) of 27 MHz may be transmitted unknowingly and these can fall into other user's bands. Where trouble of this nature occurs, low pass filters in the aerial or supply leads can help, and should be fitted in base station aerials as a matter of course. In stubborn cases it may be necessary to call for assistance from the licensing authority, or, if possible, to have the equipment checked by the manufacturers.

Interference received on the CB set from the vehicle equipment is, fortunately, not usually a severe problem. The precautions outlined previously for radio/cassette units apply, but there are some extra points worth noting.

It is common practice to use a slide-mount on CB equipment enabling the set to be easily removed for use as a base station, for example. Care must be taken that the slide mount fittings are properly earthed and that first class connection occurs between the set and slide-mount.

Vehicle manufacturers in the UK are required to provide suppression of electrical equipment to cover 40 to 250 MHz to protect TV and VHF radio bands. Such suppression appears to be adequately effective at 27 MHz, but suppression of individual items such as alternators/dynamos, clocks, stabilisers, flashers, wiper motors, etc, may still be necessary. The suppression capacitors and chokes available from auto-electrical suppliers for entertainment receivers will usually give the required results with CB equipment.

Other vehicle radio transmitters

Besides CB radio already mentioned, a considerable increase in the use of transceivers (ie combined transmitter and receiver units) has taken place in the last decade. Previously this type of equipment was fitted mainly to military, fire, ambulance and police vehicles, but a large business radio and radio telephone usage has developed.

Generally the suppression techniques described previously will suffice, with only a few difficult cases arising. Suppression is carried out to satisfy the 'receive mode', but care must be taken to use heavy duty chokes in the equipment supply cables since the loading on 'transmit' is relatively high.

42 Heater motor unit – removal and refitting

1 Disconnect the battery earth lead.
2 Carefully prise free the plastic screen cover between the windscreen and the bulkhead.
3 Unscrew the nuts and remove the motor cover (photo).
4 Unclip and remove the resistor leaving the wires connected (photo).
5 Remove the screw from the resistor holder (photo).
6 Withdraw the motor by tilting it on its side, then disconnect the wiring (photo).

42.3 Remove the heater motor cover

42.4 Unclip the heater motor resistor ...

42.5 ... then unscrew and remove the resistor holder and securing screw

42.6 Heater motor removal

42.7 Heater motor installed with wiring reconnected

7   Refitting is a reversal of removal. Check that the wiring connections are secure before refitting the motor cover (photo).

Note: *For details concerning the heater control cables and the heater unit refer to Chapter 12, Sections 36 and 37.*

43 Heater control switch – removal and refitting

1   Disconnect the battery earth lead.
2   Pull free the heater and fresh air control knobs.
3   Where fitted remove the radio, otherwise unclip and withdraw the glovebox above the heater controls.
4   Prise free and remove the rocker switch trim panel (below the heater unit).
5   Remove the retaining screws and withdraw the heater control panel.
6   The control switch wire multi-connector can now be detached, the switch retaining clips compressed and the control switch withdrawn from the panel.
7   Refit in the reverse order to removal.

44 Heated rear screen – care and repair

1   Care should be taken to avoid damage to the element for the heated rear window.
2   Avoid scratching with rings on the fingers when cleaning, and do not allow luggage to rub against the glass.
3   Do not stick labels over the element on the inside of the glass.
4   A voltmeter or ohmmeter can be used to assist with location of defects. Look for an open-circuit or a sudden change in voltage, reading along the resistance wires.
5   If the element grids do become damaged, a special conductive paint is available from most motor factors to repair it.
6   To repair, degrease the affected area and wipe dry.
7   Apply tape at each side of the conductor, to mask the adjacent area.
8   Shake the repair paint thoroughly, and apply a thick coat with a fine paint brush. Allow to dry between coats, and do not apply more than three.
9   Allow to dry for at least one hour, before removing the tape.
10 Rough edges may be trimmed with a razor blade if necessary, after a drying time of some hours.
11 Do not leave the heated rear window switched on unnecessarily, as it draws a high current from the electrical system.
12 If the driver's exterior rear view mirror is electrically heated, this operates only during the period when the rear screen element is switched on.

45 Wiring diagrams – description

1   The wiring diagrams included at the end of this Manual are of the current flow type where each wire is shown in the simplest line form without crossing over other wires.
2   The fuse/relay panel is at the top of the diagram and the combined letter/figure numbers appearing on the panel terminals refer to the multi-plug connector in letter form and the terminal in figure form.
3   Internal connections through electrical components are shown by a single line.
4   The encircled numbers along the bottom of the diagram indicate the earthing connecting points as given in the key.

46 Fault diagnosis – electrical system

Symptom	Reason(s)
Starter fails to turn engine	Battery discharged or defective Battery terminal and/or earth leads loose Starter motor connections loose Starter solenoid faulty Starter brushes worn or sticking Starter commutator dirty or worn Starter field coils earthed Starter armature faulty Automatic stop/start system fault (where applicable)
Starter turns engine very slowly	Battery discharged Starter motor connections loose Starter brushes worn or sticking
Starter noisy	Pinion or ring gear teeth badly worn Mounting bolts loose
Battery will not hold charge	Plates defective Electrolyte level too low Alternator drivebelt slipping Alternator or regulator faulty Short in electrical circuit
Ignition light stays on	Alternator faulty Alternator drivebelt broken
Ignition light fails to come on	Warning bulb blown Warning light open circuit Alternator faulty
Instrument readings increase with engine speed	Voltage stabilizer faulty
Fuel on temperature gauge gives no reading	Wiring open circuit Sender unit faulty
Fuel on temperature gauge gives maximum reading all the time	Wiring short circuit Sender unit or gauge faulty
Lights inoperative	Bulb blown Fuse blown Switch faulty Wiring open circuit Connection corroded
Failure of component motor	Fuse blown Wiring loose or broken Brushes sticking or worn Armature shaft bearings seized Field coils faulty Commutator dirty or burnt Armature faulty
Failure of an individual component	Wiring loose or broken Fuse blown Switch faulty Component faulty

Chapter 11 Suspension and steering

For modifications, and information applicable to later models, see Supplement at end of manual

Contents

Specifications

Front suspension
Type .... Independent with coil spring struts incorporating telescopic shock absorbers, lower wishbones and anti-roll bar

Rear suspension
Type .... Transverse torsion axle incorporating trailing arms, telescopic shock absorbers with externally mounted coil springs

Steering
Type .... Rack-and-pinion, tie-rods connected to coupling attached to rack, power assistance or steering damper fitted to some models

Turning circle .... 10.7 m (35.1 feet)

Power steering
Overall ratio .... 18.5 to 1
Steering wheel turns lock to lock 3.45
Pump fluid type .... ATF Dexron
Capacity .... 0.65 litre (1.1 Imp pint)

Front wheel alignment
Total toe-in .... +10' ± 10' (1.0 ± 1.0 mm/0.04 ± 0.04 in)
Toe angle difference, left and right, at 20° lock .... -50' ± 30'
Camber .... -40' ± 30'
Maximum camber difference between sides .... 30'
Castor .... +30' ± 30'
Maximum castor difference between sides .... 30'

Rear wheel alignment
Camber .... -1° 40' ± 20'
Maximum camber difference between sides .... 30'
Total toe-out .... 25' ± 15'
Maximum toe-out difference between sides .... 25'

Wheels
Type .... Pressed steel or light alloy
Size .... 5J x 13 or 5½ J x 13

Tyres
Size .... 165 SR 13 82S or 185/70 SR 13 84 S
Pressures – bar (lbf/in²) cold tyres:

	Front	Rear
Half load	1.8 (26)	1.8 (26)
Full load	1.9 (27)	2.3 (33)*
*Rear pressure, full load, Estate model		2.6 (37)

Note: Increase pressures by 0.2 bar (3 lbf/in²) for winter grade tyres

Torque wrench settings

	Nm	lbf ft
Front suspension		
Strut to body	60	44
Strut bearing to piston rod	50	37
Shock absorber screw cap	150	110
Suspension balljoint to strut	50	37
Suspension balljoint to wishbone	65	48
Wishbone to subframe	60	44
Subframe to body	70	52
Anti-roll bar	25	18
Splash plate to wheel bearing housing	10	7
Rear suspension		
Trailing arm bracket to body	45	33
Trailing arm to bracket pivot bolt	70	52
Shock absorber to rear axle	70	52
Shock absorber to body nut	35	25
Brake backplate/stub axle	60	44
Steering		
Flange tube (manual) to pinion	25	18
Flange tube (power assisted) to pinion	30	22
Steering wheel	40	30
Column tube bolt (cheese head)	20	15
Steering lock bolt	10	7
Coupling bolts (power assisted)	25	18
Flange tube to coupling clamp (power assisted)	30	22
Bearing flange (power assisted)	10	7
Steering gear to body nut	35	26
Steering gear to side body nut	20	15
Tie-rod end to bracket nut	45	33
Tie-rod end balljoint nut	30	22
Tie-rod end balljoint lock nuts	40	30
Damper to steering gear bolt	35	26
Steering gear adjuster plate bolts	20	15
Power steering pressure line union	40	30
Power steering return line union	30	22
Power steering valve body bolts	20	15
Roadwheel bolts	110	81

1 General description

The front suspension is of independent type, incorporating coil spring struts and lower wishbones. The struts are fitted with telescopic shock absorbers and both front suspension units are mounted on a subframe. An anti-roll bar is fitted to the lower wishbones (Figure 11.1).

The rear suspension consists of a transverse torsion axle with trailing arms rubber bushed to the body. The axle is attached to the lower ends of the shock absorbers, which act as struts, since they incorporate mountings for the coil springs (Figure 11.2).

The steering is of rack-and-pinion type mounted on the bulkhead. The tie-rods are attached to a single coupling which is itself bolted to the steering rack. Power assistance is fitted to some models, and a steering damper is fitted to some models with manual steering.

Fig. 11.1 Front suspension and steering layout (Sec 1)

Tie rod, adjustable

Steering damper

Rack and pinion steering

Front bush for wishbone

Suspension strut

Safely steering column

Camber adjusting screw

Wishbone

Rear bush for wishbone

Anti-roll bar

Drive shaft

Caliper

Subframe

Fig. 11.2 Rear suspension layout (Sec 1)

Strut mounting

Strut

Shock absorber

Bonded rubber mounting

Stub axle

Trailing arm

Axle beam

Bracket with bonded rubber bush

2   Maintenance – suspension and steering

The following routine maintenance procedures should be under-taken at the specified intervals given at the start of this manual.

Tyres
1   Check and if necessary adjust the tyre pressures. Check the condition and general wear characteristics of the tyres and if wearing unevenly have the steering and suspension alignment checked. Refer to Section 24 for further details on wheels and tyres.

Fig. 11.3 Tyre tread wear indicator strips show when tyres need renewal (Sec 2)

2.2 Front suspension and steering check points (arrowed)

Suspension
2   Raise and support each end of the vehicle in turn and inspect the suspension and steering components for signs of excessive wear or damage. Inspect the suspension balljoints for wear and the dust covers for any signs of splits or deterioration. Renew if necessary. Check the wishbone and anti-roll bar mounting/pivot bushes for signs of excessive wear and/or deterioration and again renew if necessary. Check the shock absorbers for signs of leakage and the suspension to body mountings for signs of corrosion (photo).

Fig. 11.4 Power steering fluid reservoir (Sec 2)

Steering
3   Inspect the steering tie-rod end balljoints for signs of excessive wear and the dust covers for splits or deterioration and leakage. Inspect the steering gear bellows for signs of leakage or splitting. Check that all steering joints and mountings are secure.

Power assisted steering
4   Check the power steering reservoir fluid level and top up using only the specified type of fluid if necessary. Check the power steering hoses and joints for condition and security. Check the condition and tension adjustment of the power steering pump drivebelt. Adjust or if necessary renew it as described in Section 22.

3   Front suspension strut – removal and refitting

1   Prise the cap from the centre of the roadwheel, then unscrew the driveshaft nut. *This is tightened to a very high torque and no attempt to loosen it must be made unless the full weight of the car is on the roadwheels.*
2   Loosen the four bolts securing the roadwheel.
3   Jack up the car and support the body securely on stands, or wood blocks.
4   Remove the roadwheel.
5   Remove the brake caliper with reference to Chapter 9, but do not disconnect the hydraulic hose. Support the caliper on a stand without straining the hose.
6   Detach the hose bracket from the strut.
7   Unscrew and remove the suspension balljoint clamp bolt, noting that its head faces forward (photo).
8   Using a balljoint removing tool, as described in Section 14, unscrew the nut and disconnect the tie-rod end from the strut/wheel bearing housing.

3.7 Suspension balljoint and clamp bolt (viewed from rear)

9   Unscrew the anti-roll bar mounting bolts and remove the bar, with reference to Section 6.
10   Remove the driveshaft nut, then push the wishbone down from the strut.
11   Using a hub puller, press the driveshaft out of the front wheel hub.
12   Support the suspension strut from below, then, working in the engine compartment, pull off the dust cap and unscrew the nut from the top of the shock absorber piston rod. It will be necessary to hold the piston rod stationary with an Allen key while unscrewing the nut (photo).

3.12 Removing the front suspension strut dust cap

Fig. 11.5 Front suspension strut and associated components (Sec 3)

13 Lower the suspension strut from under the car.

14 Refitting is a reversal of removal. However, refer to Chapter 8 when installing the driveshaft, Chapter 9 when installing the brake caliper, and Section 6 when installing the anti-roll bar. Tighten all nuts and bolts to the specified torque. The upper rubber damping ring should be dusted with talcum powder before fitting.

4 Front suspension strut – dismantling and reassembly

1 Do not attempt to dismantle the suspension strut unless a spring compressor has been fitted. If you have no special compressor, take the strut to a garage for dismantling.

Fig. 11.6 Exploded view of the front suspension strut (Sec 4)

1   Coil spring
3   Anti-roll bar
4   Mounting bush (anti-roll bar)
5   Mounting bush (anti-roll bar)
6   Clamp
7   Bolt
8   Nut
9   Clamp
10 Wheel bearing housing/strut
10A Cap
11 Upper spring seat
12 Upper spring seat (heavy duty type)
13 Rubber stop
14 Rubber stop (heavy duty type)
15 Boot
16 Bellows (heavy duty type)
17 Stop
18 Retainer
19 Ring
20 Washer
21 Washer (heavy duty type)
22 Cap
23 Retainer (heavy duty type)
24 Shock absorber
25 Nut

2   With the spring compressor in place on the spring, clamp the wheel bearing housing in a vice.

3   Compress the spring until the upper spring retainer is free of tension, then remove the slotted nut from the top of the piston rod. To do this, a special tool is available (Fig. 11.7). However it is possible to hold the piston rod stationary with an Allen key, and use a peg spanner to unscrew the slotted nut.

4   Remove the strut bearing, followed by the spring retainer.

5   Lift the coil spring from the strut with the compressor still in position. Mark the top of the spring for reference.

6   Withdraw the bump stop components from the piston rod, noting their order of removal.

7   Move the shock absorber piston rod up and down through its complete stroke and check that the resistance is even and smooth. If there are any signs of seizing or lack of resistance, or if fluid has been leaking excessively, the shock absorber should be renewed. To do this, unscrew the screw cap using a hexagon box spanner, or the special VW tool No 40-201 A. The cap is very tight, so the tool used must fit accurately.

8   Pull the shock absorber from the strut.

9   If the strut wheel bearing housing is to be renewed, remove the wheel bearing as described in Section 5 then fit the bearing and hub to the new housing, with reference to the same Section.

10 Clean all the components, in particular the shock absorber recess in the wheel bearing housing. Note that the coil springs are normally colour coded, and therefore new springs must always bear the same code as those removed. Check the strut bearing for wear, and if necessary, renew it.

11 Reassembly is a reversal of removal, but tighten the screw cap and slotted nut to the specified torques.

Fig. 11.7 Using the special tool to unscrew the slotted nut from the front suspension. A peg spanner and Allen key will suffice if necessary – see text (Sec 4)

5   Front hub and bearing – removal and refitting

1   Remove the front suspension strut as described in Section 3.

2   Remove the cross-headed screw and tap the brake disc from the hub (Figure 11.8).

Fig. 11.8 Front hub and bearing components (Sec 5)

3 Remove the screws and withdraw the splash guard.
4 Support the wheel bearing housing with the hub facing downward, and press or drive out the hub, using a suitable mandrel. The bearing inner race will remain on the hub, and therefore, once removed, it is not possible to re-use the bearing. Use a puller to remove the inner race from the hub.
5 Extract the circlips, then, while supporting the wheel bearing housing, press or drive out the bearing, using a mandrel on the outer race.
6 Clean the recess in the housing, then smear it with a little general purpose grease. Where a new wheel bearing kit has been obtained, the kit will contain a sachet of Molypaste. Smear some Molypaste onto the bearing seat (not the bearing).
7 Fit the outer circlip, then support the wheel bearing housing and press or drive in the new bearing, using a metal tube *on the outer race only*.
8 Fit the inner circlip making sure that it is correctly seated.
9 Position the hub with its bearing shoulder facing upward, then press or drive on the bearing and housing, using a metal tube *on the inner race only*.
10 Refit the splash guard and brake disc, then refit the front suspension strut, as described in Section 3.

6 Anti-roll bar – removal and refitting

1 Jack up the front of the car and support it on axle stands. Apply the handbrake.
2 Unscrew the nuts and extract the front mounting clamps which secure the anti-roll bar to the subframe (photo).

6.2 Anti-roll bar front mounting

3 Unscrew the nuts and extract the side mounting clamps which secure the anti-roll bar to the suspension wishbones. Withdraw the anti-roll bar from under the car.
4 Refitting is a reversal of removal, but make sure that the anti-roll bar is fitted the correct way round, with the offset away from the wishbones (Fig. 11.9). Initially, the mounting bolts must be only partially tightened. Then the car should be lowered to the ground and 'bounced' a few times to settle the mountings, before fully tightening the bolts to the specified torque with the full weight of the car on its wheels.

7 Front suspension wishbone – removal, overhaul and refitting

1 Remove the anti-roll bar as described in Section 6.
2 Remove the relevant roadwheel.

Fig. 11.9 Position of offset on correctly fitted anti-roll bar (Sec 6)

3 Unscrew and remove the suspension balljoint clamp bolt, noting that its head faces forward.
4 Tap the wishbone downward to release the balljoint from the strut.
5 Unscrew and remove the pivot bolts from the subframe, noting the position of their heads, then lower the wishbone and withdraw it (photo).
6 Check the balljoint for excessive wear, and check the pivot bushes for deterioration. Also examine the wishbone for damage and distortion. If necessary, the balljoint and bushes should be renewed.
7 To renew the balljoint, first outline its exact position on the wishbone. This is important as the holes in the wishbone are elongated to allow camber adjustment. Unscrew the nuts and remove the balljoint and clamp plate. Fit the new balljoint in the exact outline, and tighten the nuts.
8 To renew the pivot bushes, use a long bolt together with a metal tube and washers to pull each bush from the wishbone eyes. Fit the new bushes using the same method, but first dip them in soapy water.
9 Refitting the wishbone is a reversal of removal, but delay tightening the pivot bolts until the weight of the car is on the suspension. Refer to Section 6 when refitting the anti-roll bar. Have the front wheel camber angle checked and, if necessary, adjusted by a VW dealer.

7.5 Front suspension wishbone pivot bolt (arrowed)

8   Rear axle – removal and refitting

1   Jack up the rear of the car, and support it with axle stands positioned beneath the underbody. Chock the front wheels and remove the rear wheels.

2   Unhook the rubber mounting rings and lower the rear exhaust silencer as far as possible. Support the silencer on an axle stand.

3   Unscrew the nut from the handbrake lever rod and remove the compensator bar.

4   Prise the handbrake cable guide bushes from the underbody brackets, and remove the cables from the rear brackets and trailing arm pivot retainer each side (photo).

5   Remove the brake fluid reservoir filler cap and tighten it down onto a piece of polythene sheeting placed over the reservoir filler hose in order to prevent the loss of fluid. Alternatively fit brake hose clamps to both rear brake hoses.

6   Disconnect both rear brake hoses from the trailing arms by unscrewing the rigid brake line union nuts, while holding the hose end unions stationary with a spanner. Remove the clamp plates (photo).

7   Loosen the nuts on the pivot bolts at the front of the trailing arms.

8   Unhook the brake pressure regulator spring from the rear axle.

9   Support the rear axle with a trolley jack, and place axle stands beneath the trailing arms.

10   Unscrew and remove the rear shock absorber lower mounting bolts.

11   Unscrew the nuts and remove the pivot bolts from the trailing arms.

12   With the help of an assistant if necessary, lower the rear axle to the ground while guiding the handbrake cable over the exhaust pipe.

13   If necessary, remove the stub axles, with reference to Section 11, also remove the brake lines and handbrake cables, if required. The pivot bushes may be renewed using a long bolt and nut, metal tube, and packing washers, but make sure that the bush gaps are in line with the trailing arms and press the bushes in flush (Figure 11.10).

14   The trailing arm pivot brackets can be removed from the chassis member each side by unscrewing the three retaining nuts. If the brackets are to be refitted to the trailing arms prior to refitting the rear

Fig. 11.10 Diagram showing correct positioning of rear axle pivot bushes (Sec 8)

8.4 Handbrake cable locating retainer on trailing arm pivot (arrowed)

8.6 Detach the handbrake cable and brake line from trailing arm

Fig. 11.11 Pivot bushes installed dimension (a) (Sec 8)

a = 61.6 to 62.0 mm (2.42 to 2.44 in)

Fig. 11.12 Bracket to axle angle must be 15 to 19°. Adjust using VW tool 3021 if available (Sec 8)

9.1 Detach the rear shock absorber upper mounting trim cover (Estate shown) ...

axle unit, they must be secured at an angle of between 15 to 19° to the axle as shown in Figure 11.12.

15 Refitting is a reversal of removal, but delay tightening the rear axle and shock absorber mounting bolts until the weight of the car is on the suspension. Bleed the hydraulic system and adjust the handbrake cable, as described in Chapter 9.

9 Rear suspension strut/shock absorber – removal and refitting

1 Detach the trim cover from the top of the shock absorber within the luggage compartment (photo). On early Saloon models it will be necessary to remove the rear seat, backrest and parcel shelf to gain access to the upper end of the strut mounting. On later models produced from March of 1982 the rear parcel shelf was modified in that it has a diagonal 'break line' at each forward corner and it can be prised up at this point and hinged back to provide access to the strut upper mounting.

2 Unscrew the nut from the top of the shock absorber piston rod and remove the dished washer and rubber bearing (photo).

3 Jack up the rear of the car using a trolley jack beneath the rear axle, and support the car with axle stands positioned beneath the underbody. Chock the front wheels.

4 Lower the rear axle until the coil spring is no longer under tension then unscrew and remove the shock absorber lower mounting bolt. The shock absorber can now be lowered from the car, together with the coil spring and damping ring (photo).

5 Remove the damping ring, coil spring, bump stop components and spring retainer from the shock absorber, but mark the position of the retainer if the shock absorber is to be re-used. **Note:** *Both shock absorbers should not be disconnected from the rear axle at the same time, as the rear brake hydraulic hoses and the axle beam bushes may be damaged.*

6 Clean all the components, and examine them for wear and damage. Note that the coil springs are normally colour coded, and therefore new springs must always bear the same code as those removed. With the shock absorber vertical, move the piston rod up and down through its complete stroke and check that the resistance is even and smooth. If there are any signs of seizing, or lack of resistance, or if fluid has been leaking excessively, the shock absorber should be renewed. Renew all components as necessary.

7 Before fitting new shock absorbers check their action when vertical – after being stored on their sides for some time, it is necessary to operate the piston rods through several full strokes, in order to purge any trapped air.

8 Refitting is a reversal of removal, but dust the upper rubber bearings with talcum powder before fitting them. Delay tightening the shock absorber lower mounting bolt to the specified torque until the weight of the car is on the suspension.

9.2 ... for access to the retaining nut

9.4 Rear suspension strut and coil spring

Fig. 11.13 Rear suspension and strut assembly components (Sec 9)

Cover for strut mounting
Upper spring seat
Plug
Self-locking nut
Bellows
Plate
Upper bearing
Protective cap
Spacer
Lower bearing
Washer
Ring
Circlip
Bump stop
Coil spring
Stub axle
Axle beam
Thickness of V section
Packing
Lower spring seat
Shock absorber
Studs
Handbrake cable bracket
Bracket for regulator spring
Bonded rubber bush
Bracket
Spring for handbrake cable

Fig. 11.14 Rear wheel hub and bearing components (Sec 10)

10 Rear wheel bearings – removal, refitting and adjustment

1 Chock the front wheels, then jack up the rear of the car and support it on axle stands. Remove the rear roadwheel, and release the handbrake.

2 Remove the cap from the centre of the brake drum by tapping it on alternate sides with a screwdriver or blunt chisel (Figure 11.14).

3 Extract the split pin and remove the locking ring.

4 Unscrew the nut and remove the thrust washer.

5 Withdraw the brake drum, making sure that the outer wheel bearing does not fall out. If the brake drum binds on the shoes, insert a small screwdriver through a wheel bolt hole and lever up the wedged key in order to release the shoes – refer to Chapter 9, if necessary.

6 Remove the outer wheel bearing inner race and rollers from the brake drum/hub.

7 Lever the oil seal from the inner side of the brake drum/hub and withdraw the inner wheel bearing inner race and rollers.

8 Using a soft metal drift, drive the outer races from each side of the brake drum/hub.

9 Clean the bearings and brake drum/hub with paraffin, and also wipe the stub axle clean. Examine the tapered rollers, inner and outer races, brake drum/hub, and stub axle for wear and damage. If the bearing surfaces are pitted, renew them. Obtain a new oil seal.

10 Pack the bearing cages and tapered rollers with a lithium based grease, and also pack the grease into the brake drum/hub inner cavity.

11 Using a length of metal tube, drive the outer races fully into the brake drum/hub.

12 Insert the inner bearing race and rollers, then locate the oil seal with the sealing lip facing inward, and drive it in with a block of wood until flush. Smear a little grease on the oil seal lip then wipe clean the outer face of the seal.

13 Locate the brake drum/hub on the stub axle and fit the outer wheel bearing, followed by the thrust washer and nut (photos).

10.13A Lubricate the hub and stub axle ...

10.13B ... locate the bearing ...

10.13C ... the thrust washer and nut

10.14 Check that the thrust washer can still be rotated after fitting the nut

10.15 Fit the lock ring and split pin to secure ...

10.16 ... then refit the grease cap

14   Tighten the nut firmly while turning the drum/hub, then back off the nut until the thrust washer can *just* be moved by pressing on it with a screwdriver. Do not lever or twist the screwdriver in an attempt to move the thrust washer (photo).
15   Fit the locking ring without moving the nut, and install a new split pin (photo).
16   Tap the grease cap onto the drum/hub (photo).
17   Refit the roadwheel and lower the vehicle to the ground.

11   Rear stub axle – removal and refitting

1   Proceed as described in the previous Section in paragraphs 1 to 5 inclusive.
2   Remove the brake shoes as described in Chapter 9, Section 7.
3   Remove the brake fluid reservoir filler cap, and tighten it down onto a piece of polythene sheeting over the reservoir filler hole in order to prevent the loss of fluid in the following procedure. Alternatively fit a brake hose clamp on the hydraulic hose between the rear axle and underbody.
4   Unscrew the brake pipe union on the rear of the wheel cylinder.
5   Unscrew the bolts and withdraw the brake backplate and stub axle from the rear axle mounting plate, at the same time disconnecting the handbrake cable.
6   Refitting the stub axle is a reversal of the removal procedure, but make sure that the mating faces are clean. Tighten the bolts to the specified torque. Refit the rear brake shoes referring to Chapter 9.
7   Refit the brake drum and adjust the wheel bearings as described in the previous Section.
8   Bleed the brake hydraulic system as described in Chapter 9 then depress the footbrake pedal firmly to set the rear brake shoes.
9   Refit the roadwheel and lower the vehicle to the ground.

12   Steering wheel – removal and refitting

1   Centralise the front wheels to the straight-ahead position.
2   Prise free the horn bar from the centre of the steering wheel.
3   The indicator (turn signal) switch should be in the neutral position.
4   Mark the steering wheel and inner column in relation to each other, then unscrew and remove the retaining nut and washer (photo).
5   Withdraw the steering wheel from the inner column splines. If it is tight, ease it off by rocking from side to side.
6   Refitting is a reversal of removal, but align the previously made marks, and tighten the retaining nut to the specified torque. Make sure that the turn signal lever is in neutral, otherwise the switch arm may be damaged.

12.4 Unscrew and remove the steering wheel nut

13 Steering column – removal, overhaul and refitting

1 Disconnect the battery earth lead.
2 Remove the steering wheel as described in Section 12.
3 Detach and remove the lower trim panel beneath the dashboard.

4 Remove the lower shroud from the upper end of the steering column. The shroud is secured by recessed screws.
5 Disconnect the multi-plugs from the ignition switch and combination switch.
6 Remove the three screws, and withdraw the combination switch (Figure 11.15).

Steering wheel
Horn bar
Steering column switch
Slip ring
Trim
Lock washer
Spring
Contact ring
Steering lock housing
Support ring
Choke knob
Column tube
Cheese head screw
Shear bolt
Flange tube
Trim
Bush
Steering column
Clamp
Grommet

Fig. 11.15 Steering column assembly components – manual steering (Sec 13)

Fig. 11.16 Lower steering column components – power steering models (Sec 13)

7   On manual steering models unscrew and remove the clamp bolt securing the flange tube to the steering gear pinion, then, using a soft metal drift, drive the flange tube upward until it is disconnected from the inner steering column. If necessary the flange tube can be removed completely by removing the clamp and pulling it through the grommet (photo).

8   On power-assisted steering models mark the relative positions of the pinion and flange tube coupling, then remove the coupling flange clamp bolt and self-locking nut. Note that all steering column self-locking nuts must be renewed on reassembly. Unscrew the column mounting bolts – one of these requires an Allen key, and the remaining shear-bolt requires the use of an 8.5 mm drill to remove the head, after which the shank can be unscrewed (photo).

9   Withdraw the steering column assembly.

13.7 Manual steering flange tube clamp and bolt (arrowed)

13.8 Column tube mounting showing shear-bolt

10 Commence dismantling the steering column by prising off the lockwasher and removing the spring.

11 Lever off the contact ring.

12 Withdraw the inner column from the outer column, and remove the rubber support ring.

13 Unscrew the clamp bolt from the steering lock housing and slide the housing from the outer column.

14 Note that the steering column on power-assisted steering models will have an additional bearing at its bottom end, but is otherwise the same as on manual models.

15 Clean all the components, and examine them for wear and damage. Obtain new components as necessary, including a new shear-bolt and lockwasher.

16 Reassembly and refitting are a reversal of the dismantling and removal procedures, but the following points should be noted. Push the steering lock housing fully onto the outer column before tightening the bolt. Press the lockwasher onto the inner column so that it compresses the spring and contact ring against the stop. Before tightening the column mounting bolts make sure that the inner column is fully entered in the flange tube, and the flange tube is connected to the steering gear pinion. Except where Teflon sleeves are fitted, lubricate the flange tube bushes with a little molybdenum disulphide grease. If the flange tube is dismantled on power-assisted steering models, note that the bearing flange must be refitted with the lug towards the centre of the vehicle (Figure 11.17).

14.3A Using ball-joint separator tool to remove tie-rod from strut

Fig. 11.17 Bearing flange lug must point to centre of vehicle (Sec 13)

14.3B Steering tie-rod end showing rubber boot

14 Tie-rod — removal and refitting

1 The left-hand tie-rod is adjustable for length, but the right-hand tie-rod may not be adjustable on some models.

2 Apply the handbrake, jack up the front of the car, and support it on axle stands. Remove the roadwheel.

3 Unscrew the balljoint nut from the outer end of the tie-rod and use a separator tool to detach the tie-rod from the strut (photos).

4 Disconnect the inner end of the tie-rod by unscrewing the locking nuts and withdrawing the stud plate from both tie-rod inner ends. The self-locking nuts must be renewed on reassembly (photo).

5 If renewing the end of an adjustable tie-rod, measure the distance between the two ends before screwing the old tie-rod end out, and then screw in the new one to the same dimension, otherwise the front wheel alignment will be disturbed.

6 Refitting is a reversal of removal. Tighten the nuts and bolts to the specified torque, but delay tightening the tie-rod inner mountings until the weight of the car is on the suspension. Check and, if necessary, adjust the front wheel alignment as described in Section 23.

14.4 Steering tie-rod inner connections and damper unit

15 Steering gear unit – removal and refitting

1   Apply the handbrake, jack up the front of the car, and support it on axle stands. Remove the roadwheels.
2   Disconnect the inner ends of the tie-rods with reference to Section 14, paragraph 4.
3   Where applicable, remove the bolt securing the steering damper to the tie-rod bracket.
4   Detach and remove the lower trim panel on the driver's side.
5   Disconnect the lower steering column from the steering gear pinion as described in Section 13.
6   On models equipped with power assisted steering, place a suitable container beneath the steering gear, then unscrew the union nut and bolt, and detach the hydraulic feed and return lines. Recover the washers, plug the hoses and the ventilation hole in the fluid reservoir cover to prevent leakage and the ingress of dirt.
7   Undo the mounting bolts and on manual steering models, withdraw the steering gear through the aperture in the side panel. On power steering models the steering gear unit is removed from underneath together with the hose and reservoir (as applicable).

8   Refitting is a reversal of removal. Renew all self-locking nuts. Delay tightening all nuts and bolts until the weight of the car is on the suspension. Check and, if necessary, adjust the front wheel alignment as described in Section 23.
9   On power steering models unplug the hoses and reservoir cap ventilation hole, connect the hoses taking care not to let dirt enter the system. Top up the system fluid as described in Section 20 and check for any signs of leakage on completion.

16 Steering damper – testing, removal and refitting

1   A steering damper is fitted to models which do not have power steering, and it is connected between the tie-rod bracket and the side of the engine compartment (see photo 14.4).
2   Repair of the steering damper is not possible. If the steering is sensitive to road shocks, remove the damper and check its operation. The damper is attached by a bolt at each end.
3   Test the damper by moving the piston in and out by hand, over the whole range of its travel. If the movement is not smooth and with a uniform resistance, fit a new damper.

Fig. 11.18 Steering gear unit and associated components – manual steering (Sec 15)

Notched ring

Seal retainer

Hose clip

Bellows

Pressure line

Return flow line

Retaining ring

Valve body

Seal

Circlip

Ball bearing

Axial needle bearing

Thrust washer

O-ring

Intermediate cover

O-rings

O-ring

Tie rod bracket

Self-locking nuts

Steering rack seal

Cap

O-ring

Self-locking nut

Thrust piece

Steering rack

Steering gear housing

Cheese head bolt

Self-locking nut

Fig. 11.19 Steering gear unit and associated components – power assisted steering (Sec 15)

17 Steering gear bellows – renewal

1 The steering gear bellows can be removed and refitted with the steering gear unit in situ or removed from the vehicle.
2 Unbolt the tie-rod bracket from the end of the steering rack.
3 Prise the bellows from the retaining ring, then remove the ring.
4 Release the clip and slide off the bellows.
5 Smear the rack with steering gear grease, then fit the new bellows, clip, and ring. If necessary, a worm drive clip may be fitted in place of the crimped type, with the screw toward the bulkhead.
6 Refit the tie-rod bracket, and tighten the bolts to the specified torque.

18 Steering gear (manual) – adjustment

1 If there is any undue slackness in the steering gear, resulting in noise or rattles, the steering gear should be adjusted as follows, with reference to photo 18.1.
2 Loosen the locknut and, with the wheels in the straight-ahead position, turn the adjusting screw until it just touches the thrust washer. On some models an Allen key will be required.

18.1 Manual steering gear adjustment locknut (1) and adjusting screw (2)

3   Tighten the locknut while holding the adjusting screw stationary.
4   Turn the steering from lock to lock, and make sure that there are no tight spots.

19 Power steering – filter renewal

1   If any component in the steering system is renewed, or if the fluid in the steering system is changed, a new filter should be fitted.
2   The filter is fitted in the bottom of the fluid reservoir and can be renewed as follows.
3   Remove the reservoir cover and lift out the spring (Figure 11.20).
4   Lift off the filter cover and take out the filter.
5   Fit a new filter and sealing ring using a reversal of the removal procedure.

Fig. 11.20 Power steering fluid reservoir and filter components (Sec 19)

Labels: Cap, Seal, Cover, Seal, Filter cover, Filter, Suction line connection, Return flow line connection

20 Power steering – fluid draining and refilling

1   Disconnect the feed hose from the steering fluid reservoir and drain the reservoir.
2   Disconnect the return hose from the reservoir and put its open end into a jar. Turn the steering wheel from lock to lock to expel as much fluid as possible.

3   Discard the fluid which has been drained off.
4   After fitting a new filter (Section 19), ensure that all hoses are in place and their clips tightened, and then fill the system with fresh fluid of the approved specification.
5   Fill the reservoir to the top with fluid and then start the engine and switch off as soon as it fires, repeating the starting and stopping sequence several times; this will cause fluid to be drawn into the system quickly.
6   Watch the level of fluid and keep adding fluid so that the reservoir is never sucked dry. When the fluid ceases to drop as a result of the start/stop sequence, start the engine and allow it to run at idling speed.
7   Turn the steering from lock to lock several times, being careful not to leave the wheels on full lock because this will cause the pressure in the system to build up.
8   Watch the level of the fluid in the reservoir and add fluid if necessary to keep the level at the MAX mark.
9   When the level stops falling and no more air bubbles appear in the reservoir, switch the engine off and fit the reservoir cap. The level of fluid will rise slightly when the engine is switched off, but the rise should not exceed 10 mm (0.39 in).

21 Power steering – checking for fluid leaks

1   With the engine running, turn the steering to full lock on one side and hold it in this position to allow maximum pressure to build up in the system.
2   With the steering still at full lock, check all joints and unions for signs of leaks, and tighten if necessary. To check the steering rack seal, remove the inner end of the rack bellows from the steering gear, and pull it back to reveal the seal.
3   Turn the wheel to full lock on the other side and again check for leaks.
4   If a leak is found from the steering pinion, the valve housing seal and intermediate cover O-rings must be renewed.
5   If a steering rack seal in the housing is suspected, loosen off the bellows hose clip and slide the bellows to one side. If there is fluid in the bellows then the rack seals and O-rings must be renewed. The steering gear unit must be removed and dismantled to renew the seals.

22 Power steering pump – removal, refitting and adjustment

1   The power steering pump and associated fittings will differ according to engine type, see Figure 11.22 or 11.23 as applicable. If the drivebelt is in need of adjustment proceed as described in paragraph 8.
2   If the pump is suspected of malfunctioning it is advisable to check the pressure and flow limiting valve. Inspect the valve pistons and pump housing drillings for wear and any signs of dirt. The pistons must operate freely in the housing drillings. Do not dismantle the valve unit. Renew it if found to be defective and use a new washer (Figure 11.24).
3   It is also possible to obtain a repair kit of seals which can be fitted after removing the pump backplate. More serious defects will require the renewal of the pump as follows.
4   First remove the alternator drivebelt (Chapter 10) and on five-cylinder models remove the retaining screws and detach the pump drivebelt cover.
5   Remove the pump drivebelt by loosening off the unit retaining bolt and nuts and the tensioning bolt.
6   Place a container beneath the pump, then unscrew the union nut or bolt from the hydraulic lines. Do not twist the union nut line – if necessary unscrew the pump from the line when it is removed. Unscrew and remove the pivot bolt, and remove the pump.
7   Refitting is a reversal of removal, but tension the drivebelt as described in paragraph 8 and top up with new fluid and bleed the system as described in Section 20.

Adjusting the drivebelt tension
8   To adjust the drivebelt tension, the pump unit retaining nuts and bolts should be loosened. Also loosen the adjuster bolt locknut on the pump bracket. Turn the tensioning bolt until the belt can be depressed approximately 10.0 mm (0.4 in) under firm thumb pressure midway between the crankshaft and pump pulleys. Tighten the adjusting bolt locknut when the tension is correct. Also tighten the pump retaining nuts and bolts (Figure 11.25 or 11.26 as applicable).

Fluid reservoir (with filter)

Return flow line

Valve body

Pressure chambers

Steering rack

Suction line

Piston

Work cylinder

Vane type pump

Pressure and flow limiting valve

Pressure line

Fig. 11.21 Power steering layout and hydraulic circuits (Sec 21)

Rear pivot bracket

Pressure hose

Bracket

Front pivot bracket

Bracket

Tensioner bracket

Suction hose

Vane type pump

Pressure and flow limiting valve

Drive belt

Tensioning bolt

Belt pulley

Fig. 11.22 Power steering pump and associated components – four-cylinder models (Sec 22)

288

Bracket
Front pivot bracket
Tensioning bolt
Tapping screw
Drive belt cover

Speed nut
Bracket

Drive belt

Drive belt pulley

Rear pivot bracket

Suction hose

Vane type pump

Pressure hose

Pressure and flow limiting valve

Washer

Tensioning bracket

Fig. 11.23 Power steering pump and associated components – five-cylinder models (Sec 22)

Fig. 11.24 Power steering valve piston tolerance group marking must be the same if renewed (Sec 22)

Fig. 11.25 Power steering pump tensioning bolt – four-cylinder models (Sec 22)

Fig. 11.26 Tension power steering pump drivebelt by slackening nuts (1) and turning tensioning bolt (2) – five-cylinder models (Sec 22)

23 Wheel alignment – checking and adjusting

1   Accurate wheel alignment is essential for good steering and slow tyre wear. The alignment details are given in the Specifications and can be accurately checked by a suitably equipped garage. However, front wheel alignment gauges can be obtained from most motor accessory stores, and the method of using one is as follows.

2   Check that the car is only loaded to kerbside weight, with a full fuel tank, and the tyres correctly inflated.
3   Position the car on level ground, with the wheels straight-ahead, then roll the car backwards 12 ft (4 m), and forwards again.
4   Using a wheel alignment gauge in accordance with the manufacturer's instructions, check that the front wheel toe-out dimension is as given in the Specifications. If adjustment is necessary, loosen the locknuts or clamp bolts, as applicable, and turn the tie-rod (or tie-rods) as required, then tighten them. Where both tie-rods are adjustable, both must be turned by equal amounts. Make sure that the tie-rod end balljoints are central in the arcs of travel before tightening the locknuts or clamp bolts.
5   If, after adjustment, the steering wheel spokes are no longer horizontal when the front roadwheels are in the straight-ahead position, then the steering wheel must be removed (see Section 12) and repositioned.
6   Although the camber angle of the front wheels can be adjusted this is a task best entrusted to your VW dealer.

24 Roadwheels and tyres – general

1   Clean the insides of the roadwheels whenever they are removed. If necessary, remove any rust and repaint them, where applicable.
2   At the same time, remove any flints or stones which may have become embedded in the tyres. Examine the tyres for damage and splits. Where the depth of tread is almost down to the legal minimum renew them.
3   The wheels should be rebalanced half way through the life of the tyres to compensate for loss of rubber.
4   Check and adjust the tyre pressures regularly, and make sure that the dust caps are correctly fitted. Do not forget to check the spare tyre.
5   Do not interchange roadwheels (steel or alloy rims) or the retaining bolts, with pre 1981 Passat models.

25 Fault diagnosis – suspension and steering

Symptom	Reason(s)
Excessive play in steering	Worn steering gear
	Worn tie-rod end balljoints
	Worn tie-rod bushes
	Incorrect rack adjustment
	Worn suspension balljoints
Wanders, or pulls to one side	Incorrect wheel alignment
	Worn tie-rod end balljoints
	Worn suspension balljoints
	Uneven tyre pressures
	Weak shock absorber
	Broken or weak coil spring
Heavy or stiff steering	Seized steering or suspension balljoint
	Incorrect wheel alignment
	Low tyre pressures
	Leak of lubricant in steering gear
	Power steering faulty (where applicable)
	Power steering pump drivebelt broken (where applicable)
Wheel wobble and vibration	Roadwheels out of balance
	Roadwheels damaged
	Weak shock absorbers
	Worn wheel bearings
Excessive tyre wear	Incorrect wheel alignment
	Weak shock absorbers
	Incorrect tyre pressures
	Roadwheels out of balance

Chapter 12 Bodywork and fittings

For modifications, and information applicable to later models, see Supplement at end of manual

Contents

1 General description

The body is of unitary all-steel construction, and incorporates computer calculated impact crumple zones at the front and rear, with a central safety cell passenger compartment. During manufacture the body is undersealed and treated with cavity wax injection. In addition all open box members are sealed.

There are two body styles available for the Passat, the four-door Hatchback and four-door Estate. The Santana model is only available as a four-door Saloon.

2 Maintenance – bodywork and underframe

1 The general condition of a vehicle's bodywork is the one thing that significantly affects its value. Maintenance is easy but needs to be regular. Neglect, particularly after minor damage, can lead quickly to further deterioration and costly repair bills. It is important also to keep watch on those parts of the vehicle not immediately visible, for instance the underside, inside all the wheel arches and the lower part of the engine compartment.

2 The basic maintenance routine for the bodywork is washing – preferably with a lot of water, from a hose. This will remove all the loose solids which may have stuck to the vehicle. It is important to flush these off in such a way as to prevent grit from scratching the finish. The wheel arches and underframe need washing in the same way to remove any accumulated mud which will retain moisture and tend to encourage rust. Paradoxically enough, the best time to clean the underframe and wheel arches is in wet weather when the mud is thoroughly wet and soft. In very wet weather the underframe is usually cleaned of large accumulations automatically and this is a good time for inspection.

3 Periodically, except on vehicles with a wax-based underbody protective coat, it is a good idea to have the whole of the underframe of the vehicle steam cleaned, engine compartment included, so that a thorough inspection can be carried out to see what minor repairs and renovations are necessary. Steam cleaning is available at many garages and is necessary for removal of the accumulation of oily grime which sometimes is allowed to become thick in certain areas. If steam cleaning facilities are not available, there are one or two excellent grease solvents available which can be brush applied. The dirt can then be simply hosed off. Note that these methods should not be used on vehicles with wax-based underbody protective coating or the coating will be removed. Such vehicles should be inspected annually, preferably just prior to winter, when the underbody should be washed down and any damage to the wax coating repaired. Ideally, a completely fresh coat should be applied. It would also be worth considering the use of such wax-based protection for injection into door panels, sills, box sections etc, as an additional safeguard against rust damage.

4 After washing paintwork, wipe off with a chamois leather to give an unspotted clear finish. A coat of clear protective wax polish will give added protection against chemical pollutants in the air. If the paintwork sheen has dulled or oxidised, use a cleaner/polisher combination to restore the brilliance of the shine. This requires a little effort, but such dulling is usually caused because regular washing has been neglected. Care needs to be taken with metallic paintwork, as special non-abrasive cleaner/polisher is required to avoid damage to the finish. Always check that the door and ventilator opening drain

2.4 Door drain holes must be kept clear

holes and pipes are completely clear so that water can be drained out (photo). Bright work should be treated in the same way as paintwork. Windscreens and windows can be kept clear of the smeary film which often appears by the use of a proprietary glass cleaner. Never use any form of wax or other body or chromium polish on glass.

5   Where a sunroof is fitted, refer to Section 31 for maintenance details.

3   Maintenance – upholstery and carpets

Mats and carpets should be brushed or vacuum cleaned regularly to keep them free of grit. If they are badly stained remove them from the vehicle for scrubbing or sponging and make quite sure they are dry before refitting. Seats and interior trim panels can be kept clean by wiping with a damp cloth. If they do become stained (which can be more apparent on light coloured upholstery) use a little liquid detergent and a soft nail brush to scour the grime out of the grain of the material. Do not forget to keep the headlining clean in the same way as the upholstery. When using liquid cleaners inside the vehicle do not over-wet the surfaces being cleaned. Excessive damp could get into the seams and padded interior causing stains, offensive odours or even rot. If the inside of the vehicle gets wet accidentally it is worthwhile taking some trouble to dry it out properly, particularly where carpets are involved. *Do not leave oil or electric heaters inside the vehicle for this purpose.*

4   Minor body damage – repair

The photographic sequences on pages 294 and 295 illustrate the operations detailed in the following sub-sections.

Repair of minor scratches in bodywork

If the scratch is very superficial, and does not penetrate to the metal of the bodywork, repair is very simple. Lightly rub the area of the scratch with a paintwork renovator, or a very fine cutting paste, to remove loose paint from the scratch and to clear the surrounding bodywork of wax polish. Rinse the area with clean water.

Apply touch-up paint to the scratch using a fine paint brush; continue to apply fine layers of paint until the surface of the paint in the scratch is level with the surrounding paintwork. Allow the new paint at least two weeks to harden: then blend it into the surrounding paintwork by rubbing the scratch area with a paintwork renovator or a very fine cutting paste. Finally, apply wax polish.

Where the scratch has penetrated right through to the metal of the bodywork, causing the metal to rust, a different repair technique is

required. Remove any loose rust from the bottom of the scratch with a penknife, then apply rust inhibiting paint to prevent the formation of rust in the future. Using a rubber or nylon applicator fill the scratch with bodystopper paste. If required, this paste can be mixed with cellulose thinners to provide a very thin paste which is ideal for filling narrow scratches. Before the stopper-paste in the scratch hardens, wrap a piece of smooth cotton rag around the top of a finger. Dip the finger in cellulose thinners and then quickly sweep it across the surface of the stopper-paste in the scratch; this will ensure that the surface of the stopper-paste is slightly hollowed. The scratch can now be painted over as described earlier in this Section.

Repair of dents in bodywork

When deep denting of the vehicle's bodywork has taken place, the first task is to pull the dent out, until the affected bodywork almost attains its original shape. There is little point in trying to restore the original shape completely, as the metal in the damaged area will have stretched on impact and cannot be reshaped fully to its original contour. It is better to bring the level of the dent up to a point which is about $\frac{1}{8}$ in (3 mm) below the level of the surrounding bodywork. In cases where the dent is very shallow anyway, it is not worth trying to pull it out at all. If the underside of the dent is accessible, it can be hammered out gently from behind, using a mallet with a wooden or plastic head. Whilst doing this, hold a suitable block of wood firmly against the outside of the panel to absorb the impact from the hammer blows and thus prevent a large area of the bodywork from being 'belled-out'.

Should the dent be in a section of the bodywork which has a double skin or some other factor making it inaccessible from behind, a different technique is called for. Drill several small holes through the metal inside the area – particularly in the deeper section. Then screw long self-tapping screws into the holes just sufficiently for them to gain a good purchase in the metal. Now the dent can be pulled out by pulling on the protruding heads of the screws with a pair of pliers.

The next stage of the repair is the removal of the paint from the damaged area, and from an inch or so of the surrounding 'sound' bodywork. This is accomplished most easily by using a wire brush or abrasive pad on a power drill, although it can be done just as effectively by hand using sheets of abrasive paper. To complete the preparation for filling, score the surface of the bare metal with a screwdriver or the tang of a file, or alternatively, drill small holes in the affected area. This will provide a really good 'key' for the filler paste.

To complete the repair see the Section on filling and re-spraying.

Repair of rust holes or gashes in bodywork

Remove all paint from the affected area and from an inch or so of the surrounding 'sound' bodywork, using an abrasive pad or a wire brush on a power drill. If these are not available a few sheets of abrasive paper will do the job just as effectively. With the paint removed you will be able to gauge the severity of the corrosion and therefore decide whether to renew the whole panel (if this is possible) or to repair the affected area. New body panels are not as expensive as most people think and it is often quicker and more satisfactory to fit a new panel than to attempt to repair large areas of corrosion.

Remove all fittings from the affected area except those which will act as a guide to the original shape of the damaged bodywork (eg headlamp shells etc). Then, using tin snips or a hacksaw blade, remove all loose metal and any other metal badly affected by corrosion. Hammer the edges of the hole inwards in order to create a slight depression for the filler paste.

Wire brush the affected area to remove the powdery rust from the surface of the remaining metal. Paint the affected area with rust inhibiting paint; if the back of the rusted area is accessible treat this also.

Before filling can take place it will be necessary to block the hole in some way. This can be achieved by the use of aluminium or plastic mesh, or aluminium tape.

Aluminium or plastic mesh is probably the best material to use for a large hole. Cut a piece to the approximate size and shape of the hole to be filled, then position it in the hole so that its edges are below the level of the surrounding bodywork. It can be retained in position by several blobs of filler paste around its periphery.

Aluminium tape should be used for small or very narrow holes. Pull a piece off the roll and trim it to the approximate size and shape required, then pull off the backing paper (if used) and stick the tape over the hole; it can be overlapped if the thickness of one piece is insufficient. Burnish down the edges of the tape with the handle of a screwdriver or similar, to ensure that the tape is securely attached to the metal underneath.

Bodywork repairs – filling and re-spraying

Before using this Section, see the Sections on dent, deep scratch, rust holes and gash repairs.

Many types of bodyfiller are available, but generally speaking those proprietary kits which contain a tin of filler paste and a tube of resin hardener are best for this type of repair. A wide, flexible plastic or nylon applicator will be found invaluable for imparting a smooth and well contoured finish to the surface of the filler.

Mix up a little filler on a clean piece of card or board – measure the hardener carefully (follow the maker's instructions on the pack) otherwise the filler will set too rapidly or too slowly.

Using the applicator apply the filler paste to the prepared area; draw the applicator across the surface of the filler to achieve the correct contour and to level the filler surface. As soon as a contour that approximates to the correct one is achieved, stop working the paste – if you carry on too long the paste will become sticky and begin to 'pick up' on the applicator. Continue to add thin layers of filler paste at twenty-minute intervals until the level of the filler is just proud of the surrounding bodywork.

Once the filler has hardened, excess can be removed using a metal plane or file. From then on, progressively finer grades of abrasive paper should be used, starting with a 40 grade production paper and finishing with 400 grade wet-and-dry paper. Always wrap the abrasive paper around a flat rubber, cork, or wooden block – otherwise the surface of the filler will not be completely flat. During the smoothing of the filler surface the wet-and-dry paper should be periodically rinsed in water. This will ensure that a very smooth finish is imparted to the filler at the final stage.

At this stage the 'dent' should be surrounded by a ring of bare metal, which in turn should be encircled by the finely 'feathered' edge of the good paintwork. Rinse the repair area with clean water, until all of the dust produced by the rubbing-down operation has gone.

Spray the whole repair area with a light coat of primer – this will show up any imperfections in the surface of the filler. Repair these imperfections with fresh filler paste or bodystopper, and once more smooth the surface with abrasive paper. If bodystopper is used, it can be mixed with cellulose thinners to form a really thin paste which is ideal for filling small holes. Repeat this spray and repair procedure until you are satisfied that the surface of the filler, and the feathered edge of the paintwork are perfect. Clean the repair area with clean water and allow to dry fully.

The repair area is now ready for final spraying. Paint spraying must be carried out in a warm, dry, windless and dust free atmosphere. This condition can be created artificially if you have access to a large indoor working area, but if you are forced to work in the open, you will have to pick your day very carefully. If you are working indoors, dousing the floor in the work area with water will help to settle the dust which would otherwise be in the atmosphere. If the repair area is confined to one body panel, mask off the surrounding panels; this will help to minimise the effects of a slight mis-match in paint colours. Bodywork fittings (eg chrome strips, door handles etc) will also need to be masked off. Use genuine masking tape and several thicknesses of newspaper for the masking operations.

Before commencing to spray, agitate the aerosol can thoroughly, then spray a test area (an old tin, or similar) until the technique is mastered. Cover the repair area with a thick coat of primer; the thickness should be built up using several thin layers of paint rather than one thick one. Using 400 grade wet-and-dry paper, rub down the surface of the primer until it is really smooth. While doing this, the work area should be thoroughly doused with water, and the wet-and-dry paper periodically rinsed in water. Allow to dry before spraying on more paint.

Spray on the top coat, again building up the thickness by using several thin layers of paint. Start spraying in the centre of the repair area and then, using a circular motion, work outwards until the whole repair area and about 2 inches of the surrounding original paintwork is covered. Remove all masking material 10 to 15 minutes after spraying on the final coat of paint.

Allow the new paint at least two weeks to harden, then, using a paintwork renovator or a very fine cutting paste, blend the edges of the paint into the existing paintwork. Finally, apply wax polish.

5 Major body damage – repair

Where serious damage has occurred or large areas need renewal due to neglect, it means that complete new panels will need welding in, and this is best left to professionals. If the damage is due to impact, it will also be necessary to completely check the alignment of the bodyshell, and this can only be carried out accurately by a VW dealer using special jigs. If the body is left misaligned, it is primarily dangerous as the car will not handle properly, and secondly, uneven stresses will be imposed on the steering, suspension and possibly transmission, causing abnormal wear, or complete failure, particularly to such items as the tyres.

6 Door rattles – tracing and rectification

1   The most common cause of door rattles is a striker plate which is worn, loose, or misaligned, but other causes may be:

    (a) *Loose door handles, window winder handles, door hinges, or door stays*
    (b) *Loose, worn or misaligned door lock components*
    (c) *Loose, or worn remote control mechanism*
    (d) *Loose window glass*

2   If the striker catch is worn, as a result of door rattles, fit a new striker before adjusting the door.
3   If door hinges are worn significantly, new hinges should be fitted.

7 Front door trim panel – removal and refitting

1   Unscrew and remove the locking knob.
2   If a manual door mirror adjuster is fitted, pull free the adjuster knob. On models with an electrically operated door mirror/heater, detach the battery earth lead, lever up and remove the switch from the door panel. Detach the lead connectors from the switch (Figure 12.1).
3   Prise back the door pull handle retaining screw cover, undo the screw and remove the handle by pulling it downwards (photo).
4   Remove the door catch release bezel by pushing it rearwards (photo).
5   Remove the retaining screw and withdraw the window regulator handle and escutcheon (manual window regulator type).
6   On earlier models, withdraw the door pocket after removing its retaining screws. On later models the pocket is secured to the panel from inside, but where a radio speaker unit is fitted into the pocket, it can be prised free and the wires disconnected.
7   On earlier models, where the door speaker unit is fitted direct to the door trim panel, the speaker can be left in position and the speaker wires detached after partial removal of the panel.
8   Unscrew and remove the trim panel retaining screws on the leading and trailing edges (one screw to each edge). On later models the bottom edge is also secured by a retaining screw.
9   It should now be possible to pull the trim panel away from the

Fig. 12.1 Electrically operated door mirror switch removal from trim panel (Sec 7)

7.3 Removing an armrest retaining screw

7.4 Removing the door release catch bezel

Fig. 12.2 Door trim removal tool dimensions (Sec 7)

a	= 130 mm (5.1 in)	d	= 2 mm (0.08 in)
b	= 100 mm (3.9 in)	e	= 0.5 mm (0.02 in)
c	= 18 mm (0.70 in)	f	= 30 mm (1.18 in)

door enabling it to be lifted clear. If the panel is reluctant to move, fabricate a trim removal tool to the dimensions shown in Figure 12.2. Prise free the panel with the tool by inserting it between the trim panel and the door/window seal aperture at the appropriate points indicated. Avoid levering at those points indicated with an asterisk (at fixed corner windows). These points will have to be carefully pulled free from the window slot seal (Figures 12.3, 12.4 and 12.5).

Fig. 12.3 Front door clip locations (Sec 7)

a	=	30 mm (1.18 in)
b	=	300 mm (11.8 in)
c	=	330 mm (12.9 in)

Fig. 12.4 Rear door clip locations (Sec 7)

a	=	30 mm (1.18 in)	c	=	330 mm (12.9 in)
b	=	300 mm (11.8 in)			

Fig. 12.5 Lever with clip to release door trim panel (Sec 7)

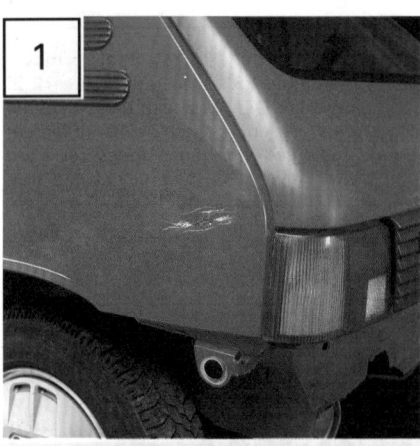

1 This photographic sequence shows the steps taken to repair the dent and paintwork damage shown above. In general, the procedure for repairing a hole will be similar; where there are substantial differences, the procedure is clearly described and shown in a separate photograph.

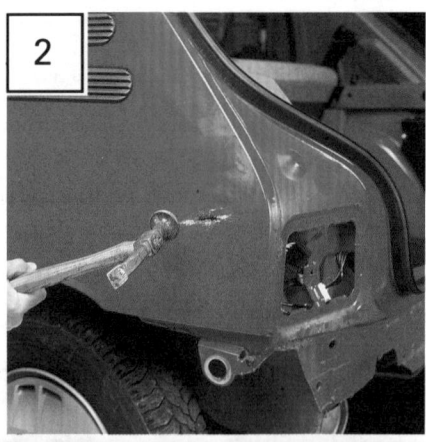

2 First remove any trim around the dent, then hammer out the dent where access is possible. This will minimise filling. Here, after the large dent has been hammered out, the damaged area is being made slightly concave.

3 Next, remove all paint from the damaged area by rubbing with coarse abrasive paper or using a power drill fitted with a wire brush or abrasive pad. 'Feather' the edge of the boundary with good paintwork using a finer grade of abrasive paper.

4 Where there are holes or other damage, the sheet metal should be cut away before proceeding further. The damaged area and any signs of rust should be treated with Turtle Wax Hi-Tech Rust Eater, which will also inhibit further rust formation.

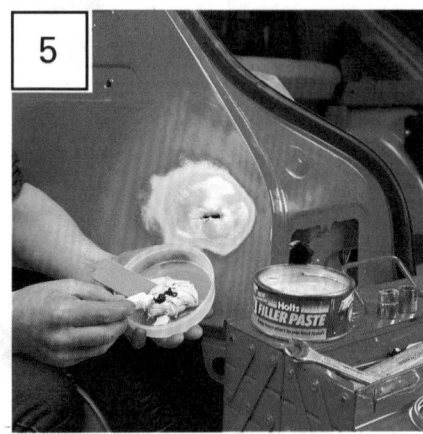

5 *For a large dent or hole* mix Holts Body Plus Resin and Hardener according to the manufacturer's instructions and apply around the edge of the repair. Press Glass Fibre Matting over the repair area and leave for 20-30 minutes to harden. Then ...

5A ... brush more Holts Body Plus Resin and Hardener onto the matting and leave to harden. Repeat the sequence with two or three layers of matting, checking that the final layer is lower than the surrounding area. Apply Holts Body Plus Filler Paste as shown in Step 5B.

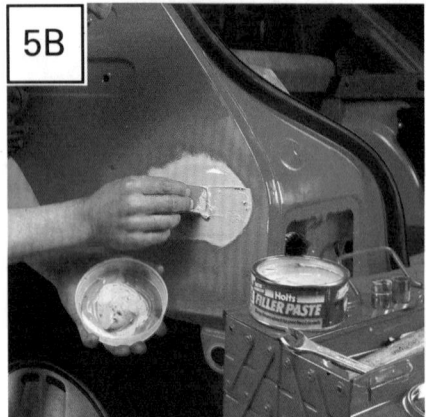

5B *For a medium dent*, mix Holts Body Plus Filler Paste and Hardener according to the manufacturer's instructions and apply it with a flexible applicator. Apply thin layers of filler at 20-minute intervals, until the filler surface is slightly proud of the surrounding bodywork.

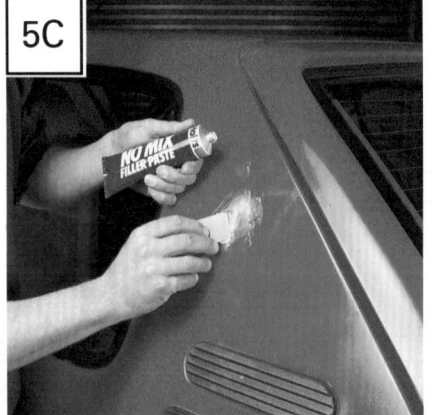

5C *For small dents and scratches* use Holts No Mix Filler Paste straight from the tube. Apply it according to the instructions in thin layers, using the spatula provided. It will harden in minutes if applied outdoors and may then be used as its own knifing putty.

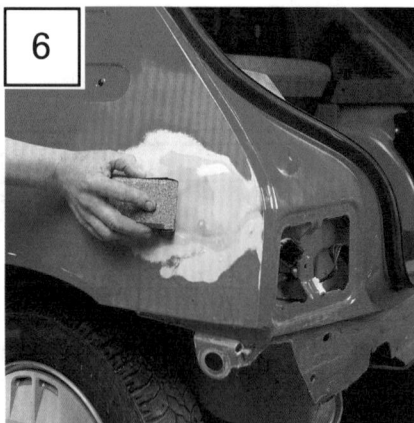

6 Use a plane or file for initial shaping. Then, using progressively finer grades of wet-and-dry paper, wrapped round a sanding block, and copious amounts of clean water, rub down the filler until glass smooth. 'Feather' the edges of adjoining paintwork.

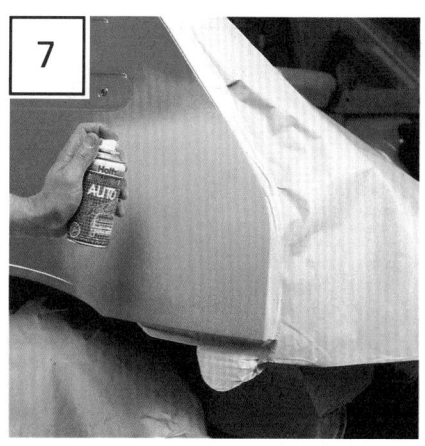

Protect adjoining areas before spraying the whole repair area and at least one inch of the surrounding sound paintwork with Holts Dupli-Color primer.

Fill any imperfections in the filler surface with a small amount of Holts Body Plus Knifing Putty. Using plenty of clean water, rub down the surface with a fine grade wet-and-dry paper – 400 grade is recommended – until it is really smooth.

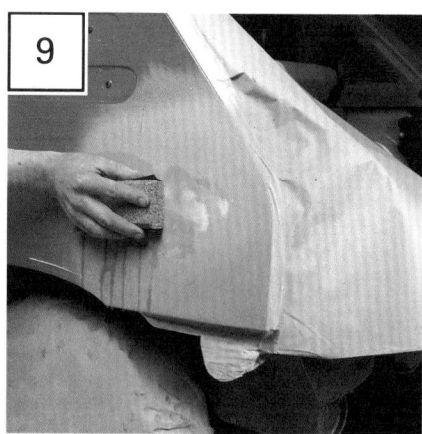

Carefully fill any remaining imperfections with knifing putty before applying the last coat of primer. Then rub down the surface with Holts Body Plus Rubbing Compound to ensure a really smooth surface.

Protect surrounding areas from overspray before applying the topcoat in several thin layers. Agitate Holts Dupli-Color aerosol thoroughly. Start at the repair centre, spraying outwards with a side-to-side motion.

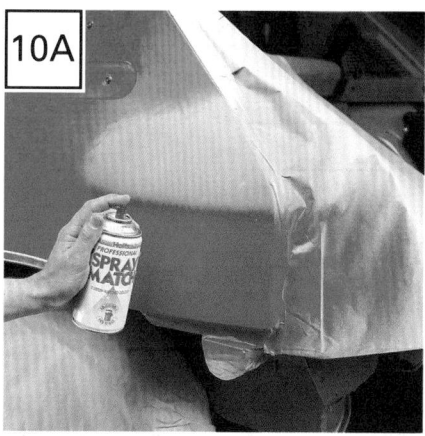

If the exact colour is not available off the shelf, local Holts Professional Spraymatch Centres will custom fill an aerosol to match perfectly.

To identify whether a lacquer finish is required, rub a painted unrepaired part of the body with wax and a clean cloth.

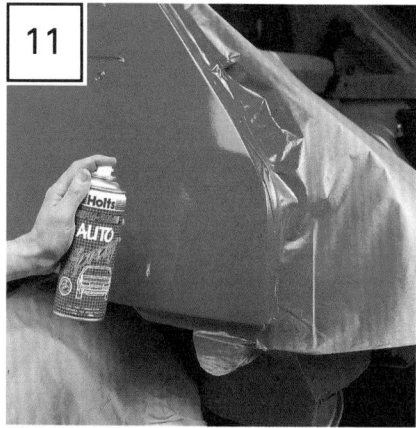

If *no* traces of paint appear on the cloth, spray Holts Dupli-Color clear lacquer over the repaired area to achieve the correct gloss level.

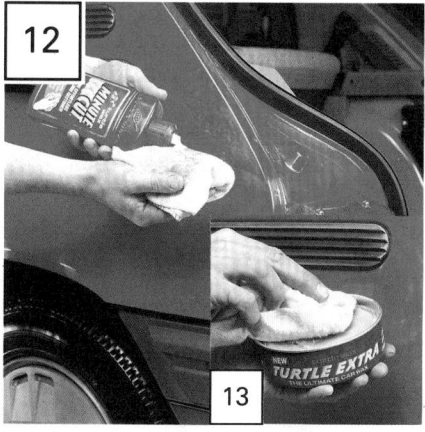

The paint will take about two weeks to harden fully. After this time it can be 'cut' with a mild cutting compound such as Turtle Wax Minute Cut prior to polishing with a final coating of Turtle Wax Extra.

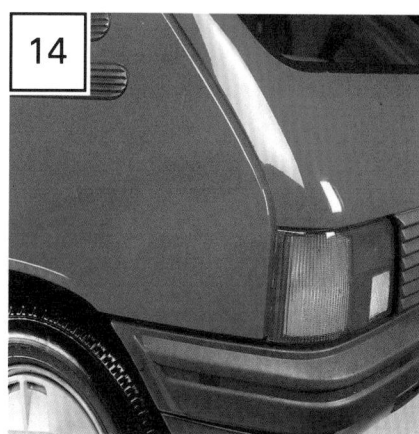

When carrying out bodywork repairs, remember that the quality of the finished job is proportional to the time and effort expended.

7.10A Remove the sponge insulator from the window regulator shaft ...

7.10B ... and peel back the waterproof sheet

8.1 Front door lock location

10 With the panel removed, withdraw the spring insulator from the window regulator shaft (where applicable) and peel back the waterproof sheet for access to the inner door (photos).

11 Refitting is the reverse of removal. Make sure that the panel clips are aligned with the holes before tapping them in with the palm of the hand.

8 Front and rear door locks – removal and refitting

1 Using an Allen key unscrew and remove the two lock retaining screws (photo) and withdraw the lock approximately 10 to 12 mm (0.4 to 0.5 in).

2 Insert a screwdriver through the hole in the bottom of the lock to retain the lock lever in the 90° position.

3 Unhook the remote control rod from the lock lever.

4 Pull the lock out of the sleeve and disconnect the operating rod.

5 Refitting is a reversal of removal (Figures 12.6 and 12.7).

9 Door exterior handles – removal and refitting

1 Prise the plastic insert from the handle, starting from the front.

2 Remove the handle retaining screws, one from the front of the handle and the other from the edge of the door. The handle can now be withdrawn from the door (Figure 12.8).

3 Refitting is a reversal of removal.

Fig. 12.7 Door lock installation showing rod (3), sleeve (4) and pullrod (50 (Sec 8)

Fig. 12.6 Inner view of door lock showing screwdriver inserted through hole (E) to retain the lock lever (A) (Sec 8)

Fig. 12.8 Exterior door handle retaining screw locations (Sec 9)

Fig. 12.9 Exploded view of front door (Sec 10)

10 Front door – dismantling and reassembly

1   Remove the door trim panel and the external door handle as described in Sections 7 and 9.

2   On models with power operated windows and door locks, remove the relevant components as described in Sections 34 and 35.

3   Remove the door lock inner control latch by pulling the retaining cleat from the location hole in the inner panel then sliding the control latch unit forwards. The latch seal can be pulled free (photo).

4   Remove the door lock as described in Section 8, also the lock rod and sleeve.

5   Lower the window so that the regulator lifter to window attachment, on its lower edge, is accessible through the inner door aperture. Undo the two screws to disengage the window from the lifter and lower it into the door cavity (photo).

6   Unscrew the four bolts retaining the window lifter (regulator) unit and remove the lifter unit (photos).

7   Remove the door mirror as described in Section 25.

8   Remove the window inner slot seal.

9   Detach the window guide channel. This is secured by a screw and washer at the top and a bolt and washer at the bottom. Remove the channel on early models. On later models lower it into the door cavity (Figure 12.10).

10.3 Door lock inner control latch showing retaining cleat (1) and latch unit (2)

10.6B Window lifter upper retaining bolt

10.5 Window lifter to lower attachment screws

Fig. 12.10 Front door window guide channel fixing screw locations (arrowed) (Sec 10)

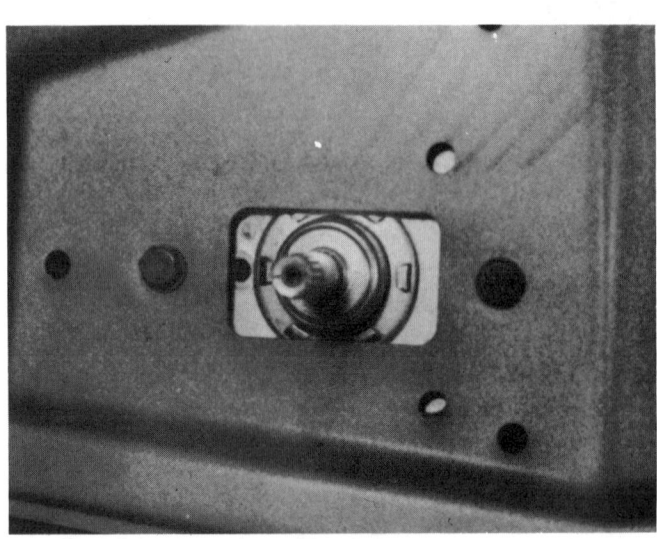

10.6A Window lifter (regulator) retaining bolts

10 Unclip the corner window seal lip in the trim moulding area, then carefully remove the window and seal.

11 Pull free and remove the trim moulding together with the outer slot seal.

12 If still in position carefully lever free the door mirror mounting packing which is secured with double sided adhesive tape.

13 Bend back the tab securing the outer window surround trim moulding at the top rear corner and using a suitable plastic wedge tool prise free the moulding which is secured with double sided adhesive tape. Remove the window channel (Figures 12.11 and 12.12).

14 Tilt the window and remove it from the door.

15 Remove the door check strap by prising free the pivot pin retaining clip and drifting out the pin. Withdraw the rubber cover in the door cavity and remove the check strap retaining bolts. Withdraw the strap unit (photos).

16 Reassembly is a reversal of dismantling. Check the operation of the door catch, lock and window lifter prior to refitting the trim panel.

Fig. 12.11 Door window surround securing tab (arrowed) (Sec 10)

10.15B Door check strap

Fig. 12.12 Lower trim moulding with plastic wedge to remove (Sec 10)

10.15A Door check strap cover

11 Rear door trim panel — removal and refitting

1   Unscrew and remove the locking knob.
2   Unclip the press fit trim strip from the armrest then unscrew the retaining screws and withdraw the armrest.
3   On models with manually operated windows, fully close the window and note the position of the regulator handle. Prise the plastic cover from the centre of the handle, remove the screw, and pull off the handle, together with the bezel.
4   Remove the door catch bezel by pushing it rearwards and disengaging it.
5   The trim panel is secured by two screws, one on the leading and one on the trailing edge. Remove the screw caps and undo each screw.
6   Referring to Section 7, make up the tool described in paragraph 9, then carefully prise free the rear door trim panel from the points indicated in Figure 12.4.
7   With the trim panel removed, peel back the waterproof sheet for access to the inner door.
8   Refitting is a reversal of removal. Make sure that the panel clips are aligned with the holes before tapping them in with the palm of the hand.

12 Rear door — dismantling and reassembly

1   Remove the door trim panel, the exterior door handle and door lock as described in previous Sections.
2   Unclip and detach the remote control catch and remove the seal.
3   On models with power windows and door locks remove the relevant components with reference to Sections 34 and 35.
4   Unclip the cranked lever and locking rod from the inner door cavity at the front end, detach the long locking rod, withdraw the lever and short locking rod. Withdraw the long rod separately (Figure 12.14).
5   Lower the window and working through the inner door aperture detach the window from the lifter (regulator) by undoing the two retaining screws and spring washers. Lower the window into the door cavity.
6   Remove the four retaining bolts with spring washers and withdraw the window lifter (regulator) unit.
7   Prise free and remove the inner window slotted seal and the outer seal.
8   Undo the bolt securing the bottom end of the guide channel and the screw at the top, and remove the channel upwards.
9   Release the corner window seal lip from the trim moulding and remove the corner window complete with seal.
10 Extract the window channel from the frame. To remove the window, tilt it and lift it out.

Corner window with seal

Window guide channel

Door window

Trim moulding

Locking knob

Window channel

Outer window slot seal

Door handle

Inner window slot seal

Locking rod – long

Door lock

Remote control seal

Remote control

Cranked lever with locking rod – short

Window lifter

Door check strap

Fig. 12.13 Exploded view of rear door (Sec 12)

Fig. 12.14 Rear door cranked lever unit and associated components (Sec 12)

5 *Locking knob*
6 *Spreader rivet*
7 *Locking rod (long)*

8 *Cranked lever*
9 *Locking rod (short)*

13.4 Door hinge unit

between the edge of the door and the body pillars. When door alignment is correct, tighten the hinge screws fully, if necessary, adjust the striker as described in the following Section.

14 Door striker – adjustment

1   Mark round the door striker with a pencil, or a fine ballpoint pen (photo).
2   Fit a spanner to the hexagon on the striker and unscrew the striker about one turn so that the striker moves when tapped with a soft-headed hammer.
3   Tap the striker towards the inside of the car if the door rattles, or towards the outside of the car if the door fits too tightly, but be careful to keep the striker in the same horizontal line, unless it also requires vertical adjustment. Only move the striker a small amount at a time; the actual amount moved can be checked by reference to the pencil mark made before the striker was loosened.
4   When a position has been found in which the door closes firmly, but without difficulty, tighten the striker.

11 To remove the door check strap, prise free the pivot pin retaining clip and drive out the pin. Pull free the rubber cover within the door cavity then undo the two retaining bolts and spring washers. Withdraw the check strap unit.
12 Reassemble in the reverse order to dismantling. Check the operation of the door catch, lock and window regulator prior to refitting the trim panel.

13 Doors – removal and refitting

1   Remove the trim panel as described in Sections 7 or 11.
2   On models fitted with the centralised locking system, disconnect the vacuum hose from the door switch element, detach the protective bellows and withdraw the hose from the door. If the same door is to be refitted, mark round the hinges on the door, using a pencil or a fine tipped ballpoint pen. This simplifies realignment of the door.
3   Remove the retaining clip from the pin in the door check strap and tap out the pin. Fit the pin and clip back into the clevis to prevent their being lost.
4   With an assistant supporting the weight of the door, or with the bottom of the door propped, remove the screws from the hinges and take the door off (photo).
5   Refitting is a reversal of removal. If the same door is refitted, screw the screws in until they are just tight and line the hinges up with the marks made prior to removal. If using a different door, screw the hinge screws in until they are just tight, close the door and push it into the position which aligns its edge with the body contour. Move the door up and down or sideways as necessary to give an even gap

14.1 Front door striker location

15 Front grille – removal and refitting

1   Undo and remove the single screw securing the grille lower side section (right or left will do), then pull free the side section from the grille.
2   Unclip the grille at the top edge and withdraw it from the opposing lower side grille section.
3   Refit in the reverse order to removal.

16 Bonnet – removal, refitting and adjustment

1   Support the bonnet in its open position, and place some cardboard or rags beneath the corners by the hinges.
2   Disconnect the windscreen washer pipe from the bonnet (photo).
3   Mark the location of the hinges with a pencil (photo).
4   With the help of an assistant, unscrew the nuts and withdraw the bonnet from the car.
5   Refitting is a reversal of removal, but adjust the hinges to their original positions so that the bonnet is level with the surrounding bodywork. If necessary the front of the bonnet height may be adjusted by screwing the striker located beneath the bonnet in or out.

16.3 Bonnet hinge and retaining nuts

17 Bonnet lock release cable – removal and refitting

1   Raise and support the bonnet. Remove the front grille (Section 15).
2   Reaching down through the aperture in the front cross panel unscrew and loosen off the cable to bonnet catch clamp screw.
3   Working from the front unscrew and remove the cable retainer securing screw to the left of the catch.
4   Unclip the cable from the retainers in the engine compartment (Figure 12.15).
5   Detach the cable from the release handle inside the vehicle and pull the cable through the bulkhead grommet and remove it (photo).
6   Refit in the reverse order to removal, but adjust the cable so that when the clamp screw is tightened the cable is not under tension. Bend the excess wire over. Pull the release lever to operate and check the satisfactory operation of the catch before closing the bonnet.

18 Boot lid – removal, refitting and adjustment

1   Support the boot lid in its open position, and place some cardboard or rags beneath the corners by the hinges.

2   Disconnect the wiring loom and lower lock hose, as necessary, then mark the location of the hinges with a pencil.
3   With the help of an assistant, unscrew the nuts and withdraw the boot lid from the car.
4   Refitting is a reversal of removal, but adjust the hinges to their original positions so that the boot lid is level with the surrounding bodywork.

Fig. 12.15 Bonnet lock release cable routing (Sec 17)

1   Cable retaining clips   3   Clip
2   Seal grommet

17.5 Bonnet release handle and cable

19 Boot lid lock – removal, refitting and adjustment

1   Open the boot lid and, working through the inner panel aperture, drive out the eccentric retaining pin.
2   Detach and remove the lock housing assembly, the component parts of which are shown in Figure 12.16.
3   Insert the key to remove the lock cylinder from its housing.
4   Refit in the reverse order to removal. On completion adjust the lid lock by loosening off the striker plate so that it is located, but not fully

Eccentric

Pin

Housing

Sealing ring

Spring

Lock cylinder housing

Housing ring

Sealing ring

Lid lock

Striker plate

Spring
for lock cylinder
housing

Lock cylinder
(Insert key to remove)

Fig. 12.16 Boot lid lock components (Sec 19)

tightened. Close the boot lid to centralise the striker plate, then re-open the lid and fully tighten the striker plate securing screws. If necessary readjust the rubber stops.

20 Tailgate (Hatchback) – removal, refitting and adjustment

1   Disconnect the battery negative lead.
2   Open the tailgate and support it.
3   Disconnect the cable for the rear light cluster.
4   Unclip and detach the luggage shelf stays from the tailgate.
5   Detach the rear window demister lead connector.
6   Get an assistant to support the tailgate, then disconnect the tailgate support struts (Figure 12.17).
7   Prise free the tailgate hinge covers from the rear end of the roof headlining.
8   Mark the location of the hinges with a pencil, then, with the help of an assistant, unscrew the nuts and withdraw the tailgate from the car.
9   Refitting is a reversal of removal, but adjust the hinges to their original positions. Use the adjustment of the hinges on the tailgate to

position the tailgate in relation to the rear panel, and the adjustment of the hinges on the roof panel to position the tailgate in relation to the side panels.

21 Tailgate rear flap lock (Hatchback) – removal and refitting

1   Raise and support the tailgate and remove the trim panel from it.
2   Referring to Figure 12.19, unclip and detach the lock operating rod.
3   Unclip and disengage the spreader rivets from the cranked lever, then detach the left and right-hand operating rods.
4   Remove the screws securing the lock to the rear flap, withdraw the lock and disengage the operating rod by pressing in direction indicated in Figure 12.20.
5   To remove the lock cylinder and housing, prise free the securing circlip A, then with the key in the cylinder, pull out the lock cylinder. Prise free the second circlip B and pull out the lock cylinder housing (Figure 12.21).
6   Refitting is a direct reversal of the removal procedure.

Fig. 12.17 Tailgate components – Hatchback (Sec 20)

1	Tailgate	8	Screw	13	Washer	19	Gasket
2	Hinge	9	Grommet	14	Washer (concave)	19A	Spacer shim
3	Gasket	10	Rubber stop	15	Lockwasher	19B	Clip
4	Washer	10A	Spacer	16	Spacer	20	Deflectors (spoiler)
5	Bolt	11	Washer	17	Pin	21	Washer
7	Lock ring washer	12	Gas-filled strut	18	Spring washer	22	Nut

Fig. 12.18 Tailgate (rear flap) lock components – Hatchback (Sec 21)

Fig. 12.19 Tailgate lock components (Sec 21)

1   Operating rod
2   Cranked lever
3   Operating rod
4   Operating rod

Fig. 12.20 Remove tailgate lock (5) by pressing rod (6) down in direction of arrow (Sec 21)

Fig. 12.21 Tailgate lock cylinder showing circlips (A) and (B)

(Sec 21)

22 Tailgate (Estate) – removal and refitting

1 Disconnect the battery earth lead.

2 Open the tailgate and prise free the trim panel from it.

3 Detach the wiring connections from the number plate light and the rear window wiper.

4 Attach a suitable length of strong cord to the end of the dismantled wires and withdraw them from the tailgate by pulling through. Disconnect the cord and leave it in position in the tailgate, so that the procedure can be reversed to relocate the wires when refitting the tailgate.

5 Get an assistant to support the tailgate, then detach the gas-filled struts from the tailgate by levering down the spring clip and pulling the socket from the ball (photo).

6 Mark the location of the hinges with a pencil. Prise free the plastic

Fig. 12.22 Tailgate and associated components (Estate) (Sec 22)

1	Tailgate	10	Stop	17	Striker plate	24	Eccentric
2	Hinge	11	Number plate cover	18	Screw	25	Spacer
3	Gasket	12	Speed nut	19	Rubber stop	26	Washer
4	Washer	13	Washer	20	Seal washer	27	Concave washer
5	Bolt	14	Screw	21	Lock unit	28	Lock washer
7	Spring washer	15	Lock unit	22	Key	29	Strut
8	Screw	16	Screw	23	Roll pin	30	Ball mounting
9	Grommet					31	Gasket

22.5 Tailgate strut-to-body attachment

22.6A Mark the hinge positions (tailgate) then ...

22.6B ... remove the hinge securing bolts

covers from the headlining at the rear to expose the tailgate hinge bolts (photos).

7   With the assistant firmly supporting the tailgate, unbolt and remove the tailgate.

8   Refitting is reversal of removal, but adjust the hinges to their original positions. Use the adjustment of the hinges on the tailgate to position the tailgate in relation to the rear panel, and the adjustment of the hinges on the roof panel to position the tailgate in relation to the side panels.

9   Reattach the wires to the cord and pull them carefully into position through the tailgate, detach the cord and reconnect the wires. Check the number plate lights and the rear wiper for satisfactory operation before refitting the trim panel.

10   To adjust the tailgate striker loosen off the retaining screws and move the striker in the required direction then retighten the screws (photo).

22.10 Tailgate striker (Estate)

23   Tailgate lock (Estate) – removal and refitting

1   Open the tailgate and remove the rear trim panel by prising free the plastic clips.

2   Compress the retaining lugs of the grip on the inside (photo) and withdraw the lock cylinder unit and grip.

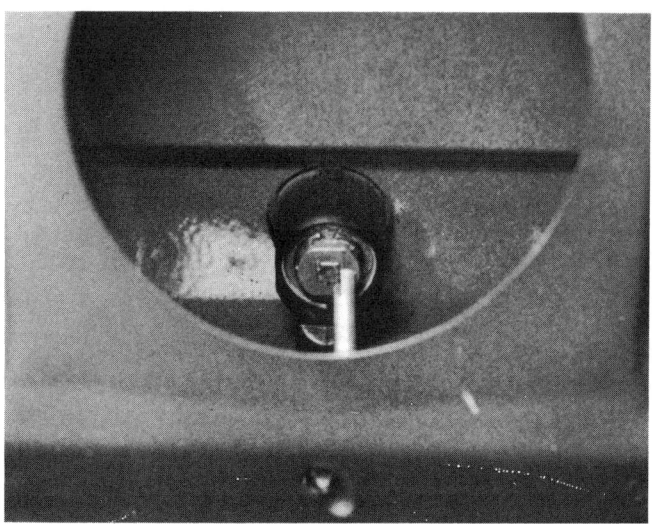

23.2 Tailgate lock cylinder viewed through inner panel aperture

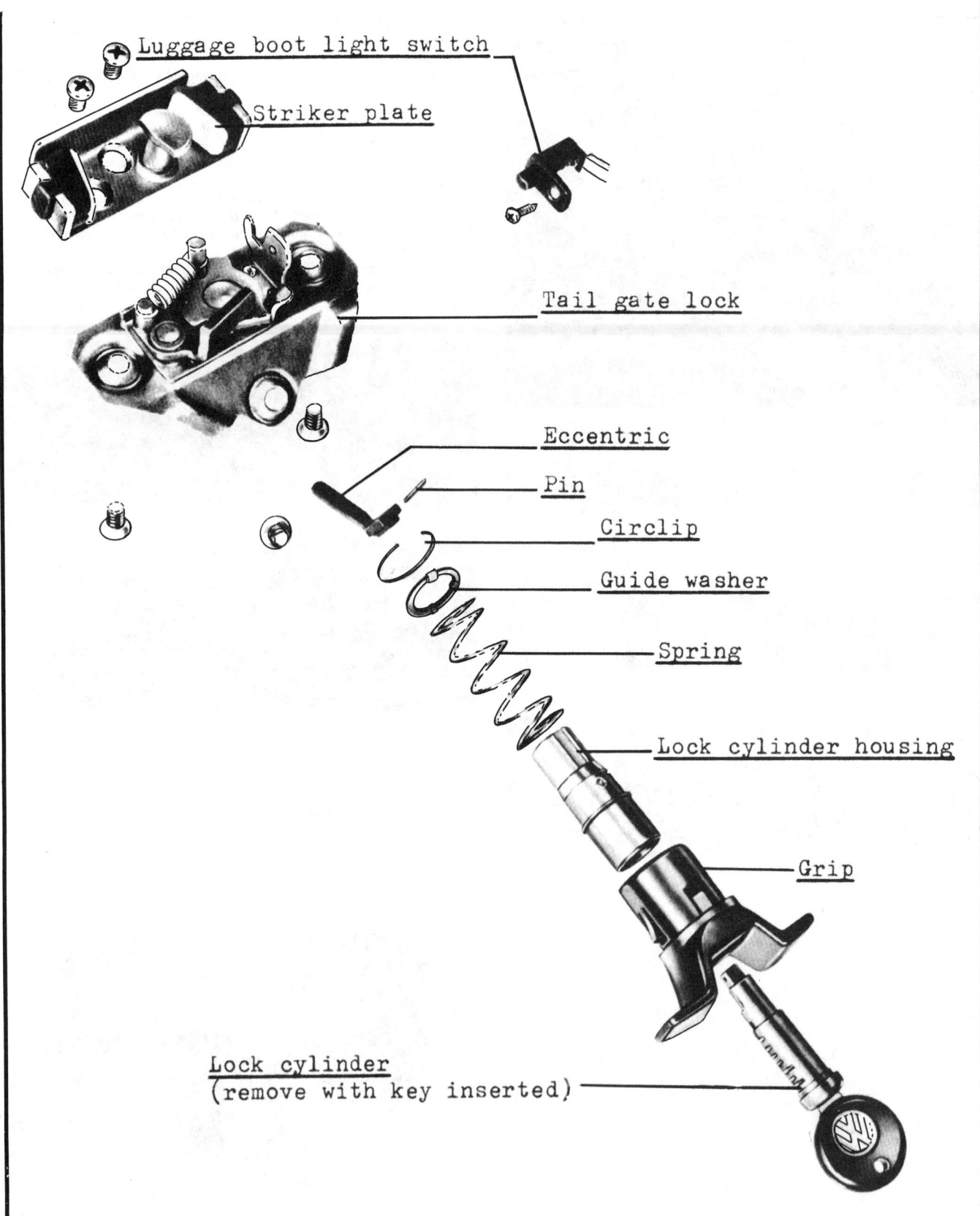

Fig. 12.23 Tailgate lock assembly components (Estate) (Sec 23)

Luggage boot light switch

Striker plate

Tail gate lock

Eccentric

Pin

Circlip

Guide washer

Spring

Lock cylinder housing

Grip

Lock cylinder
(remove with key inserted)

3 To remove the lock from the grip drive out the roll pin securing the eccentric to the lock, withdraw the eccentric.
4 Extract the circlip, the guide washer and spring and separate the lock cylinder housing from the grip (Figure 12.23).
5 Undo the three retaining screws to remove the lock unit (photo).
6 Refit in the reverse order to removal. Apply a ring of sealant to the lock seal.

23.5 Tailgate lock unit and three securing screws

24 Tailgate/rear hatch support struts – removal and refitting

1 Raise and support the tailgate/rear hatch. An assistant or suitable support will be necessary if both struts are to be removed.
2 Prise free the circlips, remove the single washer at the top of the strut, two washers at the bottom end and remove the strut.
3 The strut is gas filled and no attempt must be made to repair or dismantle the strut. Renew if defective.
4 Refit in the reverse order of removal.

25 Door mirror – removal and refitting

Standard type
1 Prise free the trim cover.
2 Remove the retaining screws, withdraw the mirror and packing piece.
3 Refit in reverse order of removal. Adjust by pressing on glass as required.

Manual adjustment (internal) type
4 Pull free the adjusting knob and bellows.
5 Remove the door trim panel as described in Section 7.
6 Unscrew and remove the adjuster locknut then pass the adjuster through the retainer (Figure 12.24).
7 Prise free the mirror internal cover, remove the three retaining screws together with the trim retainers whilst supporting the mirror.
8 Withdraw the mirror and feed the adjusting knob assembly up through the door cavity.
9 Refit in reverse order of removal and adjust mirror.

Fig. 12.24 External mirror and adjuster components – mechanical (Sec 25)

Fig. 12.25 Electrically adjusted external door mirror components (Sec 25)

Fig. 12.26 Electrically adjusted/heated door mirror wiring clip (1) and connector (2) locations (Sec 25)

26.2 Front bumper retaining bolts

Electrically operated type

10 Disconnect the battery earth lead.
11 Remove the door trim panel as described in Section 7.
12 Disconnect the heated rear window/exterior rear view mirror and mirror adjuster switch lead connectors (Figure 12.25).
13 Detach the mirror as described in paragraph 7 and withdraw the mirror feeding the cables up through the door cavity (Figure 12.26).
14 Refit in reverse order of removal and adjust the mirror.

26 Bumpers – removal and refitting

1 Disconnect the direction indicator/rear number plate wiring and headlight washer equipment from the bumper, as applicable.
2 Unscrew and remove the centre mounting bolts located on the front underframe or in the rear luggage compartment (photo).
3 Slide the bumper from the side guides, keeping the bumper parallel to the front of the car.
4 If necessary, remove the screws and withdraw the corner sections, then unclip the cover from the bumper.
5 Refitting is a reversal of removal.

27 Windscreen and rear window glass – removal and refitting

The windscreen and rear window are directly bonded to the metalwork, and the removal and fitting of this glass should be left to your VW dealer or a specialist glass replacement company.

28 Facia – removal and refitting

1 Disconnect the battery earth lead.
2 Remove the steering wheel as described in Chapter 11.
3 Undo the two screws securing the central trim panel in position, withdraw the panel and detach the cigarette lighter lead.
4 Referring to Figure 12.27, undo and remove the five passenger side trim panel retaining screws. Pull the trim back to release it from the lower retaining clip A and remove it.
5 Where a manual choke system is fitted, drive out the roll pin securing the choke control knob, remove the knob and the ring nut (Figure 12.28).
6 Referring to Figure 12.31, undo the three securing screws and pull the lower trim panel free from its lower edge retaining clip.
7 Remove the radio (if fitted) referring to Chapter 10 for details.
8 Pull free the heater and ventilation control knobs then carefully press out the trim and detach the controls.
9 Undo the screws from the locations arrowed in Figure 12.30 then partially withdraw the instrument panel, detach the switch and warning lamp leads and remove the panel trim (photo).
10 Detach the main wiring loom connections and the speedometer cable by reaching behind the instrument panel and compressing the cable connector securing lugs.
11 Undo the upper securing screw and remove the instrument panel and detach the vacuum gauge from the rear face of the fuel consumption gauge.
12 Press the fresh air vent out (with care).
13 Unscrew and remove the screws from the positions shown in Figure 12.31.

Fig. 12.27 Passenger side trim retaining screw locations (arrowed), and clip (A) – left-hand drive shown (Sec 28)

Fig. 12.28 Manual choke control grip (D), ring nut (E) and sleeve (C) (Sec 28)

Fig. 12.29 Driver's side trim retaining screw locations (arrowed) and clip (B) – left-hand drive shown (Sec 28)

Fig. 12.30 Instrument panel retaining screw positions (left-hand drive shown) (Sec 28)

Fig. 12.31 Facia panel retaining screw positions (Sec 28)

28.9 Disconnect the switch and warning lamp leads and connections from earthing strip

Fig. 12.32 Plenum chamber nut location (arrowed) (Sec 28)

14 Peel back and remove the door A pillar trim.
15 Raise the bonnet and working at the bulkhead end undo and remove the two nuts from the plenum chamber (Figure 12.32).
16 Withdraw the facia panel unit, detaching from the body attachment points and remove it through the door aperture.
17 Refitting is a reversal of the removal procedure.

29 Central console – removal and refitting

1 Disconnect the battery earth lead.
2 Remove the single retaining screw each side of the console (under the facia), and the single securing screw from the console rear end directly to the rear of the gear lever.
3 Prise free and release the gear lever gaiter from the console.
4 Lift the console partly clear, detach the wiring to the console switches as necessary and lift the console clear over the gear lever.
5 Refit in the reverse order to removal.

30 Seats – removal and refitting

Front seat – all models
1 Prise free the lower runner cover and clip, towards the rear end of the seat.
2 Pull the cover from the runner and then pull the seat forwards (Figure 12.33).

Fig. 12.33 Front seat removal – upper runner cover (Sec 30)

3 Referring to Figure 12.34, unscrew the cap nut, remove the washer and cheese head screw. Then releasing the securing rod, remove the seat rearwards.
4 Refitting is a reversal of the removal procedure, but the cap nut must be tightened to the manufacturer's recommended torque setting of 1.5 Nm (1.10 lbf ft).

Fig. 12.34 Front seal securing rod and associated components (Sec 30)

Fig. 12.35 Pressure points (arrowed) for removal of rear seat cushion (Sec 30)

Rear seat – Saloon
5 Remove the seat cushion by pressing on the pressure points each side at the front lower edge of the cushion, and lift the cushion out (Figure 12.35).
6 Rotate the headrest guide sleeves through 90° and remove the headrests by pulling them upwards from the backrest.
7 At the bottom end of the seat backrest, bend the retaining tabs up (one each side), pull the backrest retainers out and upwards and remove the seat backrest.
8 Refitting is a reversal of the removal procedure, but ensure that the backrest retaining hooks fully engage.

Rear seat – Hatchback and Estate
9 Refer to Supplement.

Fig. 12.36 Sunroof drain channel locations (Sec 31)

31 Sunroof – general

1 The sunroof requires little in the way of periodic maintenance apart from the following:

(a) *Clean out the drain channels occasionally by passing a suitable length of flexible cable (inner speedo cable is ideal) through the channels shown in Figure 12.36. The drain hoses at the front are housed in the A pillars and the cleaning cable should be passed downwards through them from the roof panel opening. The rear hoses are located within the body side panel apertures and should be cleaned by passing the cleaning cable upwards through them.*

(b) *The guide plates should be lubricated liberally with grease periodically to ensure ease of operation when opening and closing the roof panel.*

(c) *Check the sunroof panel for adjustment and adjust if necessary as described in Section 32.*

2 If for any reason the sunroof panel is to be removed refer to Section 33. Removal and refitting of the associated fixed trim components around the aperture should be entrusted to your VW dealer as special gauges are required during assembly.

3 Where an electrically operated sunroof is fitted the following procedures should be followed to open or close the roof panel should it malfunction at any time.

(a) *Prise free the interior light/roof panel switch cover frame from the inner roof by inserting a suitable lever (ignition key will do) into the slot in the right-hand side of the light cover and levering it free.*

(b) *Remove the interior light by pressing the spring in towards the centre of the light (at the opposite end to the switch).*

(c) *Press out the roof panel switch from the inside.*

(d) *Work through the large aperture and push the spring clips at the trim panel front end rearwards and remove the panel.*

(e) *Extract the manual crank from its location within the panel.*

(f) *Unhook the pin (2 in Figure 12.37) and rotate it rearwards, then engage the manual crank and wind it accordingly to open or close the roof panel.*

Fig. 12.37 Electric sunroof showing emergency manual operation (Sec 31)

1 *Unhook pin and swing it to rear*

2 *Take crank off rear panel*

3 *Insert crank in gear and turn*

32 Sunroof – adjustment only

1 The sunroof panel is correctly adjusted when it is positioned as shown in Figure 12.38. If adjustment is necessary first remove the trim panel from the sliding/tilting roof as described in Section 33.

2 Prise the lock washer from the water guide plate retaining pin then detach the water deflector plate operating lever from the pin. This is necessary to ensure accurate adjustment.

3 Referring to Figure 12.39, slacken off the mounting screws A and turn the central adjuster screw B to adjust the panel. With adjustment made recheck the height adjustment pushing up the roof panel slightly to allow for the trim panel. Retighten the mounting screws an equal amount and check that the front guide rail pin is flat against the adjuster screw.

Fig. 12.38 Sunroof height adjustment (Sec 32)

Fig. 12.39 Sunroof mounting screws (A) and adjusting screw (B)
(Sec 32)

Fig. 12.40 Sunroof guide plate mounting screws (arrowed)
(Sec 32)

4   Loosen off the guide plate mounting screws and push the rear edge of the roof panel to the correct height, then retighten the screws (Figure 12.40).
5   If the roof fails to open and close in a parallel manner, the cable drive and rear guides are probably in need of adjustment. Special gauges are required to make this adjustment and such adjustments must be entrusted to your VW dealer.

33 Sunroof — removal, refitting and adjustment

1   Tilt the sunroof using the crank.
2   Using a length of welding rod or similar make up a hook to the dimensions shown in Figure 12.42.
3   Carefully prise down the roof panel trim and insert the hook rod to unhook the coil spring from the trim, but take care not to damage the paintwork.
4   Shut the roof panel, unclip the trim panel from the front guide. Push the panel rearwards.
5   Unhook the tilt mechanism on the right-hand side and disconnect the connecting rods to remove them then pull the left side mechanism free (Figure 12.43).
6   Prise free the locking washer from the water guide plate retaining pin and press the water guide plate operating lever from the pin.
7   Undo and remove the roof panel to front guide retaining screws.
8   Move the roof panel forwards using the crank to slide the rear guide pin out of the plate then remove the roof panel.
9   Commence refitting by positioning the roof panel into place, then crank the rear guide back to engage the guide pin with the guide plate.
10   Locate and hand tighten only the roof panel to front guide securing screws.
11   The roof panel must now be adjusted for position to provide an equal clearance at the front and rear as shown in Figure 12.38.
12   Slacken off the guide plate retaining screw and push the water deflector plate into position so that it engages with the retainer pin then fit the locking bolt to secure. Tighten the guide plate retaining screw.
13   Press the left side tilt mechanism into the guide plate so that it engages on the rear guide pin then push the tilt mechanism connecting rod into engagement (on the central pins).
14   Crank the roof panel to the tilt position then refit the coil spring using the previously made hook tool.
15   Refit the roof panel trim by moving the panel forwards to provide a gap at the front edge of 10 to 15 mm (0.4 to 0.6 in) between the panel and the roof aperture edge. Push the trim panel up a fraction at the front and simultaneously slide it forwards to engage the four retaining clips with the front guide.
16   Using the special hooked tool reconnect the coil spring with the panel trim.

34 Central door locking system — general

1   Certain models are equipped with a central door locking system which automatically locks all doors and the rear tailgate/boot lid in unison with the manual locking of either front door.
2   The system is vacuum operated by means of a bi-pressure pump which is electrically controlled. The system layout is shown in Figure 12.44.
3   Any fault in the system is most likely to be caused by a leak in one of the hoses, in which case the hose and connections should be checked and repaired as necessary. Access to the appropriate actuator is generally fairly straightforward after removal of the relevant trim panel.
4   The bi-pressure pump unit is located behind the left side trim panel in the luggage compartment and is housed in a left and right-hand bracket (Figure 12.45).
5   In the event of a system fault first check that the fuse S7 is in good condition and securely connected before removing any part of the system.
6   If the fuse is in good condition but the pump fails to operate, the electrical part of the system can be checked using a 12V test light. Remove the side trim panel for access to the pump then detach the wiring multi-connector from the pump unit.
7   With the driver's door lock knob in the open position, connect up the test light leads to the right-hand and central contacts of the

A–Self-tapping screw

B–Special M 4 screw

Front water drain hoses

Cable guide

Wind deflector

Cable drive

Cover

Wind deflector arm

Cover

Crank

Front guide

Guide rail

Guide plate

Fillister head screw

Sliding/tilting roof panel trim

Guide rail end section

Clips

Connecting rod

Arm

Sliding/tilting roof panel

Water drain plate

Rear guide with cable (one part)

Spring

Water drain plate lever

Rear water drain hose

Fig. 12.41 Exploded view of the sunroof and associated components (Sec 33)

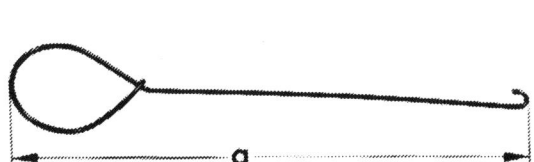

Fig. 12.42 Sunroof coil spring removal hook (Sec 33)

a = 300 mm (11.8 in)

Fig. 12.43 Sunroof and associated components prior to removal (Sec 33)

2   Panel trim
3   Front guide
4   Connecting rod
5   Tilt mechanism

Off-set grommet

Tank flap switch element

Tailgate switch element

X connector

Bi-pressure pump

Rear left door switch element

Bellows

Front left door switch element

Rear right door switch element

Bellows

Front right door switch element

Bellows

T connector

X connector

Bellows

Fig. 12.44 Central locking system layout (Sec 34)

Fig. 12.45 Central locking system bi-pressure pump and connections (Sec 34)

1   Four-way connector
2   Tank filler flap hose
3   Door switches hose
4   Tailgate hose
5   Retaining clips

Fig. 12.46 Tailgate switch element (central locking system) showing retaining screws (1), hose connection (2) and connecting rod (3) (Sec 34)

Fig. 12.47 Central locking system fuel tank filler flap switch retaining rivet locations in luggage compartment. Use 10 mm dia. drill at points shown (Sec 34)

a = 20 mm (0.78 in)   b = 25 mm (0.98 in)

Fig. 12.48 Central locking system fuel tank filler flap element location (Sec 34)

1   Retaining screws
2   Hose
3   Connecting rod (on element)

Fig. 12.49 Central locking system rear door switch element (Sec 34)

1   Retaining screws
2   Connecting hose
3   Connecting rod

Fig. 12.50 Central locking system front door switch element (Sec 34)

1   Retaining screws
2   Connecting hose
3   Connecting rod

Fig. 12.51 Central locking system bi-pressure pump wiring connector terminals – test light check (Sec 34)

connector (Figure 12.51). If the test lamp fails to light then the driver's door switch element is defective or there is a wiring fault. If the test lamp lights up the driver's door switch unit or the bi-pressure pump is defective.

8   To find out which, connect the test lamp up between the left-hand and central connector terminals with the door lock knob in the closed position. If the test lamp fails to light then the door switch element or wiring are at fault, but if the lamp does light up then the pump unit is defective.

9   It should be noted that if the vehicle has not been used for a long period or where a new bi-pressure pump unit has been fitted the system may have to be activated several times before becoming operational. Under normal circumstances the system locks should operate within two seconds of actuation. As a general guide if the pump operates for a longer period than five seconds a leak may be present in the system. Do not operate the pump for periods in excess of thirty five seconds (continuously).

35 Power operated windows – general

1   Certain models are equipped with power (electric) operated windows which can be raised or lowered when the ignition is switched on.

Fig. 12.52 Power operating window mechanism (Sec 35)

1   Window lifter unit
2   Washer (concave)
3   Bolt
4   Washer (concave)
5   Nut
6   Washer
7   Screw
8   Shake-proof washer
9   Switch
11   Relay plate
12   Relay
13   Fuse box
14   Fuse
15   Bellows
16   Bracket
17   Connector housing

Fig. 12.53 Power window securing screws (1) (Sec 35)

2   If a fault develops, first check that the system fuse has not blown.
3   Access to the electric motors and regulator mechanism is gained by removing the door trim panels as described in Sections 7 or 11.
4   The window lifter (regulator) unit which consists of the motor, cables and guide rail can be removed by first undoing the window securing bolts and lowering the window down into the door cavity (Figure 12.52).
5   Detach the wiring connector then undo and remove the window lifter retaining screws shown in Figure 12.53. Lower and remove the window lifter unit from the lower door aperture.
6   Refitting is a reversal of the removal procedure, but route the upper cable under the guide rail securing bracket.
7   Check window operation before refitting the door trim panel.

36 Heater unit – removal and refitting

Note: *If the heater/fresh air blower motor unit only is to be removed, refer to Chapter 10, Section 42.*
1   Disconnect the battery negative lead.
2   Drain the cooling system as described in Chapter 2.
3   Disconnect the heater hoses at the bulkhead.
4   Detach the temperature control cable from the heater valve.

Fresh air blower

Control valve cable

Cut-off flap cable

Gasket

Grommet

Cover

Gasket

Resistance for blower

Screw and washer

Control valve

Flow direction

closed

Connection

Fresh air and heater controls

Knob

Knob

Control flap cable

Conection

Double grommet

Window vent cover

Vent, centre

Fresh air box

Rear duct

Vent, right

Air duct, right

Gasket

Fig. 12.54 Heater assembly components (Sec 36)

5   Remove the central console and the left and right trim from below the facia.
6   Pull off the heater and fresh air control knobs.
7   Prise out the control panel, then remove the screws securing the controls.
8   Remove the screws and withdraw the central facia panel.
9   Disconnect and remove the air ducts from the heater.
10 Remove the large heater retaining clip, and detach the cowl from the air plenum.
11 Working in the engine compartment remove the heater mounting bolts located either side of the motor, then lower the heater unit from inside the car. Since there will still be a quantity of water in the heater, place some polythene sheeting, or rags, on the floor to protect the floor covering.
12 Refitting is a reversal of the removal procedure. Check that the control valve fitting direction is correct as indicated by an arrow mark on the valve body which must point to the front of the vehicle.
13 If the coolant hose location grommet has been removed from the bulkhead, apply a suitable rubber adhesive to the contact surface groove. Aid fitting by inserting a length of cord in the grommet sealing groove and pull it into position from within the vehicle. Lubricate the hoses with washing-up liquid to ease their fitting through the grommet.
14 Before refitting the central console and the trim panels, check the adjustment of the heater control cables as described in the following Section.

37 Heater control cables – adjustment

Control valve cable
1   Move the lower control lever fully to the left.
2   Press the control valve lever to the closed position, then secure the control cable.

Cut-off flap cable
3   Move the upper right control lever fully to the left.
4   Press the cut-off control flap up and secure the control cable.

Control flap cable
5   Move the upper left lever fully to the right.
6   Press the control flap in the direction of the engine and secure the control cable (photo).

38 Air conditioning system

1   This is an option on certain models.
2   Whenever overhaul of a major nature is being undertaken to the engine and components of the air conditioning system obstruct the work and such items of the system cannot be unbolted and moved aside sufficiently within the limits of their flexible connecting pipes, to avoid such obstruction the system should be discharged by your dealer or a competent refrigeration engineer.
3   As the system must be completely evacuated before recharging, the necessary vacuum equipment to do this is only likely to be available at a specialist.
4   The refrigerant fluid is Freon 12 and although harmless under normal conditions, contact with the eyes or skin must be avoided. If Freon comes into contact with a naked flame, then a poisonous gas will be created which is injurious to health.
5   The air conditioner is designed so that it will not operate if the outside temperature is below 5°C (41°F).
6   In hot weather, a pool of water may be found under the vehicle after it has been standing. This is normal and is caused by condensation dripping from the evaporator.
7   Regularly inspect the condition of the system hoses and check the tightness of the unions.
8   Check the compressor drivebelt for wear and condition and keep the belt correctly tensioned. The belt is correctly tensioned when it can be deflected through 10.0 mm (0.39 in) at the mid-point of its longest run under moderate thumb pressure.
9   On four-cylinder engined models the drivebelt tension is adjusted by unbolting the two halves of the compressor pulley and removing or adding spacer shims.
10 On five-cylinder models, the compressor bracket can be moved after releasing the pivot and adjuster slot bolts.

37.6 Heater control flap cable connection

The revised VW Passat range introduced in 1985

Chapter 13 Supplement:
Revisions and information on later models

Contents

1 Introduction

This Supplement contains information which has become available since the manual was first produced, in particular for the period from late 1984 to 1986. However some information also applies to pre-1984 models.

In order to use the Supplement to the best advantage it is suggested that it is referred to before the main Chapters of the manual; this will ensure that any relevant information can be noted and incorporated within the procedures given in Chapters 1 to 12. Time and cost will therefore be saved and the particular job will be completed correctly.

2 Specifications

These are revisions of, or supplementary to, the Specifications at the beginning of each of the preceding Chapters.

Four-cylinder engine
1.6 and 1.8 litre carburettor engines (1986-on model year)

	1.6	1.8
Valve timing at 1 mm lift/zero clearance:		
Inlet opens BTDC	3°	3°
Inlet closes ABDC	19°	33°
Exhaust opens BBDC	27°	41°
Exhaust closes ATDC	5°	5°

Fuel and exhaust systems
2.0 litre fuel injection engine (from March 1986)

System pressure	5.6 to 6.0 bar (81.2 to 87.0 lbf/in²)
Idle speed	850 ± 50 rpm
Fuel octane requirement (minimum)	98 RON
CO content	1.0 ± 0.5%

Ignition system
Spark plugs

Type (1986 models on):	
1.6 litre engine	Bosch W8DTC, Champion N9BYC
1.8 and 2.0 litre engine	Bosch W6DTC, Champion N7BYC
Spark plug electrode gap	0.8 mm (0.032 in)

Clutch
Cable free play (at clutch pedal)

1986-on models	Approximately 20.0 mm (0.787 in)

Type

(January 1985-on five-cylinder models with 093 gearbox)	Hydraulic actuation

Clutch fluid type (hydraulic clutch)

	Hydraulic fluid to FMVSS 116 DOT 3 or DOT 4 (Duckhams Universal Brake and Clutch Fluid)

Manual gearbox and final drive
Ratios – gearbox 093 code 7K

Final drive	4.70 : 1
1st	2.85 : 1
2nd	1.52 : 1
3rd	0.97 : 1
4th	0.70 : 1
5th	0.56 : 1
Reverse	3.17 : 1

Automatic transmission and final drive
Code numbers/letters – application

089/KAB (October 1982 to August 1983)	Fitted to 1.6 litre engine models

Ratios (089/KAB)

Final drive	3.73 : 1
1st	2.71 : 1
2nd	1.50 : 1
3rd	1.00 : 1
Reverse	2.43 : 1

Electrical system
Alternator drivebelt tension

Toothed rack nut torque	9.0 Nm (6.6 lbf ft)

Suspension and steering
Front wheel alignment

Toe angle difference, left and right, at 20° lock – power steering models from January 1984, chassis No. 33ZEE 125984	− 1° ± 30'
Castor – power steering models from January 1984 chassis No. 33ZEE 125984	+ 1° ± 20'

Torque wrench settings

	Nm	lbf ft
Front anti-roll bar link	20	15
Front suspension subframe:		
Stage 1	35	26
Stage 2	Further 90° turn	Further 90° turn

3 Engine

1.6 and 1.8 litre carburettor engines (1986-on) – modifications

1   As from the 1986 model year, 1.6 and 1.8 litre carburettor engines are fitted with hydraulic tappets which automatically take up the clearance between the valve stems and camshaft. Engines so equipped have a sticker as shown in Fig. 13.1 on the cylinder head cover.

2   Instead of an oil deflector inside the cylinder head cover, a full length plate is located over the camshaft bearing cap nuts. The camshaft runs in four bearings instead of the previous five, and the former No. 4 camshaft bearing location serves as an oil return for the hydraulic tappets.

3   A different camshaft is fitted to hydraulic tappet engines due to the modified bearing arrangement and the valve timing (see 'Specifications'). For engines fitted with hydraulic tappets, the camshaft is identified by a letter 'B' located between the No. 1 cams on the 1.6 litre engine, and a letter 'H' in the same position for 1.8 litre engines.

4   Engines manufactured before January 1985 have an oil pump with 26.0 mm (1.024 in) wide gears. However, all hydraulic tappet engines must be fitted with the later increased capacity oil pump with 30.0 mm (1.181 in) wide gears.

Hydraulic tappets – checking and renewal

5   When starting the engine from cold there may be a little noise from the tappets until the normal oil pressure is re-established. However, if the noise persists, a faulty tappet is indicated. To locate the tappet, run the engine to normal operating temperature indicated by the electric cooling fan switching on, increase the speed to 2500 rpm for 2 minutes, then stop the engine.

6   Remove the cylinder head cover, then turn the engine until the peak of cam No. 1 is pointing upwards.

Fig. 13.1 Diagram of cylinder head cover sticker depicting engines fitted with hydraulic tappets (Sec 3)

7   Using a tapered wooden or plastic rod, press on the tappet (Fig. 13.3). If the amount of free travel exceeds 0.1 mm (0.004 in), the tappet is faulty and should be renewed.

8   Repeat the procedure on the remaining tappets noting the results as necessary.

Note: *After fitting new hydraulic tappets the engine must not be started for approximately 30 minutes, otherwise there is a danger of the valve heads touching the pistons.*

Valves – servicing

9   Due to the working tolerances of the hydraulic tappets it is important to observe the minimum dimensions between the end of the valve stems and the cylinder head upper surface, as shown in Fig. 13.4, when re-grinding the valve heads and seats. If the dimension is less than the minimum, the hydraulic tappets will not function correctly and the end of the valve stem must be ground squarely to correct it.

Fig. 13.2 Oil deflector plate for engines fitted with hydraulic tappets (Sec 3)

1 Engine oil filler cap	3 Oil deflector plate
2 Cylinder head cover	

Fig. 13.3 Checking the free travel of a hydraulic tappet (Sec 3)

Fig. 13.4 Minimum dimension 'a' between valve stem and cylinder head surface (Sec 3)

Inlet valve 33.8 mm (1.331 in)
Exhaust valve 34.1 mm (1.343 in)

Fig. 13.5 Ohmmeter connection to the idle switch (Sec 5)

4 Cooling system

Water pump sealing ring – modifications
1 When fitting a VW reconditioned water pump, it is important to fit the correct size sealing ring. On some exchange pumps the sealing ring groove is enlarged for fitting of a 5 mm diameter ring instead of the standard 4 mm diameter ring.
2 Water pumps with this modification have the number '5' stamped on the housing next to the mounting flange.

5 Fuel and exhaust systems

Pressure surge switch (fuel injection models) – checking
1 Disconnect the wiring plug from the idle switch (see next sub-section) and connect an ohmmeter across the plug terminals (Fig. 13.5).
2 Open the throttle and check that zero resistance is obtained. If not, adjust or if necessary renew the idle switch as described in the next sub-section.
3 Disconnect the wiring plug from the pressure surge switch and connect a voltmeter between the plug No. 1 terminal and earth (Fig. 13.6).
4 With the ignition switched on, open the throttle and check that battery voltage is indicated on the voltmeter. If not, there is an open circuit in the supply wire.
5 Switch off the ignition and connect an ohmmeter across the pressure surge switch terminals. With the throttle closed, infinite resistance should be registered indicating open contacts.
6 Run the engine, then open the throttle quickly. A resistance of 1 ohm should be registered briefly.
7 Disconnect the wiring plug from the cold start valve and connect a voltmeter between the cold start valve plug No. 1 terminal and earth (Fig. 13.6).
8 Run the engine then open the throttle quickly. The voltage should rise and fall between 1 and 10 volts. If not, there is an open circuit in the supply wire.
9 Connect the voltmeter across the cold start valve plug terminals (1 and 2), then operate the starter motor. With the engine cold, battery voltage should be registered. However, with the engine coolant temperature above 40°C (104°F), zero voltage should be registered. If not, there may be an open circuit in the supply wire, or the thermo-time switch may need checking as described in Chapter 3, Section 31.

Fig. 13.6 Wiring plug terminal identification (Sec 5)

1 and 2 See text

Fig. 13.7 Ohmmeter connection to the pressure surge switch (Sec 5)

Idle switch (fuel injection models) – checking

10 The idle switch is located on the throttle lever, and is part of the digital idle stabilizer (DIS) system. To check it, first secure a suitable protractor and pointer as shown in Fig. 13.8 – the protractor must be on the first stage throttle shaft.

11 Disconnect the wiring from the idle switch, and connect an ohmmeter across the switch terminals.

12 Open the throttle approximately 20°, then close it slowly. Between 2.5° and 1.0° from the closed position the ohmmeter should register infinite resistance, indicating that the contacts have opened. If not, either adjust the position of the switch or renew it. To adjust the switch, it is necessary to remove the throttle housing (see Chapter 3).

Carburettor (Type 2E2) – choke valve plate gap adjustment

13 The choke valve plate gap may be altered if necessary by bending the operating lever with a suitable slotted tool (Fig. 13.9).

14 Remove the choke cover and using a rubber band, hold the choke valve plate closed.

15 Hold the primary throttle valve plate open at 45°. A nut of suitable size (M6) fitted between the diaphragm unit rod and the fast idle speed screw will facilitate setting the valve plate (Fig. 13.10).

16 Check the valve plate opening using a twist drill of suitable diameter. The gap should be between 6.0 and 6.6 mm (0.23 to 0.26 in).

17 If adjustment is needed, grip one end (A) of the operating lever while bending at (B) – see Fig. 13.11.

18 Finally, check the choke pull-down system as described in Chapter 3.

K-Jetronic fuel injection system – modifications

19 As from March 1986, the following modifications have been made to the fuel injection system.

20 When ordering spare parts, make sure that the production date of the car is specified.

   (a)   Higher injector pressures
   (b)   Conical seat connections instead of banjo type unions
   (c)   Metal fuel lines to injectors
   (d)   Modified pressure accumulator, thermo-time switch and cold start valve

Fig. 13.8 Adjusting the idle switch (Sec 5)

Fig. 13.9 Special tool for adjusting choke operating lever (Sec 5)

a   80.0 mm (3.12 in)   c   2.5 mm (0.10 in)
b   8.0 mm (0.31 in)   d   2.0 mm (0.08 in)

Fig. 13.10 Using nut to hold primary throttle valve plate open (Sec 5)

x   = 10.0 mm (0.39 in)

Fig. 13.11 Choke operating lever bending points A and B (Sec 5)

6 Ignition system

Distributor rotor arm – modifications

1 As from the 1986 model year, 1.6 and 1.8 litre engines with hydraulic tappets are fitted with a distributor rotor arm incorporating a centrifugal speed limitation cut-out. When the engine speed reaches between 6150 and 6450 rpm the contacts on the rotor arm separate and the HT circuit to the spark plugs is broken until the engine speed drops. The speed limitation is necessary to prevent damage to the hydraulic tappets.

7 Clutch

Hydraulic clutch – general description

With effect from January 1985, five-cylinder engine models with the 093 gearbox are fitted with a hydraulic clutch.

The clutch pedal pushrod acts on the piston in the master cylinder which is connected by a hydraulic line to the slave cylinder located on the clutch housing. The slave cylinder piston then acts on the release lever via a further pushrod. The release lever pivots on a ball-stud and forces the release bearing against the clutch diaphragm spring fingers. The system is self-adjusting.

On LHD models the brake fluid reservoir doubles as a reservoir for the clutch hydraulic system.

Clutch pedal and bracket (RHD models) – removal and refitting

1 Working inside the car, remove the screws and withdraw the trim panels below the facia on the driver's side.
2 Remove the clevis pin securing the brake pedal pushrod to the relay lever.
3 Refer to Chapter 11 and remove the steering column.
4 Prise the clip from the end of the brake pedal pivot then remove the pedal together with the pushrod.
5 Unbolt the cable holder from the bracket.
6 Remove the clevis pin securing the intermediate brake rod to the relay lever.
7 Unscrew the clutch master cylinder mounting bolts.
8 Extract the clip and remove the clevis pin securing the pullrod to the clutch pedal. Note the location of the washer against the pedal extension.
9 Pull the clutch master cylinder to the rear from the bracket and release the pushrod.
10 Unbolt the bracket assembly and lower it from the bulkhead.
11 Extract the clips and clevis pin to remove the over-centre spring unit, and extract the clip to remove the clutch pedal. If necessary the two small brackets may be unbolted from the main bracket.
12 If necessary the pedal and relay lever bushes can be renewed using a soft metal drift to remove them, and a vice to press the new ones into position. Check the brake pedal return rubber stop and renew it if necessary.
13 Refitting is a reversal of removal, but lubricate the bearing surfaces with grease. Make sure that the brake pedal pushrod is inserted

Fig. 13.12 Diagram of hydraulic clutch components (Sec 7)
LHD model shown

through the hole in the pedal bracket. When assembling the small brackets, tighten the side mounting bolt before the upper nut.

Clutch hydraulic system – bleeding

14 Remove the rubber cap from the bleed screw on the top of the slave cylinder located on the clutch housing. Fit a suitable bleed tube to it with the free end submersed in a little brake fluid in a jar.

15 Check that the clutch fluid reservoir is topped up with fluid and have some additional fluid ready to top it up during the bleeding process. On LHD models the brake fluid reservoir also supplies the clutch hydraulic system, but on RHD models a separate reservoir is located in the heater inlet chamber on the right-hand side of the bulkhead.

16 Unscrew the bleed screw half a turn and have an assistant fully depress the clutch pedal three or four times. Tighten the bleed screw with the clutch pedal depressed then top up the fluid reservoir using new fluid only.

17 Repeat the procedure in paragraph 15 two or three times then check that the clutch pedal movement is correct.

18 Disconnect the bleed tube and refit the rubber cap.

Clutch slave cylinder – removal, overhaul and refitting

19 The slave cylinder is retained in the clutch housing by a roll pin which engages the annular groove of the cylinder. First remove the clip, then use a suitable drift to drive out the roll pin.

20 Slide out the slave cylinder, together with the pushrod.

21 Loosen the hydraulic pipe union and unscrew the cylinder from the pipe. Plug the pipe to prevent loss of fluid.

22 Clean the cylinder, then prise off the rubber boot and remove the pushrod.

23 Withdraw the piston and spring from the mouth of the cylinder.

24 Clean the components and examine them for wear and deterioration. If the piston and bore are worn excessively, renew the complete cylinder, but if they are in good condition remove the seal from the piston and obtain a repair kit.

25 Dip the new seal in brake fluid and fit it on the piston using the fingers only to manipulate it into position. Make sure that the seal lip faces the spring end of the piston.

26 Insert the spring in the cylinder then dip the piston in brake fluid and carefully insert it.

27 Locate the small end of the rubber boot in the groove in the pushrod and fit the retaining ring.

28 Apply molybdenum disulphide grease to the ends of the pushrod, then fit it together with the boot to the slave cylinder.

29 Refitting is a reversal of removal, but finally bleed the hydraulic system as described in paragraphs 14 to 18.

Clutch master cylinder – removal, overhaul and refitting

30 Working inside the car, remove the screws and withdraw the trim panels below the facia on the driver's side.

Fig. 13.13 Clutch pedal and bracket components – RHD models (Sec 7)

Pushrod, long

Pin

Circlip

Bush

Relay lever

Clip

Pushrod, short

Additional bracket

Pin

R.P.MAIN

Self-locking nut

Locking clip

Brake pedal

Pedal bracket

Bush

Clip

H9514

Fig. 13.14 Brake pedal and bracket components – RHD models (Sec 7)

31 Disconnect the pushrod clevis from the pedal (LHD models) or relay lever (RHD models).
32 Disconnect and plug the hydraulic fluid supply hose, then unscrew the outlet union and disconnect the pressure line.
33 Unbolt and remove the master cylinder.
34 Clean the cylinder then prise off the rubber boot and remove the pushrod.
35 Extract the circlip from the mouth of the cylinder and withdraw the washer, piston and spring, noting that the smaller end of the spring contacts the piston. Prise the inlet grommet from the cylinder.
36 Clean the components and examine them for wear and deterioration. If the piston and bore are worn excessively, renew the complete cylinder, but if they are in good condition remove the seals from the piston and obtain a repair kit.
37 Dip the new seals in brake fluid and fit them on the piston using the fingers only to manipulate them into position. Make sure that the seal lips face the spring end of the piston.
38 Smear the inlet grommet with brake fluid and locate it in the cylinder aperture.
39 Insert the spring in the cylinder large end first, then dip the piston in brake fluid, locate it on the spring, and carefully insert it.
40 Locate the washer, then fit the circlip in the groove.
41 Fit the pushrod and rubber boot, making sure that the boot is correctly located in the grooves. Apply a little grease to the pushrod end.
42 Refitting is a reversal of removal, but finally bleed the hydraulic system as described in paragraphs 14 to 18. Lubricate the clevis pin with a little grease. On LHD models, adjust the master cylinder pushrod if necessary so that the clutch pad is about 10.0 mm (0.40 in) higher than the brake pedal pad when fully returned. On RHD models the pushrod must be adjusted so that the clevis pin can be easily inserted with the pedal resting on the rubber stop and the pushrod just touching the master cylinder piston.

Clutch release bearing and lever – removal and refitting
43 The release lever on the hydraulically operated clutch is shown in Fig. 13.14; it pivots on a ball located in the bottom of the clutch housing and is held on the ball by a spring plate.
44 To remove the bearing, prise out the springs and remove the clips, then slide the bearing from the plastic guide sleeve.
45 Pull the release lever against the spring plate and remove it from the ball.
46 Check the bearing, as described in Chapter 5. Inspect the release lever, pivot ball and cap for wear and damage and renew them if necessary.
47 Refitting is a reversal of removal, but lubricate the pivot ball with molybdenum disulphide grease. **Do not**, however, lubricate the plastic cap or plastic guide sleeve.

8 Manual gearbox and final drive

Shift rod coupling – modification
1 As from late 1984, five-cylinder engine models with the 093 gearbox are equipped with a modified shift rod coupling (Fig. 13.18) incorporating additional rubber bushes to reduce the transmission noise inside the car.
2 Modified replacement couplings are also available for the 014 and 013 gearboxes, although new cars are currently being fitted with the earlier type.
3 Unlike the earlier type, the modified shift rod coupling cannot be dismantled for repair, and must therefore be renewed complete if worn excessively or damaged.

Gearshift linkage – lubrication
4 As from late 1984 the gearshift linkage is lubricated with molybdenum disulphide based grease instead of white lubricating paste. When reassembling earlier linkages all traces of paste should be removed before applying the new grease.

Gearbox – removal and refitting
5 When removing the gearbox on models fitted with a hydraulically operated clutch (see Section 7) it will be necessary to remove the clutch slave cylinder from the clutch housing and tie it to one side, leaving the hose still attached. References in Chapter 6 to the clutch cable are not, of course, applicable.

9 Automatic transmission and final drive

Accelerator pedal and linkage (087 transmission) – adjustment
1 Move the selector lever to P.
2 Apply the handbrake then run the engine to normal operating temperature.
3 With the engine switched off, loosen the knurled adjusting nut at the transmission end of the throttle cable.
4 Check that the choke is fully open on carburettor engines and that the throttle is closed.
5 Disconnect both rods fom the throttle relay lever.
6 Turn the relay lever fully anti-clockwise, then adjust the length of the pullrod (engine side of relay lever) so that the socket is aligned with the ball. Tighten the locknuts, and refit the rod to the relay lever.
7 Refit the pushrod then loosen its clamp bolt, check that both the transmission and throttle levers are in their idle position, and tighten the clamp bolt again.
8 Have an assistant fully depress the accelerator pedal to the kickdown position then turn the knurled nut until the transmission lever contacts the stop, and tighten the locknut.
9 Check that, with the accelerator pedal at the full throttle position, the throttle is fully open without compressing the spring in the pushrod. With the accelerator pedal at the kickdown position the spring must be compressed (Fig. 13.19).

Accelerator pedal and linkage (089 transmission) – adjustment
10 Move the selector lever to P.
11 Apply the handbrake, then run the engine to normal operating temperature.
12 With the engine switched off, loosen the knurled adjusting nut at the transmission end of the accelerator pedal cable.
13 On carburettor engines remove the air cleaner.
Engines with 2E2 carburettor and overrun cut-off
14 Turn the warm-up lever so that the throttle valve operating pin is not making contact, then retain the warm-up lever in this position with a screwdriver (Fig. 13.20).
15 Pull the vacuum hoses from the three-point vacuum unit then connect a vacuum pump to outlet A (Fig. 13.21) and plug outlet B.
16 Operate the vacuum pump until the diaphragm pushrod stays in the overrun position and is not touching the cold idle adjusting screw.
Engines without 2E2 carburettor and overrun cut-off
17 Check that the throttle is closed and on carburettor engines that the choke is fully open.
All engines
18 Loosen the locknuts at the bracket on the engine and adjust the outer cable position to eliminate all play. Tighten the locknuts.
19 Have an assistant fully depress the accelerator pedal to the kickdown position, then turn the knurled adjusting nut until the transmission lever contacts the stop, and tighten the locknut.
20 Check that, with the accelerator pedal at the full throttle position, the throttle is fully open without compressing the spring at the carburettor. With the accelerator pedal at the kickdown position the spring must be compressed (Figs. 13.22 and 13.24).
21 Remove the vacuum pump and reconnect the hoses on engines with the 2E2 carburettor and overrun cut-off.

10 Electrical system

Battery – maintenance
1 On some later batteries the cell plugs are initially locked in position and a special procedure is necessary to remove them for checking the electrolyte level. Before removing the plugs however, check any conditions given in the battery warranty restricting their removal.
2 Using a small screwdriver, pierce the plastic skin (Fig. 13.25) and turn the top part of the plug as far as possible.
3 The plug can now be unscrewed and refitted in the normal manner.

Fig. 13.15 Pedal and hydraulic components – LHD models (Sec 7)

332

Plate washer

Pin

Clip

Clevis

Pushrod

Retaining ring

Pushrod

Piston

Grooved cup

Circlip

Washer

Secondary seal

Piston

Primary seal

Slave cylinder

Reservoir

Angled connection

Grommet

Master cylinder

Pressure line

Bleed screw

Pressure hose

Fig. 13.16 Master and slave cylinder components – RHD models (Sec 7)

Slave cylinder

Retaining clip

TDC sensor adapter for clutch 228 mm ∅

TDC sensor adapter for clutch 215 mm ∅

Push rod

Roll pin

Ball cap

Leaf spring

Retaining plate

Plastic guide sleeve

Clutch release lever

Retaining spring

Retaining clip

Release bearing

Fig. 13.17 Clutch release bearing and lever components for hydraulic clutch (Sec 7)

Fig. 13.18 Modified shift rod coupling (Sec 8)

Fig. 13.19 Throttle pushrod dimension for kickdown
position on 087 transmission (Sec 9)

a   = 10.5 mm (0.413 in)

Fig. 13.20 Accelerator pedal and linkage adjustment on
the 2E2 carburettor (Sec 9)

A   Warm-up lever   *C   Lever*
B   Throttle valve operating pin   *D   Screwdriver*

Fig. 13.21 Vacuum pump connected to outlet A with
outlet B plugged (Sec 9)

Fig. 13.22 Kickdown dimension on non-2E2 carburettor
engines (Sec 9)

A   = 8.0 mm (0.315 in)

Fig. 13.23 Kickdown dimension on fuel injection engines
(Sec 9)

A   = 8.0 mm (0.315 in)

Fig. 13.24 Kickdown dimension on 2E2 carburettor engines (Sec 9)

a = 8.0 mm (0.315 in)

Alternator drivebelt (from April 1985) – adjustment
4   With effect from April 1985, 1.6 and 1.8 litre engines are fitted with a toothed rack for tensioning the alternator drivebelt (photo). The tension is set by using a torque wrench on the nut located on the clamp bolt.
5   First loosen all pivot and adjustment bolts so that the alternator is free to move in and out from the engine.
6   Using a socket and torque wrench, turn the tensioning nut anti-clockwise until a torque of 9.0 Nm (6.6 lbf ft) is indicated.
7   Tighten the pivot bolt while checking that the alternator remains in the same position, then tighten the adjustment bolt and adjustment rail pivot bolt.

Bosch 75 and 90 amp alternator – description
8   The Bosch 75 and 90 amp alternator fitted from January 1985 is shown in Fig. 13.26 and apart from a few minor components is identical to the previous type. The servicing procedures are as given in Chapter 10.

Instrument panel cluster (later models) – description
9   The instrument panel cluster components for later models are

shown in Figs. 13.27 and 13.28. Removal and refitting procedures are as given in Chapter 10.

Headlamp and foglamp units (later models) – removal and refitting
10   Remove the screw and withdraw the trim strip from under the headlamp and foglamp units (photo).
11   With the bonnet open, disconnect the wiring from the foglamp, sidelamp and headlamp bulbs (photos).
12   Unscrew the top and bottom mounting screws and withdraw the lamp unit complete (photos).
13   To remove the headlamp unit from the frame, unscrew the beam adjustment screw (photo) and turn the retaining clips through 90°. To remove the foglamp unit turn the three clips through 90° (photos).
14   Refitting is a reversal of removal, but finally adjust the headlamp beam with reference to Chapter 10. Make sure that the 'TOP' mark on the foglamp cap is uppermost.

Headlamp range control – description, removal and refitting
15   The headlamp range control is an optional extra on certain models as from January 1986. It consists of a facia mounted range control and two adjuster motors mounted on the rear of the headlamps. The control only functions on dipped beam and it is only possible to *lower* the beam from the normal setting (ie when carrying a heavy load).
16   Before adjusting the headlamp beam it is important to check that the range control is at its basic setting.
17   To remove the control from the facia, first disconnect the battery negative lead, then prise out the control and disconnect the wiring plug.
18   To remove the motors, working in the engine compartment, disconnect the wiring plugs from both adjuster motors.
19   Disengage the motors from the headlamp frames by turning the right-hand motor anti-clockwise and the left-hand motor clockwise.
20   Remove the headlamp units as previously described, then unscrew the adjustment screws and withdraw the motors.
21   Refitting is a reversal of removal.

Lamp bulbs – renewal
Side marker lamp
22   Using a thin screwdriver or a piece of plastic sheet, depress the plastic tab from the rear end of the lamp (photo). Use a piece of card or rag to prevent damage to the paintwork.
23   Ease out the rear of the lamp and unhook the front tab from the hole.
24   Pull out the bulbholder, then extract the wedge type bulb from the holder (photos).
25   Refitting is a reversal of removal.

Fig. 13.25 Plastic skin to pierce when removing the battery cell plugs (Sec 10)

10.4 Alternator adjusting link with toothed rack

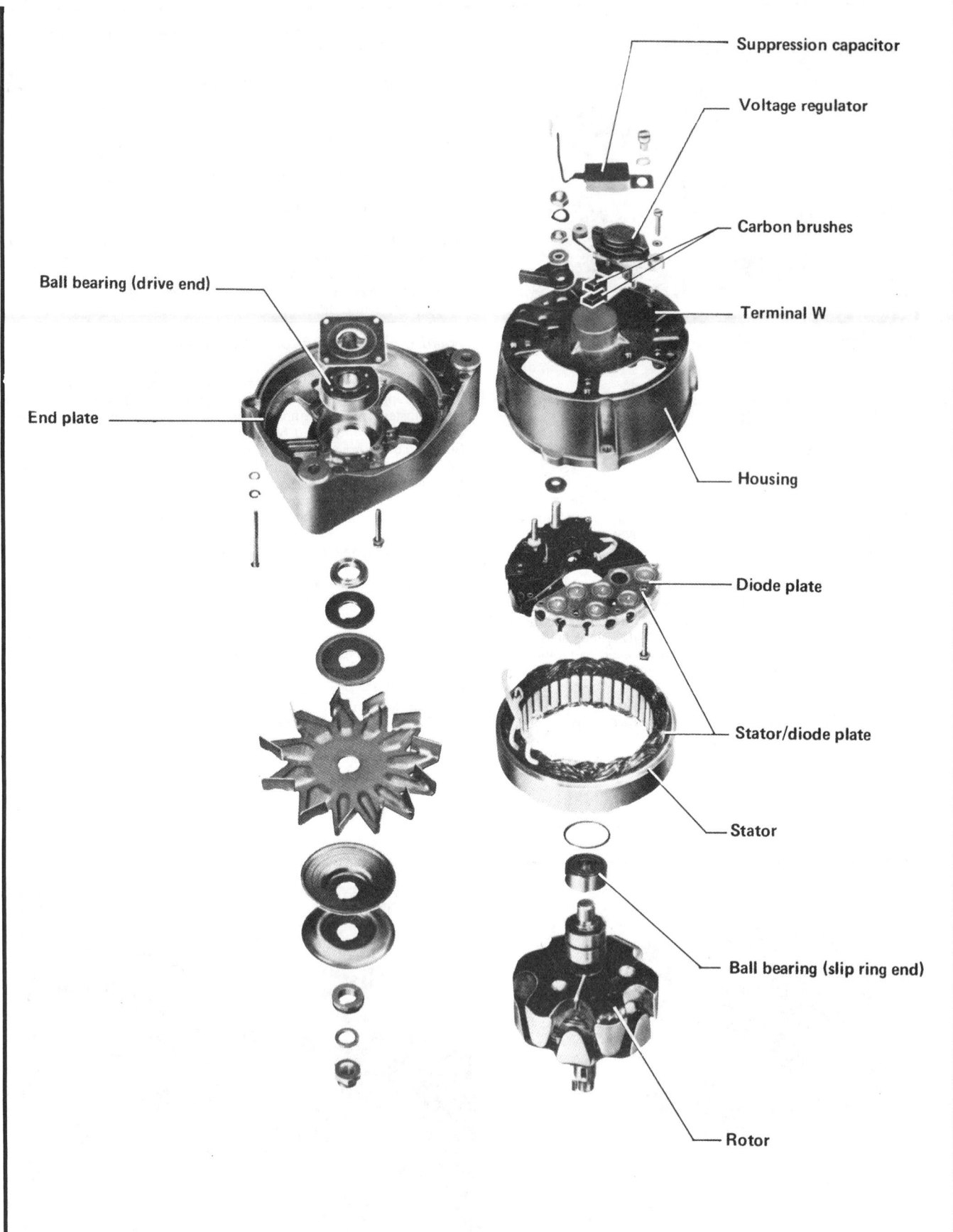

Suppression capacitor

Voltage regulator

Carbon brushes

Ball bearing (drive end)

Terminal W

End plate

Housing

Diode plate

Stator/diode plate

Stator

Ball bearing (slip ring end)

Rotor

Fig. 13.26 Exploded view of later type Bosch 75 and 90 amp alternator (Sec 10)

Speedometer

Switch unit (printed circuit)
For optical and acoustic oil
pressure warning system

Bulb for instrument
lighting

Speedometer housing
and optical and acoustic oil
pressure warning system

Screw
For speedometer housing
and switch unit for optical
and acoustic oil pressure
warning system

Voltage stabilizer

Printed circuit

Screw

Fig. 13.27 Instrument panel components
fitted to certain models after July 1983
(Sec 10)

10.10 Removing headlamp trim strip

Printed circuit

Bulb for instrument lighting

Voltage stabilizer

Heat sink

Housing for speedometer and switch
unit for oil pressure warning system

Switch unit (printed board)
for oil pressure warning system

Coolant temperature gauge

Warning lamp housing

Speedometer

Rev counter

LEDs

Retaining plate

Fuel gauge

Bulb

Cap (blue)

Diode holder

Dash insert

Digital clock

**Fig. 13.28 Instrument panel components fitted to certain models after January 1985
(Sec 10)**

10.11A Disconnecting foglamp wiring

10.11B Disconnecting sidelamp wiring

10.11C Disconnecting headlamp wiring

10.12A Unscrew the top mounting screws ...

10.12B ... inner bottom screws ...

10.12C ... and outer bottom screws ...

10.12D ... and withdraw the lamp unit

10.12E Complete lamp unit showing mounting frame

10.13A Headlamp beam adjustment screw location

10.13B Foglamp unit top mounting clips ...

10.13C ... and bottom mounting clip

Fig. 13.29 The foglamp cap 'Top' mask must be uppermost
(Sec 10)

Fig. 13.30 Prising out the headlamp range control
(Sec 10)

Fig. 13.31 Disconnecting a wiring plug (1) from a
headlamp range control adjuster motor (Sec 10)

10.22 Depressing the retaining tab on the side marker lamp

10.24A Pull out the bulbholder ...

10.24B ... and extract the wedge type bulb

Rear lamp cluster – saloon
26 Open the boot lid, then squeeze together the plastic tabs as shown in Fig. 13.32 and withdraw the bulbholder.
27 Push and twist the bulb to remove it.
28 Refitting is a reversal of removal.
Rear lamp cluster – hatchback models (January 1985-on)
29 Open the tailgate and remove the inner trim panel from the body corner or tailgate inner panel. Where necessary turn the fastener 90° and pull off the trim cover (photo).

30 Squeeze together the plastic tabs and remove the bulbholder (photos).
31 Depress and twist the bulb to remove it.
32 To remove the lamp body, unscrew the inner nuts and withdraw the lamp from the rear of the car (photos).
33 Refitting is a reversal of removal.

Fig. 13.32 Rear lamp cluster retaining tab locations on Saloon models (Sec 10)

10.29 Removing inner trim panel cover for access to the tailgate rear lamp cluster

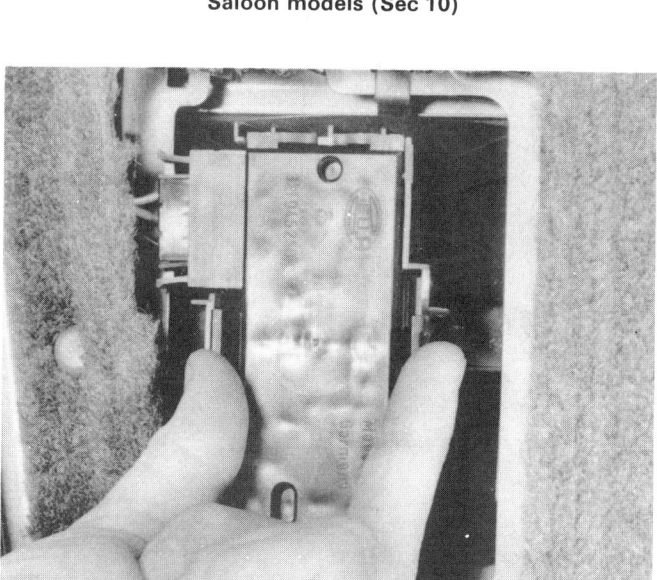

10.30A Squeeze together the plastic tabs ...

10.30B ... and remove the tailgate bulbholder

Window for luggage compartment illumination

Cover for tail light
– only for towing hitch –

Bulb for luggage compartment illumination

Bulb holder

Reversing light bulb

Rear fog light bulb

Tail light bulb

Brake light bulb

Turn signal bulb

Seal

Reversing light

Rear fog light

Tail light

Brake light

Turn signal light

Fig. 13.33 Rear lamp cluster components on Saloon models (Sec 10)

Bulb holder

Reversing light bulb

Rear fog light bulb

Turn signal bulb

Seal

Tail/brake light bulb

Rear fog light ⎫
⎬ ON TAILGATE
Reversing light ⎭

Turn signal light ⎫
⎬ ON BODY
Tail/brake light ⎭

Fig. 13.34 Rear lamp cluster components on hatchback models from January 1985 (Sec 10)

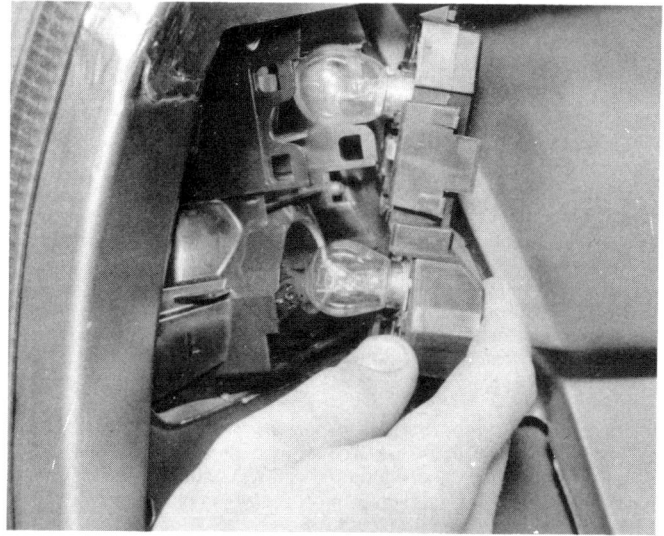

10.30C ... or body corner bulbholder

10.32A Unscrew the inner nuts ...

10.32B ... and remove the lamp body

10.34A Number plate light mounting screws

10.34B Separating the bulbholder from the lens

10.44 Prise off the cover ...

Number plate light – Hatchback models (January 1985-on)
34 Remove the cross-head screws and withdraw the number plate light from the tailgate (photos).
35 Separate the bulbholder, then depress and twist the bulb to remove it.

Interior light – later models
36 Press the spring (Fig. 13.35) towards the switch and remove the light.
37 Renew the bulb as described in Chapter 10.

Rear reading lamp
38 Release the lamp by inserting a screwdriver in the direction shown in Fig. 13.36 against the retaining spring.
39 Renew the bulb as described for the interior light.
40 When refitting the lamp, insert the switch end first.

Luggage compartment light
41 On hatchback models, prise the light from the trim. On saloon models, depress the plastic tab and remove the lens.
42 Remove the festoon type bulb from the spring contacts.
43 Refitting is a reversal of removal.

Door mounted speakers – removal and refitting
44 Carefully prise off the speaker cover with a screwdriver (photo).
45 Remove the cross-head mounting screws, withdraw the speaker from the door trim panel, and disconnect the wiring plug, noting which way round the wires are connected (photo).
46 Refitting is a reversal of removal.

10.45 ... for access to the door mounted speaker

Fig. 13.35 Press the spring as shown to remove the interior light (Sec 10)

Fig. 13.36 Insert a screwdriver as shown to remove the rear reading lamp (Sec 10)

Fig. 13.37 Luggage compartment light on hatchback models (Sec 10)

Fig. 13.38 Luggage compartment light removal on Saloon models (Sec 10)

Headlamp dim-dip system

47 This system is fitted to later models (1986 on) to meet current UK regulations. The system is designed to prevent the vehicle being driven with only parking lamps on.

Fuses and relays – general

48 From July 1982 a revised fusebox and relay plate is fitted to all models. The new unit comprises a main relay plate and auxiliary plate clipped together to form one unit. On the main relay plate there is provision for 22 fuses and 11 relays. Additional fuses and relays are carried on the auxiliary plate, according to model, year and options fitted. Details of the fuse locations and circuits protected are given in the Specifications at the beginning of Chapter 10. The relay locations and circuits controlled are given with the appropriate wiring diagrams at the end of this Supplement.

11 Suspension and steering

Front hub and bearing – modification

1 As from December 1985, new front wheel bearing kits no longer included a sachet of Molypaste as described in Chapter 11, Section 5. The Molypaste was originally provided for application to the bearing seat, in order to prevent slight movement of the bearing which sometimes occurred with the front wheels on full lock. This problem has now been cured by increasing the outside diameter of the bearing.

Anti-roll bar – description, removal and refitting

2 As from January 1984 on power-assisted steering models, the ends of the anti-roll bar are attached to the front suspension wishbones by angled links.
3 When fitting the links, make sure that the shoulders are at right-angles to the surfaces of the wishbone and anti-roll bar.
4 The bushes in the anti-roll bar and wishbone can be renewed using the procedure described in Chapter 11, Section 7, but first cut off the collars with a hacksaw.

Front suspension subframe – general

5 The front suspension subframe mounting bolts should be renewed when removing and refitting the subframe.
6 The correct sequence for tightening the bolts is as follows:

Rear left
Rear right
Front left
Front right

7 Originally a torque of 70 Nm (44 lbf ft) was specified for the subframe bolts (see Chapter 11), but this has now been changed to 35 Nm (26 lbf ft) plus angle tightening of 90°. This applies to all model years.

Front shock absorber – renewal

8 New vehicles are installed at the factory with 'wet' type front suspension struts where the shock absorber consists of a piston and rod acting directly in the strut which is filled with hydraulic fluid.
9 The original piston, rod and seals cannot be renewed, but they can be replaced by a shock absorber cartridge. To do this, remove the piston and rod, as described in Chapter 11, then drain the fluid from the strut wheel bearing housing and clean the recess thoroughly.
10 Insert the new cartridge and tighten the screw cap.
11 With the cartridge upright fully operate the shock absorber piston rod through several strokes to purge it of any trapped air.

Steering wheel – removal and refitting

12 The accompanying photos show the steering wheel on a later model and the removal and refitting procedure is as given in Chapter 11.

Wheels and tyres – general care and maintenance

13 Wheels and tyres should give no real problems in use provided that a close eye is kept on them with regard to excessive wear or damage. To this end, the following points should be noted.
14 Ensure that tyre pressures are checked regularly and maintained correctly. Checking should be carried out with the tyres cold and not immediately after the vehicle has been in use. If the pressures are checked with the tyres hot, an apparently high reading will be obtained

Anti-roll bar mounting

Anti-roll bar

Self-locking nut

Bush

Link

Anti-roll bar rubber mounting

Drive shaft

Bush

Wheel bearing housing

Rubber mounting for wishbone

Bolt

Wheel bolt

Brake caliper

Self-locking nut for wheel hub to drive shaft

Fig. 13.39 Front suspension components showing anti-roll bar with angled link (Sec 11)

11.12A Prise off the centre pad ...

11.12B ... for access to the steering wheel retaining nut

owing to heat expansion. Under no circumstances should an attempt be made to reduce the pressures to the quoted cold reading in this instance, or effective underinflation will result.

15 Underinflation will cause overheating of the tyre owing to excessive flexing of the casing and the tread will not sit correctly on the road surface. This will cause a consequent loss of adhesion and excessive wear, not to mention the danger of sudden tyre failure due to heat build-up.

16 Overinflation will cause rapid wear of the centre part of the tyre tread coupled with reduced adhesion, harsher ride, and the danger of shock damage occuring in the tyre casing.

17 Regularly check the tyres for damage in the form of cuts or bulges, especially in the sidewalls. Remove any nails or stones embedded in the tread before they penetrate the tyre to cause deflation. If removal of a nail *does* reveal that the tyre has been punctured, refit the nail so that its point of penetration is marked. Then immediately change the wheel and have the tyre repaired by a tyre dealer. Do *not* drive on a tyre in such a condition. In many cases a puncture can be simply repaired by the use of an inner tube of the correct size and type. If in any doubt as to the possible consequences of any damage found, consult your local tyre dealer for advice.

18 Periodically remove the wheels and clean any dirt or mud from the inside and outside surfaces. Examine the wheel rims for signs of rusting, corrosion or other damage. Light alloy wheels are easily damaged by 'kerbing' whilst parking, and similarly steel wheels may become dented or buckled. Renewal of the wheel is very often the only course of remedial action possible.

19 The balance of each wheel and tyre assembly should be maintained to avoid excessive wear, not only to the tyres but also to the steering and suspension components. Wheel imbalance is normally signified by vibration through the vehicle's bodyshell, although in many cases it is particularly noticeable through the steering wheel. Conversely, it should be noted that wear or damage in suspension or steering components may cause excessive tyre wear. Out-of-round or out-of-true tyres, damaged wheels and wheel bearing wear/maladjustment also fall into this category. Balancing will not usually cure vibration caused by such wear.

20 Wheel balancing may be carried out with the wheel either on or off the vehicle. If balanced on the vehicle, ensure that the wheel-to-hub relationship is marked in some way prior to subsequent wheel removal so that it may be refitted in its original position.

21 General tyre wear is influenced to a large degree by driving style – harsh braking and acceleration or fast cornering will all produce more rapid tyre wear. Interchanging of tyres may result in more even wear, but this should only be carried out where there is no mix of tyre types on the vehicle. However, it is worth bearing in mind that if this is completely effective, the added expense of replacing a complete set of tyres simultaneously is incurred, which may prove financially restrictive for many owners.

22 Front tyres may wear unevenly as a result of wheel misalignment. The front wheels should always be correctly aligned according to the settings specified by the vehicle manufacturer.

23 Legal restrictions apply to the mixing of tyre types on a vehicle. Basically this means that a vehicle must not have tyres of differing construction on the same axle. Although it is not recommended to mix tyre types between front axle and rear axle, the only legally permissible combination is crossply at the front and radial at the rear. When mixing radial ply tyres, textile braced radials must always go on the front axle, with steel braced radials at the rear. An obvious disadvantage of such mixing is the necessity to carry two spares tyres to avoid contravening the law in the event of a puncture.

24 In the UK, the Motor Vehicles Construction and Use Regulations apply to many aspects of tyre fitting and usage. It is suggested that a copy of these regulations is obtained from your local police if in doubt as to the current legal requirements with regard to tyre condition, minimum tread depth, etc.

12 Bodywork and fittings

Plastic components – repair

1 With the use of more and more plastic body components by the vehicle manufacturers (eg, bumpers, spoilers, and in some cases major body panels), rectification of damage to such items has become a matter of either entrusting repair work to a specialist in this field, or renewing complete components. Repair by the DIY owner is not really feasible owing to the cost of the equipment and materials required for effecting such repairs. The basic technique involves making a groove along the line of the crack in the plastic using a rotary burr in a power drill. The damaged part is then welded back together by using a hot air gun to heat up and fuse a plastic filler rod into the groove. Any excess plastic is then removed and the area rubbed down to a smooth finish. It is important that a filler rod of the correct plastic is used, as body components can be made of a variety of different types (eg, polycarbonate, ABS, polypropylene).

2 If the owner is renewing a complete component himself, he will be left with the problem of finding a suitable paint for finishing which is compatible with the type of plastic used. At one time the use of a universal paint was not possible owing to the complex range of plastics encountered in body component applications. Standard paints, generally speaking, will not bond to plastic or rubber satisfactorily. However, it is now possible to obtain a plastic body parts finishing kit which consists of a pre-primer treatment, a primer and coloured top coat. Full instructions are normally supplied with a kit, but basically the method of use is to first apply the pre-primer to the component concerned and allow it to dry for up to 30 minutes. Then the primer is applied and left to dry for about an hour before finally applying the special coloured top coat. The result is a correctly

12.3A Pull off the knob ...

12.3B ... and cover from the manual door mirror adjuster

12.3C Unscrew the locking knob ...

12.3D .. and remove the plastic cover

12.3E Disconnect the wiring from the door mounted speaker

12.4 Removing a trim strip from the front grille

12.5A Depress the plastic tabs with a screwdriver ...

12.5B ... to release the top of the grille from the crossmember ...

12.6 ... then unhook the bottom from the valance

coloured component where the paint will flex with the plastic or rubber, a property that standard paint does not normally possess.

Front door trim panel (1984-on models) – removal and refitting

3   The accompanying photos show minor differences for the removal and refitting of the front door trim panel on later models. The basic procedure remains as given in Chapter 12, Section 7.

Front grille (later models) – removal and refitting

4   Remove the two screws and slide the twin trim strips outwards from under the headlamp units (photo).
5   Release the top of the grille from the crossmember using a screwdriver to depress the plastic tabs (photos).

6   Unhook the bottom of the grille from the valance (photo).
7   Refitting is a reversal of removal, but press in the top of the grille until the clips snap into place.

Tailgate (Hatchback) – removal, refitting and adjustment

8   The procedure is as given in Chapter 12, Section 20. However, the following additional points should be noted.
9   Pull off the luggage shelf stays to disconnect them (photo).
10   Disconnect the tailgate support struts by prising out the retaining clips (photo).
11   When shut, the tailgate should be firmly in contact with the weatherstrip and rubber stop. To achieve this adjust the side strikers (or lock plates) as necessary, and also ensure that the locks engage the strikers centrally (photos).

12.9 Disconnecting a luggage shelf stay

12.10 Disconnecting a tailgate support strut

12.11A Tailgate rubber stop

12.11B Tailgate lock side striker

12.11C Tailgate lock

Fig. 13.40 Front head restraint pillar, bezel and spring clip (Sec 12)

Seat belts
12 The front and rear seat belts are of inertia reel type.
13 Examine the belts regularly for signs of fraying or damage. If evident, renew the complete belt assembly. The belt should also be renewed if the belts have been strained due to the vehicle having been involved in a front end collision.
14 Clean the belts using only a damp cloth and liquid detergent. Never use solvents of any kind.
15 Whenever a seat belt is removed and refitted, the anchor bolt components (wave washer, spacer, anchor plate) must be fitted in their originally installed sequence.

Head restraints
16 To adjust the height of the head restraints, simply grip the sides and pull up or push down.
17 To remove a front head restraint, push the spring clips out of the grooved bezels at the base of the head restraint pillars. Pull the head restraint up and out.
18 When refitting, press the spring clips into the bezel grooves so that the straight parts of the clips are towards the rear of the car. Insert the head restraint pillars into their holes.
19 To remove a rear head restraint from Hatchback versions, release the backrest and tilt it forwards, then remove the head restraint by giving it a sharp jerk upwards.
20 To remove a rear head restraint from the Saloon, twist both bezels at the base of the pillars until the slots in the bezels point to the side. Pull the head restraint upwards and out.
21 After refitting the Saloon rear head restraints, twist the bezels until their slots point towards the front.

Rear seat (Hatchback and Estate) – removal and refitting
22 To remove the rear seat, pull the cushion loop upwards and fold the seat cushion forwards.
23 Release the seat back and fold it forwards. The side pivot bracket screws may now be removed and the seat cushion and back withdrawn from the vehicle.
24 On certain later Hatchback and Estate models, the rear seat is of asymmetrical (60/40) split type but the removal procedure is similar to that described earlier.

Fig. 13.41 Using a screwdriver to release the door mirror glass locking ring (Sec 12)

Grab handles
25 The interior grab handles which are located above the door apertures can be removed if the end caps are prised out and the fixing screws extracted.

Exterior door mirror glass (electrically heated and adjustable type) – renewal
26 The mirror glass can be renewed without removing the complete mirror assembly from the door, using the following procedure.
27 Using a small screwdriver inserted through the slot in the base of the mirror body, engage the locking ring teeth and turn the locking ring anti-clockwise (Fig. 13.41).
28 With the locking ring released, withdraw the glass, disconnect the wiring and remove the glass from the mirror body.
29 Refitting is the reverse sequence to removal.

Conversion factors

Length (distance)
Inches (in)	X	25.4	= Millimetres (mm)	X 0.0394	= Inches (in)
Feet (ft)	X	0.305	= Metres (m)	X 3.281	= Feet (ft)
Miles	X	1.609	= Kilometres (km)	X 0.621	= Miles

Volume (capacity)
Cubic inches (cu in; in³)	X	16.387	= Cubic centimetres (cc; cm³)	X 0.061	= Cubic inches (cu in; in³)
Imperial pints (Imp pt)	X	0.568	= Litres (l)	X 1.76	= Imperial pints (Imp pt)
Imperial quarts (Imp qt)	X	1.137	= Litres (l)	X 0.88	= Imperial quarts (Imp qt)
Imperial quarts (Imp qt)	X	1.201	= US quarts (US qt)	X 0.833	= Imperial quarts (Imp qt)
US quarts (US qt)	X	0.946	= Litres (l)	X 1.057	= US quarts (US qt)
Imperial gallons (Imp gal)	X	4.546	= Litres (l)	X 0.22	= Imperial gallons (Imp gal)
Imperial gallons (Imp gal)	X	1.201	= US gallons (US gal)	X 0.833	= Imperial gallons (Imp gal)
US gallons (US gal)	X	3.785	= Litres (l)	X 0.264	= US gallons (US gal)

Mass (weight)
Ounces (oz)	X	28.35	= Grams (g)	X 0.035	= Ounces (oz)
Pounds (lb)	X	0.454	= Kilograms (kg)	X 2.205	= Pounds (lb)

Force
Ounces-force (ozf; oz)	X	0.278	= Newtons (N)	X 3.6	= Ounces-force (ozf; oz)
Pounds-force (lbf; lb)	X	4.448	= Newtons (N)	X 0.225	= Pounds-force (lbf; lb)
Newtons (N)	X	0.1	= Kilograms-force (kgf; kg)	X 9.81	= Newtons (N)

Pressure
Pounds-force per square inch (psi; lbf/in²; lb/in²)	X	0.070	= Kilograms-force per square centimetre (kgf/cm²; kg/cm²)	X 14.223	= Pounds-force per square inch (psi; lbf/in²; lb/in²)
Pounds-force per square inch (psi; lbf/in²; lb/in²)	X	0.068	= Atmospheres (atm)	X 14.696	= Pounds-force per square inch (psi; lbf/in²; lb/in²)
Pounds-force per square inch (psi; lbf/in²; lb/in²)	X	0.069	= Bars	X 14.5	= Pounds-force per square inch (psi; lbf/in²; lb/in²)
Pounds-force per square inch (psi; lbf/in²; lb/in²)	X	6.895	= Kilopascals (kPa)	X 0.145	= Pounds-force per square inch (psi; lbf/in²; lb/in²)
Kilopascals (kPa)	X	0.01	= Kilograms-force per square centimetre (kgf/cm²; kg/cm²)	X 98.1	= Kilopascals (kPa)
Millibar (mbar)	X	100	= Pascals (Pa)	X 0.01	= Millibar (mbar)
Millibar (mbar)	X	0.0145	= Pounds-force per square inch (psi; lbf/in²; lb/in²)	X 68.947	= Millibar (mbar)
Millibar (mbar)	X	0.75	= Millimetres of mercury (mmHg)	X 1.333	= Millibar (mbar)
Millibar (mbar)	X	0.401	= Inches of water (inH₂O)	X 2.491	= Millibar (mbar)
Millimetres of mercury (mmHg)	X	0.535	= Inches of water (inH₂O)	X 1.868	= Millimetres of mercury (mmHg)
Inches of water (inH₂O)	X	0.036	= Pounds-force per square inch (psi; lbf/in²; lb/in²)	X 27.68	= Inches of water (inH₂O)

Torque (moment of force)
Pounds-force inches (lbf in; lb in)	X	1.152	= Kilograms-force centimetre (kgf cm; kg cm)	X 0.868	= Pounds-force inches (lbf in; lb in)
Pounds-force inches (lbf in; lb in)	X	0.113	= Newton metres (Nm)	X 8.85	= Pounds-force inches (lbf in; lb in)
Pounds-force inches (lbf in; lb in)	X	0.083	= Pounds-force feet (lbf ft; lb ft)	X 12	= Pounds-force inches (lbf in; lb in)
Pounds-force feet (lbf ft; lb ft)	X	0.138	= Kilograms-force metres (kgf m; kg m)	X 7.233	= Pounds-force feet (lbf ft; lb ft)
Pounds-force feet (lbf ft; lb ft)	X	1.356	= Newton metres (Nm)	X 0.738	= Pounds-force feet (lbf ft; lb ft)
Newton metres (Nm)	X	0.102	= Kilograms-force metres (kgf m; kg m)	X 9.804	= Newton metres (Nm)

Power
Horsepower (hp)	X	745.7	= Watts (W)	X 0.0013	= Horsepower (hp)

Velocity (speed)
Miles per hour (miles/hr; mph)	X	1.609	= Kilometres per hour (km/hr; kph)	X 0.621	= Miles per hour (miles/hr; mph)

Fuel consumption*
Miles per gallon, Imperial (mpg)	X	0.354	= Kilometres per litre (km/l)	X 2.825	= Miles per gallon, Imperial (mpg)
Miles per gallon, US (mpg)	X	0.425	= Kilometres per litre (km/l)	X 2.352	= Miles per gallon, US (mpg)

Temperature

Degrees Fahrenheit = (°C x 1.8) + 32

Degrees Celsius (Degrees Centigrade; °C) = (°F - 32) x 0.56

It is common practice to convert from miles per gallon (mpg) to litres/100 kilometres (l/100km), where mpg (Imperial) x l/100 km = 282 and mpg (US) x l/100 km = 235

Index

357

Symbols used in current flow diagrams

358

Note:
All **switches** and **contacts** are illustrated in the **mechanical off position**. The various contacts in a switch are shown in the current track to which they belong by function.

This area represents the relay plate with fuse holder

Wire cross section in mm²

Wiring colour codes
Primary colour
Tracer colour

Numbers in squares indicate that a wire is discontinued in the diagram and refer to the current track where it is continued.

Numbers/number combinations
These indicate the individual contacts in a multi-point connector, e.g. T 10/4
T 10 = ten-point connector
/4 = contact 4

Terminals with the numbers which are on the actual parts.

Wiring codes

black – sw
blue – bl
brown – br
green – gn
grey – gr
lilac – li
red – ro
white – we
yellow – ge

Symbols
(in this case: bulb)

Parts designation
Using the legend you will be able to find which part in the current flow diagram is referred to by this symbol,
e.g. W = interior light

Internal connections (thin lines)
These connections are **not** to be found in the form of wires. Internal connections are however current-carrying connections. They make it possible to check the flow of current within a component or unit.

Numbers in circles indicate the locations of earthing points (see legend)

Current track numbers
to help you find the parts in the current flow diagram
(see legend)

Instructions for using current flow diagrams

Specimen legend

The same part designations are used in all current
flow diagrams.

E.g.: A is always used for the battery or N for the
ignition coil

		in current track
Designation		
		4
A	— Battery	5, 6, 7, 8
B	— Starter	3
C	— Alternator	3
C 1	— Voltage regulator	2
F 2	— Door contact switch	10, 11
N	— Ignition coil	8
N 6	— Series resistance (for coil)	10, 11, 12, 13
O	— Distributor	11, 12, 13
P	— Spark plug connector	11, 12, 13
Q	— Spark plugs	
S 7	— Fuse in fuse box	
T 10	— Connector, ten-point, on instrument panel insert	1
W	— Interior light	

① — Earthing strap, battery/body

② — Earthing strap, alternator/engine

③ — Earthing strap, gearbox/chassis

Explanation of where a
connection is to be found on
the vehicle.

Number of current track
to help you locate the part in the
current flow diagram.
Current track numbers are not
given for fuses, wiring connections
and earthing points.

Instructions for using current flow diagrams (continued)

Wiring diagram for all models from September 1981 (Part 1A)

361

Wiring diagram for all models from September 1981 (Part 1B)

Wiring diagram for all models from September 1981 (Part 1C)

Key to Part 1 of wiring diagram for all models from September 1981

Designation		In current track
A	Battery	5
B	Starter	6,7
C	Alternator	2-4
C1	Voltage regulator	2-4
D	Ignition switch	14-18
E1	Lighting switch	30-40
E4	Dip and headlight flasher switch	50-52
E15	Heated rear window switch	41-42
E19	Parking light switch	16,17
E20	Instrument lighting rheostat**	40
E23	Fog and rear fog light switch*	58,60
F2	Door contact switch front left	21
F3	Door contact switch front right	22
F5	Switch for boot light*	19
G40	Hall sender	9,10
J5	Fog light relay*	60,62
J59	Relief relay (for X contact)	30,31
K10	Heated rear window warning lamp	41
K17	Fog light warning lamp	58
L1	Twin filament headlight left	53,55
L2	Twin filament headlight right	54,56
L8	Digital clock light (only vehicles with rev counter)	24
L9	Lighting switch light	30
L10	Dash insert light	25,26
L20	Rear fog light*	59
L22	Fog light left	61
L23	Fog light right*	62
L28	Cigarette lighter light*	29
M1	Parking light left	49
M2	Rear light right	47
M3	Parking light right	46
M4	Rear light left	48
N	Ignition coil	12
N41	TCI switch unit	8-12
O	Distributor	11-13
P	Spark plug connector	11-13
Q	Spark plug	11-13
R	Connection for radio (behind dash insert)	24,27
S1-S5,S7,S12-S14	Fuses in fuse box	
S28	Separate fuse for fog lights	62

Designation		In current track
T1a	Connector single in engine compartment near left wheel housing	
T1b	Connector single in engine compartment near battery	
T1d	Connector single behind dash	
T1e	Connector single behind dash	
T1g	Connector single in boot rear left	
T1h	Connector single behind dash	
T1j	Connector single behind dash	
T1k	Connector single behind dash	
T1l	Connector single behind dash	
T1v	Connector single in boot rear left	
T2a	Connector two point behind dash	
T2c	Connector two point behind dash	
T2k	Connector two point behind dash	
T3b	Connector three point behind dash	
T4	Connector four point behind dash	
T14/	Connector 14 point on dash insert	
T29/	Connector 29 point behind dash	
U1	Cigarette lighter**	28
W3	Boot light*	19
W6	Glove box light*	57
X	Number plate light	44,45
Y2	Digital clock (only vehicles with rev counter)	23
Z1	Heated rear window	43

Earth points

- ① Earth strap from battery via body to gearbox
- ② Earth wire alternator to engine block
- ⑨ Earth point on relay plate bracket
- ⑩ Earth point behind dash (earth plate secured to dash)
- ⑮ Earth point in insulating sleeve of front loom
- ⑯ Earth point bound with insulating tape in dash loom
- ⑰ Earth point in insulating sleeve of rear loom
- ⑱ Earth point roof cross member upper right
- ⑳ Earth point roof cross member upper left

* only GL models
** only L and GL models
*** only 55 kW engine

Colour code key

black	=	sw
blue	=	bl
brown	=	br
green	=	gn
grey	=	gr
lilac	=	li
red	=	ro
white	=	we
yellow	=	ge

Wiring diagram for all models from September 1981 (Part 2A)

Wiring diagram for all models from September 1981 (Part 2B)

N23

N25

bl S15 ro S10

M18
J31
M17 M19 M21 M26 M20

D6 E19 F16 C18 F19 A6 G1 G6 H D19 C5 C6 C16 C13 C9 E16 E15 E21 E18 E8 G2 E20 E7 C17

1.0 1.0 1.0 1.0 2.5 2.5 2.5 1.0 1.0 1.0 1.0 1.0 1.0 1.0 0.5 1.0 0.5 1.0

sw/we sw/gn sw/we ro/sw br gn br/sw gn/ro gn/ro

sw/gn sw/we ro sw/gr gn sw/gr gn/ge

gn/ge gn/ge gn/ro

gn/sw gn/sw

T297

1.5

49a E9

E2 III II I

L 1.5 1.5 1.5

1.0 ge/sw

sw/we T2b T1f T2b T1n T1u

T29/26 we

sw/we 1.0

1.5

L F18 N23

K6 ge

58b 31 1.5 53b 53

0.5 0.5 0.5 2.5 J L T

br ro/sw 53a 53e 21T0J

40 ge E22

BL BL BL BL 53 53b 53a 53e

gr/bl

L21 M8 M7 M6 M5 V7 V2 V V5

T2g T2h 31

1.0 1.0

T2g T2h

0.5 1.0 1.0 2.5 1.5 0.5 1.0

br br br br br br br

(10) (10) (9) (15) (16) (17)

00 101 102 103 104 105 106 107 108 109 110 111 112 113 114 115 116 117 118

Wiring diagram for all models from September 1981 (Part 2C)

Key to Part 2 of wiring diagram for all models from September 1981

Designation		In current track
E2	Turn signal switch	100
E3	Emergency light switch	97-102
E9	Fresh air blower switch	109,110
E22	Intermittent wiper switch (only GL model with intermittent operation)	114-117
F	Brake light switch	95,96
F1	Oil pressure switch	90
F4	Reversing light switch	63
F6	Brake system warning light switch*	91
F9	Handbrake warning light switch*	92
F18	Thermoswitch for coolant fan	108
F26	Thermo switch for automatic choke ***	68
F35	Thermo switch for manifold preheating ***	69
F62	Vacuum switch for gearchange indicator	71
F68	Gear switch for gearchange and consumption indicator	74
G	Fuel gauge sender	89
G1	Fuel gauge	84
G2	Coolant temperature gauge sender	88
G3	Coolant temperature gauge	85
G5	Rev counter	78
G51	Gearchange and consumption indicator	76
H	Horn controls	65
H1	Horn	66
J2	Emergency flasher relay	99,100
J6	Voltage stabilizer	84
J31	Relay for wash/wipe intermittent facility*	112-115
J81	Relay for manifold preheating***	69,70
J98	Control unit for gearchange indicator	71-73
K1	High beam warning lamp	79
K2	Generator warning lamp	81
K3	Oil pressure warning lamp	80
K5	Turn signal warning lamp	82
K6	Emergency flasher system warning lamp	103
K7	Dual circuit brake and handbrake warning lamp*	93,94
K28	Coolant temperature warning lamp (too hot, red)	87
K48	Gearchange indicator lamp	77
L21	Heater lever light**	102
M5	Turn signal front left	107
M6	Turn signal rear left	106
M7	Turn signal front right	105
M8	Turn signal rear right	104
M9	Brake light left	97
M10	Brake light right	96
M16	Reversing light left	64
M17	Reversing light right	63
N1	Automatic choke***	68
N3	By-pass air cut-off valve	67
N23	Ballast resistance for fresh air blower	110
N51	Heater element for intake manifold preheating***	66
N52	Heater element (part throttle passage heating – carburettor)	66
N60	Solenoid valve for gearchange and consumption indicator	75
S6,S8,S9,S10,S11,S15	Fuses in fuse box	

Designation		In current track
T1c	Connector single behind dash	
T1f	Connector single behind dash	
T1m	Connector single in engine compartment near carburettor	
T1n	Connector single behind dash	
T1o	Connector single in engine compartment near carburettor	
T1p	Connector single behind dash	
T1r	Connector single behind dash	
T1s	Connector single behind dash	
T1t	Connector single in engine compartment near carburettor	
T1u	Connector single behind dash	
T2b	Connector two point behind dash	
T2d	Connector two point behind dash	
T2e	Connector two point behind dash	
T2f	Connector two point in engine compartment near servo	
T2g	Connector two point near right headlight	
T2h	Connector two point near left headlight	
T3a	Connector three point in engine compartment near battery	
T3b	Connector three point behind dash	
T4	Connector four point behind dash	
T6/	Connector six point on dash insert	
T14/	Connector 14 point on dash insert	
T29/	Connector 29 point behind dash	
V	Wiper motor	111-113
V2	Fresh air blower	109
V5	Windscreen washer pump	118
V7	Radiator fan	108

Earth points:

⑨	Earth point on fuse box bracket
⑩	Earth point behind dash (earth plate secured to dash)
⑭	Earth wire steering gear
⑮	Earth point in insulating sleeve of front loom
⑯	Earth point bound with insulating tape in dash loom
⑰	Earth point in insulating sleeve of rear loom
⑱	Earth point on rear cross member (driver's side)
㉑	Earth point on earth strap from battery via body to gearbox

* only GL models
** only L and GL models
*** only 55 kW engine

Colour code key

black	=	sw
blue	=	bl
brown	=	br
green	=	gn
grey	=	gr
lilac	=	li
red	=	ro
white	=	we
yellow	=	ge

Key to Part 1 of wiring diagram for Passat C, CL and GL5 models and Santana LX, GX and GX5 models from
August 1982

Designation		In current track
A	Battery	7
B	Starter	10–12
C	Alternator	4, 6
C1	Voltage regulator	4, 6
D	Ignition/starter switch	25–29
E1	Lighting switch	59–69
E4	Headlight dimmer/flasher switch	76, 77
E19	Parking light switch	27, 28
E20	Instrument/instrument panel lighting control	69
F1	Oil pressure switch (1.8 bar)	46
F2	Front left door contact switch	53
F3	Front right door contact switch	54
F5	Luggage boot light switch (only Variant)	50
F10	Rear left door contact switch	52
F11	Rear right door contact switch	55
F22	Oil pressure switch (0.3 bar)	47
F26	Thermoswitch for choke	24
F35	Thermoswitch for intake manifold preheating	23
F62	Gearshift indicator vacuum switch	48
F68	Gear switch for gearshift and consumption indicator	49
G	Fuel gauge sender	45
G1	Fuel gauge	40
G2	Coolant temperature gauge sender	44
G3	Coolant temperature gauge	41
G5	Rev. counter	35
G40	Hall sender	14, 15
G51	Consumption indicator	39, 40
J6	Voltage stabilizer	40
J59	Relief relay (for x contact) (relay 8)	60–63
J87	DIS (idling stabilisation) switch unit (relay 4)	14, 15
J98	Gearshift indicator control unit	48, 49
J114	Oil pressure monitor control unit	33–34
K1	Main beam warning lamp	37
K2	Alternator warning lamp	30
K3	Oil pressure warning lamp	32
K5	Turn signal warning lamp	36
K28	Coolant temp. warning lamp (overheating, red)	43
K48	Gearshift indicator warning lamp	38
L1	Twin filament headlight bulb left	78, 80
L2	Twin filament headlight bulb right	79, 81
L8	Clock light	64
L10	Instrument panel insert light	65, 66
L28	Cigarette lighter light	59
M1	Side light left	75
M2	Tail light right	73
M3	Side light right	72

Designation		In current track
M4	Tail light left	74
N	Ignition coil	18, 19
N1	Automatic choke	24
N3	By-pass air cut-off valve	23
N41	TCI control unit	13–16
N51	Heater element for intake manifold preheating	21
N52	Heater element (part throttle channel heating/carburettor)	22
N60	Solenoid valve for consumption indicator	39
P	Spark plug connector	16–19
Q	Spark plugs	16–19
R	Radio connection	
S3, S5, S7-S10, S17, S20-S22	Fuses in fuse box	
T1	Connector, single near battery	
T1a	Connector, single engine compartment front left	
T1b	Connector, single engine compartment centre	
T1c	Connector, single near battery	
T1d	Connector, single behind dash on right	
T1e	Connector, single near relay plate	
T1f	Connector, single behind dash on left	
T1v	Connector, single in tailgate	
T2k	Connector, two point behind dash	
T3a	Connector, three point engine compartment centre	
T3b	Connector, three point near battery	
T4	Connector, four point behind dash	
T14	Connector, 14 point on dash insert	
T29	Connector, 29 pin behind dash	
U1	Cigarette lighter	58
W	Interior light, front	51–53
W3	Luggage boot light	50
X	Number plate light	70, 71
Y2	Digital clock	56

Earth points:

①	Earth strap from battery to body
⑨	Earth point on fuse box bracket
⑩	Earth point behind dash (earth plate secured to dash)
⑮	Earth point in insulating sleeve of front loom
⑯	Earth point bound with insulating tape in dash loom
⑰	Earth point in insulating sleeve or rear loom

For relay locations see key on page 378

Colour code key

black	=	sw
blue	=	bl
brown	=	br
green	=	gn
grey	=	gr
lilac	=	li
red	=	ro
white	=	we
yellow	=	ge

Wiring diagram for Passat C, CL and GL5 models and Santana LX, GX and GX5 models from August 1982 (Part 1A)

Wiring diagram for Passat C, CL and GL5 models and Santana LX, GX and GX5 models from August 1982 (Part 1B)

Wiring diagram for Passat C, CL and GL5 models and Santana LX, GX and GX5 models from August 1982 (Part 1C)

Wiring diagram for Passat C, CL and GL5 models and Santana LX, GX and GX5 models from August 1982 (Part 1D)

Wiring diagram for Passat C, CL and GL5 models and Santana LX, GX and GX5 models from August 1982 (Part 2A)

Wiring diagram for Passat C, CL and GL5 models and Santana LX, GX and GX5 models from August 1982 (Part 2B)

375

Wiring diagram for Passat C, CL and GL5 models and Santana LX, GX and GX5 models from August 1982 (Part 2C)

Wiring diagram for Passat C, CL and GL5 models and Santana LX, GX and GX5 models from August 1982 (Part 2D)

Key to Part 2 of wiring diagram for Passat C, CL and GL5 models and Santana LX, GX and GX5 models from
August 1982

Designation		In current track
E2	Turn signal switch	100,101
E3	Emergency light switch	95-103
E9	Fresh air blower switch	115,116
E15	Heated rear window switch	93
E22	Intermittent wiper switch	121,122
E23	Fog light and rear fog light switch (only GL models)	87,88
F	Brake light switch	108,109
F4	Reversing light switch	112
F9	Handbrake warning system switch (only GL models)	127
F18	Radiator fan thermoswitch	114
F34	Brake fluid level warning contact (only GL models)	126
F66	Coolant shortage indicator switch (from 63 kW engine)	135
H	Horn control	130
H1	Dual horns (only GL models)	132,133
J2	Emergency light relay (relay 12)	98-100
J4	Dual tone horn relay (only GL models) (relay 6)	130,131
J5	Fog light relay (only GL models) (relay 7)	86,88
J31	Intermittent wash/wiper relay (relay 10)	121–124
J39	Headlight washer system relay (only GL models) (relay 15)	124,125
J120	Switch unit for coolant shortage indicator (from 63 kW engine) (relay 18)	134,135
K6	Emergency light system warning lamp	103
K7	Dual circuit brake and handbrake warning lamp (only GL models)	128
K10	Heated rear window warning lamp	92
K17	Fog light warning lamp (only GL models)	89
L9	Lighting switch light	129
L20	Rear fog light (only GL models)	84
L21	Heater controls light	102
L22	Fog light left (only GL models)	82
L23	Fog light right (only GL models)	83
L39	Heated rear window switch	91
L40	Front and rear fog light switch (only GL models)	90
M5	Front left turn signal	105
M6	Rear left turn signal	104
M7	Front right turn signal	107

Designation		In current track
M8	Rear right turn signal	106
M9	Brake light left	111
M10	Brake light right	110
M16	Reversing light left	113
M17	Reversing light right	112
N23	Series resistance for fresh air blower	116
S1, S2, S4, S6, S11-S16, S18, S19	Fuses in fuse box	
S27	Separate fuse for rear fog light	
T1f	Connector, single behind dash	
T1g	Connector, single in boot rear left	
T1l	Connector, single behind relay plate	
T1m	Connector, single behind dash	
T1s	Connector, single behind relay plate	
T2b	Connector, two point behind dash	
T2g	Connector, two point engine compartment front right	
T2h	Connector, two point engine compartment front left	
T2k	Connector, two point engine compartment front	
T2l	Connector, two point behind relay plate	
T3a	Connector, three point engine compartment left	
T3b	Connector, three point engine compartment centre	
T29	Connector 29 pin behind dash	
V	Windscreen wiper motor	117-120
V2	Fresh air blower	115
V5	Windscreen washer pump	123
V7	Radiator fan	114
V11	Headlight washer pump (only GL models)	125
Z1	Heated rear window	94

Earth points:

⑨ Earth point on fuse box bracket
⑩ Earth point behind dash (earth plate secured to dash)
⑭ Earth wire, steering box
⑮ Earth point in insulating sleeve of front loom
⑯ Earth point bound with insulating tape in dash loom
⑰ Earth point in insulating sleeve of rear loom

Fuse colour/capacities
S_1 – green – 30A
S_{14} – yellow – 20A
S_4 – S_6, S_{11} – S_{13} and S_{16} – blue – 15A
S_2, S_3, S_7 – S_{10} and S_{17} – S_{22} – red – 10A

Colour code key
black	=	sw
blue	=	bl
brown	=	br
green	=	gn
grey	=	gr
lilac	=	li
red	=	ro
white	=	we
yellow	=	ge

Relay locations:
1 Vacant
2 Intake pre-heating relay
3 Vacant
4 Switch unit for gearshift indicator
5 Vacant
6 Duel horn relay
7 Fog light relay
8 Relief relay for X contact
9 Vacant
10 Relay for wash-wipe intermittent facility
11 Vacant
12 Emergency light relay
13 Vacant
14 Vacant
15 Headlight washer relay
16 Vacant
17 Vacant
18 Switch unit for coolant shortage indicator

Relay locations for Passat C, CL and GL5 models and Santana LX, GX and GX5 models from August 1982

Key to Part 1 of wiring diagram for the Passat CL5, GL5 and Santana LX5 and GX5 from August **1983**

Designation		In current track
E3	Turn signal switch	96-97
E3	Emergency light switch	94-99
E9	Fresh air blower switch	112
E15	Heated rear window switch	92
E22	Intermittent wiper switch	115-117
E23	Fog light and rear fog light switch	86-88
F	Brake light switch	104,105
F4	Reversing light switch	108
F9	Handbrake warning system switch	126
F18	Radiator fan thermo switch	110
F34	Brake fluid level warning contact	127
F66	Coolant shortage indicator switch	123
H	Horn button	129
H1	Horn	131,132
J2	Emergency light relay	95-96
J4	Dual tone horn relay	129,130
J5	Fog light relay	85-87
J31	Intermittent wash/wiper relay	115-118
J39	Headlight washer system relay	119-120
J120	Switch unit for coolant shortage indicator	122,123
K6	Emergency light system warning lamp	99
K7	Dual circuit brake and handbrake warning lamp	124
K10	Heated rear window warning lamp	92
K17	Fog light warning lamp	88
L9	Lighting switch light bulb	128
L20	Rear fog light bulb	83
L21	Heater controls light bulb	98
L22	Fog light bulb, left	81
L23	Fog light bulb, right	82
L39	Heated rear window switch bulb	90
L40	Front and rear fog light switch bulb	89
M5	Front left turn signal bulb	101
M6	Rear left turn signal bulb	100
M7	Front right turn signal bulb	103
M8	Rear right turn signal bulb	102
M9	Brake light bulb, left	107
M10	Brake light bulb, right	106
M16	Reversing light bulb left	109
M17	Reversing light bulb right	108
N23	Series resistance for fresh air blower	112

Designation		In current track
S1, S2, S4, S6, S11-S19	Fuses in fuse box	
S27	Separate fuse for rear fog light	84
T1f	Connector single, behind dash panel	
T1g	Connector single, in luggage boot, left	
T1l	Connector single, in engine compartment, left	
T1m	Connector single, behind dash panel	
T1s	Connector single, behind relay plate	
T1u	Connector single, behind relay plate	
T1x	Connector single, behind relay plate	
T2	Connector two pin, behind relay plate	
T2a	Connector two pin, in engine compartment, front	
T2b	Connector two pin, behind dash panel	
T2g	Connector two pin, in engine compartment, front right	
T2h	Connector two pin, in engine compartment, front left	
T2k	Connector two pin, near dual tone horns	
T2v	Connector two pin, in engine compartment, front right	
T3a	Connector three pin, in engine compartment, left	
T3b	Connector three pin, in engine compartment, centre	
T29/	Connector 29 pin, behind dash panel	
V	Windscreen wiper motor	113,114
V2	Fresh air blower	111
V5	Windscreen washer pump	118
V7	Radiator fan	110
V11	Headlight washer pump	121
Z1	Heated rear window	93

Earth points:

⑨ Earthing point near relay plate

⑮ Earthing point in insulating hose of front wiring loom

⑯ Earthing point in insulating hose of dash panel wiring loom

⑱ Earthing point in insulating hose of wiring loom for instruments

⑲ Earthing point near handbrake

⑳ Earthing point in a tailgate/boot lid

For relay locations and connections see page 385

Colour code key

black	=	sw
blue	=	bl
brown	=	br
green	=	gn
grey	=	gr
lilac	=	li
red	=	ro
white	=	we
yellow	=	ge

Wiring diagram for the Passat CL5, GL5 and Santana LX5 and GX5 from August 1983 (Part 1A)

Wiring diagram for the Passat CL5, GL5 and Santana LX5 and GX5 from August 1983 (Part 1B)

Wiring diagram for the Passat CL5, GL5 and Santana LX5 and GX5 from August 1983 (Part 1C)

30
15
X
31
a
b

2/30
⑧
3/87

S₇ ro   S₈ ro   S₂₀ ro   S₁₀ ro S₉ ro   S₂₂ ro S₂₁ ro

A9 M1   B27   B26   A24   A26 G9 E1 C14 E18 E9 C4 B23 M2 A21 B22 C17 C16   C5   C6

1,5   0,5   0,5   0,5   0,5 0,5 0,5 0,5 0,5 0,5 0,5 1,0   1,5 1,5 1,5 1,5 1,5 1,5
e/sw   gr/sw   gr/sw   gr/gn gr/gn gr/gn gr/gn gr/ro gr/ro gr/sw gr/sw ro/ge ge we we/sw we ge/sw ge

T₂₉/₁₇

119

T₁ᵥ

76   25   26   61

1,5   0,5   0,5   1,5
we/sw   gr/sw   gr/sw

56   58L   58R   58   30   56

E₂⊗W₆   E₄

58b

gr/bl

0,5   0,5   56a   56b
0,5 gr/bl   gr   gr/bl
T₂ₖ   0,5
          T₂₉/₁₁ T₂₉/₁₈

0,5   0,5
gr/bl   gr/bl

T₇/₆   0,5 br
                                                                         0,5 br
⊗L₈ ⊗L₁₀ ⊗L₁₀   gr/gn   1,5

                    0,5   56a   56b
                 58 58 58 58
            ⊗X ⊗   ⊗M₃ ⊗M₂ ⊗M₄ ⊗M₁   ⊗L₁ ⊗L₂   ⊗L₁ ⊗L₂

89   97   0,5 sw   br
            0,5   1,0   c
                                                                   d
                     br
                     1,0   1,5
            0,5
            sw   1,0   1,5
                      br   br   br

⑯   ⑳   ⑰   ⑮   ⑮

60 61 62 63 64 65 66 67 68 69 70 71 72 73 74 75 76   77 78 79 80

Wiring diagram for the Passat CL5, GL5 and Santana LX5 and GX5 from August 1983 (Part 1D)

Key to Part 2 of wiring diagram for the Passat CL5, GL5 and Santana LX5 and GX5 from August 1983

Designation		In current track
A	Battery	7
B	Starter	9-11
C	Alternator	5,6
C1	Voltage regulator	5,6
D	Ignition/starter switch	23-27
E1	Lighting switch	59-67
E4	Headlight dimmer/flasher switch	75,76
E19	Parking light switch	25,26
E20	Instrument/instrument panel lighting control	67
F1	Oil pressure switch (1.8 bar)	44
F2	Front left door contact switch	51
F3	Front right door contact switch	52
F5	Luggage boot light switch	47
F10	Rear left door contact switch	50
F11	Rear right door contact switch	53
F22	Oil pressure switch (0.3 bar)	43
F26	Thermo time switch	17,18
F62	Gearshift indicator vacuum switch	45
F68	Gear switch for gearshift and consumption indicator	46
F89	Switch for acceleration enrichment	18
F92	Pressure switch	18
G	Fuel gauge sender	20
G1	Fuel gauge	37
G2	Coolant temperature gauge sender	41
G3	Coolant temperature gauge	38
G5	Rev. counter	32
G6	Electric fuel pump	19
G40	Hall sender	12,13
G51	Consumption indicator	36
J6	Voltage stabilizer	37
J17	Fuel pump relay	19-22
J59	Relief relay for x contact	58-60
J98	Gearshift indicator control unit	45,46
J114	Oil pressure monitor control unit	30,31
K1	Main beam warning lamp	34
K2	Generator warning lamp	28
K3	Oil pressure warning lamp	29
K5	Turn signal warning lamp	33
K28	Coolant temperature warning lamp	39
K48	Gearshift indicator warning lamp	35
L1	Twin filament bulb, headlight left	77,79
L2	Twin filament bulb, headlight right	78,80
L8	Clock light bulb, headlight	61
L10	Instrument panel insert light bulb	62,63
L28	Cigarette lighter light bulb	57
M1	Side light bulb, left	74
M2	Tail light bulb, right	72
M3	Side light bulb, right	71
M4	Tail light bulb, left	73
N	Ignition coil	15
N9	Warm-up valve	21
N17	Cold start	18

Designation		In current track
N21	Auxiliary air valve	22
N41	TCI control unit	12-15
N60	Solenoid valve for consumption indicator	36
O	Ignition distributor	14,15
P	Spark plug connector	14-16
Q	Spark plugs	14-16
R	Radio connection	
S3, S5, S7-S10, S17, S20, S21, S22 Fuses in fuse box		
T1	Connector single, engine compartment, left	
T1d	Connector single, behind dash panel, right	
T1e	Connector single, behind relay plate	
T1f	Connector single, behind dash panel, left	
T1m	Connector single, behind relay plate	
T1v	Connector single, in luggage boot, left	
T1x	Connector single, in engine compartment, centre	
T2k	Connector two pin, behind dash panel	
T2u	Connector two pin, in engine compartment, right	
T2x	Connector two pin, in engine compartment, front	
T3a	Connector three pin, in engine compartment, left	
T3b	Connector three pin, in engine compartment, centre	
T4	Connector four pin, behind dash panel	
T7/	Connector seven pin, on dash panel insert	
T7a/	Connector seven pin, on dash panel insert	
T7b/	Connector seven pin, on dash panel insert	
T7c/	Connector seven pin, on dash panel insert	
T29/	Connector 29 pin, behind dash panel	
U1	Cigarette lighter	56
W	Interior light, front	49-51
W3	Luggage boot light	47
W6	Glovebox light	68
W11	Reading lamp, rear left	54
W12	Reading lamp, rear right	48
X	Number plate light	69,70
Y2	Digital clock	55

Earth points:

①	Earthing strap from battery	
⑨	Earthing point near relay plate	
⑮	Earthing point in insulating hose of front wiring loom	
⑯	Earthing point in insulating hose of dash panel wiring loom	
⑰	Earthing point in insulating hose of rear wiring loom	
⑱	Earthing point in insulating hose of wiring loom for instruments	
⑳	Earthing point on tailgate/boot lid	
㉑	Earthing point on gearbox	

For relay locations and connections see page 385

Colour code key

black	=	sw
blue	=	bl
brown	=	br
green	=	gn
grey	=	gr
lilac	=	li
red	=	ro
white	=	we
yellow	=	ge

Relay locations

Connections

Relay locations

1	Vacant
2	Relay for fuel pump
3	Vacant
4	Gearchange and consumption indicator
5	Vacant
6	Relay for dual tone horns
7	Relay for front and rear fog lights
8	Relief relay for X contact
10	Intermittent wash/wipe relay
11	Vacant
12	Turn signal flasher relay
13	Vacant
14	Vacant
15	Headlight washer relay
16	Vacant
17	Vacant
18	Switch unit for coolant shortage indicator
19	Vacant
20	Vacant
21	Rear fog light fuse (S 17/10A)
22	Vacant
23	Vacant
24	Vacant

Relay connections

A	Multi-pin connector (blue) for dash wiring loom
B	Multi-pin connector (red) for dash wiring loom
C	Multi-pin connector (yellow) for engine compartment loom left
D	Multi-pin connector (white) for engine compartment loom right
E	Multi-pin connector (black) for rear wiring loom
G	Single connector
H	Multi-pin connector (brown) for air conditioner wiring loom
K	Multi-pin connector (transparent) for belt warning system loom
L	Multi-pin connector (black) connection for lighting switch terminal 56 and dip and flasher switch terminal 56b
N	Single connector, connection for separate fuse (glow plugs or heater element for manifold)
P	Single connector – terminal 30
R	Not in use

Fuse colours

30A	–	green
20A	–	yellow
15A	–	blue
10A	–	red

Relay locations and connections for Passat CL5, GL5 and Santana LX5 and GX5 from August 1983

Wiring diagram for the Passat CL5, GL5 and Santana LX5 and GX5 from August 1983 (Part 2A)

4/31

K 12

S₂ ro   S₁₅ ro   S₁ gn

1 3 5 8
⑤
4 7 2 6

A7 A20 D11 E6 C19 E11 C8 D25 C3 C1 E16 D16 C20 C21 E12 D19 C7 H4 H2 H6 H3 H1

1,0 w/gn 1,0 sw/we   1,0 sw/we 1,0 sw/gn 1,0 1,0 sw/ro 1,0 1,0 sw/ro 1,0 1,0 sw 2,5 ro

sw/we sw/gn

sw/gr

T3b
49a
E₂
R L   1,0 sw
R L   T3a
T29/27 T29/26   1,0
1,5 1,5   F4
R L   1,0
K₆   1,0 T3a
E₃   1,0
58b 31   T3b   ϑ F18
67 0,5 br   F   ro/sw
gr/bl   1,0   2,5
0,5   T2a T2a T2b
L₂₁ T2h T2g   1,0 sw   T2a ge
sw BL BL BL   54 54 RF RF   1,5 ge
0,5 M₆ M₅ M₈ M₇ M₁₀ M₉ M₁₇ M₁₆ V₇   V₂

0,5 1,0 1,0   2,5 br 1,5 br T1m
T2h T2g
1,0 br 1,0 br

18 15 15   104 105 106 107 15   16

96 97 98 99 100 101 102 103 104 105 106 107 108 109 110 111

Wiring diagram for the Passat CL5, GL5 and Santana LX5 and GX5 from August 1983 (Part 2B)

Wiring diagram for the Passat CL5, GL5 and Santana LX5 and GX5 from August 1983 (Part 2C)

Wiring diagram for the Passat CL5, GL5 and Santana LX5 and GX5 from August 1983 (Part 2D)

Wiring diagram for electric window lifters

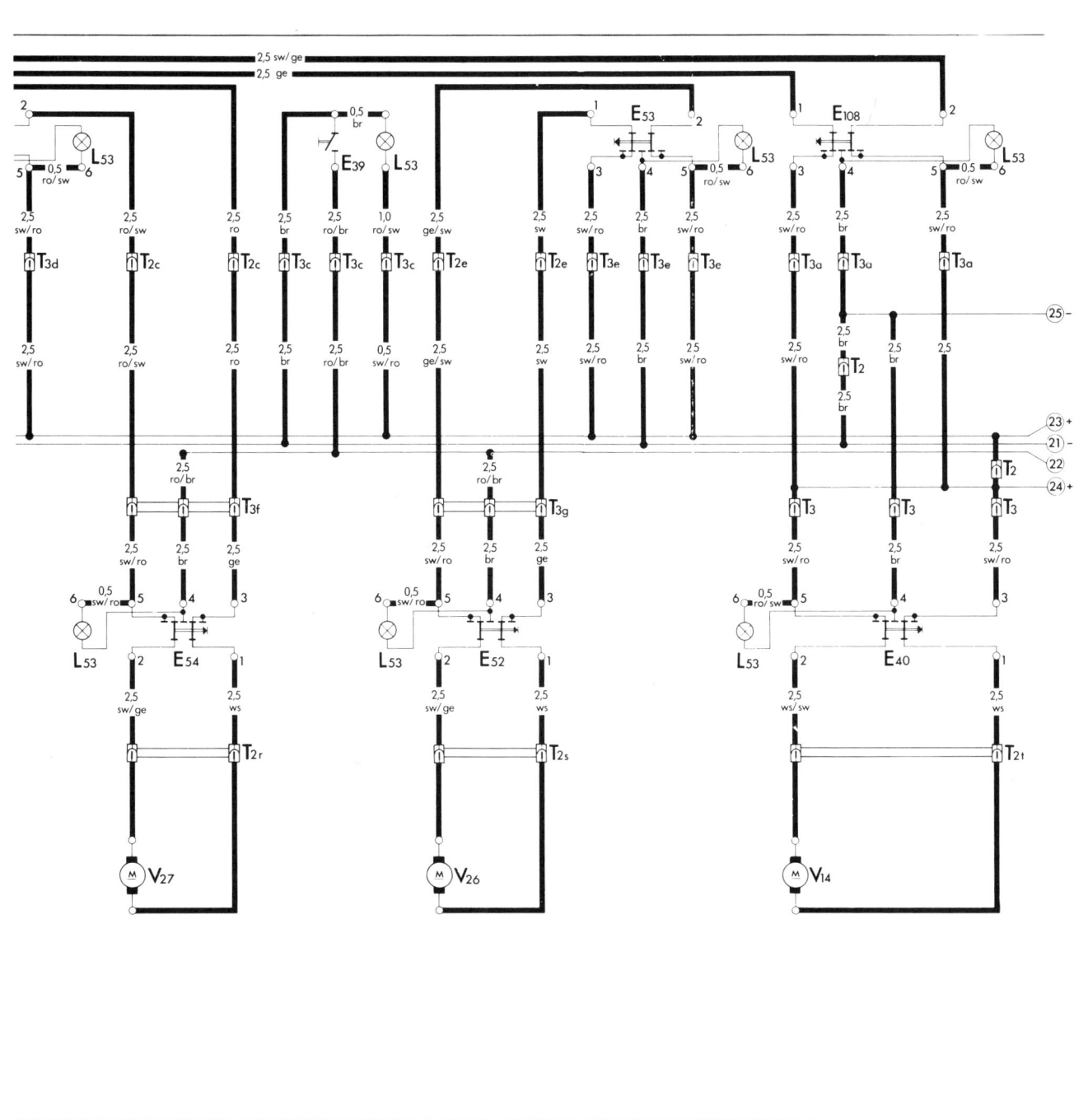

Wiring diagram for electric window lifters (continued)

Key to wiring diagram for electric window lifters

Designation		In current track
E39	Window lifter switch	13
E40	Window lifter switch, left	22-26
E41	Window lifter switch, right	3-5
E52	Rear left window lifter switch (in door)	15-17
E53	Rear left window lifter switch (in console)	18-20
E54	Rear right window lifter switch (in door)	10-12
E55	Rear right window lifter switch (in console)	6-8
E108	Window lifter switch, right (in driver's door)	22-24
J51	Window lifter relay	1, 2
L53	Bulb – for window lifter switch light	2
S12	Fuse in fuse box	
S37	Separate fuse for window lifter (Automatic fuse)	2
T1	Connector single, behind relay plate	
T2	Connector 2 pin, behind relay plate	
T2a	Connector 2 pin, in driver's door	
T2b	Connector 2 pin, behind relay plate	
T2c	Connector 2 pin, behind console	
T2e	Connector 2 pin, behind console	
T2i	Connector 2 pin, in front right door	
T2r	Connector 2 pin, in rear right door	
T2s	Connector 2 pin, in rear left door	

Designation		In current track
T2t	Connector 2 pin, in front left door	
T3	Connector 3 pin, behind dash	
T3a	Connector 3 pin, behind dash	
T3b	Connector 3 pin, behind dash	
T3c	Connector 3 pin, behind console	
T3d	Connector 3 pin, behind console	
T3e	Connector 3 pin, behind console	
T3f	Connector 3 pin, on B pillar	
T3g	Connector 3 pin, on B pillar	
V14	Window lifter motor, left	22
V15	Window lifter motor, right	3-5
V26	Window lifter motor, rear left	15
V27	Window lifter motor, rear right	

Earth crimped connections
⑩	Earth point, near relay plate	
㉑	Earth point, in crimped connector of window lifter loom	
㉒	Crimped connector in window lifter loom	
㉓	Crimped connector in window lifter loom	
㉔	Crimped connector in window lifter loom	

Relay locations
16	Window lifter relay	
20	Automatic fuse for window lifter	

Colour code key

sw	=	black	ro	=	red
ge	=	yellow	ws	=	white
br	=	brown			

Key to wiring diagram for stereo radio and electric aerial – January 1985 on

Designation		In current track
E20	Instrument/instrument panel lighting control	4
L28	Cigarette lighter light bulb	5
R	Radio	2-10
R2	Front left loudspeaker	6
R3	Front right loudspeaker	7
R4	Rear left loudspeaker	8
R5	Loudspeaker, rear right	9
S3	Fuse in fuse box	
T2	Connector 2 pin, on A pillar	
T2a	Connector 2 pin, in driver's door	
T2b	Connector 2 pin, on A pillar	

Designation		In current track
T2c	Connector pin, in passenger's door	
T2o	Connector 2 pin, behind relay plate	
T4/	Connector 4 pin, on radio	
U1	Cigarette lighter	1
V44	Electric aerial	11, 12
W3	Luggage boot light	3
W15	Interior light with delay switch	2
Y2	Digital clock	4

Earth points
⑩	Earth point, near relay plate	
⑯	Earth point, in insulating sleeve of dash loom	

Colour code key

ws	=	white	ge	=	yellow
sw	=	black	gn	=	green
ro	=	red	gr	=	grey
br	=	brown	bl	=	blue

Wiring diagram for stereo radio and electric aerial – January 1985 on

Colour code key

ws	=	white
sw	=	black
ro	=	red
br	=	brown
ge	=	yellow
gn	=	green
gr	=	grey
bl	=	blue

Wiring diagram for radiator fan – January 1985 on

Designation		In current track
2 Speed radiator fan wiring		
F18	Radiator fan thermo switch	1, 2
S1	Fuse in fuse box	1
T3	Connector 3 pin	
V7	Radiator fan	1, 2
Single speed radiator fan wiring		
F18	Radiator fan thermo switch	3
S1	Fuse in fuse box	3
V7	Radiator fan	3

Designation		In current track
250 W and 200 W radiator fan wiring		
C	Alternator	5
F18	Radiator fan thermo switch	4-7
J26	Radiator fan relay	6, 7
S1	Fuse in fuse box	7
S42	Separate fuse for radiator fan	5
T1	Connector single	
T2	Connector 2 pin	
T3	Connector 3 pin	
V7	Radiator fan	4-6
V35	Radiator fan II	8
Earth point		
(15)	Earthing point in insulating sleeve of front wiring loom	

30
15
X
31

S15
10A

D16 E12 C20 D19 C21   C18 B8 D24

1,0   1,0   1,0   4,0
sw   sw   sw/gr   ro/sw

T3b   T3b   T3b

D

RF   E17   50   D2   1

15   50A   P   R   N   D   2   1A

0,5   4,0
                      ro/sw

C   A   C   T3a

2,5   16,0   2,5
ro   sw   ro

T1b

4,0
ro/sw

58   58   50

          RF   RF
M2   M4   M16   M17   L19   30   B

1,0 sw   M

1,0 br

1,0   0,5
br   br

(17)   (21)

1   2   3   4   5   6   7   8   9   10

Wiring diagram for automatic transmission – August 1985 on

Colour code key

ws	=	white
sw	=	black
ro	=	red
br	=	brown
ge	=	yellow
gn	=	green
gr	=	grey
bl	=	blue
li	=	lilac

Designation		In current track
A	Battery	7
B	Starter	7-9
C	Alternator	6, 8
D	Ignition/starter switch	10
E17	Starter inhibitor and reversing lights switch	3-10
L19	Speed selector light bulb	5
M2	Tail light bulb, right	1
M4	Tail light bulb, left	1
M16	Reversing light bulb left	2

Designation		In current track
M17	Reversing light bulb right	4
S15	Fuse in fuse box	
T1	Connector single, in engine compartment, left	
T3a	Connector 3 pin, behind dash panel	
T3b	Connector 3 pin, behind dash panel	

Earth point

(17)	Earth point in rear wiring loom
(21)	Earth point next to starter inhibitor switch

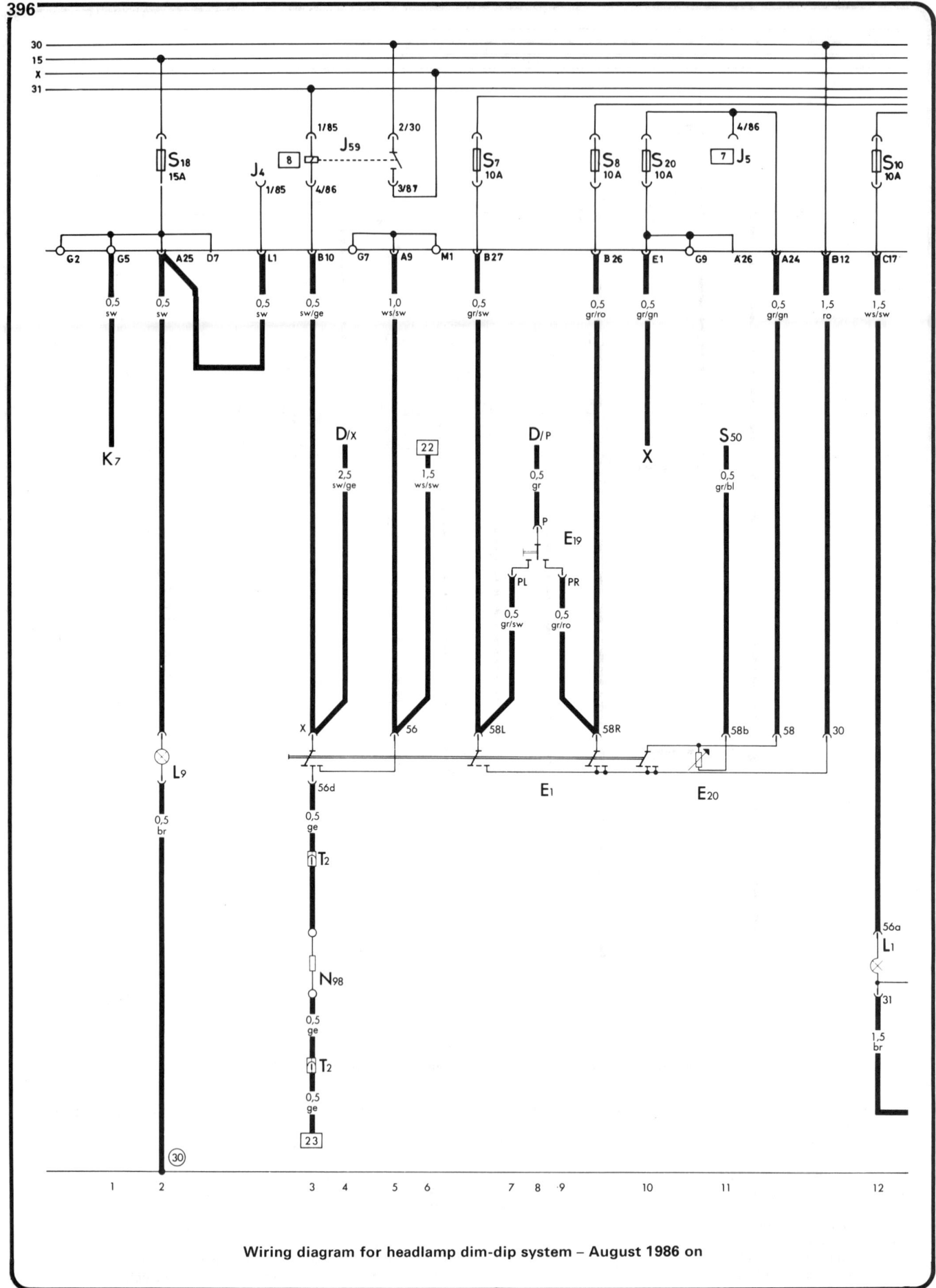

Wiring diagram for headlamp dim-dip system – August 1986 on

30
15
X
31

4/86

7 J5

S10
10A

S21
10A

S22
10A

S9
10A

G9 A26 A24 B12 C17 C5 C4 E9 E18 C14 C6 C16 A2B B23 M2 A21 B22

0,5
gr/gn

1,5
ro

1,5
ws/sw

1,5
ge/sw

0,5
gr/sw

0,5
gr/sw

0,5
gr/ro

0,5
gr/ro

1,5
ge

1,5
ws

0,5
bl/ws

1,0
ro/ge

1,5
ge

0,5
ge

1,5
ws

S50

0,5
gr/bl

K1

6

3

1,5
sw/ws

58b 58 30

E20

30 56

E4

56a 56b

56a 56b 58 58 58 58 56b 56a

L1 L1 M1 M4 M2 M3 L2 L2

31 31 31 31 31 31

1,5
br

1,5
br

1,5
br

1,5
br

1,5
br

1,5
br

(12) (93) (86) (12)

11 12 13 14 15 16 17 18 19 20 21 22 23

Wiring diagram for headlamp dim-dip system – August 1986 on (continued)

Key to wiring diagram for headlamp dim-dip system – August 1986 on

Designation		In current track
D	Ignition/starter switch	4, 7
E1	Lighting switch	3-11
E4	Headlight dimmer/flasher switch	21, 22
E19	Parking light switch	8
E20	Instrument/dash panel lighting control	11
J4	Dual tone horn relay	3
J5	Foglight relay	11
J59	Relief relay for x contact	3, 4
K1	Main beam warning lamp	20
K7	Dual circuit brake and handbrake warning lamp	1
L1	Twin filament bulb, left	12, 13
L2	Twin filament bulb, right	18, 19
L9	Lighting switch light bulb	2
M1	Sidelight bulb, left	14
M2	Tail light bulb, right	16
M3	Sidelight bulb, right	17
M4	Tail light bulb, left	15
N98	Series resistance – dim-dip lights	3
S7-S10, S18, S20-S22	Fuses in fuse box	
S50	Fuse, terminal 58B	11
T2	Connector 2 pin behind dash panel	
X	Number plate light	10

Earth points

- (12) Earth point, in engine compartment, left
- (30) Earth point, next to relay plate
- (86) Earth connection -1-, in rear wiring loom

Relay locations

- [7] Foglight relay
- [8] Relief relay for x-contact

Colour code key

bl	=	blue
br	=	brown
ge	=	yellow
gn	=	green
gr	=	grey
li	=	lilac
ro	=	red
sw	=	black
ws	=	white

Printed by
J H Haynes & Co Ltd
Sparkford Nr Yeovil
Somerset BA22 7JJ England